Wakefield Press

Irish South Australia

Also in this series

A Case to Answer: The story of Australia's first European war crimes prosecution
David Bevan

Ashton's Hotel: The journal of William Baker Ashton, first governor of the Adelaide Gaol
Rhondda Harris

Behind the Wall: The Women of the Destitute Asylum Adelaide, 1852–1918
Mary Geyer

Colonialism and its Aftermath: A history of Aboriginal South Australia
Peggy Brock and Tom Gara (editors)

Emigrants and Historians: Essays in honour of Eric Richards
Philip Payton

Foundational Fictions in South Australian History
Carolyn Collins and Paul Sendziuk (editors)

In the Land of the Magic Pudding: A gastronomic miscellany
Barbara Santich (editor)

Mary Lee: The life and times of a 'turbulent anarchist' and her battle for women's rights
Denise George

Miss Marryat's Circle: A not so distant past
Cheryl Williss

One Common Enemy: The Laconia Incident: A survivor's memoir
Jim Mcloughlin with David Gibb

Pens and Bayonets: Letters from the Front by soldiers of Yorke Peninsula during the Great War
Don Longo

South Australia on the Eve of War
Melanie Oppenheimer, Margaret Anderson, Mandy Paul (editors)

The Last Protector: The illegal removal of Aboriginal children from their parents in South Australia
Cameron Raynes

Turning Points: Chapters in South Australian history
Robert Foster, Paul Sendziuk (editors)

Irish South Australia

New histories and insights

Edited by
**SUSAN ARTHURE, FIDELMA BREEN,
STEPHANIE JAMES, DYMPHNA LONERGAN**

Wakefield Press

Wakefield Press
16 Rose Street
Mile End
South Australia 5031
www.wakefieldpress.com.au

First published 2019

Copyright © this collection Susan Arthure, Fidelma Breen, Stephanie James,
Dymphna Lonergan, 2019
Copyright in individual chapters remains with the respective authors

All rights reserved. This book is copyright. Apart from
any fair dealing for the purposes of private study, research,
criticism or review, as permitted under the Copyright Act,
no part may be reproduced without written permission.
Enquiries should be addressed to the publisher.

Cover designed by Liz Nicholson, designBITE
Edited by Margot Lloyd, Wakefield Press
Typeset by Michael Deves, Wakefield Press

ISBN 978 1 74305 619 6

A catalogue record for this
book is available from the
National Library of Australia

This publication has been assisted by
the History Trust of South Australia –
Wakefield Press History Initiative.

   Wakefield Press thanks
Coriole Vineyards for
continued support

For David Fitzpatrick

Contents

Foreword by His Excellency Breandán Ó Caollaí	ix
Map	x
Preface	xi
Timeline of the Irish in South Australia before Federation	xvii
G.S. Kingston and other pioneer Irish in South Australia *Dymphna Lonergan*	1
Irish settlement in the Mount Barker region, 1836–1891 *Ann Herraman*	12
Fortune and misfortune: Early Irish colonists in the Clare Valley *Rory Hope and Stephanie James*	23
The unexpected Irishmen: How David Power and Anthony Sutton established an Irish colonial presence in the South East of South Australia *Neisha Wratten*	41
Kapunda's Irish connections *Susan Arthure*	58
Irish graves in Mid North South Australia, 1850–1899: An examination of cultural significance *Janine McEgan*	74
'The most thoroughly Irish centre in South Australia': Pekina from the 1870s to the 1940s *John Mannion and Stephanie James*	90
Irish women in early South Australia *Cherrie De Leiuen*	117
The 'wrong kind of immigrant': How existing prejudice on class, gender and ethnicity affected the reception of female Irish Famine orphans in South Australia under the Earl Grey Scheme *Jade Hastings*	131
Irish lawyers and judges in South Australia, 1836–1914 *Peter Moore*	143
South Australia's Irish colonial surgeons: The first 30 years, 1836–1866 *Bronte Gould*	159

St Patrick's Day in South Australia, 1836–1945 *Simon O'Reilley*	**173**
Varieties of Irish nationalism in South Australia, 1839–1950: Changing terms of engagement *Stephanie James*	**192**
Ireland, Home Rule and the Orange Order in South Australia *Fidelma Breen*	**212**
Cultural capital and Irish place names *Dymphna Lonergan*	**229**
Notes	**255**
Author biographies	**307**
Acknowledgements	**312**
Index	**314**

Foreword

It is my great pleasure to see the publication of *Irish South Australia: new histories and insights*, a very important addition to Irish Australian scholarship which will help give us a clearer picture of the Irish experience in South Australia in all its complexities and manifestations, both positive and negative. In 2016, Carmel and I were privileged to attend the first Irish Studies of Australia and New Zealand (ISAANZ) conference to be held in Adelaide – '1916–2016: Change, Commemoration, and Community' – where we met the editors and a number of the contributors to this volume. There were many excellent research papers on Irish South Australia at the conference that told a unique story about the Irish community here, and I am delighted to see many of the themes replicated and given more fulsomely here.

I commend the editors for their work in bringing this volume to fruition and wish them the best in continuing this worthwhile research.

Breandán Ó Caollaí
Ambassador of Ireland to Australia

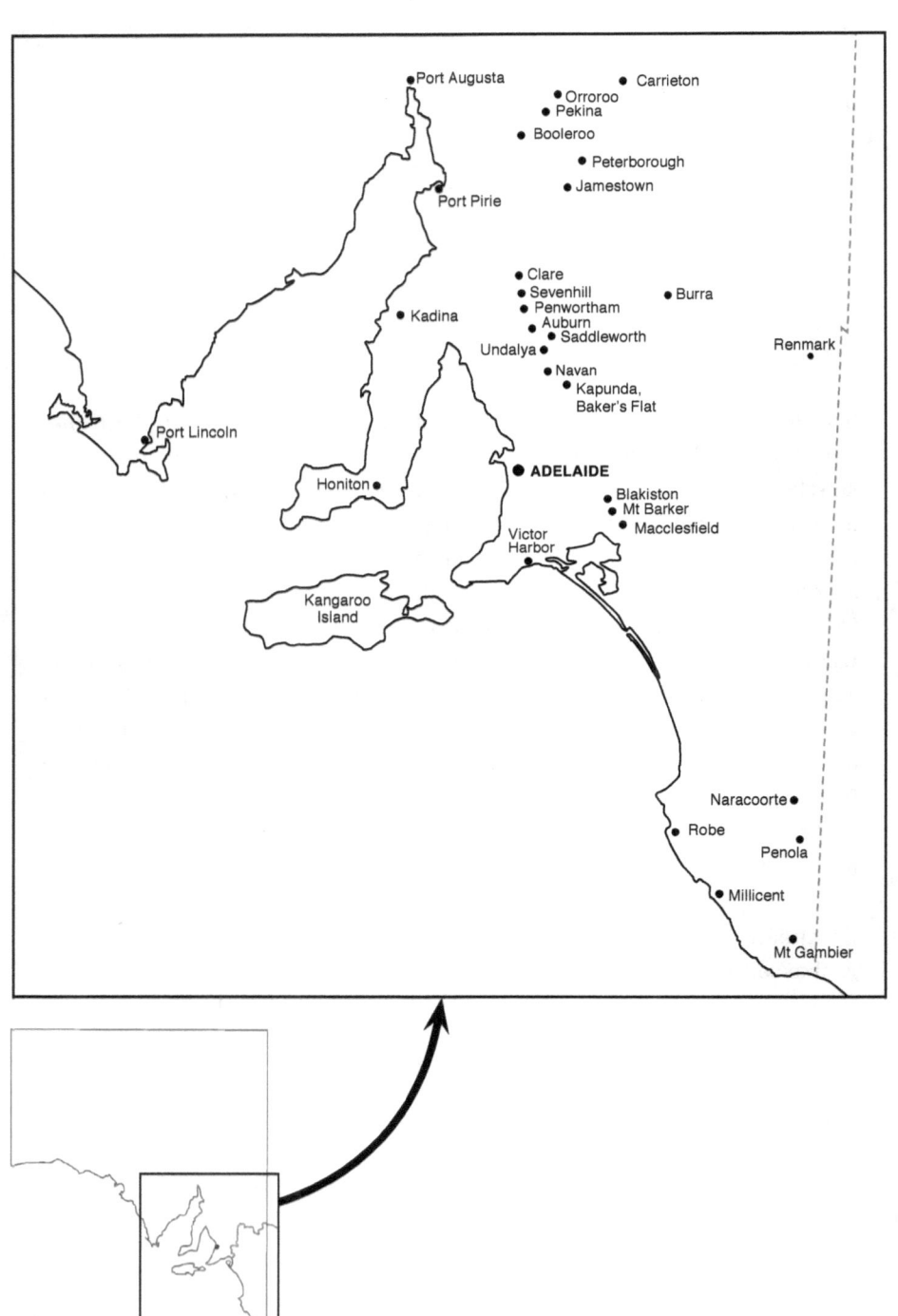

Preface

Australia, as we know it, was inhabited many thousands of years before it was colonised by the British. The Kaurna people lived in the Adelaide Plains region where metropolitan Adelaide now thrives, and where the colony of South Australia was declared in 1836. This land was first sighted by Europeans in 1627, but it would be more than 200 years before the South Australian settlement plan was enacted. In June 1829, Edward Gibbon Wakefield published *A Letter from Sydney* (penned while serving time in Newgate Prison, London) in conjunction with Robert Gouger, outlining a systematic colonisation scheme to address the pressures of Britain's growing population. Although Wakefield is credited with drafting much of the consequent South Australia Act, by the time the South Australian Association was formed in December 1833 he had, in fact, distanced himself from the colonisation project, disappointed at the low price proposed for land sales. Gouger remained enthused, however, and, alongside men like Robert Torrens and George Fife Angas, was instrumental in the formation of the South Australian Association that successfully lobbied the British parliament to pass the *South Australia Act 1834*. The Act made provision for the systematic colonisation of the province of South Australia through land sales authorised by the South Australian Colonisation Commission. Based on the Wakefield Plan, the Act determined that land sales in the colony would support an emigration fund to assist the labouring classes to emigrate. Several conditions were legislated: assisted emigrants were encouraged to bring their families with them; equal distribution of the sexes was to be sought; there was to be religious freedom and no established church; and the transportation of convicts to South Australia was prohibited.

In 1836, some nine ships carried 636 people to the colony on behalf of the South Australian Company formed by George Fife Angas. The first settlement was at Kangaroo Island, but after Colonel Light's initial survey most of this group moved to the mainland where the province was proclaimed by Governor Hindmarsh at Holdfast Bay in December 1836. The settlement of South Australia was initially conceived as a joint venture between the Crown and the Commission, but the British government assumed full control of South Australia as a Crown colony and abolished the commission in 1842.

Paradise?

From its foundation, South Australia's early character differentiated it from the other Australian colonies. While conceived as a free colony, it has been argued that it was no paradise since its economic formation made it virtually impossible for the labouring class to purchase land.[1] Rather, those with means advanced their power by taking up the most arable and profitable lands. The result was that some of those seeking a new, freer way of life instead encountered disappointment in a world that was cruder and aesthetically different to their homeland, and differed little in its economic bonds.

Despite the picture of South Australia as a place of great opportunity conveyed through the medium of contemporary immigration literature, social inequality remained a feature. On the surface, and by reputation, the colony was indeed a working man's paradise – there was opportunity, which, combined with hard work, luck and forbearance, could give one a space to call one's own. But British societal structures had been firmly established in the principles of the colony's foundation by men who were influenced by the rise of economic and political liberalism in 1830s Britain. The 'tourism brochure' view of the colony sat in stark contrast to the reality of colonial society. There was a very visible gentry class that participated in debutante balls and fox hunts and frequented the Adelaide Club.[2] In a study of some pastoral families, Eleanore Williams claims that what appeared

> paradoxical in a society which has been described as wholly middle class, egalitarian, and affected little, if at all, by class differences, was the considerable social and political influence wielded by the owners of ...

large estates ... Their attitudes and mode of living helped to reproduce the British class structure in South Australia ... consciously hierarchical and definitely not egalitarian.[3]

In his study of succession-duty records, Michael Shanahan also provides data that disputes the comparative equality of South Australia's society. 'By 1911 ... land ownership had become a source of great wealth for select members of society, as well as the foundation for the local gentry's culture'.[4] South Australia's egalitarianism did not represent equality but socialism of a diluted kind: a central authority over health, public works, education and the destitute represented a genuine effort to provide a uniformity of benefits to all, but ultimately control was held by large pastoralists and gentlemen. William Rounsevell, Assembly Member for both Burra and Port Adelaide, and one of Irish Home Rule's long-term supporters in South Australia, once stated that he did not wish the colony to be 'entirely democratic', indicating that a certain boundary was placed on social equality in the minds of those of his standing.[5] A paradise of dissent perhaps, but Utopia, South Australia was not.

Established by free men and women, and inherently British in outlook and feeling from the outset, South Australia did not have the convict 'stain' of the other colonies. It also did not have a substantial Irish population. David Fitzpatrick states that throughout its first century South Australia 'had the lowest proportion of Catholics and the smallest Irish component of the immigrant population'.[6] In the early 1880s the Irish-born in South Australia represented 6.52 per cent of the colony's population, compared with an average of 9.55 per cent across Australasia.[7] The assisted passage scheme was utilised heavily by the Irish and between 1873 and 1885 nearly a quarter of those assisted to South Australia were Irish, the peak year being 1885 when 67 per cent of assisted immigrants were categorised as Irish.[8] The Irish population of South Australia reached its peak of 10 per cent in 1861.[9] But even though they formed only a small portion of South Australia's population, the Irish-born were, in fact, the third largest national group in the colony.[10] They resided alongside the English who represented 21.14 per cent of the total, the Scottish at 3.80 per cent, and Germans and Austrians at 3.21 per cent, the remainder being mostly Australian-born (59.83 per cent) and small numbers of Chinese and French.[11]

While hailed as a paradise for dissenters following a successful recruitment campaign in the Home Counties directed at non-Conformists, South Australia was also regarded, if only by its own population, as a 'fair state ... founded and colonised by honourable, law-abiding, peaceful and industrious Britons'.[12] The exclusive Adelaide Club, a gentlemen's club which still exists today, continued the traditions of its predecessor, the South Australian Club, set up just 17 months after the colony's foundation.[13] It was every inch the colonial mirror of the exclusive London Club. With liveried footmen, an all-male membership and an alleged underground passage between its premises on North Terrace and the state parliament building, the Adelaide Club represented a seat of 'English' power. C.H. Cudmore, chairman of the club at its centenary, attributes South Australia's difference from other colonies to the 'class and type of people who came here as its founders' adding that the 'almost continuous infusion of the mellow thought, as well as the latest ideas, from the English seats of learning ... has had a continuous and beneficial effect'.[14] Of the 121 members listed in the club's centenary history, just 10 appear to be Irish-born.[15]

Research on the Irish in Australia

Irish Australia became a popular area of academic study in the late 1980s and remains so. The literature has been dominated by individuals such as Patrick O'Farrell, Malcolm Campbell, Oliver MacDonagh, Trevor McClaughlin and David Fitzpatrick and has in the main been broadly based, focused on the Catholic Irish, and mostly concerned with the eastern states of New South Wales and Victoria. While respecting these works, this volume promotes the view that South Australia, despite its comparatively small Irish population, warrants closer inspection, and the following chapters attempt to redress the dearth of research into the South Australian Irish community. Until now, this group has not been fully investigated, exposed or synthesised into the larger picture of Irish Australia. Further research in this area can only assist in understanding more fully the Irish-Australian contribution to the state's history and that of Australia as a whole, and may also highlight to other researchers the possibilities which may exist in other states for similar work.

A substantial body of research exists on the economic profile of early immigrants and their descendants, as illustrated by Eric Richards's expansive corpus of work on the nature of Australian immigration as well as the character of the South Australian population from its earliest years.[16] He notes that the Irish in South Australia 'faced the established and unquestionable primacy of Anglo-Scottish colonisation'.[17] The development of the Catholic Church, which appears to be inextricably intertwined with the existence of Irish communities, is well documented in the work of Margaret Press.[18] Fitzpatrick notes the 'uniquely low proportion of non-Catholics within the small Irish minority' in South Australia, where 78 per cent of the Irish community were Catholic compared to 70 per cent of the Irish in Victoria;[19] several chapters in this book reflect that identity. Ann Herraman's work on Irish settlement in Mount Barker in the 1850s and 1860s illustrates the effect of early migration from Ireland on the growth of South Australia's Irish population, as do her calculations of the effect on that area's birth rate after the assimilation of 225 Irish orphan girls.[20] More recent works such as Stephanie James's thesis focusing on the Irish in the Clare Valley,[21] and Susan Arthure's archaeological work on the Irish of Baker's Flat,[22] lay out the nature of particularly Irish and Catholic areas of settlement within the colony. Fidelma Breen's 2013 thesis acknowledges the importance of the local Irish community in securing widespread colonial support for Irish Home Rule in the form of both money, and good sentiment, during visits by Irish parliamentarians from the early 1880s onwards.[23]

A number of individuals appear in several of the chapters of this book – George Strickland Kingston, Charles Harvey Bagot and Edward Burton Gleeson, among others – indicating their standing and influence in colonial society. It is likely that many of Adelaide's current residents are unaware of the Irish ancestry of either the colonial judge, John Jeffcott, or the government surveyor and colonial architect, George Kingston. Admittedly, they were of the Anglo-Irish elite to which some may say the colonial Irish could lay no claim. Dymphna Lonergan notes that many earlier settlers were recorded as 'British',[24] yet the website of Kingston House claims that Kingston often boasted of being 'the first Irishman to set foot in the colony'.[25] 'Irishness' has many guises and interpretations – several chapters in this book interrogate these various forms of identity. While it may have been a label which denoted trouble where the Irish orphan girls were concerned and perhaps a benign element of identity for the Irish lawyers discussed here, it was one worn with pride by many others. South Australia's Irish achievers are numerous.

This book had its genesis in the 22nd Australasian Irish Studies Conference held in Adelaide in December 2016 under the auspices of the Irish Studies Association of Australia and New Zealand. The editors of this volume – Susan Arthure, Fidelma Breen, Stephanie James and Dymphna Lonergan – were also convenors of the conference. Many contributors presented at that conference and responded to an invitation to submit their work for consideration for this refreshing account of Irish South Australia.

It is our hope that this book will fulfil a purpose and provide pleasure for many different readers. We anticipate that it will introduce the history of the Irish in South Australia to novice historians and general readers, while supplementing the knowledge of researchers in the field. Family historians and genealogists will enjoy the biographical sketches of the many individuals herein while those interested in various professions or organisations with Irish origins will also find chapters of interest. This volume provides an expanse of new source materials and knowledge about Irish people in South Australia which has been missing from previous works. Each author has made an original contribution to the historiography of the state, and it is our collective hope that further research occurs and adds to this body of work in the future.

Susan Arthure, Fidelma Breen, Stephanie James and Dymphna Lonergan
August 2018

Timeline of the Irish in South Australia before Federation

The timeline presented below aims to locate the Irish population within the broader sweep of colonial life. The reader will see that the Catholic Church in terms of dioceses, bishops, churches and education predominates here, a reflection of the fact that Catholicism represents the religion of the majority of the incoming Irish. Documenting the ways that the Protestant Irish established their stamp on colonial life has proved far more difficult to chronicle, and we leave this as a challenge for the next round of researchers.

1829   Edward Gibbon Wakefield's *A Letter from Sydney* is published in London

1832   Wakefield suggests the possible benefits of Irish emigration to the colonies during the 1830s

1833   South Australian Association is formed by Robert Gouger in England

1834   South Australia Act is assented to in August

1835   Board of Colonisation Commissioners appointed in May, Robert Torrens as chairman; South Australian Company is established in October; Robert Torrens publishes the *Colonization of South Australia* in which he proposes emigration as a solution to the poverty in Ireland

1836   Letters patent issued in February – creating the Province of South Australia legally and establishing boundaries; the first officials are appointed and a council of government set up; European voyagers land on Kangaroo Island in July and August, and at Holdfast Bay in November

1837 First land allotments in Adelaide made and survey of country land on Adelaide Plains begins in April; Port Adelaide is declared a port; a whaling station is established at Encounter Bay

1839 August, 300 Irish families in the colony as result of indentured labourer scheme; priests Francis Murphy (Meath) and Michael Ryan (Galway) arrive in Sydney; Robert Richard Torrens arrives to take up appointment as collector of customs

1840 George Kingston organises the first St Patrick's Day celebration at local hotel; Captain Bagot arrives on the *Birman* with 224 emigrants mostly from County Clare

1841 Bankruptcy of commissioners in England leads to financial crisis in colony with public spending slashed; assisted passages are halted; by December, one in seven of the population relies on official relief; Governor Grey plans for city wage earners to move to rural areas where their cheap labour would help develop agriculture; one third of Adelaide's houses deserted; Glen Osmond Wheal Gawler mine opens extracting silver-lead ore; Father Benson (Dublin) arrives

1842 Civil registration of births, deaths and marriages begins; census shows 17 per cent masters and 78 per cent servants; inaugural meeting of Sons of Erin with G.S. Kingston as secretary; discovery of copper at Kapunda by Captain Bagot's son Charles and Francis Stacker Dutton; British government abolishes Board of Colonisation Commissioners; South Australia now has same legal/political status as other colonies

1843 Flourishing agricultural industry established by year's end; Irish hold a football match on St Patrick's Day at Thebarton

1844 Fr Edmund Mahoney (Cork) arrives in January; first colonial census records a population of 17,366, Catholics are 6 per cent; Kapunda copper mine opens as a surface mine; 300 Catholic families have arrived; Fr Francis Murphy becomes first Bishop of Adelaide; English convert, Mr Leigh, donates 100 acres or £4000 for a church; Bishop Murphy living in old city cottage, a former hotel; St Mary's Church, Morphett Vale, opens as first colonial Catholic church

1845 Copper discovered at Burra; assisted passages reinstated due to prosperity linked to Burra and Kapunda mines; Fr Ryan begins visiting Mount Barker; Bishop Murphy moves into his Kingston-designed West Terrace residence; Mary Lee, a leading figure in Adelaide's women's suffrage movement, marries in Ireland

1846 Opening of Morphett Vale Church; census shows 7.4 per cent (1,846) of population is Catholic; the governor announces churches will receive grants of land and money based on numbers, amounts contributed and zeal; Bishop Murphy visits Ireland for priests and emigrants; first hundreds proclaimed to regulate the occupation of Crown lands

1847 The bishop returns with priest and deacon; Morphett Vale gets resident priest; planning for a Willunga church; Daniel Brady (Cavan) donates land for a church at Dry Creek or Salisbury; state to provide grants to schools; report in Tasmanian newspaper of Orange Order in Adelaide

1848 Six hundred and twenty-one Irish girls receive assisted passages; Orphans' Guardian Board is established with church and government members, their responsibilities include reception of the girls, and supervision of apprenticeships to worthy citizens; between 1848 and 1858, 15,448 Irish arrive in the colony; resident priest at Mount Barker and Clare; two Austrian Jesuits arrive

1849 St Patrick's Society formed to increase numbers of Irish colonists, R.R. Torrens, G.S. Kingston, Bishop Murphy and Fr Ryan founding members; foundations of Clare church blessed; *South Australian Register* reports Orange Lodge formed in Adelaide

1850 Four hundred and thirty Irish female orphans are employed as domestic servants; church foundations at Kapunda and Gawler are blessed; church opened at Mount Barker; Willunga parish established

1851 Education Act removes funding from church schools; first vines planted at Sevenhill (wine pressed in 1853); Captain William Littlejohn O'Halloran (Limerick) is made auditor-general

1852 Discovery of alluvial gold in Victoria leads to population exodus – an estimated 10,000 leave South Australia between 1851 and 1855;

the bishop instructs Fr Ryan to raise money at the diggings; St Patrick's Society unsuccessfully suggests immigration of female Irish paupers to replace labourers leaving for Victoria; Education Act changes control of schools, the new Central Board has no Catholic representatives; Bishop Murphy draws a line from the River Murray and all areas north under care of Sevenhill Jesuits; District Councils Act

1853 South Australia becomes a major wheat producer; Sevenhill construction begins (church completed in 1875); masses said in private homes at Mintaro, Upper Wakefield, Saddleworth and Burra; first district councils formed

1854 Resident priest in South East; Bishop Murphy confirming in Burra, Clare and Sevenhill; church foundations blessed at Mintaro; St John's church at Kapunda opened; significant numbers of Irish migrants arrive at Kapunda and settle at Baker's Flat

1855 Census shows 9.8 per cent (8335) of population Catholic; 43 per cent of assisted immigrants are Irish; 5000 domestic servants sent to colony, 74 per cent are Irish; country depots for Irish girls at Clare, Mount Barker, Gawler Town, Kapunda, Port Elliot, Port Lincoln and the South East; Port Adelaide parish established; opening of Mount Gambier church; Richard Graves MacDonnell (Dublin) becomes South Australian governor

1856 Colony's population exceeds 100,000; opening of churches at Yankalilla and Mintaro; Sevenhill College opens as day and boarding school to provide classical education

1857 Newly constituted colonial government tries to limit immigration abuses by introducing 'Proportions Regulations' to restrict Irish-Catholic inflow but little effect in ensuring fair proportions of Catholic and Protestant emigrants; Fr Julian Tenison Woods is ordained in January; Salisbury church opened in March; in November, Bishop Murphy reports there are 14,000 Catholics, 7 chapels and 12 priests

1858 Of the 2395 assisted passage applications, 1643 are Irish; Dr Robert Waters Moore (Cork) is appointed as colonial surgeon; death of Bishop Murphy; St Francis Xavier's Cathedral blessed and opened in July; churches under construction at Marion and Port Adelaide

1859   Copper found at Wallaroo, mining begins in 1860; Armagh in the Hundred of Clare is officially proclaimed; Bishop Patrick Bonaventure Geoghegan (Dublin) arrives in October and is greeted by a crowd of 2000; churches opened at Marion and Penola

1860   Bishop Geoghegan's pastoral letter increases pressure on Catholics to contribute to establishing their schools, and for government assistance to education – this suggests 'tolerant peaceful coexistence' between different churches no longer exists; Sevenhill Jesuits visit Kadina, Wallaroo and Moonta in response to growth of mining population; church opens at Robe; Hibernian Society founded to provide for social and financial needs of Catholic men and their families

1861   Between 1851 and 1861, 14,350 Irish immigrants reached the colony, but in 1861 only 12,694 were living in South Australia; slightly more than 10 per cent of the population are Irish born, Catholics make up 14 per cent (38 per cent are locally born)

1862   Sir Dominick Daly (Galway) becomes the colony's first Catholic governor, he dies in office in 1868; St Patrick's Day celebrated with a regatta at Port MacDonnell (named after Governor MacDonnell); Bishop Geoghegan leaves in February to attend bishop's meeting in Sydney before sailing to Europe (he dies there in May 1864); the bishop's 1860 urging that priests set up schools in their parishes leads to schools in the city (St Patrick's Girls and Boys near West Terrace and in hall of new Cathedral), also at North Adelaide, Port Adelaide, Queenstown, Marion, Bowden, Thebarton, Marybank, Virginia, Clare, Penola, Morphett Vale, Kapunda and Sevenhill

1863   Bishop Geoghegan's report to the Congregation of the Propagation of the Faith in Rome describes the faithful as 'chiefly of Irish origin with a sprinkling of Germans and Poles' and some Scotch Catholics in the South East; opening of church at Hectorville

1864   Severe drought begins; opening of church at Kanmantoo

1865   Goyder's line of rainfall drawn to show southern reach of drought and extent of country likely to get reliable rainfall, helping government allocate assistance to farmers; church opens at Virginia, Polish immigrants at Polish Hill River in Clare Valley

1866   Half of the population live in rural areas, 45 per cent locally born,

8.9 per cent Irish born and 14.5 per cent Catholic; Mary MacKillop founds Sisters of St Joseph of the Sacred Heart in Penola – committed to teaching the poor; Laurence Bonaventure Sheil (Wexford) becomes colony's third bishop, Fr Tenison Woods his secretary and director of Catholic education; opening of churches at Kadina, Lower Wakefield, Kapunda and Hamley Bridge

1867 Twenty-eight per cent of colonial landholdings are only 50–99 acres, 35 per cent between 100 and 199 acres, resulting in two thirds of farmers unlikely to get good returns, even if all land cropped; Bishop Sheil sails for Europe in April; churches opened at Blumberg, Port Wakefield, Greenock, Stockport and Wallaroo; public meetings in May outline proposed Catholic Education structure; arrival of Sisters of St Joseph in June (by December there are 10 in the community); Catholic orphanage is set up; in September the *Southern Cross and South Australian Catholic Herald*, edited by Fr Woods, is published; birth of Daisy Bates (Tipperary), who first arrives in Australia in 1884 (from 1912, she plays a significant role in South Australian Indigenous communities)

1868 Sisters of St Joseph take charge of orphanage in January; June sees the opening of Mitcham Catholic Female Refuge; churches open at Bowden and Kooringa; South Australian Benefit Society set up as provident institution, 350 members in six months; establishment of Catholic Book Depot to provide approved texts to Catholic schools; seven Irish Dominican sisters arrive in December to set up school for girls

1869 Waste Lands Amendment (Strangways) Act in January allows large farming blocks to be bought with 20 per cent deposit – this opens up northern areas south of Goyder's line, southern Eyre Peninsula and Mount Gambier area to the less affluent; legislation results in counties such as Gawler, Light, Stanley, Victoria and Frome with previous high proportions of Catholics losing numbers to places like Pekina, Georgetown, Caltowie, Jamestown and Narridy, which develop as new centres of largely Irish-Catholic clustering; February opening of Dominican day and boarding schools for girls, first female secondary education in colony; opening of churches at North Adelaide, Glenelg, Port Lincoln, Riverton, Saddleworth and Moonta; 44 Catholic schools in diocese; Providence for aged, infirm and destitute adults opens in city

1870　Churches opened at Norwood, Mitcham and Manoora

1871　Census shows 7.7 per cent of colony's population are Irish-born (14,255), 15.4 per cent are Catholic (28,668); Bishop Sheil returns from Europe; he excommunicates Mary MacKillop, 42 schools are operated by her sisters who withdraw from 17 in response to Bishop's edict; Loyal Orange Institution of South Australia established

1872　Bishop Sheil dies in March; Fr Woods and members of Central Education Board depart following Bishop's commission investigation into diocesan affairs; opening of churches at Hill River, Yorketown and Georgetown; between 1872 and 1886 South Australian government does not send travelling inspector of emigrants to Ireland but does to other parts of UK

1873　Christopher Reynolds (Dublin) becomes Adelaide's bishop; 34 Josephite schools operating; Mary Lee arrives in Adelaide

1874　University of Adelaide receives its charter (teaching begins in 1876); assisted passages reintroduced until 1884

1875　Education Act introduces compulsory schooling for 7- to 13-year-olds but full-time attendance not required; Orangeman, Thomas Cowan from County Tyrone elected as MP for Yatala in House of Assembly; churches open at Pekina, Yatina, Appila-Yarrowie, Melrose, Port Pirie, Caltowie, Narridy, Whyte Yarcowie, Maitland, Mallala and Tarlee; opening of St Joseph's Convent, Kensington

1876　Census shows slight drop in Catholic numbers to 15.3 per cent; churches open at Warooka, Redhill, Orroroo, Crystal Brook and Farrell's Flat

1877　Burra copper mine closes; churches open at Jamestown and Lower North Adelaide (known as Irishtown)

1878　Colony's population exceeds 250,000; closure of Kapunda copper mine for major mining; four Irish Christian Brothers arrive to open day and boarding schools for boys; church opens at Willochra

1879　Christian Brothers College (CBC) opens in January; Bishop Reynolds travelling from July 1879 to June 1881, first to Rome then to Ireland to secure more religious orders and seminary places for South Australia; formation of Home Rule Association in Adelaide, and also St Patrick's Literary Society; December public meeting initiates major focus on Irish Famine distress and leads to success of Australia-wide fundraising across denominations raising £90,000, South Australia donates £8000

1880 Sisters of Mercy arrive from Dublin, open a school and House of Mercy to assist immigrant girls; church opens at Echunga; colony extended 150 miles north of Clare, the furthest point in 1869 when Strangways Act opened land sales; wheat and flour replace wool as prime export items

1881 Census shows 18,246 Irish born or 6.5 per cent, Catholics now 15.2 per cent or 42,628; Bishop Reynolds returns from Europe; five Carmelite priests arrive; Mercy boarding school opens in Mount Gambier; churches open in Lancelot, Warnertown and Strathalbyn; first Irish Parliamentary Party delegate, John W. Walshe, reaches Melbourne in June, this leads to formation of Land League in Australia and funds regularly flowing back to Ireland

1882 Third year of drought in North halts wheat farming expansion; churches open in Port Pirie, Gladstone, Carrieton, Terowie, Craddock, Stirling East and Thebarton

1883 Economic depression stops assisted immigration; churches open in Pirie St, Undalya, Colton, Petersburg, Port Augusta, Yongala and Quorn; CBC has 200 students; English Dominican sisters arrive in August; visit of Irish Parliamentary Party envoys John and William Redmond; South Australia sends J.V. O'Loghlin, P. Whelan, F.B. Keogh and William Dixon to first Irish-Australian Convention in Melbourne; Irish National League (INL) set up

1884 Churches open at Narracoorte and Millicent; INL branches open in Adelaide, Pekina, Carrieton, Petersburg, Millicent and Mount Gambier

1885 Churches open at Hawker, Hookina, Dawson, Bordertown, Mount Gambier (St Paul's) and Allendale

1886 Dominican boarding school moves from Franklin St to Cabra at Goodwood; Jesuit College at Sevenhill closes

Timeline of the Irish in South Australia before Federation

1887 Northern Diocese established with Port Augusta as centre, John O'Reily (Kilkenny) the first bishop
1889 July publication of *Southern Cross*; April visit of Irish Parliamentary Party envoys, John Dillon (greeted by 400 friends), John Deasy and Sir Thomas Esmonde; Irish MP J.R. Cox visits
1891 Census figures show 14,369 Irish-born or 4.5 per cent, Catholics at 14.7 per cent or 47,179; J.R. Cox visits again; Irish National Federation (INF) replaces INL
1894 South Australian women gain the right to vote and sit in parliament
1895 Michael Davitt visits
1896 Premier Charles Cameron Kingston is joined by second-generation Irish-Australians, J.V. O'Loghlin and P.P. Gillen as ministers; John O'Reily becomes Adelaide's archbishop
1899 Membership of Loyal Orange Lodges said to be 379
1900 United Irish League (UIL) replaces INF
1901 Census shows Irish-born are 11,243 or 3.1 per cent of population, Catholics 52,193 or 14.4 per cent

G.S. Kingston and other pioneer Irish in South Australia

DYMPHNA LONERGAN

Founding year, 1836

George Strickland Kingston (1807–1880), deputy surveyor to Colonel Light, the founder of Adelaide, was born and raised in Bandon, County Cork. His father and mother were in the timber business and owned a great deal of land and property.[1] George Kingston, however, would not enjoy much of his family's fortune. His father died when he was 10 years old, his sister when he was 11, and his mother when he was 13.[2] The estate then passed to his eldest brother William who was 21. Eleven years later George was married and living in London. Although in 1830 his son was baptised in Bandon (posthumously, having only lived five hours),[3] Kingston was to say goodbye to his Ireland home within a few years, and as with many other migrants, never returned. For all that, George Strickland Kingston never forgot his ethnic heritage. He was proud to be an Irishman in South Australia, not least because as an Irishman, he said, 'he could not be expected to have much modesty'[4] and so had a licence to boast about his achievements, and they were many.

G.S. Kingston was one of a small number of visionary men in London in the early 19th century who believed in the proposed new colony in South Australia. Having trained as a civil engineer in Birmingham,[5] he was keen to put his skills to work. Through answering a newspaper advertisement in 1834 he worked voluntarily for the South Australian Colonisation Commission. His reward was to be chosen as Colonel Light's right-hand man, arriving at Holdfast Bay on the *Cygnet* in 1836.[6] In November of that year, while Colonel Light sailed north to look for a suitable harbour in Spencer Gulf, 29-year-old George Kingston set out from the Holdfast Bay campsite to find a suitable site for the city of Adelaide.[7]

Kingston was young, keen, and, above all, fit enough to negotiate in the summer heat the dense forest of what was later named Hindley Street.[8] On 6 November 1836, his thirsty dog came across what turned out to be the River Torrens;[9] it was subsequently named after the Derry-born chairman of the South Australian Colonisation Commission, Colonel Robert Torrens.[10] Although he was convinced that the flat area supplied by the Torrens was an ideal site for a city, Kingston needed confirmation from his superior, Colonel Light, who, on viewing the area from a distance because he was too exhausted to travel any further inland, agreed with Kingston's choice.[11] Light then informed the just-arrived Governor Hindmarsh, who thought it was too far from the harbour, and suggested an alternative site near present-day Torrensville. Light agreed with this suggestion, but Kingston cautioned that Light see Hindmarsh's site for himself. On 30 December, Kingston went with Light to the site and promptly pointed out that the area Hindmarsh had in mind was subject to flooding. Light then returned to Kingston's first proposal and the next day endorsed it as the best spot for the city of Adelaide.[12]

Although it became known as Light's Vision, the city plan for Adelaide was largely drawn up in London before Colonel Light came on the scene. During the two years of preparation, Kingston led a team that looked at building requirements and provided 'proposals for a town and government buildings' on a 'permanent plan'.[13] Kingston went on to design many of Adelaide's early buildings when he set himself up as a private architect in Adelaide in 1838.[14] While Kingston's experience as an architect was largely book-based, he applied himself to serving the fledgling city's needs, and many of his building designs still stand: older parts of Government House, the Catholic Bishop's House (West Terrace), Adelaide Gaol, St Francis Xavier Roman Catholic Cathedral, Ayers House, the Braes in Reynella, and his own Kingston House in the suburb of Marino.

While it seems that Kingston has stood in the shadow of Colonel Light in Adelaide's early history, he was never shy of promoting his achievements. As a politician in the 1850s, this was necessary, but as an old colonist who lived to tell many a tale, Kingston was often given the opportunity to share his knowledge of early Adelaide. Kingston was very clear, if qualifying, in 1877, in a letter to the *South Australian Register* about his role in the founding of Adelaide when he acknowledged that (in so far as fixing on the site and founding the city may be considered synonymous terms) 'the foundation of the city took place on December 31, 1836'.[15]

Kingston cultivated Irish networks in Adelaide; he founded a group called the Sons of Erin in 1840.[16] In 1849, he was a founding member of the St Patrick's Society that lobbied for increased Irish immigration to South Australia.[17] Kingston ultimately represented Burra and Clare in the Legislative Council; in 1857 he became the first speaker of the House of Assembly in South Australia.[18] His son, Charles, became premier of South Australia in 1893. In a history of the Irish in South Australia that aims to acknowledge the early numbers of Irish-born who played a role in the establishment of the state, Sir George Strickland Kingston certainly holds the prominent position of being the first European to have set foot in 1836 in what was to become known as Adelaide. His major contribution to the development of South Australia was likened in his obituary to having been 'almost the history of the colony' with 'none of its pioneers possessing in a higher degree a better claim to public recognition and general regard'.[19] Place names associated with Kingston include Kingston-on-Murray.

A number of lesser-known Irish immigrants feature in South Australia's formative years. In 1836, the *Cygnet* also carried Hugh Quin who joined the *Cygnet*'s crew in Rio de Janeiro.[20] Captain Quin was born and raised in Newry, County Down, and, as with George Kingston, the death of Quin's father at an early age was to see his Irish childhood brought to an end, and his future mapped out far from an Irish coastline. At the age of 13 he sailed with his mother and sisters to New York and shortly afterwards began his working life at sea. When he joined the *Cygnet* in 1836 his marine skills were soon noticed and he was promoted to second mate before the end of the voyage. Quin brought much-needed maritime experience to the new colony, becoming first a river pilot, then superintendent of the government tug, and finally a long-serving and much-beloved harbour master at Port Adelaide. He was known as the 'Grand Old Man of the Port',[21] serving for almost 50 years. While there is no mention of his Irish background in the newspaper account of his impressive funeral – 'three mourning coaches and thirty vehicles'[22] – his place of birth is mentioned in an earlier edition recording his death.[23] Although he had left Ireland at a young age, his Irishness was important to him. In 1856 he was one of the stewards at the annual St Patrick's Day dinner.[24]

John Jeffcott from Tralee, County Kerry, also arrived in Adelaide's inaugural year of 1836 on the *Isabella* to take up the position of the colony's first judge.[25] Jeffcott had been chief justice of Sierra Leone and the Gambia before his appointment and had the unfortunate claim of being part of the last duel to be fought in Exeter, England, during which he fatally wounded a Dr Peter Hennis from Youghal, County Cork. Hennis was such an esteemed local doctor in Exeter that his death was recorded in a broadsheet with the poem 'Weep! Weep! Exorians! Mourn your loss severe, / Poor Hennis lies within the general bier'.[26] Jeffcott was brought to trial but the case was dismissed when the prosecution refused to bring their case.[27] John Jeffcott's new life in the colony was short-lived. Within a year of his arrival in Adelaide, he drowned in the Murray River when an overladen boat capsized. He was 41 years of age. Although he only had a short time to make his mark in South Australia, Jeffcott was a member of the first state legislature, and was a member of the committee that named Adelaide's earliest streets. His choices included Jeffcott Street, Kermode Street, and O'Connell Street,[28] all in North Adelaide. Kermode was the surname of his fiancée, Anne, in Van Diemen's Land. Jeffcott is also remembered in the naming of Jeffcott Chambers on North Terrace, and in Mount Jeffcott.[29]

The *Lady Liverpool* brought 22-year-old Patrick Boyce Coglin from Ballymote, Sligo, in 1836. Coglin was to make a long contribution to South Australia, first as a timber merchant in Hindley Street where he supplied the colonial engineer,[30] then as landlord of the first Napoleon Hotel (that he also built), [31] next as a pastoralist on the west coast where he had a sheep station on Rapid Bay that was found to have silver deposits and became the Wheal Coglin Mine, and finally as a local and state politician. A creek, a town, and a hundred are named after him.[32] He gave 55 of his years to the colony of South Australia.

While some early Irish settlers made their homes in Adelaide, more pushed north and south to find opportunities for farming and tillage. Twenty-one-year-old John Clarke from Killarney arrived in Adelaide on the *Tam O'Shanter* in 1836.[33] On arrival in Adelaide he bought an acre of land and imported a horse and dray from Van Diemen's Land. Later he built a home at Wattle Flat to which he took his bride, Cork-born Catherine Taggart.[34] The Clarkes earned their livelihood in the southern areas of Yankalilla, Myponga, and Wattle Flat. The steep hill at Myponga was named for the family. One of their children described the harsh times travelling on these roads: 'up the steep Clark's [sic] Hill, down the other side to the flooded creek, we had to push the coach and horses through this' on and on until they arrived at the Myponga Hotel 'covered in mud and muck'.[35] As with Paddy Coglin, John Clarke gave a long life to the young colony. He died at Wattle Flat in 1890. Catherine died three years later.

South Australia's first colonial chaplain was 29-year-old Reverend Charles Beaumont Howard,[36] a Dubliner and Trinity College Dublin graduate. He and his wife Grace arrived on the *Buffalo* into Holdfast Bay on 28 December 1836, where the Reverend conducted the first religious service on New Year's Day 1837. He brought his parsonage with him on the ship; early days in the colony meant that the Reverend had to transport it the seven miles to the city himself, using a hand truck.[37] Thereafter he travelled by horse to surrounding districts and later imported 'an Irish jaunting-car'.[38] He was the only clergyman in the colony until 1840. He too played a part in developing the social and civic fabric of Adelaide as a board member for the hospital, botanic gardens, and Aboriginal Protection. He also played the violin and reportedly entertained the other passengers on the journey out.[39]

From 1837 to 1839

In 1837, the *Cygnet* brought from Van Diemen's Land Daniel and Mary (Nihill) Cudmore.[40] The Cudmores were Limerick Quakers who had received assisted passage to Tasmania because of their poor circumstances. Two years later, they decided to try their luck in Adelaide. Their first home was a reed hut built by Daniel near today's Government House.[41] The fledgling city needed building and Daniel became a successful pisé-house builder. With the money made from that enterprise, he established breweries in Adelaide and Kapunda. Later, with money from an Irish legacy, the Cudmores spread north to take up pastoral leases where 'the improvements they effected on their Yongala and Riverland leaseholds paved the way for the later success of numerous small-holders'.[42] Their children continued expanding the family holdings, and the big houses associated with them became famous: the names Tara, Adare, and Avoca reflecting their Irish heritage. Paringa Hall, once owned by James Francis Cudmore, is now part of Sacred Heart College, Somerton Park.

On board the *Rajasthan* in 1838 was Thomas Shuldham O'Halloran. The O'Hallorans were from Limerick and father and sons were army careerists, most notably in the Indian army. Two sons immigrated to South Australia. Thomas arrived first, building 'Lizard Lodge' on what is now known as O'Halloran Hill from a prefabricated Manning house he brought out on the *Rajasthan*. Lizard Lodge was so named because the lizard is represented on the O'Halloran family crest. O'Halloran's positive nature is summarised in lines from a song composed in his honour: 'Major O'Halloran, soldier, statesman / He was a farmer at the end; / A noble, Irish, true gentleman, / Every worthy poor man's friend'.[43] In 1839, he was a justice of the peace for the province.[44] In June 1840, he was appointed South Australia's first commissioner of police.[45] He was a founding member and president of the St Patrick's Society. His grounds at O'Halloran Hill became known as a resting point for Indigenous people travelling between Encounter Bay and Adelaide. There they would find 'a fresh supply of blankets and rations'.[46] He promoted farming and industry in the southern area, and while he was a founding member of Christ Church in O'Halloran Hill and is buried there, he showed his support for the local Irish-Catholic community in being present at St Mary's, Morphett Vale, when it opened. At a St Patrick's Day celebration in 1851 he claimed himself 'an Irishman to the heart's core but equally a South Australian'.[47] Majors Road, an arterial road at O'Halloran Hill, is named after T.S. O'Halloran, as is Mount O'Halloran.[48]

The same year Thomas O'Halloran arrived, the *Lady Goderich* brought William and Sarah Oldham from Dublin. Twenty-seven-year-old William started teaching English to the Indigenous children in Adelaide and then moved north: first to Gawler where he was a tutor to the Reids, an Irish family,[49] and then to Kapunda where his contribution to that developing town included being postmaster and bank manager. Later he was mine captain at Kapunda. In Kapunda, Oldham also served as a Congregational minister and was the conductor of the Kapunda Philharmonic Society.[50] Oldham House, his 1860s home in Kapunda, currently operates as a bed and breakfast.

Moving in the same circles as his cousin William Oldham would have been Edward Burton Gleeson, who also arrived in 1838, on the *Emerald Isle* from Calcutta where he had been working in the Indian Civil Service. He bought his first block of land in Adelaide from the Reverend Howard.[51]

He is credited with being the 'first person to reap a crop of grain in South Australia'.[52] By 1840, he had 17,300 sheep, 550 cattle, and 24 horses, but lost it all during an economic downturn.[53] Gleeson recovered his fortunes and moved north where he became known as 'Paddy Gleeson, King of Clare'[54] having named the 500 acres he purchased in the County of Stanley 'Clare' after his home county, and his house, Inchiquin, after his old home.[55] From a district of fewer than 100 people in 1842, the South Australian town grew out of Gleeson's Village, and was known as Clare from 1846.[56] Gleeson's home was host to Adelaide dignitaries, and was 'the hub of Clare': as Clare's first mayor, Gleeson often held meetings in his home, which was also Clare's first post office.[57] Paddy Gleeson was called 'a true specimen of the fine old Irish gentleman' later in life, and his funeral was attended by 100 horsemen and the same number of people on foot, as well as 80 vehicles.[58]

According to the memorial plaque unveiled by the City of Onkaparinga in Morphett Vale in 1973, 'town patriarch' Alexander Anderson[59] from 'Northern Ireland' [sic] arrived in 1839 on the *Recovery* with his wife Catherine (née Creighton) and two children. The family headed south to take up farming in Morphett Vale. Alexander Anderson is listed in the *South Australian Almanac* in 1841 as one of the 'district's first men of substance'.[60] He was also the licensee of the Emu Hotel, Morphett Vale.[61] The hotel served as a post office with Anderson the first postmaster, and it also served as an early court.[62] Although a non-Catholic, he sold[63] an acre of his land at Morphett Vale to the Catholic Church and subsequently attended the opening of St Mary's Help of Christians,[64] South Australia's first purpose-built church still in use. He was also a founding member of the St Patrick's Society in 1849.

The *Orleana* in 1839 brought both the Reid family from Rostrevor, County Down, who were to become the first settlers in Gawler,[65] and John Hope from Derry. The McEllisters from Tralee sailed in on the *Delphi*, and from Wicklow came Patrick and Sarah Butler and Mortimer Nolan on the *Prince Regent*. John Brennan was a labourer from Cashel, County Tipperary, and Henry Clarke from Newry was on the *Charles Forbes*. Soon we see Brennan labouring for John Morphett at Glenelg,[66] Hope, Butler, and Nolan farming in the Mid North, the latter sponsoring Irish migrants,[67] the McEllisters running the Irish Harp hotel,[68] and the Reid family growing wheat, maize, melons, and potatoes at Clonlea, Gawler:[69] a wealth of Irish enterprise and labour in the early years of the colony. Many of these 'new chums' became bedrocks in their communities. Patrick Butler's barn served as a church before Clare's Catholic church was built; the Reids' Rostrevor House later became Rostrevor College and their land the basis for the eastern Adelaide suburb; John Hope grazed almost 20,000 sheep at Koolunga and is noted as a pastoral pioneer. He too was a member of the St Patrick's Society, and his Walkerville cemetery gravestone bears the name of Maghera, Derry, his birth place.[70] Edward McEllister also publicly proclaimed his ethnic heritage in his 1844 newspaper advertisement that welcomed race time with a 'Cead Mille Fealte'[71] and the cheer of 'Erin go Bragh'.[72] Also a founding member of the St Patrick's Society in 1849, his other public service included being a mounted policeman, merchant, member of parliament representing Burra and Clare from 1858 to 1860, Yatala from 1860 to 1862, and a member of the Legislative Council from 1863 to 1866.

From 1840 to 1842
In Ireland, the Poor Law was enacted in 1838 and boards of guardians were charged with looking after the poor in the resulting workhouses. It would have been cheaper to pay a ship's passage for a suitable resident than to keep him or her in the workhouse, and opportunities available in the new colony of South Australia were promoted in the Irish newspapers and in meetings. The steady stream of immigration increased and the 1840s were to see the arrival of three ships in particular, the *William Nichol*, *Mary Dugdale*, and the *Brightman*, which carried a great number of the Irish who were to characterise Irish South Australia in the 19th century. Most notable were Robert Richard Torrens from Cork, the son of Colonel Robert Torrens, and Captain Harvey Bagot from Kildare, emigration agents for hundreds of mainly County Clare immigrants.

R.R. Torrens arriving on the *Brightman* in 1840 became collector of customs in South Australia, but he is best known for his land reform initiative, the Torrens Title.[73] He entered South Australian politics, achieving the highest office of premier in 1857.[74] Also on the *Brightman* that year was William Littlejohn O'Halloran, the brother of Thomas Shuldham.

William became the auditor-general for South Australia. Like his brother, he named his property after an aspect of the O'Halloran coat of arms: Clanfergil was the name he gave to the estate that eventually became Daw Park Repatriation Hospital.[75] The *Mary Dugdale* brought the O'Sullivans from Kerry. Honora and Ignatius settled into farming in Morphett Vale and were key to the suburb's development. Stone from their property was used to build St Mary's Help of Christians,[76] and both Honora and Ignatius are buried in the church cemetery

The *William Nichol* (1840) was the first ship to sail directly from Ireland for South Australia. Edward and Mary Cain from Sligo started their life in the colony in Stanley Street, North Adelaide, part of which was sometimes called Irishtown. Catherine Taggart from Cork was on board the *William Nichol* with her parents, brother, John, and sisters, Margaret and Mary.[77] On the *Birman* that year was labourer John O'Dea who was to develop the suburb of Glandore, named after his home in County Cork.[78] The ship was chartered by Captain Harvey Bagot whose son, Charles Samuel, later found the green stone that proved to be evidence of copper at Kapunda and led to the establishment of the Kapunda mine. C.H. Bagot came up with 'an ingenious and novel plan' to transport the mined copper by making a track between Kapunda and Port Adelaide using a plough.[79] When the plough broke, he continued the track using the forked branch of a she-oak tree. Bagot first farmed at the foot of the Adelaide Hills. Later he built a big house on Stanley Street, North Adelaide, and named it Nurney House after his family estate in Kildare. Nurney House was known for its hospitality, and Mrs Bagot was a sympathetic ear for newly arrived Irish immigrants.[80] Charles Harvey Bagot served in public life between 1844 and 1859 as a nominee of the Legislative Council, member for Light, and as a sitting member.[81] He was also a founding member of the St Patrick's Society. His grandson John married Lucy, the daughter of Sir Henry Ayers.[82]

Reverend Howard, the colonial chaplain, would have been relieved at the arrival of another clergyman in 1840, but more so because the Reverend James Farrell who arrived on the *Lysander* was another Irishman: from Longford, but also a graduate of Trinity College Dublin. The Reverend Farrell became the first rector of Holy Trinity Church on North Terrace (named for Trinity College) and was vice-president in 1849 of the St Patrick's Society along with the Catholic vicar-general, Michael Ryan. Also on the *Lysander* were Thomas and Ellen Higgins from Clonmore, County Offaly, who were to farm at Gawler and Virginia.

Daniel and Rose (née Rudden) Brady sailed in on the *Diadem* in 1840 to begin a full and busy life. Daniel received a land grant in 1845 and selected 100 acres between Dry Creek and the Little Para north of Adelaide. In 1849, he was the licensee of the Cross Keys hotel.[83] He too headed for the Mid North, farming in Dry Creek and Clare, and in 1848 sponsored two families from Ballyjamesduff, County Cavan, the Keelans and the Bradys.[84] In all, the Bradys sponsored around 500 people over 20 years.[85] From small beginnings, buying a cow a month for two years, Daniel and Rose's wealth accumulated, but at the same time their marriage deteriorated and they were legally separated in July 1860.[86] The place names Cavan, Cross Keys, and Virginia were named by Daniel Brady.

The remainder of the decade brought Michael Kenny from County Clare via Van Diemen's Land in 1842 where he once walked from Hobart to Launceston with a double-barrelled gun over his shoulder.[87] He married Brigid Purtle from Kerry who had arrived in 1840 on the *Mary Dugdale* and who had become widowed early in Morphett Vale. Kenny was a keen sportsman and won a silver cup when his horse Faugh-a-balla (Irish *fág a beallach*, 'clear the way') won the first 'Wheatsheaf Cup'. There was no cup, but Michael insisted on one and waited the two years it took to arrive from England.[88] The Kennys (Michael, Brigid, four sons and a daughter) farmed extensively all over the state. His obituary on 7 May 1892[89] sets out his contribution to public life: a founding member of 'the Light Farmer's Club at Freeling, which did much in the interest of land reform ... a member of the first district council in Southern Yorke's Peninsula'. The Kennys also sponsored hundreds of Irish migrants and were some of the leading proponents of chain migration to South Australia.[90] Their wheat and sheep property in Colton was named Bally (Ir. *baile* 'home') Mckenny.[91]

Conclusion

These immigrants did not come to South Australia as a recognisable Irish group in the way that the Irish Orphans did in later years. Their Irishness, however, was important if they sponsored others or were sponsored themselves, with one place in Ireland being a common denominator. The early years in South Australian settlement show small Irish networks with immigrants settling where there were other Irish, and individual families assisting in the development of social infrastructure such as churches and schools. Membership of committees and councils were another way Irish immigrants contributed toward the development of their new home. Greater service came in membership of state government or in taking up important posts. Successful Irish men such as Bagot, Brady, Gleeson, Kingston, and Torrens knew each other and paved the way for newcomers by their example and often through direct assistance such as sponsorship. Irishness is also reflected in those place names that were chosen for new homes in South Australia. These early Irish in South Australia were no better or worse than those who came from other parts of the Empire, but for many, being Irish was important: it was a strength and source of pride.

Irish settlement in the Mount Barker region, 1836-1891

ANN HERRAMAN

A gradual progression

Emigrants from Ireland were participants in all stages of European settlement across the broad Mount Barker region following the implementation of the Special Survey land distribution opportunity in 1839.[1] In a gradual progression from near invisibility in the census of 1841, the Irish slowly expanded their presence.[2] By 1881 the numbers of Irish settlers scattered through the small settlements of Mount Barker, Hahndorf, Nairne, Echunga, Strathalbyn and Macclesfield had increased from 0.1 per cent of the 819 settlers recorded in 1841 to 15 per cent of the 15,567 settlers enumerated within the encompassing Counties of Hindmarsh and Sturt.[3] This population expansion had resulted from further migration infusions, expansion of mining and other employment opportunities, family formation and natural increase.[4]

Over time, the Irish presence in the Mount Barker region was acknowledged by descriptive names such as the Dublin Castle Hotel located in the tiny settlement of Little Dublin near Nairne. The Catholic precinct, including presbytery, church and cemetery built on rising ground above the main Mount Barker town, was locally known as Paddy's Hill. In one rural settlement in the heart of the Davenport Special Survey of 1839, the township of Macclesfield became known as Paddy's Town or the Hibernian Capital of South Australia where the traditions and issues of the Irish homeland were celebrated on an annual basis.[5]

The characteristics of the Irish settlers within the Mount Barker region have emerged through demographic analyses of census enumerations and the registers of marriages, births and deaths, primarily drawn from the records of the Catholic Church. Personal papers, diaries and family histories have provided rich sources of personal information, adding life and colour to the raw numbers. Enlivening with personal stories has not only affirmed the success of the Wakefield colonisation model and the importance of the Special Survey intervention, but has also highlighted the migration strategies and experiences of some of the Irish settlers themselves and their ongoing patterns of mobility and adaptation within the colony.

In small settlements such as Macclesfield the numbers of Irish gradually increased and small communities grew and consolidated. Supported by the locally based institutions of the Sisters of St Joseph and the Church of St James the Less, they were able to extend their influence and highlight their presence through public activities which reflected their cultural traditions and memories of home.[6]

Personal participation

Irish participants listed in the first census of 1841 when settlers were enumerated by name represented only 0.1 per cent of the 819 settlers listed. The only name which could be confidently traced to Ireland was that of Ann Hall, an assisted immigrant from County Tipperary, who had arrived in the colony in 1840. Her husband, William Hall, employed as a stonemason, had arrived in the colony as an assisted immigrant from Hampshire in England one year earlier. Both were members of the Catholic faith. It is possible that they had met and married following their arrival in the colony. Ann Hall's employment skills were in 'plain work'.[7]

Two other Catholic families listed in the 1841 census were John and Sarah Saby with their three children who were resident in Macclesfield, and Patrick and Christina Hughes who resided with their four children at Mount Barker. Six other Catholics were adult males in labouring positions in Mount Barker and Balhannah. Another 19 listed as members of the Catholic Church did not record their places of origin. At this entry point the settlers were predominantly from England (225), Scotland (140) and Prussia (242).[8]

For the Irish this was a very small beginning, but evidence from a Protestant source suggests that another Irish family would arrive within the year. Although not included in the 1841 census, the records of the

Anglican Church of St James near Blakiston reveal the presence of a notable Anglo-Irish settler.[9] Henry Seymour, a former lawyer from Dublin, had migrated with his wife and family of three on board the *Siam* in 1841. Seymour purchased a smallholding near the settlement of Littlehampton, through the agency of John Wraithall Bull. He named his property 'Tara'.[10]

Disappointed by the difficulties of establishing a profitable farm on land which he described as 'the tail end of gum scrub', Seymour moved his family and investments to the South East where he established extensive pastoral properties – Killanoola near Bool Lagoon and Mount Benson near Robe. Sadly, the first burial in the Blakiston cemetery was his son Henry Seymour Jnr who was fatally wounded by the accidental discharge of a shotgun in 1846.[11] While the presence of the Seymour family was relatively brief, they played a formative role in the development of the Anglican community. Henry Seymour himself was instrumental in the development of the first Church of England outside the primary settlement of Adelaide.[12]

While the inclusion of the Seymour family in the early Irish tally lifted the number from one to six, the real benefit of this small increase was in the contribution of immigrants with professional expertise, capital resources, and a willingness and capacity to support social and religious development in every region of their engagement. The ongoing migration trajectory of the Seymour family demonstrated a typical pattern of initial testing, informed changes to the original plan, and ongoing expansion of influence and social and economic capacity through family growth and intermarriage with like-minded and well-resourced settlers. The subsequent marriage of Elizabeth Seymour to George Hawker linked two prominent pastoral families, strengthening the regional links between the South East and the Mid North, with the Hawker family established at Bungaree. The birth of 16 children to George and 'Bessie' Hawker, who had spent some of her youth in Mount Barker, was a major contribution to the local population in another part of the colony.[13]

An influx of Irish girls

Between 1848 and 1849 assisted migration was re-activated when labour shortages and sympathy for the Irish famine victims supported migration of female orphans to South Australia.[14] The *Roman Emperor*, *Inconstant* and the *Elgin* brought 621 young Irish women to Adelaide where the majority found employment.[15] One passenger on the *Inconstant* eventually found employment and a husband at Mount Barker. On 31 December 1853, Margaret Lewis married Henry Taylor at the Anglican Church of St James, Blakiston.[16]

With limited success and many complaints about the quality of the Irish female immigrants, the strategy was abandoned until 1853 when the government returned to Ireland as a source of female domestic servants and farm labourers. The Irish component of immigrant arrivals increased from 10 per cent of 4500 immigrants in 1853 to 27 per cent of 9000 immigrants in 1854. Between 1850 and 1855 the gender ratio shifted, with 3644 Irish females outnumbering 2094 Irish males among the 5738 Irish immigrants. Once again the balance between demand and supply was addressed.[17] The Mount Barker region would benefit from the infusion of 225 female immigrants dispersed into local employment through a depot established in Hutchinson Street, Mount Barker.[18]

Marie Steiner's calculations show that 238 immigrant girls were sent into service from the depot and that 246 females were sent to the depot by 28 January 1856.[19] While there were some Scottish women in the group, the majority were Irish. The impact of their arrivals can be observed through the records of the Mount Barker Catholic Mission where marriage and baptism registers show increasing numbers of marriages and births from 1855 and 1856.[20] Steiner's study of seven immigrant depots in rural South Australia shows that Mount Barker Immigrant Depot received the largest number of Irish girls between 1855 and 1856. Steiner concluded, 'There can be no doubt that Mount Barker Depot was the largest and the most successful country depot'.[21]

Despite initial misgivings and resistance to an influx of unsupported Irish-Catholic females, particularly from the Davenport family, who feared the potential Catholic influence on young Protestant men, the Mount Barker community had responded positively to both employment needs and the opportunities afforded. The successful absorption of 246 Irish girls over a relatively short period could be accounted for on a range of levels: relative proximity to Adelaide, diversity of the regional economy, and the range of employment prospects available. The numbers of small towns in the region which had well established local communities by this time, and the strength of the regional Catholic Church and the support provided by

Father Michael O'Brien, himself an Irish immigrant from Waterford, were among the many factors which accounted for this success. Local histories such as Faull's study of Macclesfield show the influx and influence of Irish settlers through this deliberate migration strategy.[22]

Macclesfield's story

Mount Barker population statistics calculated from the census of 1861 reveal that the number of births in the Macclesfield district was among the highest in the region, and at 43.1 per thousand was equal to the South Australian rate.[23] Local historian Jim Faull noted two important and complementary elements in population growth at Macclesfield. The first was the initial and ongoing support provided by the Davenport family in providing employment and a range of land purchase options which assisted young families including Irish-Catholic settlers. This was a positive change of attitude by the Davenport brothers. The second was the weight of numbers and longevity of some families including the Calaby and Anderson families in populating the district.[24] The experience and influence of the Milligan and Anderson partnership illustrate how these two factors came into play.[25]

Anderson and Milligan – migration, marriage and settlement

In 2009 family historian Tom Dyster collated the records of the Anderson and Milligan families, revealing their converging migration and settlement patterns. Alexander Anderson, formerly of Berwick on the border of Scotland and England, had been employed as a block-master before he married Mary Greathurst around 1810. Born on 29 April 1785, Mary Anderson died in September 1858 aged 73 years. Mary and Alexander Anderson produced eight children, including William, born in High Street, Middlesex on 12 November 1811. William was trained as a cabinet-maker, but also found employment as a farmer and slate-quarry worker. He was also apprenticed as a mariner seaman for three years – an unusual range of skills, which he used to advantage in South Australia. He married Elizabeth Reeves who died after only four months of married life. The date of marriage and cause of death are unknown.[26]

William Anderson's decision to emigrate followed a heated argument with his father over a game of skittles on Good Friday 1840. Taking decisive action he found employment as a ship's carpenter and sailed for South Africa, and then to South Australia on board the *Courier*. In July he was on the high seas. Toward the end of the voyage Anderson and another seaman, Ned Pront, disputed the ship's course with the captain, and took charge of the vessel, arriving safely at Port Adelaide in July 1840. Anderson and Pront deserted immediately, taking a store of peas to sustain them in hiding. Three weeks later, when the vessel departed, they found employment at the Willunga slate quarries. Anderson moved from Willunga to Flaxley using his cabinet-making skills in constructing cedar doors and windows at Robert Davenport's new home, Battunga. There he met Mary Eliza Milligan, a maid or governess in the Davenport household.[27]

Mary Eliza Milligan was an Irish girl, born on 4 August 1821, in Belfast, Ireland. Eldest daughter of Melville and Sarah Milligan, Mary Eliza lived for some time with two spinster aunts and two bachelor uncles at Seaford, where they kept the post office. Mary Eliza's father was known to be a staunch Orangeman with a liking for taunting Catholics. Family history suggests this triggered a desire or need to emigrate.[28]

In July 1840, Melville Milligan arrived with his wife and daughter at Port Adelaide on board the *William Nichol*, captained by Captain William Elder. Mary Eliza was 19 years of age and, although they sighted the *Courier*, she did not meet her future husband for several years. Melville Milligan, formerly a shopkeeper in Belfast, took up land at Blakiston and Bugle Ranges. Mary Eliza found employment with the Davenports at Battunga, Macclesfield.

Mary Eliza Milligan and William Anderson married on 23 July 1844 at Holy Trinity Church, North Terrace, Adelaide, four years after their arrival in the colony. Accompanied by Melville Milligan as chaperone, Mary Eliza and William had walked from Blakiston to Adelaide staying overnight at 'The Mountain Hut' to make preparations for the wedding the following day. Discovering that the clergyman was about to depart for a country tour, the couple rushed to Holy Trinity Church where they were married before returning to Macclesfield.[29]

In January 1845 Robert Davenport advertised the property Watergate Farm with a cottage, farm premises and three good paddocks to let. This became the home of Mary Eliza and William Anderson. Their economic progress can be traced through a series of land transactions and changes of occupation. In February 1849, William Anderson was listed in Declaration of Acreage with 200 acres near Macclesfield.[30]

There were some downturns in the Andersons' fortunes. William made an unsuccessful visit to the Victorian diggings in 1854. In 1856 he was granted a slaughterhouse licence. In 1859 their farm and possessions were lost in a bush fire. Renting a second property on Meadows Road, William supplemented the family income by burning charcoal for forges, working as a blacksmith and farrier, fencing, splitting posts and rails and building sale yards. William Anderson died of colic (later thought to be appendicitis) on 14 April 1872, aged 61 years. Mary Eliza survived him by 40 years. She continued to farm on Sections 2953 and 2954 with the assistance of her sons until 1884 when she retired to Mount Barker. She died there, aged 79 years, on 29 April 1901.[31]

Descendants of Mary Eliza and William Anderson state that 'the most notable contributions to Macclesfield was their family of 16 children, many of whom subsequently married into other pioneer Macclesfield families, such as the Motts, McNamaras, Staceys and Webbs'.[32] On her death in 1901, Mary Eliza Anderson was survived by 13 of her 16 children, 60 grandchildren and eight great-grandchildren.

The Andersons produced 16 children over a period of 24 years. All but two married and raised families. Overall, this equated to a significant increase in the regional population following the union of Mary Eliza Milligan and William Anderson in 1845. The last grandchild was born in 1901 – the year of Mary Eliza Anderson's death.[33]

The *'domestic power of increase'*, Edward Gibbon Wakefield, 1829

The Anderson/Milligan partnership illustrates in great detail the economic and social benefits of a colonisation strategy which supported skilled immigrants of marriageable age. By marrying, reproducing prolifically and remaining in the region, the Anderson family affected the regional economies and communities without ever amassing significant personal wealth, providing ample evidence of Wakefield's advocacy of population growth achieved by 'the domestic power of increase'.[34]

Engaging in slate quarrying, farming, saw-milling, blacksmithing, cabinet-making, carpentry, cartage, construction and mining, the Andersons adapted their skills to prevailing opportunities. The versatility of the second generation of Andersons was evidenced by the four youngest sons who developed a saw-milling business at Macclesfield. In 1881 they purchased a 10-hp portable engine and contracted to supply 10,000 gum sleepers for the Nairne railway. In 1884 they began a steam sawmill at Mount Barker replicating their father's ability to respond to opportunities.[35]

William Anderson's success inspired other family members to migrate to Australia. His brother Alexander migrated to New South Wales as a schoolmaster. His sister Matilda took a position as postmistress at Macclesfield. Her nephew (or son) accompanied her and worked as a bookkeeper at Melrose. Melville Milligan's other children also remained in the region.[36]

Descendant and local historian Tom Dyster recorded and coordinated the Milligan and Anderson family journeys in 2009. The value of these two sets of complementary records lies in the level of detail describing the experiences of both partners prior to marriage, their common link with the Davenport family, and subsequent independent long-term success. While the primary marriage partnership was particularly successful, their qualities were typical of many families, including a range of skills acquired prior to departure, varied experiences on arrival and before settling in one place, adaptation to circumstances and the ability to respond to opportunities as they arose. These stories demonstrate the benefits of the Wakefield concepts and also illustrate the power of the Special Survey model in the hands of socially and economically committed investors such as the Davenport family.

Nurturing an Irish community
Supported by the Catholic Church, Irish settlers in small towns such as Macclesfield maintained their faith and fostered social elements of their Irish culture by their own creative energies. Annual events such as the Catholic Picnic on New Year's Day, marketed and managed by the Irish men in the town, consolidated a sense of community. The regular concerts produced by the Sisters of St Joseph ensured that Irish traditions and skills were maintained and fostered. Through these activities the intensely Irish character of Macclesfield was continually enhanced, earning it the label of Paddy's Town.

The New Year's Day tradition began in 1882 in Macclesfield when

John O'Malley, Mike Kavanagh, 'Big' Tom O'Loughlin, Bart Tobin, Patrick Kavanagh, Martin Considine and Jack Salmon arranged a community event advertised in the *Southern Argus* as

> A grand Catholic picnic [which would] take place ... under the Patronage of the HACB Society, Branch 154 on New Year's Day.[37]

Festivities began with a parade by members of the Hibernian Society marching – in full regalia with brass band accompaniment – to the Macclesfield Picnic Ground. The program of food, music, dancing and athletic events included flat and hurdle races, standing high jump, hop, step and jump, and the go-as-you-please race. The tug-of-war between six men of Macclesfield against any other six men of any district, throwing the pole, wheelbarrow races and the old favourite egg-and-spoon races entertained and challenged all-comers throughout the day. A sewing machine to the value of £2.0.0 was presented by the Reverend W. Prendergast to the best lady dancer over 40 years of age.[38]

By 1899 this New Year's Day institution drew crowds from every locality. Fathers Landy and Phelan were available all day encouraging the Catholics of the district to approach the sacraments on the first day of the year. Ninety-eight persons took Holy Communion on New Year's Day in 1899. Parliamentary candidates met their constituents. Variations of this Irish-Catholic rural institution continue today.[39]

The arrival of the Sisters of St Joseph in 1869 consolidated Irish culture and religious practices. At the instigation of Mother Mary MacKillop, the Josephite Convent attached to the Church of St James the Less at Macclesfield opened in 1869.[40] The sisters dedicated their lives to the poor Irish settlers and adapted a small building for education purposes by drawing a curtain across the church sanctuary. Following the regulated curriculum formulated by Father Julian Tenison Woods they also taught plain and fancy sewing to the girls and book-keeping to the boys.[41] Beyond their teaching responsibilities, the Sisters of St Joseph also responded to the social and spiritual needs of the lonely Irish/Catholic women and families who were scattered around the district.

The ongoing Irish influence in the district and the school is evident in the program presented by students from St Joseph's Convent, Macclesfield as reported in the Catholic newspaper, *Southern Cross* on 27 August 1897:

> After an overture and chorus by the children, Miss Maggie Kain sang 'Killarney' in a way which charmed the audience, and, in conjunction with Mr M. Kain, sang a duet, 'The Convent Bells'; towards the end of the first part of the programme, the same young lady gave 'Dublin Bay' which was decidedly the gem of the evening ... Miss E. McKearnean (a little dot, just five) then appeared, and sang 'The Cows in the Corn' and later on graced the stage to sing 'The Liquid Gem'; an encore being demanded, she sang 'Deep in the Australian Woods' ... A step dance by Master D. O'Malley and Miss Polly O'Malley was enthusiastically encored ... The concluding, and certainly the best item followed, being a drama entitled 'The Irish Heroine'. Mr Thomas Cosgrave, as Philip, acted the part of the Irish patriot in his appeal to the judges ... Miss M. Kain as 'Emily' had to appear in different capacities, among other things, entrapping the courtier, destroying the death warrant, and lastly, in her intrigue obtaining the prison keys ... Mr M. Daly as 'Denis Muldoon' was successful in keeping the audience in continual laughter. Mr Thomas Nestor, as the King's Courtier, was an ardent supporter of the Throne and very severe on all Irish rebels.[42]

The evening concluded with a vote of commendation for the diligent Sisters of St Joseph.

Conclusion

Within 40 years, the Irish settlers in the Mount Barker region had demonstrated their commitment to their new homeland, their retention of the traditions of their places of origin, and their ongoing engagement with the political issues which affected their families in Ireland.

The registers of the Mount Barker Catholic Mission had shown increases in marriages and births following the arrival of large numbers of Irish female immigrants between 1855 and 1856. The fears that an influx of Irish female immigrants would lure young Protestant men into the arms of the Catholic Church had not been realised. While Catholic population expansion had predominated, the records of Protestant families had also demonstrated the validity of Wakefield's belief in the 'domestic power of increase'.

Individual stories have coloured the statistics and confirmed the success of the Wakefield colonisation model and the importance of the

Special Survey provision in establishing communities of Protestant and Catholic immigrants across the Mount Barker region. The Davenport brothers had made a major investment in the Mount Barker region in 1839. They could not have predicted that the social vitality of the Irish settlers would recast their township of Macclesfield as the Hibernian Capital of South Australia within 40 years.

Fortune and misfortune: Early Irish colonists in the Clare Valley

RORY HOPE AND STEPHANIE JAMES

In 1836 the inhabitants of the area now known as the Clare Valley were the Ngadjuri people. As pioneering colonists moved further north, they ended up on Ngadjuri land. This chapter will focus on the local contribution of, and the interaction between, six individuals of Irish birth – Edward Burton Gleeson, John Hope, Patrick Butler, Peter Brady, Mary Ann Geary and Catherine Coffy – whose lives had some impact on the first decades of European colonisation in the Clare Valley. Census data from 1861, the first time that colonists were asked about their place of birth, reveals that with 14.7 per cent of its inhabitants born in Ireland, the Clare Valley was the most Irish area of South Australia.[1] The present study not only shows the extent of the local engagement of these individuals, but importantly, it also reveals positive relationships between some of these Irishmen and their Indigenous employees.

The six individuals came to the Clare Valley at different points between 1842 and 1855 as shown in Figure 1.[2] As a result of the privately funded Hutt Special Survey (December 1839 to January 1841),[3] the northern area was found to be 'favourable' – incorporating both flat and hilly land within a well-watered environment.[4] One of those who contributed to the £2000 survey costs was Irishman E.B. Gleeson, who reached the colony in July 1838.[5] Visiting the Hutt River briefly, he had shepherds working there by late September 1840.[6] Having experienced dramatic, and very public, insolvency in Adelaide early in 1842, Gleeson retreated north to the Hutt River. By 1843, Patrick Butler, one of Gleeson's shepherds living near Adelaide, was a 'stockholder of Inchiquin', possibly on land leased from Gleeson.[7] John Hope was in the area from 1841 and acquiring land by

1843.[8] He employed Mary Ann Geary between April 1853 and April 1859.[9] In 1851, Peter Brady took up land near Mintaro, several miles south-east of Clare. The final individual discussed here, Catherine Coffy, was one of the first residents of the servants depot in Clare, and in late July 1855 she was employed from there.

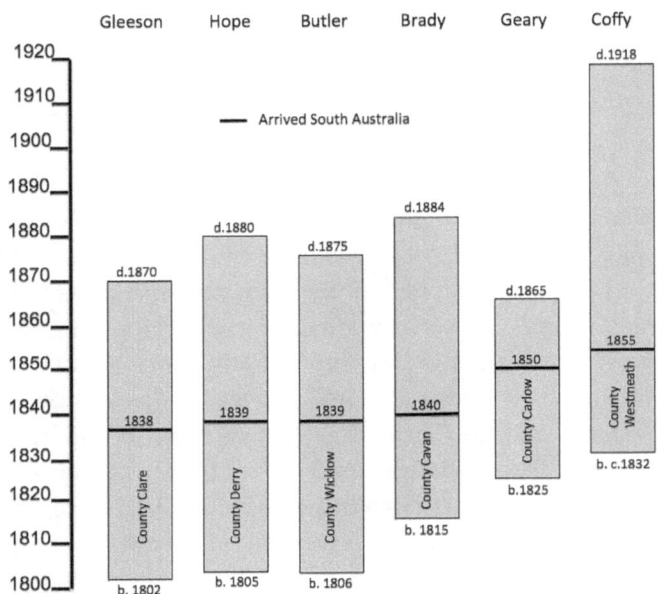

Figure 1. Diagrammatic representation of differences in County of origin, birth year, longevity, date of colonial arrival and death date for the individuals discussed in this chapter. Note the significant proportion of their lives spent in Ireland, years about which little is known, including their education and family interaction.

These six Irish individuals were differentiated by class, religion, education and gender. Gleeson and Hope, while certainly not aristocratic, represented something of a local elite, with greater access to both the top rung of colonial society, and finance. Their Protestant backgrounds ensured wider acceptance than was accorded Butler and Brady who, as Catholic Irishmen, were much less advantaged.[10] However, in a developing rural environment, the latter two arguably had opportunities which would have been closed to them in Adelaide. Both Geary and Coffy were low on the social scale in consequence of their gender, and their occupation as servants; Geary's position was probably slightly higher because she was a Protestant.[11] However, these women were far from docile and accepting of their lot; both challenged the patriarchal structures by deft use of the legal system, asserting their rights in a relatively hostile environment. Gender was not significant in determining education – all the males were educated; Mary Ann Geary was also literate,[12] and Catherine Coffy appears to have been.[13]

The 1841 colonial census did not include the Clare region; the best population estimate of '83 souls in a diameter of 14 miles' in 1842 came from a local historian.[14] The County of Stanley, in which the Clare Valley is located, was proclaimed in June 1842, a development which precipitated a basic administrative structure for the region. Peter Moore refers to early Irish immigrants as moving 'up-country [from Adelaide] in easy stages … finally to the Clare Valley and the Gleesons of Inchiquin'.[15] By 1846 the name Clare was in use, and subsequently Gleeson was credited with the village's establishment.[16] The region displayed strong Irish associations from the outset; the individuals discussed here all came from different parts of Ireland: E.B. Gleeson (see below), John Hope from Derry, Patrick and Sarah (née Naulty) Butler from Wicklow on the *Prince Regent* in 1839, Peter and Bridget (née Smith) Brady from Cavan on the *Thirteen* in 1840, Mary Ann Geary from Carlow on the *Joseph Somes* in 1850, and in 1855, Catherine Coffy, probably from Westmeath, on the *Nashwauk*.[17]

Edward Burton Gleeson
Born in 1802 either at Inchiquin in County Clare or Nenagh in Tipperary, Gleeson's background was 'within a privileged Irish culture'.[18] With lawyers and British army forebears, the Gleesons were described by one family researcher as 'a very bitter, Cromwellian family … show[ing] a typical start of a middle class English family' coming to Ireland 'as land grabbers'.[19] At 20 and 24 years respectively, Gleeson and older brother, John Hampton, joined the British exodus to India, the former becoming a keeper of the East India's correctional facilities in Calcutta, and the latter an assistant in the judge advocate's office. Both married, were then widowed and later remarried in India. In 1837 the brothers shared the proceeds of winning the Calcutta Lottery – purportedly an amount of £30,000.[20] Supported by the Australian Association of Bengal, they arrived in Adelaide with a large entourage on the *Emerald Isle*.[21] Establishing himself first in Adelaide,

E.B. Gleeson lived well, owning land and operating within the nascent capital's elite.[22] But his 1842 insolvency revealed major financial issues – so the fortuitous exclusion of his Hutt River land from his named assets during the bankruptcy proceedings enabled a tactical retreat.[23] By 1845, having regrouped, he had begun to construct Inchiquin, his homestead slightly north of Clare.[24]

The 1840s encompassed both Gleeson's semi-enforced absence from Adelaide and exalted colonial society, and later, his recovery through land purchase and agricultural success,[25] leading to his reappearance in those city circles. Intriguingly, and doubtless linked to earlier association with the colonial Irish network, the precipitating event seemed to be the April 1849 foundation meeting of the St Patrick's Society.[26] An initial committee member, he then figured as a speaker at the society's 1850 and 1851 dinners, and was later a steward at the 1856 St Patrick's Day celebration.[27] Toasting 'The Province of South Australia' in 1850, his devotion was evident. He claimed the colony followed Ireland as the 'finest country in the world', and he urged Irish colonists to avoid the 'deadly blight of sectarian dissensions' which had 'so cruelly marred' their homeland. And this was consistent with the support he provided all denominations in Clare.[28]

In Clare, Gleeson played an increasingly prominent role. In August 1850 he became Clare's first JP and magistrate.[29] He also donated land for a school in 1849.[30] He played an important role in planning for the 1851 construction of St Barnabas Anglican church and was appointed as a trustee and church warden.[31] In 1850 his name was first mentioned as a potential parliamentary candidate, and again several times in 1856.[32] He was founding chairman of Clare's district council, remaining in the position from 1853 to 1857. In that role he was instrumental in ensuring the 1855 servants depot functioned effectively; he was also an early employer – a Mary Fogarty was hired for 2/6 per week on 27 July 1855.[33] He chaired the 1856 meeting to establish the Clare Land and Building Society, and became a trustee.[34] His 1857 promotion and leadership of the Clare Agricultural Society was divisive – the organisation was perceived as pro-squatter, and, in the short term, precipitated a counter-organisation favouring smaller landholders.[35] Clearly viewed locally as a preeminent figure, his presence, often in an officiating role, was sought for significant events. So, for example, in January 1851, he was a judge at the Burra races,[36] and in

October 1854 he laid the foundation stone for Penwortham's steam mill. His address at that event ranged wide, about the need to shift from pastoral to agricultural interests, and the ways the mill would add to facilities already existing in the region. But he also focused on his love for Ireland – 'the home of my heart' – and its green flag, before emphasising Irish loyalty (the Crimean War was then underway), and urging his audience to 'meet and speak as South Australians' in 'this favoured land'.[37] In 1859, toasting Gleeson at an Auburn dinner, G.S. Kingston, fellow Irishman and parliamentarian, mentioned both had endured 'the ups and downs of colonial life', were 'thorough South Australians', and 'always delight[ed] to forward the interests of their colony of adoption'.[38] In the report of the 1865 ploughing match dinner, mention was made of 'an excellent sample of colonial wine ... the manufacture of Mr E.B. Gleeson of Inchiquin' – perhaps a fitting example of his response to the South Australian environment he had made his home.[39] When Clare became a corporation in 1868, Gleeson was its first mayor, a further recognition of his contribution to the region.

Figure 2. Portrait of E.B. Gleeson, Inchiquin, c1870. (From the photographic composite image of northern pioneers, compiled in 1908 by Mora Studio, Rundle Street, Adelaide.) Courtesy State Library of South Australia, B 6912/4

Gleeson's colonial life demonstrates resilience, the effective surmounting of early economic difficulties, and his many 'exertions ... for the welfare of Clare and the Northern districts'.[40] He moved in elite circles; the attendance of the two Irish-born colonial governors at the Northern Agricultural Society's dinner provided clear evidence, not only of Clare's regional significance, but also of Gleeson's status. These governors, Richard MacDonnell and Dominick Daly, stayed with the Gleesons at Inchiquin on their visits in February 1859 and September 1862.[41] Numerous public events reflected the strength of local respect for this 'fine old Irish gentleman'.[42] John Hope's diaries show multiple interactions with Gleeson – in social settings, on the court bench as JPs, and in local government.[43] He was also associated with both Butler and Brady as elected councillors. The importance of his ongoing relationship with his countryman, G.S. Kingston, was a consistent thread in coverage of local parliamentary matters.[44] In August 1866, Kingston's toast at the opening of Clare's town hall was to Gleeson as 'a worthy son of old Ireland'.[45] Somewhat surprisingly, when he died on 2 February 1870, neither Gleeson's Irish birth nor his lasting attachment to his homeland received comment, but his role as the 'father of Clare' was at least acknowledged.[46] He was buried in the family vault attached to the Anglican Church of St Barnabas, one of the objects of his earlier financial generosity.

John Hope

John Hope, a Presbyterian of Scottish ancestry, was born in Maghera, County Derry in 1805. Like most Irish immigrants to South Australia, little is known of his early and formative life in Ireland. Hope's father was a 'grocer, haberdasher and distributor of stamps'. After a traumatic voyage to Australia, during which he 'lost everything' when his ship foundered on the coast of South America, Hope, aged 34 years, eventually reached Adelaide in 1839.[47]

Following a short stint as tutor to the children of Irishman John Reid in Gawler Town, in 1841 Hope entered into partnership with John Watts, Adelaide's postmaster general.[48] Watts put up money for the purchase of sheep; Hope cared for them on the Wakefield River, and later on pastures north of Clare. The partnership with Watts ended soon after Hope became manager of Bungaree, his friend George Hawker's station, in 1853.[49] In the meantime, Hope had been squatting on 95 square miles of land near the Broughton River, for which he obtained an occupation licence in 1847. On this property, which he named Koolunga, he employed a manager and some 20 shepherds. It was the sale of wool from this property that provided Hope with the financial security that had motivated his desire to leave Ireland. He relinquished Koolunga in 1865.[50]

While managing Koolunga and Bungaree, Hope had become involved in community affairs. In 1857 he briefly joined Gleeson on the district council,[51] and after withdrawing from that role, was elected as a council auditor in 1860.[52] He had also been acquiring freehold land in the Clare Valley on which he built a cottage, Wolta Wolta, within walking distance of the township. This homestead was renovated and enlarged (as was his landholding), which reached an area of 2500 acres) in time for the 1859 return from Dublin of John Hope with his new bride Isabella, née Kenney.[53] John and Isabella had five children, and four generations of Hopes lived and worked at Wolta Wolta.

Figure 3. The earliest known photograph of John Hope, taken c. 1860.
(Photo courtesy Rory Hope)

In addition to his increasingly extensive property concerns and the demands of a growing family, Hope's diaries reveal that he was not only aware, but was also philanthropically involved in many community religious and other activities. There are many examples of his consistent commitment to Protestant churches; in mid 1853 he wrote of going with Charles Hawker 'to Church meeting [and taking] ... 5 sittings and pa[ying] [£]2/10/0 to Gleeson for Clergyman'.[54] But his generosity extended further. He donated land for Clare's Presbyterian manse in 1865, and was asked to lay the foundation stone,[55] just as his wife, Issie, had laid the foundation stone for the Wesleyan chapel at White Hut in 1860.[56] Perhaps more surprisingly, Hope's early 1860 diary recorded that he 'gave ... [Patrick Butler] £5 for Roman C [sic] Chapel'.[57] Then, in 1863 he subscribed £10 for the Clare school fund.[58] One diary entry for May 1863 notes: 'Went to meeting of Aborigines friends society, subscribed five pounds'.[59] (His diaries also note his willingness to employ Indigenous stockmen.)[60] Hope's account book covering the years 1863 to 1874 indicates annual subscriptions to a number of charities including, for example, 'Sailor's Home', 'Ragged School', 'Church Missionary', 'Orphan Refugees', 'Bible Society', 'Mission Calabar' [Africa] and 'Irish Society.'[61]

In the 1870s, somewhat overstretching himself financially, John Hope purchased two additional and very large properties – Para, on the Darling River near Wentworth, New South Wales, and Keeroongooloo, on Cooper's Creek, in the Channel Country of south-west Queensland. The latter property was sold soon after Hope's death.[62] In 1879, John Hope, then aged 74, together with his family, travelled to the British Isles so that he could help settle the legal and financial affairs of his brother Charles. This was a trying period for pastoralists in South Australia – wool prices were depressed and climatic conditions unfavourable. The Hopes returned to Adelaide in 1880 and John, who had taken ill on the return voyage, died at Adelaide's York Hotel on 20 June 1880.[63] His North Road Cemetery grave in Adelaide displays a large and very impressive Celtic cross.

Through John Hope's provision of advice and practical support to colleagues in the Mid North, the employment he offered on his properties, and his many and varied entrepreneurial activities and philanthropic acts, he made a substantial contribution to founding the pastoral industry in South Australia. While he exhibited a strong attachment to family life at Wolta Wolta, John and Isabella never fully embraced Australia as 'home' – that had to wait for the next generation of Hopes at Wolta Wolta. As his local obituary stated:

Figure 4. The Celtic Cross surmounting the grave of John and Isabella Hope, North Road Cemetery, Adelaide. (Photo courtesy Rory Hope)

Mr Hope was an early colonist and pioneer, and though he met with reverses during the first few years of his colonial experience he did not give up in despair. Being a shrewd businessman, and endowed with perseverance and honesty of purpose, he soon recovered himself, and was prosperous in all his undertakings.[64]

Patrick Butler

Wicklow-born Patrick Butler first worked for E.B. Gleeson on his Adelaide property, Gleeville. Gleeson's bankruptcy schedule[65] listed Butler as owed £36.4.9. Butler followed Gleeson north, seemingly untroubled by their difficult early economic association. By the mid 1840s Butler was buying and selling land in the Clare Valley region. His Catholicism explained the 1844 use of his barn for the area's first mass, and in 1858, his property was the site of Catherine Coffy's first wedding. In another link to the Church, his 1848 loan of £27 to Adelaide's Bishop Murphy demonstrated his economic progress.[66] In 1849 he became treasurer of the Clare school planning committee; E.B. Gleeson was a fellow member.[67] Demonstrating something of an entrepreneurial bent, in March 1849 he applied for a publican's licence for Armagh, appealing in 1850 when his application was again refused. He emphasised his local residency of nine years and quoted Gleeson's support but to no avail.[68] This was also the year when he both received a timber licence and was cited as 'the first discoverer of these [potentially copper lode bearing] hills' in a letter to the Royal Mining Company.[69]

Butler demonstrated his commitment to the local community in many ways. In 1853, he joined Gleeson as a founding member of the Clare council, and followed him as chairman in 1857, remaining a member until 1867. In the 1850s Butler also became publicly involved in local politics to the extent of promoting parliamentary candidates.[70] In 1859, a number of local Irishmen were among those forming the Clare committee of the South Australian Parliamentary Association (SAPA), a body committed to political change, and representing working men rather than wealthy landowners.[71] Butler became chairman, and Peter Brady a committee member; Gleeson's public opposition to the organisation reflected class differences. Butler's earlier willingness to employ a young woman from the servants depot – Mary Casey or Canese – demonstrates both responsiveness to the girls' situation, as well as his financial security.[72]

In the mid 1860s, his name was increasingly associated with district 'Ploughing Matches'.[73] In 1857 for example, he judged the best working bullock category,[74] but in other years, his employees competed, as shown in the 1864 report, which reveals as much positively about Butler as it does about contemporary societal attitudes.

> Great ... [interest] was created by an aboriginal [sic], who with a team of horses, manfully contested for a prize, and won ... £2 ... and, by the management of two powerful and very spirited horses and his plough, showing ... [his skill] ... In my opinion great credit is due to his employer, Mr Patrick Butler, for the style in which he was placed on the field.[75]

The incident provides some insights into the colonist-Indigenous relationships, but also indicates perhaps early evidence of what has been claimed elsewhere about close interaction between Irish and Indigenous.[76]

John Hope's diaries from May 1853 to September 1870 contain numerous references to Butler. The entries typically belong to three categories: Hope seeking Butler's advice or organising his assistance,[77] interaction between the two men which involved one going to see the other but without a specific purpose being nominated,[78] or the two working together on some project.[79] The Hope diaries are rich with the names of Hope's employees,[80] passing individuals,[81] and more formalised social interaction with the regional 'upper class'.[82] But his references to Butler exude deep respect, reliance and trust, without suggesting they were on the same social plane. Both Hope's account books and some letters provide evidence of loans to Butler,[83] and in 1867 Butler approached Hope about lending £1000 to Brady.[84] Late in 1855 he had written of Butler: 'he is from home'.[85] Hope interacted comfortably with Butler's sons,[86] and consistently utilised Butler's skills to deal with potential problems while absent from Clare.[87]

Butler did not remain in the Clare Valley. His wife died in September 1871, and in April 1873, like other Clare Valley farmers taking advantage of the provisions under the *Strangways Land Act 1869*, he moved further north to Canowie Belt.[88] After 30 years residence in Armagh, he was noted as an 'active and useful member of society'.[89] A widely reported court case of April 1875, heard before JPs E.B. Gleeson and others, related to a breach of promise case (£100) against him. Having admitted to 'being lonely', the name of Bridget Kelly, a single woman of Sevenhill (who claimed to have known him for 10 or 12 years) was among those suggested as potential wives. There were discussions and allegedly a wedding date fixed for late October 1874. Butler's evidence revealed concern about Bridget's debts and wanting a settlement, and also 'he had heard that she was free in drinking brandy, and that she was fond of tattling'. The verdict procured £50 for Bridget; Patrick Butler had married another Bridget, Bridget Sexton in February at Canowie.[90] Sadly, he died as a result of a dray accident near Farrell Flat on 13 April the following year.[91] His estate details revealed he had retained his Armagh house and landholdings of over 760 acres (many leased) in the Clare area.[92]

Peter Brady

The Brady family from Cavan reflected the pattern of chain migration. Peter (born in 1817) and his two brothers made significant contributions to the colony. Peter and Bridget (née Smith), were not far behind Daniel and Rose (née Rudden) in 1840, while Michael and Eleanor (née Maguire) arrived later in 1849. Both Daniel and Peter were responsible for sponsoring many others from Cavan; Bridget's father, an arrival of 1849, was just one who benefited.[93] By the time they headed to Mintaro in 1851, the Bradys were relatively experienced colonists.[94]

Figure 5. Bridget Brady (left) and Peter Brady (right).
(Photos courtesy Gerald Lally)

Like Butler, the Bradys' Mintaro house was also used as a mass centre and wedding venue from 1852. But in 1855 in an early land donation, Peter Brady offered two acres of Section 318, a prominent site just outside Mintaro, for the construction of a Catholic church.[95] He then provided 'an entertainment ... in a building temporarily erected for the purpose' on the November 1856 day of the church's blessing and opening.[96] Subsequently he provided hospitality in a 'hearty manner' to those travelling long distances to attend mass.[97] Beyond his commitment to Catholicism, the religion of most local Irishmen, Brady extended his civic benevolence toward education by offering half an acre for a schoolhouse in May 1856. Several years later, the local community benefited from his support of Mintaro's race meeting on his property's course.[98] Years later, in 1865 and 1867, newspaper reports provided evidence both of his economic position and his commitment to Mintaro. Initially he subdivided land 'into allotments with streets for building purposes'.[99] Subsequently he sold 20 half-acre lots at the expensive rate of £50 an acre, in order to break the private property barrier then strangling the town's expansion.[100]

In 1854, when first standing for council, Brady was described as a special favourite with the ratepayers of both Clare and Mintaro.[101] When he then joined the council, half the members were Irish; this did not, however, guarantee they worked as a bloc.[102] He remained a member till 1861. Like Butler, Brady's opinion was sought in the endorsement of parliamentary candidates.[103] Following the exclusive founding of the Clare Agricultural Society in 1857 – this included both E.B. Gleeson and John Hope and other major landowners – a Mintaro meeting presided over by Brady formed an oppositional group.[104] The early 1860s reflected political volatility – and at times located Butler and Brady on opposite sides of the fence despite their South Australian Political Association (SAPA) involvement. A local SAPA challenge (fully supported by Butler)[105] to prominent MP and Irishman G.S. Kingston in 1860 was successful, but in the by-election that quickly followed, Brady's endorsement of Kingston stated he 'had ever found him an upright and consistent man'.[106]

Presiding over a meeting in 1860 to farewell Mintaro's teacher, Brady was the subject of unqualified compliments. These were endorsed by 'half a dozen gentlemen'. There was 'glowing praise' of his colonial career:

> Upon his notorious generosity and hospitality, his house being a home ... [for everyone] who wanted one, irrespective of country or creed or class or anything else but the fact that they had need of assistance.[107]

Brady's community enthusiasm was reflected in his 1864 membership of Mintaro's committee which was focused on attracting a local doctor,[108] and then his role, like Butler's, in various aspects of local ploughing matches.[109] At a meeting of Mintaro and Burra residents in 1867 – following the March closure of Burra's copper mine – about extending the railway from Roseworthy, north of Gawler, Brady proposed the need for speedy construction based on work happening simultaneously at various points along the route.[110] But in June 1869, the insolvent, Peter Brady, assigned his debts to a Sevenhill farmer and a Mintaro blacksmith, and in July a

37-acre portion of Section 318 at Mintaro containing a 'Stone House ... now occupied by ... [him]' was offered for sale.[111] He died in February 1884; when Bridget died in January 1893, she was buried with him in Mintaro's Catholic cemetery.[112]

Mary Ann Geary

Mary Ann Geary was born in Carlow, probably in 1825.[113] She was in her mid 20s, when she reached Port Adelaide in 1850, after a voyage of 90 days ex Plymouth. The Emigration Fund of London paid her passage.[114] Her occupation was listed as 'cook'. Although little is known of her early life in Ireland, her time as a servant for John Hope has sufficient detail to provide some insight into the often complex relationships between young Irish immigrant women and their financially and socially powerful employers.[115] Mary was a determined woman of substantial courage and sharp wit, as shown by her life.

Mary Geary moved to Clare, and by 1852 she was employed as a servant by George Hawker on his station Bungaree.[116] She left Hawker's employment the following year when he departed on an overseas trip; in his absence, as mentioned previously, John Hope was managing Bungaree and thus became responsible for Geary's employment.[117] On Hawker's return, Hope took up residence in Wolta Wolta, the cottage he had built on freehold land nearer Clare. Mary Geary worked as a household servant intermittently for John Hope for six years.

Hope and Geary formed a close working relationship but there is nothing in Hope's diaries to show their relationship became intimate. However, these records do indicate that Geary was given substantial freedom to buy and sell goods, engage domestic staff, and organise and attend social functions, a freedom that transgressed the social norms of the time.[118] She had frequent social interactions with the Gleesons and the Hawkers, entertaining the latter at Wolta Wolta.[119]

On 2 January 1856, Mary Geary became the owner of Section 304 (117 acres), hundred of Clare in the County of Stanley, but she quickly sold this land, making a profit of £45.[120] John Hope gave Mary the money for this purchase.[121] On 1 July 1862, Mary became the owner of Allotments 40, 41, 52 and 53, in the township of South Armagh, Hundred of Clare.[122] These remained in her possession until her death.[123]

The Hope diaries show that in the period 1856 to 1857, John Hope became very concerned for Geary's deteriorating health, an illness that may have been an early symptom of the breast cancer that caused her death. Mary Geary's final mention in Hope's diaries is Thursday 3 May 1860, the year she left Clare to reside in Adelaide. This was a year after Hope returned to Wolta Wolta from Dublin with Isabella, his Irish bride.

In 1861, Mary Geary took legal action against John Hope in the Supreme Court of South Australia (Civil Sittings). The case involved a claim by Geary for the balance of wages (£50 to £60) due to her by her former employer.[124] At first glance the trial, widely reported in the Adelaide press, seems unremarkable. The dispute was straightforward, and the sum involved was relatively small for John Hope, but certainly not for Mary Geary whose wages were about £30 per annum. Yet, the case developed into an intriguing legal drama branching out in unpredictable ways. There were allegations of forgery, manipulation of financial accounts, seduction and illegitimacy. A detailed analysis of this trial, and of Mary Geary's life, is being undertaken and will be published elsewhere. The entire episode provides insights into the ways the legal system and the press dealt with power struggles in the newly founded colony. It seems remarkable that a young female servant who was in ill health and with limited resources was willing to challenge her employer, an older man with significantly greater financial and social capital. Initially Mary's success was total because the jury returned a verdict in favour of the plaintiff – Hope was ordered to pay Geary £61. But John Hope's legal team appealed and the Full Court approved a motion 'for a new trial'.[125] There is no record of a new trial taking place. Thus, Mary Geary's victory was qualified. Significantly, John Hope's reputation did not appear to suffer.[126]

Mary Geary was admitted to the Adelaide Hospital on 9 October 1863 with breast cancer and discharged 10 days later.[127] She died at Norwood on 24 January 1865, aged about 40 years, and was buried at the West Terrace Cemetery. She had no known relatives in South Australia; there is no commemorative headstone – a desolate end to a short but active life.

Catherine Coffy[128]

The final individual in this early Irish group was Catherine Coffy. Her birthplace was probably Westmeath, c. 1831.[129] Catherine's colonial arrival was traumatic; she was one of 300 single Irish women and labourers on the *Nashwauk* when it was wrecked on 13 May 1855, close to the mouth of the Onkaparinga River, south of Adelaide.[130] All were rescued. But this influx of more Irish domestic servants coincided with a peak in anti-Irish prejudice.[131] In late June, following a proposal to establish country servants depots, the opinion of rural officials, including mayors, JPs and clergy, was sought about local labour demands and the various factors involved in organising depots.[132] From Clare, unlike some areas, came overwhelmingly positive responses. Among those consulted were Gleeson as mayor; William Lennon, the Irish-born town clerk; John Hope JP; and Adelaide's Irish-born Bishop Murphy.[133] Less than four weeks later, Catherine was among the first group of 20 who endured a wet, difficult, six-day journey from Adelaide to Clare. Further groups came later; these significantly added to the area's Irish population, and a number of these young women married locally.[134]

On 27 July, three days after arriving, Coffy was hired by English-born William Hitchcox, a local saddler, and his family for 2/6 per week.[135] The arrangement lasted until some point in 1856, but in December, court records reveal an unhappy ending. Coffy took her former employer to court, accusing him of refusing her £6.7.0 after 20 weeks, despite being hired at 5/- a week and giving notice. Mrs Hitchcox disputed the claim that there had been notice, disputed the hiring conditions and claimed the payment had been £10 per annum. The young woman, perhaps surprisingly (and like Geary some years later) ready to resort to the legal pathway, was awarded £4 and costs. Without specific knowledge of her situation or support system, it seems likely she may have received encouragement from Patrick Butler, in whose Armagh barn she subsequently married Robert Henry in June 1858.[136] The couple had two daughters: Margaret in 1860 and Mary on 11 June 1864. Robert died on 21 September; two months later, Catherine married German-born Joseph Mueller. A recent widower with five children, he and Catherine later had a son. The marriage lasted till Joseph's death in 1895, Catherine remained in the area until her decline in old age. She died in 1918. The couple are buried together in the Sevenhill Catholic Cemetery. Catherine Coffy was an unusual woman for her time. While nothing is known of her early circumstances in Ireland, she survived major challenges thereafter, displaying courage, resilience and faithfulness.

Figure 6. Catherine Mueller (née Coffy, formerly Henry), previously a resident of the Clare Servant Depot, c. 1912.
(Photo courtesy of Catherine's descendants)

Conclusion

This chapter has demonstrated that Irish-born colonists had very significant impacts on the Clare Valley region. Surprisingly, the research has uncovered evidence of some productive relationships between Irish colonists and their Indigenous employees. It has also suggested that the Irish-born males interacted in various ways: on a social and legal level for the more affluent and prominent Gleeson and Hope; in the sphere of local government for Gleeson, Hope (briefly), Butler and Brady; and as supportive/skilful/knowledgeable neighbours for Hope and Butler. Female interaction was more limited, but Catholicism clearly enabled a network that facilitated Catherine Coffy's wedding at Patrick Butler's residence. Contributions from these Irish men include their commitment to the region in terms of investment in property; construction of dwellings; roles in (and donations to) Clare's churches, local government and legal system as JPs; and involvement in the success of the servants depot. The labour and skills of all six played a part in the early development of the Clare

Valley. The women highlighted labour equity issues through their legal action and played their part in the rarely recognised but critical domestic development, and their labour contributed to the local economy in many ways. These individuals, with the exception of Mary Geary, assisted in the important process of peopling the region. Gleeson, Hope, and Brady remained in the Clare Valley, although Hope undertook numerous trips back to Ireland, expanded his landholdings inter-colonially, contemplated moving to another country, and ultimately died en route to Clare.[137] Butler moved north to Canowie Belt and was killed accidentally. Geary's health forced a move to Adelaide where her death occurred, while incredibly, Coffy survived to old age and was buried in the Clare Valley. The lives of all these Irish-born individuals reflect both fortune and misfortune. Some seemed able to overcome any obstacle, while, for others, colonial life ultimately generated impassable challenges.

The unexpected Irishmen: How David Power and Anthony Sutton established an Irish colonial presence in the South East of South Australia

NEISHA WRATTEN

Judging by published histories, an unassuming reader could be forgiven for thinking that the South East district of South Australia was solely an Anglo-Scottish enclave. In her study of settlement in this region, historian Leith Macgillivray makes only perfunctory mention of the two subjects of this paper.[1] Of the published family histories, only Pam and Brian O'Connor's work on the settlers in the Mount Gambier region includes the few of Irish extraction, and, while their genealogical information is considerable, they do not place these accounts into a greater historical context.[2] When Eric Richards writes about the myths around the Irish diaspora to South Australia, he also fails to mention the region of the South East and its Gaelic settlers. He does, however, enlarge upon the threads that deserve closer examination when considering the issue of Irish settlement on foreign soil. These include land acquisition and economic independence, establishment of networks of family and friends and engagement with the community at large. He also points out that for many of the Irish in South Australia the thorniest 'sticking point' was not their nationality, but their religion – Catholicism.[3]

This chapter examines the lives of two different Irish-born pastoralists, Anthony Sutton and David Power, who settled in the region during the 'second wave' of migration to South Australia in the 1840s. It assesses their achievements, both positive and negative, in their newly chosen home, and considers how their pre-emigration experiences in Ireland, their

Left: Anthony Sutton, 1875 (State Library of South Australia B3042) and
Right: David Power (State Library of South Australia B3077)

experience of 'Irishness', impacted on their lives in a country very different from their homeland.

Background

Anthony Sutton was the older of the two men, with his Catholic baptism record dated as 28 February 1808, in the parish of Delgany, County Wicklow.[4] He married Mary Kiernan or Kirwan in 1836 and they subsequently had two sons, John and James, prior to emigrating in 1841.[5] The young family crossed to Plymouth, and sailed as assisted migrants on the *Middlesex*, arriving in Port Phillip on 30 September.[6] They promptly set sail again for Portland Bay the following month on the *Ellen and Elizabeth*, where Sutton found employment with Edward Henty, a well-known pastoralist, 'at £30 per annum and two rations'.[7] He remained in the district until 15 December 1845, when he accepted 500 merino ewes in lieu of wages and set off with Henty's brother John for the Mount Gambier district of South Australia, his family and goods packed on a bullock dray.[8] The Henty family had had a presence in the area since 1839 or 1840 as a result of establishing a sheep station at the foot of Mount Gambier. They failed, however, to secure the government licence for the property and it was lost to Evelyn Sturt around 1845.[9] John Henty soon returned to the family's Victorian holdings, having not succeeded in securing his desired acreage. Anthony Sutton remained – and took up a lease of 15 square miles, about 10 miles to the north of the original Henty station, on a piece of wet and marshy ground, known as the Dismal Swamp.'[10]

David Power was born in Carrick-on-Suir, County Tipperary, on 31 March 1813 and baptised as a Catholic. His parents were David Power, a wealthy bacon merchant, and Bridget Higgins.[11] His journey to Australia was self-funded, aboard the fast and relatively comfortable *Mellish*, which departed from London on 22 March 1840 and made the trip to Australia in record time, arriving on 29 June.[12] He was listed as having taken up a station known as Wando Dale or Three Wandos in the Portland Bay district of Victoria in December 1844, and a licence to depasture stock was advertised the following year.[13] The station covered an area of 19,806 acres (just over 30 square miles) and could accommodate 800 cattle – Power never showed an interest in sheep-farming.[14] Like Sutton, he came overland to South Australia and first appeared in the records in 1846 as having been issued an occupation licence – 'SE from Mt Muirhead' – close to where Millicent is situated today.[15]

Land ownership, independence and economic prosperity
Both Sutton and Power initially took up occupation licences in 1846 – neither had purchased land in the colony at that stage.[16] The Return of the Commissioner of Crown Lands for 1848, 1849 and 1850 described Sutton as holding 15 square miles, with 22 cattle and 830 sheep by 1848. This was increased to 34 cattle and 1800 sheep by 1850. In the same document, Power was listed as holding 120 square miles. He ran cattle only, starting with 1950 beasts in 1848, and the numbers remained stable over the next two years.[17] However, as the government of the day could resume the land for survey and sale with only a few months' notice, there was no security of tenure for either man until the 1851 introduction of the system of 14-year leases.

The regulations around these leases, which began on 1 July 1851, were gazetted in late 1850. The land was graded as first, second or third quality, with the annual rents per square mile being £1, 15 shillings or 10 shillings respectively. The lease could be terminated by the lessee, or by the government if the need for smaller agricultural blocks rather than larger

Extract from Map of the Leased Lands, South Australia, 1857-1859, showing the location of Power and Sutton's landholdings (SRSA, GRG 35/585)

pastoral areas became apparent. A hundred (an area of approximately 100 square miles) was surveyed and the land put up for sale.[18] If a pastoralist had already occupied the land, he was entitled to demand a 14-year lease – and both Sutton and Power did so.

Power took up four leases. No. 187 was 20 square miles in area and at £1 per square mile was the best class of land. This run was to the south-east of Mount Gambier and part of one of the most fertile areas in the district. The other three, Nos. 354, 355 and 356 were poorer quality land, closer to the coast. The total area of these leases was 365 square miles, all at 10 shillings per square mile.[19] Sutton took up a lease at Dismal Swamp to the north of Mount Gambier, measuring only nine square miles, also assessed at the lowest rate.[20]

Leasing was not the only way to acquire property in 1851. Seeking extra funds, the government put some land in the colony up for sale. The majority of the pastoralists, including Power, elected not to purchase at that time, perhaps relying on the distance from Adelaide as protection for their leases as suggested by Macgillivray – or possibly the interest of potential purchasers was distracted by the discovery of gold in Victoria. Sutton, however, blinked – and took up the opportunity to purchase 160 acres, at a cost of £1 per acre, the 'upset price'.[21]

For generations of Irish, the dream of owning land in the 19th century was just that – land having been rented from landlord (often absentee) to tenant farmer, down to the labourer with his 'conacre' block, in successively smaller parcels. The dispossession of the Irish commenced early in the 17th century, with over two million acres of fertile land in West Ulster being seized by the British crown and settled with English and Scots Protestants, leaving the poorer country for the native population. This became known as the Plantation of Ulster and was followed by the establishment of other plantations throughout Ireland – although none was ever as successful.[22] This situation was compounded by the invasion and victory of Oliver Cromwell in 1649, in retaliation for the revolt of the remaining Catholic landowners in Ulster in 1641. Eleven million acres of land were confiscated and awarded to his Protestant soldiers and supporters. This set the pattern for land ownership in Ireland until the early 20th century. During this time, referred to as the Protestant Ascendancy, more than 90 per cent of the country was in the hands of Protestant – and largely British – landowners.[23] In light of this history, the Irish fixation on secure land tenure becomes understandable. This characteristic seems an intrinsic part of Sutton's 'Irishness', one that travelled with him to his new home. The risk, however small, of losing hold on any part of the dream was not one he could afford to take.

The Victorian gold rush provided a healthy boost to the South Australian economy, and the situation was very different at the land sales in June 1854. City investors, speculators and agriculturalists began in earnest to compete with the pastoralists.[24] Sutton fell prey to this competition – he purchased another 100 acres at Dismal Swamp (Section 3500) for £172 at the sales, and in 1855 a further 80 acres from Thomas Magarey (one of the large investors) for £168. However, he was forced to pay speculators an inflated price of £560 (£7 per acre) in November 1854, in order to purchase a similar block that he desired.[25]

Power was more fortunate – and shrewder. In May 1852 he purchased 160 acres of what was originally the 'Compton' run from William for £300. This was arguably one of the finest pieces of land in the district and adjacent to his No. 187 run. In June of the same year, he disposed of his Victorian station.[26] The following year, he requested a survey, and in May 1854, 4356 acres of the No. 187 run were resumed. By April 1855, Power had purchased 6729 acres of land for the grand price of £16,512 – over £2 per acre. This may have seemed a steep price, but considering that he had paid £510 for 81 acres from a land agent in October 1854, perhaps he saw it as a bargain.[27] Like other landowners with capital, Power was able to secure the best parts of his lease.

The next decision of the colonial government that confronted the Irishmen was the 1858 declaration of the Hundreds of Blanche, Gambier, Grey, Hindmarsh and Young. Both Run No. 187 (Power) and Run No. 206 (Sutton) were resumed in December of 1857, prior to survey and sale by auction the following year to augment government coffers.[28] By this time, Power had cancelled his lease of Run No. 356, leaving him with only No. 355, the Avenue station.[29] He wrote, requesting a survey of his land, as did many other pastoralists, and in 1858, again purchased heavily – a total of 1397 acres for just over £1638 – in order to protect the most valuable parts of his runs.[30] Sutton did the same, obtaining 639 acres for £639.[31]

After all the land purchases in 1858, a newspaper item in October 1859 must have caused some eyebrows to be raised and moustachios to twitch – and not only those of the stockholders in the district, but even as distant as Tasmania: 'Mr David Power, of Mount Gambier, has sold his station and stock, including several thousand acres of land bought and enclosed, to Mr Charles Fisher for the sum of £60,000.'[32] This was a slight exaggeration – when the title was registered the following year, Power had sold 9863 acres to Charles Fisher and William Browne for £45,000. It was still an astonishing sum – just over $5,000,000 in today's money.[33]

Power left no record of his reasons for the sale. In February 1859, major bushfires had encroached on his property, threatening his stock, property and his total investment.[34] The continual changes in South Australian land legislation and the lack of government support for infrastructure, such as roads or a new port, would have created frustration. In addition, a worrying form of pleuropneumonia had started to affect cattle in the district, but the authorities had failed to put any resources into its management, preferring to put all their energies into controlling scab, a highly infectious mite disease of sheep.[35] Fisher had been attempting to buy property in the district for some time, so perhaps it was opportune to sell – and Power was smart enough to take advantage.[36]

Coming from a relatively affluent commercial background where land ownership was by no means uncommon, it would seem Power had no attachment to land as an emotional entity. His actions, during his sojourn in South Australia and in his later life, support this. He viewed it as an asset, to be bought and sold for his own benefit and financial security, and that of his family. The Powers and their children departed in 1860 for Adelaide. There he placed his affairs in the hands of his attorneys, Abraham and Henry Scott, and sailed for England in the following year.[37]

The Power family remained in Scotland and later England until 1871. David and his wife retired to Cloverdale, a mansion in Toorak, Melbourne, passing the reins of the family business to his son David Herbert. In his senior years, Power took a keen interest in the sport of greyhound coursing – although he did not completely abandon business pursuits. At the time of his death during a visit to Adelaide in 1884, he was the chairman of the directors of the National Bank of Australasia.[38]

Sutton remained in the South East until his death in 1879. He continued to buy land, both at government sales and from private vendors. He also sold on land – except for those sections connected with the Dismal Swamp run, which he held on to for the rest of his days and passed to his fifth son, also named Anthony. In this action, he displays an aspect of his essential 'Irishness' – placing significance on being able to pass this great treasure, this 'Holy Grail' of land, on to his family.[39]

Macgillivray, in her study of settlement and land in the South East of South Australia, stated that unsuccessful licensees lacked either capital, experience or good land.[40] To this list, should be added judgement, in knowing when or not to sell. Sutton had ample experience but limited capital and poorer land. What was possibly the defining experience of his background in Ireland created a strong emotional attachment to the soil, meaning that he could not bring himself to sell, even if it meant profit for him and his family.[41] Power was more affluent, had good land and experience from his station in Victoria. Viewing land as a commodity and having the judgement to know when to sell for maximal profit, meant comfort and financial security for the future. When Power died in 1884 and probate on his will was granted, his assets were valued at

£32,500.⁴² Sutton's estate, despite rumours, was not as substantial.⁴³ But for that Irishman, achieving the dream of independent land ownership was probably a far greater measure of success than a simple monetary figure.

Networks – family and others
Richards pointed out that one of the most successful aspects of Irish migration was the ability to re-establish close family networks and effectively utilise the assisted migration system to achieve this.⁴⁴ In light of his comments, it seems reasonable to examine the lives of both Sutton and Power, to examine how they facilitated and supported their families and close connections.

Sutton migrated with his wife, Mary, and two sons, James and John, in 1841.⁴⁵ It appears he was the first member of his family to make the Antipodean journey. Nine more children were then added to the family. Of the sons, William, Jeremiah and Anthony survived until adulthood. Charles and Samuel did not. Daughters Anne, Elizabeth, Emily and Mary all married. Pam and Brian O'Connor, the published family historians, describe how Sutton the elder assisted four of his sons to establish properties of their own. Anthony the younger, the fifth son, inherited the Dismal Swamp property. Land records support that the father was closely involved in the financial affairs of his offspring.⁴⁶

The other claim made by the O'Connors is that Sutton assisted three of his younger siblings to emigrate to Australia, a practice not uncommon among many migrant groups. John and Honora Sutton arrived via Melbourne in 1848 (during the Great Famine), and James with his wife and daughter followed in 1852, via Adelaide. All three made their way to the South East where they settled and remained. This chain migration would have been a very 'Irish' act on Sutton's part, but unfortunately Wicklow baptism records have been unable to confirm that these three were his siblings. However, given that they made their respective ways to come under his care and patronage, it seems highly likely that they were relatives, perhaps cousins, who would certainly be protected under the Irish umbrella of kinship.⁴⁷

The circumstances of Power's arrival in Port Phillip were considerably different. He landed in 1840, a bachelor, accompanied by his brother Robert Higgins Power, a surgeon, and his sister-in-law, Mary Sophia. Mary's husband (and David's brother), Thomas Herbert Power, had arrived 12 months previously. He had set up business as an auctioneer and was waiting to welcome his wife and brothers.[48] So, to some extent, Power was migrating into a social network with already-established connections.

In 1851, David married Anne, the daughter of James Pile, a Gawler pastoralist, whose property was over 300 miles from Power's listed residence, the Avenue run in the South East.[49] Their first daughter, Isabella, was born the following year, followed in quick succession by David Herbert and Mary. Three sons were lost as children. After the family left Australia for England in 1861, a further four children were added to the family – Edward, Charles, Herbert and Francis.[50]

Evidence that Power assisted other members of his family to migrate has not come to light, but there are references suggestive of support to other migrants, including the Irish, especially those in less fortunate situations than those he and his siblings enjoyed. He assisted those in his employ to advertise in newspapers for other family members arrived in the colony in the hope of reuniting them.[51] And, like his countrymen, he became an effective user of the assisted-passage system.

Under the 'nomination' scheme introduced in 1852, for every £80 spent on Crown land purchases, a settler was entitled to nominate three adult migrants for the journey to Australia. These individuals did have to be eligible under Colonial Land and Emigration Commission regulations, but the choice of the person was up to the land purchaser or his nominated agent.[52] Correspondence from the Colonial Secretary's office indicates that as Power had spent £16,512 on land, he was entitled to select 413 adult migrants. Power nominated his medical brother, Robert H. Power, who had returned to England, as his agent.[53] Due to the limited survival of South Australian shipping records, it has not been possible to confirm whether Power took advantage of this opportunity, and we do not know if any of his fellow countrymen benefited from his largesse. Given Power's other actions during his sojourn in South Australia, it is to be hoped that they did.

In 1854 and 1855, South Australia was inundated with single female immigrants, brought out to fill the colony's demands for labour. Many of these girls were Irish. But the 1854 harvest had not met expectations, and consequently, these young women were without employment and income. The situation in Adelaide was far from ideal – the girls were crammed into an inadequate and unpleasant reception facility, facing the criticism of an Adelaide public only too keen to point the deficiencies in their behaviour and their training for service. The solution was the establishment of the Female Immigration Board, which first met in October 1855. Among the many duties of this board was the facilitation and encouragement of the girls to leave the central urban depots and move rurally, not only to seek employment, but also to aid their integration into the community of the colony.[54]

The depot for the South East was established at Robe in July 1855 under the supervision of Charles Brewer, the government resident and stipendiary magistrate. Initially pessimistic about the employment prospects at Robe, he hoped to find the girls positions at inland centres, such as Mosquito Creek (Naracoorte), Penola and Mount Gambier. This proved to be the eventual outcome.[55] On 24 July, Power wrote to the Colonial Secretary, specifically on the subject of 'Irish female immigrants', stating that while he did not believe a large number would be able to be absorbed into the district, he had already communicated with Andrew Watson, the stipendiary magistrate at Penola. His hope was that the two districts, Mount Gambier and Penola, could unite to find employment for these women. Clearly, he had already been approached by Brewer. Power's identification of these young women as Irish shows an additional concern for those of his countrymen and women, beyond that of a man who felt quite strongly about social responsibility.[56]

Community engagement

Anthony Sutton's involvement with his community was primarily through his church. His obituary in the local *Border Watch* confirms this – 'he never took a prominent part in public affairs, but he was a generous supporter of his church and one of the most hospitable of men.'[57]

According to family history, the first mass in the district was celebrated at Dismal Swamp in 1847, when a priest from Victoria lost his way and was taken in by the Suttons.[58] As auspicious as this occasion was, it was trumped by the 1854 visit of the first bishop of Adelaide, the Very Reverend Francis Murphy. He stayed two weeks with the family, enduring their living conditions and performing his religious duties.[59] Sutton was already well known to Murphy, whose diary recorded that since 1851 he and his vicar-general, Michael Ryan, had taken on the role of informal bankers for the Catholic settlers of the south east, paying their leasing fees at the Treasury.[60]

It was clear that the Church, in return, viewed Sutton as a reliable donor. The O'Connors refer to a letter written in December 1857 to Julian Tenison Woods, the new resident priest at Penola, suggesting that Mr Anthony Sutton of Dismal Swamp would be happy to assist with land purchases on the Church's behalf. A few years later Sutton was a major contributor to the building fund for St Theresa's at Mount Gambier, and, in 1869, he made a £1200 interest-free loan to the parish for the purchase of the site where St Paul's church now stands.[61] It would seem, perhaps, that Sutton did not have a high regard for the priest's financial management skills, as this extract from a letter written by the local incumbent to his vicar-general the year after Sutton's demise makes clear:

> I was not aware until a few days ago that Mr Sutton had got the deeds of all the Church property in Mount Gambier, and has them deposited in his own name in the Bank. This may be awkward at some future time, so I must proceed carefully until I get out of debt, and hand them over to you. Then everything would be safe. Who gave Dean Fitzgibbon authority to hand over the Deeds? This should be looked into in good time.[62]

None of the above should be taken to mean that Sutton remained entirely on the side of the angels throughout his sojourn in the district. In 1863, he was fined £20 for depasturing 300 sheep and 250 cattle on Dismal Swamp, which was licensed under the government regulations then in force for 1000 sheep only.[63] A further charge of illegally depasturing 1000 sheep on the reserve (Crown land) at Tarpeena was dismissed in 1866 on the grounds of inconclusive evidence. In 1869, scab, the previously mentioned sheep disease that had serious economic consequences for the entire community, was discovered in his flocks. The chief inspector of sheep, Mr Valentine, was extremely critical: 'For some months past, Mr A. Sutton has risked picking up stray sheep from the proclaimed district which might have been prevented by an outlay in fencing of about £12.'[64]

Given the potentially disastrous consequences of the infection to his neighbours' sheep, let alone his own, this last event is difficult to understand. It may have been accidental or perhaps due to ignorance, both eminently reasonable explanations. No evidence has come to light of any interaction of Sutton with his non-Catholic neighbours, apart from on business matters. It could be speculated that his concept of community only embraced those of his own religious faith, something to which he was obviously so deeply committed.

David Power's engagement with his surrounding community was, on the other hand, more varied and more visible. It commenced with a donation to support the ill-fated Adelaide German and British Hospital in 1850 to be followed by his immersion in political affairs of the district in 1851 when he endorsed the conservative Captain John Hart for the Legislative Assembly. He went as far as offering his station as the site for Hart to meet the constituents – an event that did not take place.[65] By 1853, he was appointed as a justice of the peace – a role far more substantive in the legal affairs of a district so distant from the colony's principal courts than might be supposed from its modern equivalent.[66]

Power continued to serve in the above role as the decade progressed and kept up his interest in various charities and local politics. He also entertained some prominent dignitaries at his properties, including Augustus Short, the Anglican bishop of Adelaide, in 1855, and Governor MacDonnell and his party in 1856. Short did not leave a personal impression of Power the man but described his estate as 'perhaps the finest in the colony'.[67] The governor, Sir Richard MacDonnell (a fellow Irishman), was rather more effusive – after all, Power had travelled from Melbourne, where his wife had recently been confined, just to play host to the party, which included the governor's wife, at his Mount Gambier station for several days. (His Avenue station was also used as a staging post on both legs of the overland journey from Robe). In line with the 'liberal and genuine hospitality' for which Power was known, he procured a rowboat and successfully lowered it into what is now the Blue Lake in order for the governor to explore the ancient volcanic crater. The feat was able to be repeated the following day for Lady MacDonnell, and, in thanks for his efforts, Sir Richard declared that the lake should then be known as 'Lake Power'.[68] For reasons unknown this did not come to pass, and the landmark still retains its original title.

By July of the same year Power was appointed as a special magistrate, allowing him additional legal powers, but also increasing the amount of time he had to commit to the court system.[69] Two years later, he wrote to the Colonial Secretary to report the need for a resident magistrate in the district, but did not put his own name forward for the role. In his self-effacing manner, he suggested George Byng Scott, the police inspector at Penola, as the ideal incumbent.[70]

The year 1857 saw the commencement of a series of letters between David Power, JP, and the Central Board of Education in Adelaide. As the schools inspector was unable to visit, Power reported on the inadequacy of the classroom, and supervised the erection of new facilities. He also provided input around the selection and licensing of appropriate teaching staff, including the appointment of a female teacher.[71]

The Power family only just managed to escape calamity in 1859. In February, alarming bushfires threatened the Mount Gambier station on the side of the extinct volcano – and its dwellings would have been lost save for the exertions of Power and his employees. Fortunately, the damage bill was reported to be only £300, when it so nearly could have been thousands. A smaller separate conflagration also threatened Dismal Swamp. Despite this setback, Power continued his duties as special magistrate.[72] But his rather remarkable qualities came to the fore in August of that year, when the steamship *Admella* struck a reef off Carpenter Rocks.

The *Admella*'s wreck was a tragedy – from 100 crew and passengers, only 11 passengers and 13 crew members survived. Those lives lost included men, women and children. When the ship struck the reef in the early hours of 6 August, she was within sight of land. But the survivors failed to attract the attention of passing vessels, and hours passed before several sailors managed to lash a raft together and make it to shore. When Benjamin Germain, the keeper of the Cape Northumberland lighthouse, was advised of the wreck and the predicament of its survivors, the alarm was eventually raised.

Power became aware of the tragedy on the evening of 8 August and proceeded to the wreck the following day.[73] He remained there to witness the entire rescue by various boats, and continued to exhort rescue efforts by offering a £500 reward for any person who would bring someone from the wreck alive.[74] In his capacity as magistrate, he conducted a speedy inquest on the body of a sailor washed ashore, and assisted with provision

Charles Hill, Australia, 1824–1915, *Wreck of the Admella, 1859*
1860, Adelaide, oil on canvas, 55.9 x 99.1 cm, Gift of Howard L. Hill 1944
Art Gallery of South Australia

of blankets and transport to convey both the injured to medical help, and the bodies offsite.[75] His groom, Henry Smith, was one of those men who manned the repaired lifeboat of the *Admella*, and took part in the rescue – Power did not stint in his praise.[76] And when Captain McEwen was brought ashore, conscious of the fact that he could be blamed for the loss of the ship and so many lives, it was to David Power that he turned:

> Mr Power, my case is precarious; I know your character, I appoint you as my agent – act for those in whom I am concerned; act for their interests and I am satisfied. If you need advice, consult with your brother magistrates. Whatever you do I know will be conscientious and right.[77]

Power gave evidence at the subsequent commission into the loss of the ship. He was asked to identify those who should be singled out for their bravery, and also to enquire as to whether a lifeboat crew could be established at the Cape Northumberland lighthouse. His subsequent letters show that not only did he undertake the enquiries but was also fastidious in ensuring that he did not fail to mention any of the rescuers who should be recognised. His final comment in one letter, gives a personal insight into the man and his character:

In conclusion, let me request, that if any portion of my evidence before the Commission, I have in any way made it appear that I took a more active part than those who acted with me, I wish it distinctly understood I acted invariably with them.[78]

Power departed the district the following year. It is small wonder, given his conspicuous and somewhat dazzling role in the small community, that not everyone was a fan of David Power. Robert Rowland Leake, a fellow squatter belonged to that company.

Robert was the son of John Leake, a pre-eminent pastoralist in Tasmania, and had also taken up land in the South East. Reading his correspondence, it is obvious that he believes he should have been considered 'the squatter' of the region. In 1854 he unsuccessfully ran for the Legislative Council against the candidate who had Power's support, Captain Hart.[79] Leake ultimately achieved his ambition in 1857 but resigned his seat within a matter of months after only one visit to Adelaide.[80] This comment about Power was made in a letter to his father in 1859 in regard to land sales in the district:

> I shall have to buy some more land from a neighbour of mine – he's put up 10,000 acres – a Mr D. Power of Mt. Gambier, the man who visited to vilify Brown and Co. He is a bitter greedy Irishman, wants his neighbour's grounds – in my case I cannot blame him so much as I bought some of his run after it was put up for sale.[81]

Although most of the community seemed to regret Power's 1860 departure, there is an entry in one of the local papers from the 'Border Reporter' which is open to interpretation:

> THE 'PET' OF THE PUBLIC – Our Special Magistrate took his departure on Monday last. Mr Power proceeded overland to Guichen Bay, via Frontier House and Mt. Burr, in an American buggy, and, sir, for further particulars I refer you to the report of a meeting which I have cut from the Adelaide Observer.[82]

It can be difficult, given the passage of time, to understand exactly what the writer was trying to convey. The specific mention of Frontier House may shed some light – this was the residence of Leake, a man who was perhaps more likely to be celebrating rather than regretting Power's leave-taking.

Religion

Richards is clear that religion was the greatest divide between the Irish and the rest of South Australian society.[83] In light of this claim, it is important to examine both Power and Sutton's behaviour with regards to this aspect of their lives in Australia, given that both started life baptised into the Catholic faith in Ireland.

Sutton's faith was open, direct and an integral part of his relationship with his family and his new community. Power, on the other hand, was an enigma – his actions showed him to be, unlike Sutton and some of his other countrymen, ecumenically flexible. He married into the Anglican faith. The baptism records of his children have not been able to be traced. After his death in a North Adelaide railway station in 1884, he was buried in the Wesleyan section of the St Kilda Cemetery in Melbourne.[84] He entertained Augustus Short, the Anglican bishop of Adelaide, a man not known for a sympathetic attitude toward those of the Catholic faith, and he continued to socialise with Short's daughter Millicent, who had married George Glen, another pastoralist from the South East, and one of Power's neighbours.[85] While he is not mentioned in any surviving Catholic papers, he continued to discreetly support the Catholic faith by donating toward the construction of their churches in the district.[86] Even in his later life, when he returned to settle in Toorak, Melbourne, after a decade living in England and Scotland, he continued this support. In 1880, two intriguing entries were listed in competing religious newspapers. In September, Power donated £1 to the building fund of St Patrick's Cathedral, the Catholic edifice in Melbourne.[87] The following month, his wife donated the same sum to the building fund of St Paul's Cathedral, the Church of England equivalent.[88] It seems reasonable to suggest that while his adherence to his original faith was never on public display, that faith was never completely abandoned – and it was this religiously exigent attitude, that, in part, contributed to his share of success in his new country.[89]

Conclusion

The purpose of this chapter has been twofold – first, to establish an Irish presence in the history of the settlement of the South East district of South Australia, and second, to examine how these settlers reflected the characteristics of Irish settlement elsewhere in the colony. Sutton's story was that of fierce devotion to land ownership and strong commitment to members of his family and his church, but he was only involved with his surrounding community to the extent of those of the same faith, and as Richards has pointed out, it was this more than any other factor that has set the Irish apart from many of their fellow migrants. Power, by contrast, showed a high degree of commitment to his new community, even though he departed from it after a stay of just over 13 years. His behaviour, especially with regard to land ownership and faith, shows a certain degree of pragmatism – a way to respond to the changing circumstances in his life, which may be reflective of his background in Ireland – a background seemingly quite different to that of Sutton.

The Sutton family is well-remembered in the district, probably so because the family remained for several generations. The attention given to their story by the O'Connors is evidence of this.[90] Power, for all his effort, is a less familiar identity. Incomers to the state of South Australia, even in this century, are still told that there needs to be a 'wedding, baptism and burial' before they can be considered to be a true South Australian. Power had a marriage, several births and a death to his credit – but certainly not a burial. His eldest son, David Herbert, born at the Mount Gambier station, even went on to marry Elsie Mary Parsons, a great-granddaughter of George Fife Angus – considered to be one of the founding fathers of South Australia.

Perhaps if, like Sutton, his memorial stood in the Catholic section of the Lake Terrace Cemetery at Mount Gambier, ironically close to the site of the homestead that was so nearly destroyed in 1859, instead of the Methodist section of the St Kilda Cemetery in Melbourne, Power's contributions would be feted more.

It is more than time for the South East to reclaim its Irish heritage.

Kapunda's Irish connections
SUSAN ARTHURE

In the 1840s and 1850s, Irish migrants to South Australia came from all sections of society – farm labourers and mine workers, pastoralists and farmers, professionals and tradespeople, entrepreneurs and capitalists. They included landless and poor Irish Catholics, middle-class Irish Catholics, and Anglo-Irish gentry of the Protestant Ascendancy. This full range of 'Irishness' could be observed in Kapunda, 75 kilometres north of Adelaide, which was described in the mid-19th century as 'perhaps the largest secondary town in the Colony' with about 3000 inhabitants.[1]

Charles Harvey Bagot arrives in South Australia
Among the first European colonists to arrive in the Kapunda area was Charles Harvey Bagot[2] in 1841. Bagot had been born at Nurney, County Kildare, in 1788 'in the old family mansion'.[3] He was the 11th of 12 children born to Elizabeth and Christopher Bagot, somewhat impoverished members of the Anglo-Irish elite. In his memoirs (which he completed between 1851 and 1854 when he was in his 60s), Bagot reflected back on his early years in Ireland, including his experience of the 1798 rebellion when he was 10 years old. While acknowledging the toll that this rebellion took on his family's finances and health, he was sympathetic overall to the Irish rebels, noting that the Irish were 'forced into open rebellion by the horridly coercive measures' of martial law, floggings, burnings and other outrages by an 'exasperated and badly controlled soldiery'.[4]

After spending time abroad on active service in the British army, Bagot returned to Ireland in 1819 with his wife, Mary, and their growing family in the hope of settling there permanently. In 1821, his brother-in-law, Bindon

Blood (married to Bagot's sister Harriet), offered him the job of land agent for his property in County Clare. He accepted this position gladly, and his relations with the local Irish appear to have been generally benevolent; he describes his house staff as an 'uncultivated but exceedingly civil and amenable Irish peasantry' and the local people as 'a simple inoffensive people, glad to accept employment and grateful for the little attentions to their wants and their comfort it was in our power to show them'.[5] Bagot and his wife appear to have taken their responsibilities seriously, and acted as arbiters in disputes and advocates in times of trouble, seeing the local people as friends.[6] After Bindon Blood moved to a nearby property in 1823, opportunities for social interactions between the families increased, and Blood and his daughters frequently stayed with the Bagots.[7] Although he had fully expected to live in Ireland for the remainder of his days, Bagot was increasingly concerned about ongoing troubles in Ireland and particularly by the potentially negative impact of the Irish Poor Law Act in 1838. Keen to provide for his family and knowing that his sons were attracted to the Australian colonies, he made the decision to move to South Australia.[8]

In August 1840, with Mary and their five children, Bagot set sail on board the *Birman*, bound for Port Adelaide. He took with him a special survey of 4000 acres purchased by Sir Montague Chapman of County Westmeath, who had allocated to Bagot the right to select and manage the 4000 acres in return for a quarter of the land. Chapman was another member of the Anglo-Irish establishment, whose ancestry was from Leicestershire; he later travelled to South Australia in 1852 to finalise his affairs with Bagot.[9] Also travelling on the *Birman* were 224 emigrants in steerage selected by the Colonial Commissioners.[10] They included 42 married couples (84 men and women), 18 single men, 23 single women, and 99 children aged 14 years and younger.[11] Farewelling Bagot were his brothers, George and Edward, and Bindon Blood, all of whom had been staying with the Bagot family in Cork.

Bagot wrote a journal, unpublished, over the course of 1840 and 1841 describing his voyage from Cork to Port Adelaide, and his first year in South Australia.[12] Although the colonial commissioners had selected the steerage emigrants, this was at Bagot's request,[13] and it is clear that he knew at least some of them, as he laments the loss of Michael Hickey from typhus, just a day or two out at sea, 'who had been in my employment and for whom I had a sincere regard'.[14] Published research indicates that, in fact, most of the 224 Catholic emigrants were known to him[15] – although Hickey is the only one he refers to directly in his writings – and that they came from County Clare.[16] Drew states that Bagot was involved in selecting almost all of the emigrants, and that they were mainly people that he knew and trusted from his years in County Clare.[17] Following their arrival in South Australia, these migrants are reported to have moved north with other Irish migrants, some of them to join Bagot at Kapunda.[18] This would certainly fit with the positive reciprocal relationship that Bagot had developed with the Catholic Irish while living in Ireland.

The *Birman* arrived safely in Port Adelaide on 7 December 1840. By his second day in Adelaide, Bagot had already called on the home of his maternal cousin, William Oldham.[19] Oldham had been born in Dublin in 1811, educated at Trinity College Dublin, and had been living in Adelaide since 1838.[20] He accompanied Bagot on his land inspections south of Adelaide as he looked for suitable land to take up for Sir Montague Chapman.[21]

The rise and rise of Kapunda
By April 1841, after travelling great distances in search of land that met his needs, Bagot had settled at Koonunga, 80 kilometres north of Adelaide. Here he established a sheep run, farming some of the sheep on behalf of Frederick Hansborough Dutton, who owned land close by at Anlaby. His ambition of being a successful sheep farmer changed dramatically when, in 1842, his young son, Charles, and Dutton's brother, Francis Stacker Dutton, discovered a rich vein of copper.[22] Neither Bagot nor Dutton initially owned the land on which the copper was found but, through some tactical manoeuvres, they managed to buy it without anybody else realising its potential value. The copper mine opened as a surface mine in 1844[23] and the township that developed close by became known as Kapunda. One of the first instances of the area being referred to as Kapunda, in fact, was in an article in the *Adelaide Observer* in 1845, which refers to the 'Kapunda Mines'.[24]

Output and employment at the mine increased every year for many years, and, during this time, Bagot's connections with other Anglo-Irish men were well-honed. Firstly, in 1846, William Oldham was persuaded to

Figure 1. (left) Charles Bagot, by Townsend Duryea, 1872 (SLSA, B 8235/1/210); (centre) William Oldham, by Townsend Duryea, 1872 (SLSA, B 8235/1/18L); (right) Matthew Blood, unknown photographer, approximately 1860 (SLSA B9945)

come to Kapunda. He was appointed purser at the mine in 1847 and became mine manager on Bagot's retirement in 1848, a position he held until 1867.[25] Then, in 1847, Dr Matthew Henry Smyth Blood (of the County Clare Bloods) emigrated from Ireland.[26] He was appointed mine doctor by Bagot in 1848, and also became Kapunda's first medical doctor.[27]

Forth has argued that social ties and family relationships were particularly important for the Anglo-Irish in Australia and that as a result of their historic situation in Ireland, the Anglo-Irish tended to be close-knit and bound by strong feelings of solidarity.[28] This is evidenced in the case of Bagot, Oldham and Blood (Figure 1) who used their community and kinship bonds to help build successful new lives in South Australia. In Kapunda, they were acknowledged as the 'notable Irishmen' – respectable men of means, Anglo-Irish and Protestant.[29]

In 1852, the Kapunda copper mine suffered a downturn when most of the miners left for the Victorian gold rush. William Oldham later wrote how with nearly all the miners gone, it was 'with considerable difficulty' that the mine engine was kept going and the mine kept dry.[30] At one stage, only four miners remained. However, during 1854 and 'especially in the early part of 1855', Oldham recorded that large numbers of workers either returned or came to work,[31] including significant numbers of Irish migrants.[32] These migrants – Catholic, with little means, not regarded as 'respectable' – were very different from the Anglo-Irish triumvirate of Bagot, Oldham and Blood.

The Irish arrive at Baker's Flat

The year 1854 is generally accepted as the time when this wave of Irish migrants, 'almost 100 per cent Catholic in faith', began to arrive in large numbers at Kapunda, mainly to fill the demand for mine labour.[33] Oral histories, newspaper death notices, and genealogical research indicate that many came from the south-west of Ireland, in particular County Clare.[34] This also fits with statistical reports indicating that, from 1840 to 1866, Clare was the greatest single source of assisted[35] Irish immigrants to South Australia.[36]

These new Irish found a rent-free place to live near the mine – an area

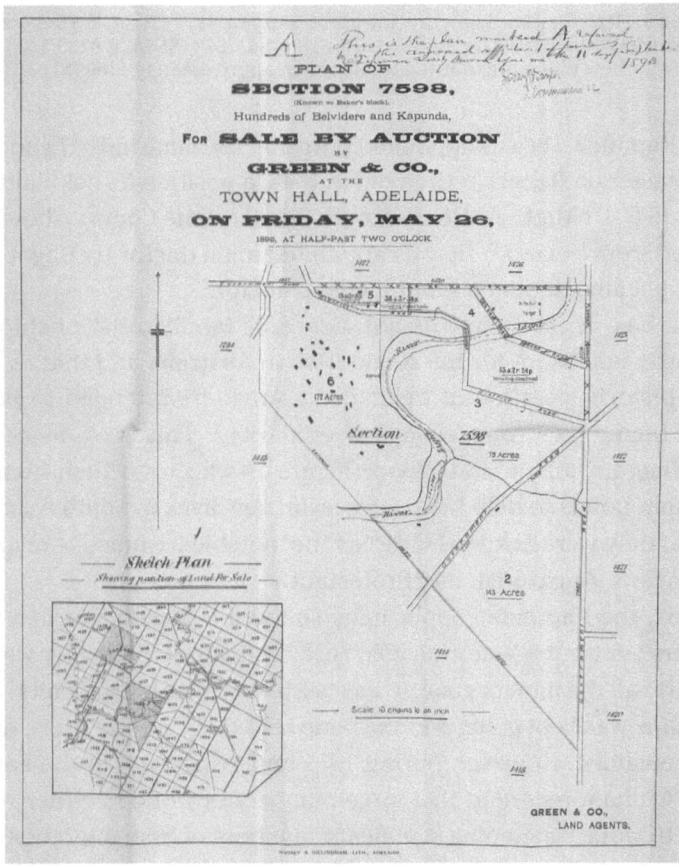

Figure 2. Survey plan of Baker's Flat, drawn in 1893
(State Records of South Australia GRG 36/54/1892/47).

of unused flat land known as Baker's Flat. And this is where an intriguing connection between Bagot, Sir Montague Chapman and the Baker's Flat Irish becomes apparent. The official name for Baker's Flat, sometimes known as Baker's Block, is Section 7598 (Figure 2). Recent research has uncovered the fact that this land, which straddles the river Light, was first surveyed in late 1841 at Bagot's request, and then selected as part of the 4000-acre Chapman selection.[37] Although Section 7598 was allocated to Chapman at that time, it was swapped in 1842 for 500 acres near Dry Creek.[38] By 1845, 490 acres of the section were owned by Mary Baker and her son John Baker (hence 'Baker's Flat'), James Poole and William Howard.[39] In the following years, John Baker sold some portions of it, but continued to be associated with Section 7598 for many years, including when the Irish arrived in 1854.[40]

Although speculative, it is possible that Bagot could have facilitated the settlement of Baker's Flat by the Irish in 1854. At that time, the landowners were absent, the land was unused yet conveniently close to the mine, which required workers, and Bagot knew the land intimately. Combined with his benevolent attitude and sense of responsibility toward the working Irish, and bearing in mind that some of the *Birman* emigrants are recorded as having joined Bagot at Kapunda,[41] it could well be that the appropriation of Baker's Flat by the Irish was not random.

Compounding this is the curious fact that, in 1845, Fr Michael Ryan celebrated mass at the Kapunda mine 'two days in succession', on February 24 and 25.[42] Fr Ryan had barely arrived in Adelaide, yet one of his first duties was 'being despatched to "The Mines"'.[43] It indicates that there were already enough Irish at Kapunda to justify a pastoral visit, and with the Bagot connection, there may already have been Irish people living on Baker's Flat. Drew certainly speculates that the Irish were squatting on Baker's Flat during the late 1840s, and that they came to the area in response to an increased demand for labour after the first horse whim[44] was erected at the mine in 1845, enabling deeper underground workings.[45] It was a similar situation which brought the Irish in the 1850s – the introduction of steam technology enabled deeper workings and led to a need for more mine workers.[46] Either way, by 1854 there were 'significant numbers' of Irish migrants living on Baker's Flat and they are recorded as having quickly formed a 'close, fiercely Irish community'.[47]

Digging in for the long haul

There are few accounts in the printed histories of the Irish settlement on Baker's Flat. A collection of memories about Kapunda was published in 1929, and it includes a description of how this 'lawless little community' evolved.[48]

> With no apparent owners about, by degrees in the course of time a number of squatters settled there, constructing for themselves shelters which developed into hovels of old iron, bags, tins and odds and ends, some with enclosures about them of a few square yards in which to pen up their geese at night. Amongst them they owned a large flock of these birds, which used to graze on the flat and disport themselves in the river. These little holdings clustered together haphazard without the slightest attempt at order or regularity. The inhabitants, squatting rent free, soon developed a community feeling quick to resent any attempted interferences with their acquired privileges.[49]

This account established the narrative for how the Baker's Flat community came to be perceived and continues to be remembered – as a hotchpotch collection of hovels, where the residents did not welcome interference of any sort. Other histories added details about 'small wattle and daub cottages with thatched roofs' where each family ran their pigs, goats and poultry without restraining fences 'of any description',[50] a state of affairs that led Baker's Flat to be viewed by the more affluent members of Kapunda society as a 'blot on the landscape'.[51]

Contemporary newspapers are littered with accounts of disorder and trouble on Baker's Flat. In 1860, for example, a letter to the editor of the *South Australian Register* drew attention to the 'almost utter absence of water-closets' among the 'hundred hovels on Baker's Flat'.[52] In 1864, a case against three men charged with using abusive and insulting language was dismissed by the magistrate as 'simply a Sunday's Baker's Flat shindy'.[53] John Lenane was charged with breaking into Mary Anne Russell's one-room mud hut in the dead of night, with a hammer in his hand, and stealing 16 shillings while she cowered next to the bed with her three children.[54] Thomas Griffy, a labourer living at Baker's Flat, was charged with being 'a pauper lunatic', after having attempted to cut his own throat while in an unsound state of mind.[55] James Neville, an old man of almost 80 years, was found in rags, barely able to move, on the floor of his 'wretched hovel on Baker's Flat', alongside a woman who was 'helplessly drunk'.[56]

Others in the community were living (or dying) according to the usual societal norms. In 1865, for example, P. Flynes of Baker's Flat made a preliminary application for a licence to teach,[57] and was apparently successful.[58] James Wood died suddenly one morning of a massive heart attack, leaving a widow and large family destitute.[59] A sum of money was found on Baker's Flat, and handed into the Rev. T. Jasper Smyth,[60] the local Anglican priest who, incidentally, was born in Ireland. Young Patrick Dundon kicked a football so hard that it broke Thomas Supple's arm, requiring the attention of Dr Blood.[61]

Irish folk traditions and customs were retained. Every Sunday afternoon hurling was played, and every evening concertinas, fiddles and flutes provided music for dancing.[62] The dance floor was 'the virgin soil, flat and smooth, and hard as cement from the thousands of feet that gaily "kept the time" to the piper's or fiddler's tune'.[63] This dance floor is also recalled in an interview with Mrs Beanland, who had lived on Baker's Flat, and who remembered dancing at the full moon and on dry nights, on a 'hard patch of earth, and fires kept going to liven the scene'.[64] A particular area of compacted ground in the northern part of Baker's Flat is still known locally today as the 'dance floor'.

Houses on the Flat varied in quality. Descriptions of mud huts and old-bags-and-tin hovels dominate. But there is also evidence of Irish-style whitewashed cottages with thatched roofs; an 1899 newspaper article describes Baker's Flat as 'dotted with picturesque white-walled cottages'.[65] In a series of interviews carried out in 1975, four Kapunda residents recalled between 30 and 60 houses on Baker's Flat that were mostly thatched, constructed as two or three rooms in a row, of whitewashed clay or stone, and given a new coat of lime and white clay every Christmas.[66] Dwellings like these were photographed by John Kauffmann on Baker's Flat in 1906 (Figure 3), and they clearly show the distinctive features of the 19th-century Irish vernacular house. Such houses were typically rectangular in design, single-storey and one room deep, with windows and doors in the long walls rather than in the gable ends. They had steeply sloped thatched roofs, and rooms that took up the full width of the house, with each room opening into the next.[67] Back in Ireland, even the one-roomed cabins occupied by the poorest labourers followed this general form, although in these instances, mud rather than stone would have been the main construction material.[68]

Figure 3. Baker's Flat houses in 1906, depicted in a series of photos taken by John Kauffmann, published in the *Christmas Observer*, 13 December 1906, Adelaide (Susan Arthure, from a copy held in the Kapunda Historical Society Museum).

It is clear from Kauffmann's images that the Irish retained their vernacular building traditions on Baker's Flat for a long period of time, since they were still intact in the early 20th century. Interestingly, though, a letter to the *Kapunda Herald and Northern Intelligencer* in 1866 hints at earlier house forms, with a statement that the residents of Baker's Flat burrowed 'like a wombat into the bowels of his mother earth' for shelter.[69] Archaeological excavations in 2016 and 2017 by the author[70] uncovered a dugout dwelling that matches this description. By digging into the slope of the hill, the builders of the dugout created walls from the calcrete bedrock.

On the tops of these walls, which were about one metre in height, they made shallow cuts which may have held the supports for a thatched roof, some remains of which were found tumbled into the structure. Recycled iron sheets, fashioned out of old kerosene tins and similar items, were used to construct taller walls on top of the ones that had been dug out. Like the cottages photographed on Baker's Flat (Figure 3), this dugout dwelling also follows the Irish vernacular tradition. It is rectangular in shape and had a thatched roof. There are channels in the floor that span the full width of the house and whose function appears to be to delineate different living zones. The excavated artefacts are consistent with domestic activities, with, for example, ceramic fragments from many plates and teacups (Figure 4), several teapots and jugs, and two chamber pots. It appears to have been lived in for an extended period, with artefacts that date from the mid 19th century and later, and a newspaper fragment with the date 1938.

Figure 4. Some of the ceramic artefacts excavated at Baker's Flat in 2017 (Photo courtesy Brendan Kearns).

The historical and archaeological evidence, then, is consistent with a long-standing, significant Irish settlement. Overall, the 1860s to 1870s appear to have been the most populous period, with estimates of between a 'hundred hovels'[71] and 170 'huts'[72] on the Flat during that time, and a 1936 article in the *Southern Cross* indicating that 'it is safe to estimate that the population of the "Flat" was five hundred for many years'.[73] By the turn of the century though, numbers had dwindled. The only known survey map, from 1893, shows 38 structures on the section (a cluster of rectangular shapes in the north-west quadrant, visible in Figure 2) and by 1902, there were just 32 occupied houses.[74] By the 1920s, only a handful of elderly people remained on Baker's Flat with the last family possibly being the O'Callahans, who had lived there since 1857.[75] Annie O'Callahan may have been the last resident; she died in 1948 at the age of 74 years, after living quietly on Baker's Flat 'the whole of her life'.[76] Her elder sister, Mary O'Callahan (Figure 5), had also lived on Baker's Flat and predeceased her in 1945.[77]

Figure 5. Miss Mary O'Callahan, one of the last residents of Baker's Flat.
(Photo courtesy Peter Swann, Kapunda).

Trouble at Baker's Flat

Baker's Flat was occupied from at least 1854 to 1948, a period of 94 years. The more raucous exploits of its residents were recorded in newspaper articles, their demises were announced in newspaper death notices, and baptisms, marriages and deaths were recorded in the registers of the Catholic Church. It could be argued that, in general, the Baker's Flat Irish lived out their lives no differently from any other member of the broader community – the respectable inhabitants would never have gained fame in the newspapers, and the drunken adventures and audacious burglaries might just have added spice to an otherwise ordinary community. But the Irish of Baker's Flat were different because they publicly advertised their Irishness in the types of houses they chose to build. They also actively controlled access to Baker's Flat, with any strangers or unauthorised visitors being obliged to 'give a satisfactory account of themselves' to the women, who were likely to react with brooms, sticks and kicks if a suitable answer was not forthcoming.[78] This helped establish the reputation of Baker's Flat as a community that was set apart and different. A further difference, which demonstrates how closely this community was intertwined, was a decades-long trouble regarding legal title to the land, where the Irish stood shoulder to shoulder in legal and physical battles against the landowners.

The catalyst for these troubles occurred in 1875 when James White, one of the legal owners at that time, decided to assert his rights to the land. After advertising that any stray horses and cattle found trespassing on Baker's Flat would be impounded, he sent his nephew and his shepherd there with a flock of sheep. The men were met by a group of women who greeted them with 'threats loud and strong',[79] armed with sticks and stones. With difficulty, and only after intercession by the local police officer, the sheep were driven off the Flat and back to the yards, with the women loud in their resolve not to allow the 'people's grass' to be eaten by Mr White's sheep.[80] Two years later, a similar question of title arose on the adjoining Section 1413, where the land had been squatted on and used for commonage for many years, with all indications that the squatters were those same Irish. Once again, James White attempted to move cattle onto the land, and once again, 'a mob of ladies' defended their rights to the land and drove the cattle off.[81]

The following three years passed fairly peacefully until 1880 when three men were sent by the landowners to erect a fence on Baker's Flat. Up to a hundred women 'turned out to drive off the would-be despoilers of their hearths and homes'.[82] The hapless fencers managed to dig a single posthole, but immediately one of the women leapt into it, declaring that any further excavation would have to be through her body. After taking counsel, the men wisely decided to retreat, and were sent on their way smartly by the women using brooms, sticks and shovels. In the court case that followed, the ringleaders were named as Ann Slattery, Mary Callaghan, Mary Lacey, Ann Hoare, Catherine Driscoll and Mary Jose.[83]

Things grumbled along until 1888 when it was reported in the *Kapunda Herald* that the legal owners intended to serve 'notices of ejectment' on the Irish occupiers.[84] The next few years were a flurry of activity, with 22 of the Irish successfully lobbying the Kapunda District Council to be inserted in the assessment book as joint owners of part Section 7598 in the Hundred of Kapunda,[85] and unsuccessfully applying to the Belvidere District Council for the same thing.[86] This group appears to have been 'D. Driscoll and others' who controlled 340 acres on Baker's Flat.[87] Across both councils, until about 1892, 35 individual Irish occupiers, in addition to those in Daniel Driscoll's group, paid rates on Baker's Flat.[88] At a total of 57 individuals, these ratepayers would have represented the majority of families living there. Driscoll was later described by the prosecution in a court case as the spokesman for the occupiers, and 'head robber – Barabbas'.[89]

A significant court case and Patrick McMahon Glynn

In 1892, legal action to reclaim the land began in the Supreme Court of South Australia over rights of possession.[90] Patrick McMahon Glynn represented the people of Baker's Flat during the case.[91] He did so for the entire duration of 10 years, as well as representing several of the occupiers in other related court cases during that time.[92]

McMahon Glynn (Figure 6) had arrived in Kapunda in 1882. He had been born in Gort, County Galway, in 1855, into a well-established Irish-Catholic family whose ancestry was a mix of merchants and old Irish aristocracy.[93] In 1880, at the age of 25, he sailed for Australia where his aunt Grace was already settled as Sister Bernard, one of the founding members of Mary MacKillop's Sisters of Saint Joseph.[94] After initial difficulties finding work, Sister Bernard recommended him to the Adelaide firm of Hardy and Davis, who wanted 'a Roman Catholic Irishman' to open a branch office for them in Kapunda.[95] It is not clear why Roman Catholicism and Irishness were specific requirements, but one can speculate that it was because of the large Irish-Catholic population at Baker's Flat. In any case, he went first to Adelaide in July 1882, and then to Kapunda the following month to open a branch office for the company.[96] He was the only Catholic lawyer in Kapunda and one of only a few in South Australia, and Gerald O'Collins, his grandson and biographer, noted that he 'quickly gained prominence with those of his own faith'.⁹⁷ He also took on the role of lead writer and editor for the local newspaper, the *Kapunda Herald*, where his articles were often pro Irish and pro land rights.⁹⁸

Figure 6. Patrick McMahon Glynn. Newspaper cutting of Glynn as MP, Junior Member for Light, 1880 (Source: SLSA B 16763/61).

Writing to his mother shortly after his arrival in Kapunda in 1882, he remarked that the Catholics 'as usual are the poorer class', while the Protestants are 'the wealthy and fashionable'.⁹⁹ McMahon Glynn was widely respected in Kapunda, both professionally and socially, and joined in with the local elite at parties, tennis, horse racing, swimming and dancing.¹⁰⁰ He was also accepted across the social divides, his biography stating that 'as a hard-riding huntsman he was the idol of the Irishmen of Baker's Flat, a ramshackle settlement on the edge of the town'.¹⁰¹ And he clearly identified as Irish, noting in his diary in 1892 that 'Of course, I was a Celt'.¹⁰²

McMahon Glynn's pro-Irish and pro-land rights principles may have influenced his decision to take on the land-rights case in 1892, but it is probable that this was also combined with a sense of obligation to his fellow Irish. Over the course of the 10-year case, the court records and newspapers recount several failed attempts at eviction, an unsuccessful auction that received no bids, another in 1893 at which some of the land was sold, including Lot 6 where the cluster of houses stood¹⁰³ (Figure 2) and the successful sale in 1894 of 143 acres south of the river to the Irish Conolan brothers, who had been occupying it for some years.[104] Even the land sold in 1893 remained problematic, with the Irish refusing to leave. When they were forced to do so they just returned as soon as practicable – Andrew Goorty, for example, was evicted from a piece of land on which he had resided for about 12 years, but returned soon afterwards; Ann Bolton received an eviction order for the land she had been living on for almost 30 years, and simply refused to go.[105] The same Ann Bolton liberated two cows and their calves from a herd of 30 that was being impounded by representatives of the Kapunda District Council, and she was represented in court by McMahon Glynn.[106] That case was dismissed.[107]

The final battle for Baker's Flat took place in 1902. After some of the land was sold to Robert Fawcett, he set about putting up fences. Over four separate evenings, about 20 men, including Daniel O'Driscoll, Thomas O'Brien, Michael O'Brien Jr, Martin O'Callahan and Andrew Griffy worked together to fill in postholes and pull down any fences that had been erected, using explosives where necessary.[108] McMahon Glynn used this case to continue the argument that his clients (the Irish occupiers) were 'rightfully in occupation' of the land.[109] The Irish lost and the case was found for the plaintiff, who was awarded £5 damages with costs. Within days, Fawcett resumed his fencing, and it was noted in the *Kapunda Herald*[110] that the 'residents of the Flat have not interfered with the fencers in any way'. This appears to have been the last time that there were any notable clashes on Baker's Flat. From that time on, most mentions of Baker's Flat in the press are confined to notices of grass fires, accidents, floods and, increasingly, the deaths of older people, as the settlement slowly wound down.

Conclusion
It is clear that in the early days of European settlement Kapunda had a significant Irish presence, albeit aligned in quite different groupings. The Anglo-Irish were part of the dominant elite, owning land and business ventures in the area. The Baker's Flat Irish lived lives characterised by poverty, Catholicism, a seeming propensity for trouble, and a willingness to engage both physically and intellectually with the legal system. Patrick McMahon Glynn, middle-class Catholic Irish, straddled both groups. But for all these differences, there was some sense of Irishness that suggests

a degree of reciprocity and responsibility for each other. The histories imply that the working Irish made a deliberate decision to join Bagot at Kapunda, and all the indications are that he facilitated, at some level, their occupation of Baker's Flat. Patrick McMahon Glynn represented the Baker's Flat Irish in extended and complex court cases long after he had left Kapunda and was living in Adelaide.

This history demonstrates that Irishness in the colony of South Australia was complex and multi-layered. The Irish community contained members who represented the elite Protestant Anglo-Irish, the middle-class Irish Catholics, and the poorest of Ireland's emigrants. The community at Baker's Flat, perhaps instigated by Bagot to supply a habitable location near the Kapunda Mines, developed into a formidable settlement, which attracted support for a lengthy legal battle aimed at securing homesteads and protecting long-settled homes. In this it demonstrates that Irish identity and concern for fellow countrymen and women was a potent element of colonial South Australia. It also illustrates how class and religious barriers were perhaps overridden by ethnic connections in times of strife and difficulty.

Irish graves in Mid North South Australia, 1850-1899: An examination of cultural significance

JANINE McEGAN

Across the continent of Australia, the Irish have left an indelible legacy, having constituted about 25 per cent of the 19th century immigrant population.[1] South Australia's Mid North became home to a large number of these new arrivals, particularly Irish migrants with connections to multiple counties.[2] According to much historical research,[3] the Irish in South Australia demonstrated a ready adjustment to their new surroundings among migrants from other nations, resulting in a diffusion of their culture. Nonetheless, archaeological investigations[4] allude to autonomy and difference being preserved in certain facets of some Irish settlements with a degree of 'Irishness' being communicated via tangible material culture in the new colony.

One way to examine Irishness, and how its presentation might alter over time, is to study gravestones, which offer a physical means of studying memorialisation practices and their changes. This chapter reports on an archaeological study of how 19th-century Irish settlers memorialised their dead over the first 50 years of Irish settlement in South Australia. In this context, memorialisation includes the iconography of the grave as represented in motifs and inscriptions, as well as the placement, form, height, style and colour of the grave marker itself.

Given that the majority of the Irish in South Australia were of the Catholic faith,[5] this study needed first to determine what aspects of memorialisation might indicate 'Irishness' as opposed to 'Catholicness'. To this end, a sub-sample of Irish-Protestant graves and non-Irish-Catholic graves was included, allowing identifiers of religious memorialisation to be separated from other cultural traits. Further, to compare change across time, memorialisation practices of first-generation immigrants and two generations of their descendants were compared. While there have been several historical studies of Irish cultural migration to South Australia,[6] none has attempted to assess Irish memorialisation practices in this context. Catholicism, being unpopular in the dissident context of the colony's attitudes to religion, resulted in a lack of representation in historical records. This under-representation, however, affords an opportunity to explore the Irish through material evidence, since gravestones are a way in which beliefs can be expressed, allowing traditions to be demonstrated rather than assumed.[7]

The study area

This chapter focuses on the Clare Valley in South Australia's Mid North, which extends from south of Kapunda as far as Peterborough in the north, covering a distance of some 150 kilometres. The cemeteries under study are situated within the counties of Stanley and Light, and particularly in or near the Mid North towns of Mintaro, Navan, Kapunda, Undalya and Saddleworth, which were all thriving communities in the 19th century (Figure 1).

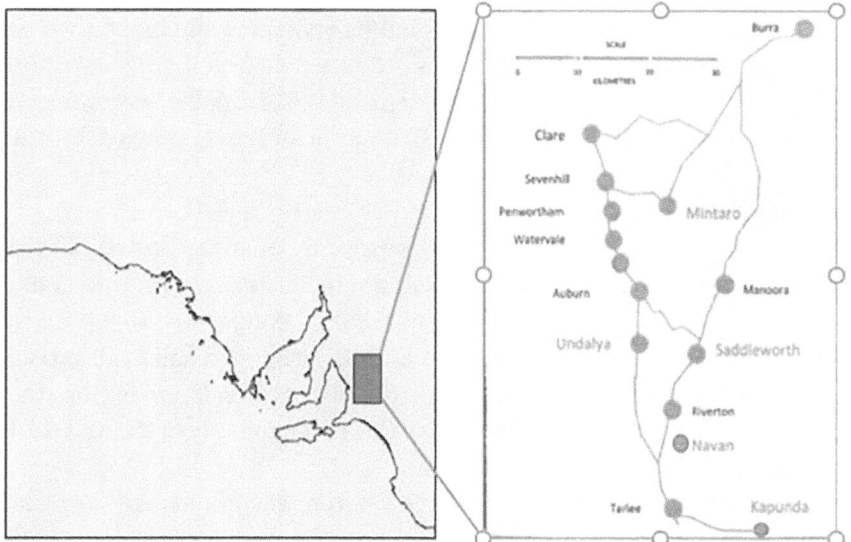

Figure 1. Clare Valley region of South Australia and towns of the Clare Valley.

Kapunda, initially an agricultural area, developed with the discovery of copper, while Mintaro grew as a result of nearby Burra's copper industry, being a transport stopover,[8] with the village established upon Joseph Gilbert's land subdivision in 1849.[9] The 1854 discovery of slate at Mintaro became a major factor in the town's survival after the ore transport bypassed it in 1857, while its development as an agricultural centre further ensured its continuance.[10] As in Kapunda, the Irish presence in Mintaro resulted in a strong community, with settlers such as Peter Brady and the Dempsey family, all of County Cavan, becoming leaders in that community.

To the south, Navan was an Irish enclave settled in the 1840s by Irish immigrants who fled the famine.[11] The establishment of a segregated Irish community such as Navan was unusual in South Australia, although, as noted by Carroll,[12] by 1876 Navan could be described as more an agricultural district than a township.[13]

Saddleworth was also settled in the 1840s, by an English farmer, James Masters. It developed in a similar way to Mintaro, being on the transport route from Burra to Adelaide.[14] Riverton, near Navan, was also established by Masters in 1856.[15] The fact that both of these communities were strongly English suggests that English immigrants may have chosen to settle away from the neighbouring Irish.

Undalya is on the border of the counties of Stanley and Light, with two of its earliest settlers being English – Captain George Lambert, who is buried in the Undalya Catholic Cemetery, and William Baker, a crewman on the *Emerald Isle*, the ship on which E.B. Gleeson and party arrived in 1838.[16]

Factors in Irish settlement
The arrival of the *Birman* in 1840 began an ongoing and significant association between County Clare and South Australia, with that county consistently providing the highest number of emigrants. Together, the counties of Clare, Tipperary, Limerick and Cork supplied half of all assisted passage arrivals after 1850.[17] However, the distribution found in this study also showed a significant percentage of Cavan immigrants in the Mid North (Figure 2).

For these immigrants, the Catholic Church was a mainstay. With low numbers of Catholics in South Australia, becoming established was difficult for the Church. Little state aid was available, mainly due to the colony

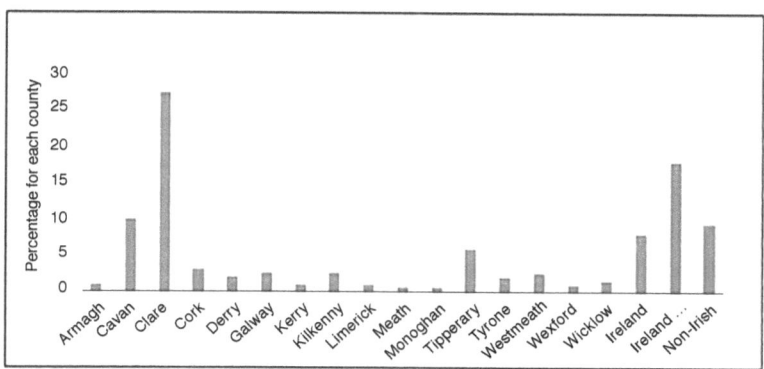

Figure 2. Birthplace of the deceased, or nearest relatives, recorded in the study.

ostensibly having no ties to a particular faith; this resulted in charitable and social organisations being created by the various faiths to finance their own churches and charitable causes. Jesuit priests, who built a centre at Sevenhill near Clare, were instrumental in Irish immigrants maintaining connections with their faith.[18] Until churches were constructed, services were often held in private homes, such as at Peter Brady's in Mintaro prior to 1855, or in Timothy Crowe's house at Undalya, where a separate room was built for religious worship. By 1871, Catholics had grown to outnumber members of the Church of England in both counties (Table 1).[19]

	Light		Stanley		Total both counties	
	1861	1871	1861	1871	1861	1871
Catholic	2163	4066	221	2794	2384	6860
Church of England	2377	2706	307	2264	2684	4970
Total in County	14980	20019	4835	9785	10904	29804

Table 1. Religion by county 1861 and 1871. (SA census: 1861 and 1871)

Stereotypically, the Irish are often portrayed as an exclusive and cohesive group,[20] and a comparison of two Irish rural settlements in the 19th century – one in Minnesota, United States, and the other in south-western New South Wales – shows similarities in both settlement patterns and the degree of integration with other migrant groups.[21] In both cases, Irish immigrants tended to work and live in urban communities prior to settling into agricultural life. Any exclusion of other cultural groups was not intentional, but rather a by-product of living in proximity to relatives or friends. With the expanse of the country and the resultant distribution of Irish settlers across many different communities, few Irish traditions were continued, save perhaps the celebration of St Patrick's Day.[22] Further overt displays of Irishness were avoided to prevent alienation or derision from the general populace.[23] With regards to South Australia, the historian Eric Richards has argued that, unlike their counterparts in Britain and North America, the Irish were not obviously marginalised, did not settle in segregated communities and were largely indistinguishable from their British equivalents.[24] More detailed historical studies in the Mid North, on the other hand, have found strong evidence for networking among Irish settlers that created family precedents for chain migration,[25] distinct traces of spatial clustering[26] throughout the 1860s and 1870s,[27] and entrenched patterns of endogamous marriage within the Irish and Catholic communities throughout the 19th century.[28] As a result, in contrast to the situation that Campbell has argued for in New South Wales, the Irish in the Mid North of South Australia were largely insular, tending to marry only other Catholics, and mostly Irish Catholics, and to live in spatially separate communities. However, with time, the Irish moved to further their opportunities and did not stay within the close confines of Irish settlements.

Significantly, particularly for those seeking to understand the ongoing construction of colonial narratives, James has argued that being Irish did not remain important for South Australia's Irish population and that therefore Irish heritage was not retained in local memory. While a clear distinctiveness was maintained until at least the turn of the 20th century in some areas, she noted a parallel neglect after 1870, erasing an earlier 'strong Irish imprint' in areas such as the Clare Valley.[29] Similarly, findings of cultural unity[30] in the United States were followed by a shift away from a distinct Irish signature from the 1880s.

In this study, the general pattern of similarity identified by Richards holds true in most areas of burial symbolism. There is, however, some archaeological evidence for distinctiveness and separation between denominations, and between the Irish and those around them. Areas of comparison and contrast are explored here in three ways: through the use of motifs of affection and grief, motifs related to religious beliefs, and overtly Irish symbols of identity.

Motifs of affection and grief

Motifs signifying affection and grief proved to have a strong religiously based difference, with Irish-Catholic graves displaying the vast majority of motifs representing affection. The use of flora was particularly dominant. Roses as a symbol of hope, and daisies, representing innocence, were the most frequently used, especially by those buried in the Mintaro and St John's cemeteries. Wreaths (of both flowers and foliage) and forget-me-nots, both portraying remembrance, were also found at the same two cemeteries.[31] In contrast, Irish-Protestant graves had more austere headstones with fewer motifs. Christchurch cemetery at Kapunda had just three emotive symbols, two of which represented grief. These were a lily with a broken stem and morning glory flowers. When looked at over time, the use of emotive symbols among Irish Catholics became more popular toward the end of the 19th century, ranging from flowers to cloth-draped urns. There was a steady escalation of such symbols, particularly those of affection, into the 1880s, with a subsequent decline in the 1890s. In contrast, only one or two were found on non-Irish graves in every decade. While there were no greater number of deaths in the 1880s than other decades, the loss of the early migrants, and thus a direct connection with Ireland, could have accounted for a surge in emotive symbols. This was, however, a choice adopted more by Irish Catholics than by Irish Protestants.

The emotional experience of death was also carried through in the language of headstone inscriptions,[32] although this was something that was shared by both Irish Catholics and Protestants. As a collective, Irish-Catholic and Protestant graves showed a significant difference in the use of emotive words compared to non-Irish burials. Figure 3 illustrates this difference, showing little use of emotive inscriptions by non-Irish, but a recognisable change in the Irish use of inscriptions relating to affection over time. So, while the choice of symbolic motifs of affection and grief distinguished Catholics from Protestants, when considered together, the use of emotive terms linked the two groups and separated them from the non-Irish around them. In other words, while Irish Catholics tended to use more affectionate terms and Irish Protestants more terms of grief, the Irish as a single group tended to be much more overtly emotive in comparison to the non-Irish.

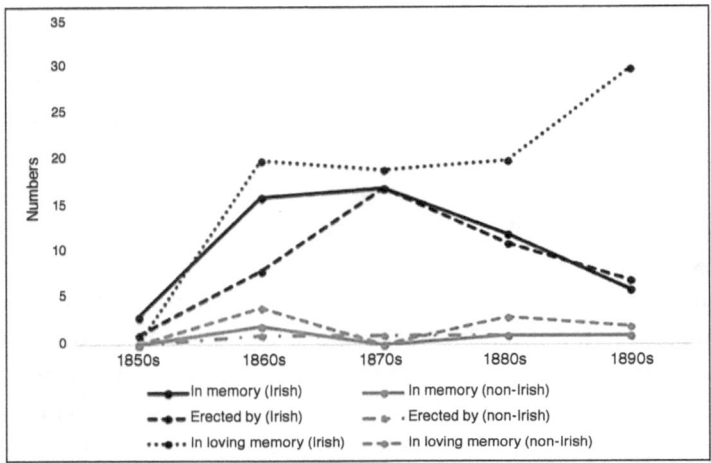

Figure 3. Irish vs non-Irish: Change over time of introductory phrases in inscriptions.

This shift is similar to that noted by Tarlow on Orkney graves, where she found that the use of emotive phrases, such as 'In loving memory' or 'Sacred to the memory', had supplanted earlier phrases such as 'In memory' by the end of the 1880s.[33]

Religious motifs

When analysing Irish-Catholic and Irish-Protestant graves, the presence or absence of religious motifs proved to be statistically significant. Symbols representing Christ (Figure 4) and the cross were predominantly on Catholic graves. In comparison, the few religious motifs found on Protestant graves related to God and the Holy Spirit. Over time, the use of religious motifs by Catholics peaked in the 1860s. The 1860s also saw the greatest use of religious words on Catholic headstones, while there were none on Protestant headstones.

These results align with other findings[34] on 19th-century Protestant observances of death, which concentrated on the judgement of a life lived, with no prospect of improvement in any afterlife, resulting in few religious symbols being included on headstones. Smith found a similar avoidance

Figure 4. Engraved stone of the Sacred Heart on Ellen Crowe's grave, 1895, Undalya Catholic Cemetery. (Photo courtesy J. McEgan)

of the cross in Protestant churches in 19th-century America,[35] since it is a symbol particularly associated with the Catholic faith. This restraint was also obvious in Protestant graves in this study.

The inscription of 'IHS'[36] on the cross was encouraged by Jesuit priests,[37] an order well-established in South Australia's Mid North. Not surprisingly, Irish Catholics in the region adopted the use of these symbols. The maintenance of such strong faith-based imagery in contrast to Protestant belief may have connoted more adherences to Catholic orthodoxy.

The use of a plain cross as a headstone form suggests interesting oppositional trends among sectors of the Irish population. Specifically, its use as a monument form declined among Irish Catholics in the 1880s, while its use by Irish Protestants increased marginally. Both groups reversed this trend in the 1890s, suggesting that something distinctive may have been occurring in the choices that each group was making. Two possible explanations are that the use of the cross by Catholics and Protestants was a result of adherence to particular religious beliefs or injunctions, or that it was an expression of wider political ideologies that influenced these two groups.

In terms of a connection between crosses and wider political beliefs, Daniel O'Connell's founding of the Repeal Association in 1840, with the aim of gaining independence from Britain, firmly aligned nationalism with Catholicism in order to unite the majority of Irish Catholics.[38] Irish nationalist political movements spread across the world, but while some partiality toward such beliefs existed, Irish migrants in Australia seemed more concerned with loyalty to family and their county of birth than with nationalist connections.[39] This attitude differed from that of Irish-American immigrants, who, according to Brown, were desperate to improve their lives to overcome 'a pervasive sense of inferiority, intense longing for acceptance and respectability'.[40] Miller suggests that the Irish believed they were 'in forced exile' from English rule, leading to a tenacious nationalism in America.[41] The involvement of Home Rule advocates in murders of English representatives in 1883 in Ireland hampered support for the movement once news reached the Australian colonies, as did the economic downturn in South Australia in the 1880s.[42] Little archaeological evidence of Irish nationalism has been found in Australia, with the exception of clay pipes sporting Irish slogans and symbols such as shamrocks and the inscription *Erin Go Bragh* (translated as 'Ireland Forever'[43]) found at the excavation of Cadman's Cottage, Sydney in 1988.[44]

An alternative explanation for the fall in popularity of cross headstones among Catholics in the 1880s may be more prosaic. The economic state of South Australia could have influenced the manner in which the departed were memorialised. The colony suffered significant droughts in the 1880s, resulting in much insolvency.[45] Since the Mid North was an agricultural area, and many of the Irish settlers were farmers, the aftermath of such weather events would have resulted in the loss of, or reduced cash flow for, the properties. A reduction in the number of cross-form headstones, given that they were among the largest and therefore most costly, could have been due to economics, as could the increasing plainness of headstones from the 1880s, as fewer engraved motifs presumably translated to lower cost. While O'Farrell found Celtic crosses to have increased in popularity on graves from about the 1880s in Australian Catholic cemeteries,[46] they were generally connected with more affluent migrants, and thus the lack of examples in this study could be an indication that the financial state of South Australia influenced headstone choices.

Figure 5. Michael Dermody's Irish-Catholic grave, 1861, St John's Cemetery, Kapunda. (Photo courtesy M. McEgan)

Figure 6. John Guiney's Catholic grave, 1883, Undalya Catholic Cemetery, showing shamrock motifs and adjacent Celtic cross. Headstone erected by his parents. (Photo courtesy J. McEgan)

Irish symbols

The use of overtly Irish symbols, such as shamrocks and the Celtic form of the cross, occurred across the timeframe of this study. From the data recorded in the study, the use of such symbols to demonstrate Irish association was primarily chosen by first-generation immigrants (Figure 5), with the lone example of a Celtic cross headstone from the second generation belonging to a 19-year-old whose parents (themselves first-generation migrants) erected the marker. The use of shamrock and Celtic cross motifs proved to be the same, with only one of five graves bearing Irish-type motifs belonging to a second-generation Irish person, whose parents also erected the memorial (Figure 6).

Celtic crosses and shamrocks figured prominently as motifs on the cast-iron surrounds of graves. The shamrock is a trifoliate leaf,[47] long associated with St Patrick, Ireland's patron saint. The plant's three leaflets are purported to have been used as a metaphor for the Holy Trinity by St Patrick on his quest to convert the Irish to Christianity in the fifth century,[48] with specimens being worn in hats to commemorate St Patrick on his holy day, as noted by Dr Caleb Threlkeld in 1726.[49] Furthermore, there is some speculation that the ancient Irish Celts revered the plant for its trefoil form, with the numeral 'three' found in many forms in Celtic materials, such as the triskele (Figure 7) and the triquetra as well as the shamrock. As noted by Mac Mathúna, Irish folklore had an inherited concept of the cosmos involving a triad of three divisions of the universe being *nem* (sky), *talam* (sea) and *muir* (earth), indicating the importance of the number 'three',[50] a belief also held by the Druids.[51] Christian belief in the Holy Trinity in many ways co-opted such beliefs and entrenched them still further.

Figure 7. Newgrange, Co. Meath showing triskele designs on entrance stone.
(Photo courtesy J. McEgan)

The dominance of the shamrock imagery on Irish-Catholic graves in the Mid North suggests strongly that the connection with religion (and thus St Patrick) was the overriding factor in its use. The Celtic Revival of 19th-century Ireland is primarily associated with the Protestant Irish,[52] in which symbols such as the Celtic cross were used 'to establish ... an Irish national identity'.[53] In contrast, traditional symbols like the shamrock and harp were well-represented among the Catholic population.[54] However, the symbols represented different ideas of an Irish heritage: Protestants used them as a means to link to traditional Irish culture in an overall context where they were politically and economically dominant, whereas Catholics associated the images with a chance to reclaim Ireland from the English and restore traditional Irish culture.[55] The results of this study substantiate such observations, as shamrocks were the dominant choice on Irish-Catholic graves with the Holy Trinity being a more probable connection than Celtic association. Celtic crosses, however, do have a probable connection with early Christianity. The shape is suggested by Bryce to have evolved from a symbol common in fourth-century Christianity – the 'chi-rho', an 'X' (chi) overlaid with a 'P' (rho), being the Greek letters of the first two letters of 'Christ' and used in combination to represent Christ.[56]

Some unique grave markers

Spatially, there was little variation in the way Irish settlers memorialised the dead in the Mid North. Headstone forms were relatively consistent in representation across the six cemeteries. Fencing designs and inscription categories showed little diversity over the study area. Motifs had the greatest fluctuation in form – religious symbols ranged from 40 to 60 per cent in the Catholic cemeteries but were much less frequent on Protestant graves. Motifs of affection had the greatest spread, ranging from 5 per cent at Undalya to 40 per cent at Saddleworth, while the other cemeteries comprised about 10 per cent. Irish symbols accounted for less than 10 per cent in all cemeteries.

However, four early grave markers were unique in style, three of which were Catholic burials at the Navan cemetery (O'Sullivan, O'Brien and Fahey) and one of which was a non-Irish-Catholic burial at the Mintaro cemetery – an iron cross for Chas Hoffmann, a blacksmith. Two of the Navan headstones, from 1858 (Fahey, Figure 8) and 1863 (O'Sullivan, Figure 10), had the same shape, but were very different to other forms. The O'Brien tablet from the 1860s (Figure 9) was the only example that appeared to be completely hand-carved. The shape of the headstone was not symmetrical, and the shapes carved around the edges were irregular. The legible text was neat, but uneven in size and distribution across the lines. Furthermore, it had spelling errors, specifically the words 'REAST' and 'AMN'. The O'Sullivan headstone had distinctive designs not seen on the other three, with two spirals decorating the space above the epitaph (Figure 11). These also appear to be hand-carved, as they are irregular. The rest of the O'Sullivan headstone had consistently sized text, though some letters had been made smaller to fit on a line, and the additional motifs were regular in form, similar to those on the Fahey stone.

Three forms of foliage decorated the O'Sullivan headstone (Figure 11), while the base of the O'Brien headstone (Figure 12) included a geometric chevron design between a cross and a chalice. It was the only example in

Figure 8. Fahey headstone, 1858, Navan Catholic Cemetery. (Photo courtesy J. McEgan)

Figure 9. O'Brien headstone, 1860s, Navan Catholic Cemetery. (Photo courtesy J. McEgan)

Figure 10. O'Sullivan headstone, 1863, Navan Catholic Cemetery. (Photo courtesy J. McEgan)

Figure 11. Sketch of motifs on the top section of the O'Sullivan headstone, 1863, Navan Catholic Cemetery (note: non-specific motifs and possible Irish spirals). (Artist: J. McEgan)

Figure 12. Sketch of the O'Brien headstone, 1860s, Navan Catholic Cemetery, showing geometric design at base. (Artist: J. McEgan)

the database to have a painted motif, and it also bore fern-like engravings similar to those on the O'Sullivan headstone.

There is no indication of who carved these headstones and they are assumed to have been made locally, by an unnamed stonemason. The O'Sullivan and Fahey headstones may have been made by the same person, since both are the same shape. They are both carved with Botonee crosses inside the rounded finials at the top of the headstone and include the same recessed panel in the centre of the epitaph. Each has unique variations, however, indicating that they were not made to precisely the same pattern. The early age of these three headstones, and their uniqueness, is likely to be indicative of a lack of a locally established masonry industry. All three examples display evidence of hand-worked symbols and inscriptions and personal inclusions representative of overt Irish symbolism. The connections made to family, with so much detail of relationships and places of birth, continued the connection with Ireland, while the symbols resembling those of Celtic ancestry, particularly the spirals and geometric designs found on the O'Sullivan and O'Brien graves, highlighted the Irish identity of these arrivals in the colony.

What does it all mean?

There is a stereotype that the Irish retain strong ties to their homeland and display these ties in overt ways, but this study of Irish graves in the Mid North does not support such an obvious scenario. In reality, the Irish immigrants studied here used subtle symbolism in motifs and words to invoke an understanding of their origins. However, their choices do link to wider stereotypes of the Irish being openly emotional and steadfastly Catholic. Furthermore, these Irish migrants demonstrated strong connections with family through their grave markers.

The three headstones at Navan that display personal influences were not mimicked in any later headstones, or at other cemeteries, with the personal symbols and details of lives and origins being particularly poignant. The inclusion of symbols associated with Celtic origins (scrolls on the O'Sullivan headstone and the geometric shape on the O'Brien marker) are indications of these early Irish migrants maintaining connections with a pre-English past. The detail with which the deceased and their origins were recorded further indicates the need for these people to continue associations with Ireland. Even the Fahey grave, while a simpler memorial, detailed the names, ages and dates of death for each member who died. These three unique graves expressed family and origins in great detail and align with Miller's argument in which he determines a commonality in Irish-Catholic society of the importance of family and tradition.[57] However, these three graves also express distinctiveness in style and motif use that differs from later memorials in the district.

The individuality of these graves indicates an opportunity for personal memorialisation that diminished in some aspects with the later standardisation of memorials. With mass production, only the choice of wording allowed some individuality, while the physical presentation of monuments became more uniform. This in itself could create a dilemma in determining the individual contribution of the family and the 'Irishness' of material culture. While individuality in graves became less apparent over time, the inclusion of family and relationships in inscriptions does show an adherence to traditions.

The significance of the use of emotion and connection to family, along with the adoption of Celtic cross and shamrock symbols, shows that the Irish of South Australia's Mid North emphasised their Irish identity in particular ways, even if not always in an overt manner. Unlike James's study, which stated that a decline in Irish association was apparent after the 1870s,[58] the archaeology indicates stability in the number of symbols and/or words associated with the Irish and a continuance in their use after this time. Emotive text and connection with Ireland or to residence in South Australia changed little. Mentioning relationships with the deceased remained relatively stable, although religious style did decrease from the 1870s. Motifs representing emotion and Ireland both increased over time, and as with the text, religious affiliation decreased. These findings indicate that representations of Irish culture did not diminish over the duration of the 19th century.

Conclusion
Recent studies have found that 19th-century Irish social identity in the Mid North was conveyed in different ways, depending on the material remains examined. While Arthure found the houses of Baker's Flat to be closely clustered, with indications of a tight-knit, set-apart community,[59] the graves

in this study suggest that the Irish were interspersed with other ethnicities. Religion was a dominant factor, however, in both studies. This grave study, while not having large numbers of Celtic-related symbols, does show a greater inclination to overtly Irish images, with religion being an evident factor. Mass-produced items such as headstones reduced the opportunity to express Irishness explicitly in the material form, but it remained evident through the use of carefully chosen text and motifs.

It is to be expected that there would be variations in the results over the time frame of this study. Traits may be shared by different groups, which are apparent in the lack of diversity in many aspects of the recorded graves, such as the proximity of family members and the form of the headstones. Differences can occur within a group (in this case, the Irish as a whole) where the type of motifs incorporated on the headstones was a point of religious difference between the two Irish groups. Affectionate symbols were favoured by the Catholics and expressions of grief by the Protestants, while religious motifs were prevalent among the Irish Catholics but not their Protestant countrymen. As suggested by Brighton, social identity evolves over time[60] – a concept that is apparent in the Irish communities of the Mid North.

'The most thoroughly Irish centre in South Australia': Pekina from the 1870s to the 1940s

JOHN MANNION AND STEPHANIE JAMES

The sale of the Pekina Catholic presbytery in October 2018 brought an end to the affiliation of the c. 1878 building with the Catholic Church.[1] The foundation stone of St Catherine's Church was laid in 1875.[2] Just inside Goyder's line of rainfall,[3] Pekina is situated in a valley between two unnamed ranges 270 kilometres north of Adelaide. Both the 1878 presbytery construction and the subsequent establishment of a school conducted by the Sisters of St Joseph underlined the importance of having resident priests and Catholic education to cater for the growing rural population. By the late 1930s, in addition to the presbytery and school, Pekina had two Catholic churches and a parish hall (the Institute, until 1937), and the Josephites briefly owned the township's hotel. While this thumbnail sketch suggests Pekina was unusual, evidence of the township's visible and widely acknowledged 'Irishness' identifies it as unique.[4]

In this chapter, 'Irishness' includes the early background of Irish colonists[5] and Pekina's continuing connection to Ireland (for example, their majority Irish-born priests,[6] with at least three of the Josephites in the first five years Irish-born;[7] membership of Irish organisations; celebration of St Patrick's Day; Irish-style dwellings; features of the cemetery; and survival of the brogue and characteristics of language), the recognised Catholic identity of the community, and an active Church presence (evident in early land ownership, the presence of the Catholic school, and ongoing construction and associated fundraising projects).[8] The book of poetry penned in 1921 by John O'Brien (Fr John Hartigan), *Around the Boree Log*, provides a consistent background reference point, showing how Pekina's Irish-Catholic community viewed itself in the early 20th century. The most important decades in this account are the 1870s and 1930s; the intervening decades are covered in less detail.

Figure 1. 'Daly's house' 2018, at the eastern base of the Hogshead Hill, near Pekina. Typical of many early dwellings the house was built in 1878 and occupied for almost 100 years. (Photo courtesy John Mannion)

Many hopeful farmers moved North (as the region was generally designated) after the *Strangways Act of 1869* simplified land purchase.[9] In response, a number of northern counties were declared in the 1870s; Dalhousie, in which Pekina was located, was proclaimed in 1871. Census figures of that year showed 212 Irish-born and 539 Catholics in that county. The former Pekina station was broken up and became a part of the Hundred of Pekina; it was surveyed in 1872 and gazetted as agricultural land in September 1873 with initial blocks having been sold in August.[10] By mid 1874 a public meeting in the Pekina district discussed the local need for a blacksmith, and 'getting a Government township surveyed'.[11] By January 1875, in advance of any township or sale, a 'subscription list' for a chapel and school had been organised, over £60 already promised.[12] Many of the early residents of the area were originally from County Clare and had been living in Irish centres such as Kapunda and the Clare Valley. The *Government Gazette* of May 1875 announced a '[n]ew township ... called Pekina', and at the following land sales, the Catholic Church Endowment Society bought eight adjoining town lots, suggesting that 'the Catholic Church ... had tremendous faith in the future of this small farming community'.[13] In 1875 Michael Duffy (County Clare) opened a post office, and by May 1876 'had just started to erect a store'.[14] Some opposition to the change in land usage was registered in the 1876 assessment of the region, which regretted that 'the exigencies of settlement and cultivation should necessitate the destruction of a really splendid property' as Pekina station, and hoped those who 'first tamed the desert' would be well compensated.[15] Adjacent townships such as Tarcowie, Caltowie, Yatina, Carrieton, Yarrowie, Cradock and Orroroo were also established in the 1870s and, excluding Orroroo, all had significant Irish populations.[16] Pekina, however, was a distinctive Irish-Catholic location between the 1870s and the 1940s.

Figure 2. Duffy's General Store 1987. Established in 1874 and built in 1876, the store was run by the Duffy family for 85 years. The business traded until 1992 (Photo courtesy John Mannion)

The 1870s

Pekina's Catholic identity preceded the town survey of 1875. In November 1874, eight Irish-born residents presented Bishop Reynolds with an address during his northern visit.[17] Describing Catholics as 'number[ing] about three fourths of the district' and hoping to be able to 'erect a chapel and establish a school', they requested 'as soon as convenient ... a resident pastor'. Blessing the people and promising a 'visit ... after harvest', the bishop expressed surprise 'at seeing so many Catholics assembled in so remote a part of the diocese'.[18] In October 1875 he returned, demonstrating a more active Church presence when he laid the foundation stone of a church intended to seat 150 to 160, and also to double as a school during the week – 'offerings on the stone amounted to nearly £80'.[19] At the bishop's 1876 dedication of the church to St Catherine, '[t]he offerings amounted to £130'.[20] In the following year, Fr Bernard Nevin, already recognised as 'Catholic parish priest of ... the Far North [from] ... 1873', became not only Pekina's first resident priest, but established the township as the area's Catholic centre.[21] When leaving four years later, responding to an address and £140 offered by the various congregations (in which 'Pekina notably ... [took] the lead'), he reminded them of changes he had witnessed since 1874:

> You were then only newly settled in what might truly be called a desert. ... You had neither a school nor a church, nor, to all appearance, any immediate prospect of having either. But from the very beginning you expressed a desire to have buildings erected ...[22]

In May 1878, the Sisters of St Joseph came to Pekina.[23] Their primary school was conducted, as planned, in St Catherine's Church. Enrolments of between 70 and 80 students were common in the early years; Pekina never had a government school, one of its unique features.[24] According to an August 1878 letter from Irish-born Sister Catherine O'Loghlin to Mother Mary MacKillop asking for money, Pekina's first convent had only two rooms. Thus, the sisters could not have boarders, and needed Fr Unsworth to buy them a clock.[25] It seems that a more substantial convent was built before 1882.[26] In the absence of any government support for Catholic education, the sisters relied on local fundraising activities, which also gathered Catholic families. Bishop Reynolds maintained his visits. In November 1878, he was greeted outside Pekina by '20 carts and buggies, and about 30 horsemen' before he administered confirmation to 20 to 25 children on Sunday.[27]

St Patrick's Day in 1877 was possibly the first of many events demonstrating the local Irish connection when a combined Catholic picnic and sports day was held.[28] Attendance that year of between 400 and 500 from 'all the surrounding townships' exceeded the previous year's similar Easter Monday event when 300 to 400 'people were on the grounds'.[29] The day's proceeds in 1877 were £10.5s, which, combined with money from the previous year, 'makes a total of about £30, which is to be devoted to Church purposes'. Comment from the local correspondent that '[s]everal parties engaged in dancing Irish jigs and reels during the afternoon', represented a description unusual for the time.[30] But neighbourhood demographics were clearly acknowledged in 1878 when a general item about the region stated, 'The land about here is principally occupied by emigrants from the Emerald Isle'.[31] In 1879, Pekina's St Patrick's Day procession from St Catherine's Church 'was headed by a nice green flag with an Irish harp worked nicely on it', and the sports were followed by a ball at the town's hotel. Numbers were not mentioned, but the proceeds were to go toward the purchase of a bell for the church.[32]

Figure 3. Panoramic view of the Pekina Catholic presbytery, church and convent, 1885 (Peterborough Catholic Church archives)

By the end of the 1870s, then, Pekina's identity was acknowledged as both the Catholic centre of the surrounding region and as a predominantly Irish location. The resident priest, according to the *Northern Argus* in mid 1880, had 'a pretty residence', and the 'Chapel [was] a nice building'.[33] Months later, the combined Pekina, Appila-Yarrowie and Ororoo Josephite school sports attracted a crowd of between 500 and 600, indicating the

'The most thoroughly Irish centre in South Australia': Pekina from the 1870s to the 1940s

region's commitment to Catholic education.[34] In the following decades – during which several events challenged the nation, including the depression of the 1890s, Federation in 1901 and World War I – changes in local Church administration also affected Irish-Catholic Pekina.

From the 1880s to the 1920s

In 1908 the *Southern Cross* informed those readers ignorant about Pekina that 'it was not a large town … it was but a village of not more than a dozen houses at the outside!'[35] According to Sands and McDougall Directories, from 1902 to 1928 the town's population was 79, and district numbers

Figure 4. 1898 Pekina Hotel calendar featuring Pope Leo XIII. The calendar design, featuring views of the Vatican reinforces the connection between Pekina and the Roman Catholic Church (Jean Colqhoun collection)

between 1914 and 1928 increased from 459 to 471. The inhabitants listed in the directories included a majority of Irish families.

During the decades between 1880 and 1930 many aspects of life in Pekina demonstrated the active role of the Church. At his farewell in 1881, Fr Nevin had felt it was his 'duty to say [he] never met a more pious, a more faithful, and a more generous people'.[36] These characteristics were visible at many points of Pekina's subsequent history. Following Fr Nevin was Fr James Maher, appointed as Pekina's priest in 1881 when the County of Dalhousie had 849 Irish-born residents; by 1901, that figure had dropped to 372. Over those decades, Catholic numbers increased from 1985 to 2153.[37] During Fr Maher's 24 years in Pekina, he chose to remain in the Northern Diocese when it was established in 1887; he became its vicar-general in 1890,[38] and in 1893 was granted the status of 'irremovable rector'.[39] Thus, in 1896 when, as Monsignor Maher, he became the second bishop of the North, he remained at Pekina rather than moving to Port Augusta where his predecessor had resided. Pekina was then, until his death in 1905, the centre of the diocese.[40] Missions at Pekina reflected an active Church. In 1889, Fr Handley encouraged 400 – 'nearly the whole of the congregation' – to take the total abstinence pledge,[41] and at the 1895 event, there were also 400 communicants.[42] The 1892 'Vatican Valley' calendar in Figure 4 also reflects the active Church framework. The *Southern Cross* judgement that Fr Maher's 'parish ... [was] one of the most Catholic', seems supported.[43] In early 1919 the creation of Booleroo Centre as a new parochial district reduced the size of Pekina's congregation.[44]

Fundraising, that quintessential part of Catholic life, further proclaimed the active role of the Church for the Pekina community. In 1890 when Bishop O'Reily decided to reduce the diocesan debt he had inherited (known as 'The Cathedral Fund'), he opened the campaign at Pekina, utilising that congregation's generosity to challenge that of other congregations. By April 1891, after unrelenting pressure, Pekina's total was £1,005.10s.0d from 'but 113 subscribers ... the great bulk is composed of small farmers and farm labourers'.[45] This precedent centring on Pekina was reactivated in 1908 by Australian-born Bishop John Norton in his campaign to clear diocesan debts.[46] In that year Pekina, Yarrowie and Yatina congregations had already raised £250 for repairs to Pekina's presbytery.[47] In all his parish visits, Bishop Norton focused on Pekina's generosity, and competitively set congregations against each other in totals subscribed. This took place after committees had assigned amounts to individuals, so that the lists of those who had paid and those who had not could be read out each week in an early ecclesiastical version of 'name and shame'.[48] This campaign seemed to be conducted much more aggressively than the first.

Figure 5. Bishop Maher's grave Pekina churchyard 2018. (Courtesy John Mannion)

Bishop Maher's death in 1906 came between these two campaigns, but it too led to financial pressure when his successor, Bishop Norton, suggested that the importance of 'at least a suitable monument ... over his grave ... [at] Pekina' should be contemplated.[49] His priests were informed the following March that, 'I am of opinion that the time is now right for this work to be carried out. ... I have already given the order for this to be done at a cost of about £100'. Although Bishop Norton decreed the diocesan donations were to be voluntary, he wanted all the details, pledging to publish them.[50]

More locally, in Pekina, this 'Catholic stronghold of the North', there was additional fundraising. The chronology and nature of Pekina's building

Figure 6. Lyons family outside their home south of Pekina, c. 1890
(Ambrose Lyons collection)

projects during these decades highlights the ongoing presence and strength of Catholicism in the township. In 1894, the presbytery needed 'additions and repairs', the chapel required 'renovation', and there were 'general improvements' to the convent; the *Southern Cross* judged that 'the congregation are much to be commended for their liberality'.[51] At the 1906 St Patrick's Day Sports (which netted £25), Fr M.J. O'Flynn linked the attendance to 'the urgent need for an Institute Hall'.[52] At the opening in November, he was credited with initially '[t]aking the matter in hand'; the committee had already raised £260, leaving a debt of only £100.[53] By the early 1920s, St Catherine's Church was found to be too small to cater for the congregation. Fundraising for a new church began in 1922, and before the foundation stone was blessed in 1925, £789 had been raised.[54] When the new St Catherine's was opened, Irishman Bishop Killian 'exhorted the people to give generously on this occasion and maintain the name they had held for a long time as the "banner" parish of the diocese'. The donations reached £519 19s 6d, not quite enough to leave the church debt free, but suggesting many of the faithful had followed clerical advice of doubling what they came prepared to give.[55] Two years later, there were more renovations and additions to Pekina's convent. (Boarding facilities for girls probably existed from then.) At the opening, Fr Morrissey spoke of the sisters' 'devotion and self-sacrificing labors', stating that 'all the necessary work in the parish had been done'. He 'hoped the people would be as generous on this occasion as they most certainly had been on all the others'; subscriptions reached £240. The *Southern Cross* item stated that, 'The block of Church buildings at Pekina is now very compact and imposing and lends an air of importance and distinction to an otherwise small township.'[56]

However, in 1928 further fundraising was needed 'to reduce the parochial debt', and in Pekina, a successful 'Bazaar and Queen Competition' was held. Over the three previous months, nine young women worked to raise money and attract votes as queens of various realms (music, shamrocks and roses for example); it was announced on the night that £760 had been raised 'despite the bad seasons … [of] the past few years'.[57] But there were additional financial demands.

The existence of the school operated by the Sisters of St Joseph presented another facet of an active Church in Pekina. In 1881, newspaper comment acknowledged that the Catholic communities of the North had been 'truly wonderful' in working for 'the education of the young, many of whom would not receive any education at all were it not for the efforts of the Catholics, with the Reverend Bernard Nevin at their head'.[58] In 1894, the *Southern Cross* recognised that the Josephite Pekina school was unique in not having any competition from a government school; the item stated there were '70 children on the roll, with an average attendance of about 50'.[59] But, in the absence of state funding for religious schools, such Church schools required financing. The extent to which the sisters relied on community support was demonstrated by picnics in the 1880s and 1890s,[60] and, from the early 1890s, annual school concerts were held in Pekina. In 1902 the hotel was used as the venue because it was the centre of the town.[61] Concerts by the Pekina students were increasingly also staged in surrounding townships, requiring enormous community organisation, and raising anything from £8 to £14.[62] This pattern continued into the 20th century with a ball at Tarcowie in 1928 netting £15, and, in 1929, as well as the children's performances, 'three of Adelaide's most popular artists' – a soprano, violinist and pianist – were also programmed. All this was followed by 'a dance … and a sumptuous supper'.[63] The education provided

Figure 7. Hinton family outside the Pekina Hotel (built 1878) in 1930s
(Mary Williams collection)

by the sisters was also of significance in consolidating the area's 'Irishness', something noted in other Irish enclaves in South Australia.[64]

The early 1880s unequivocally revealed Pekina's allegiance to Ireland. By August 1881 the 30-member branch of the Irish Land League (ILL), independently established by local Irishmen,[65] held its 'first quarterly meeting' at the Pekina Hotel, the township's only meeting place. Insisting that, 'It was their duty as Irishmen to do all in their power' to support the goal of 'better land laws for Ireland', they stated that this did not 'make them bad subjects'. A possible visit from John Walshe, the league agent from Ireland, was noted, and the secretary instructed to invite him to Pekina.[66] When Walshe's associate, Pierce Healey, visited the township a year later, league membership stood at 65, but the meeting attracted 'upwards of 200'. Healey commented that 'it was the largest ... in the North, and was certainly attended by more ladies than any other he had addressed in the country'.[67] While newspaper coverage of meetings was inconsistent, the occasional reports show sustained interest; for example, in 1887, 300 heard Irishman and colonial MP, Patrick McMahon Glynn, lecture about Ireland, the proceeds going to the local Irish National League

(INL),[68] and in July 1889, branch membership stood at 100.[69] The September 1889 meeting was notable for the admission of 10 new members, and for a motion to admit ladies 'to meetings as honorary members'. However, a large majority supported an amendment, 'it being considered better for the ladies to form a branch of their own, if desired'.[70] Writing to the *Southern Cross*, Patrick Whelan (INL Secretary) declared that 'no Irishman worthy of the name should be without his card of membership of the Irish National League'.[71] Pekina's level of commitment suggested its inhabitants were more than worthy of the name of Irishmen.

In late 1889 in the first year of *Southern Cross* publication, a series of articles highlighted Northern centres. The reporter described Pekina as 'an essentially Celtic township', wondering 'where all the people who attend Mass come from'.[72] Travelling further North he wrote, 'From Cradock to Hawker I find myself in almost a purely Irish settlement.'[73] In 1891, despite ongoing signs of an economic downturn, when J.R. Cox of the Irish Parliamentary Party (IPP) visited Pekina to raise funds for evicted Irish tenants, the *Southern Cross* reported that:

> Pekina is probably the most thoroughly Irish centre in South Australia, and as most of the people hail from Clare county [sic], they determined to give the member for Clare a right royal welcome: and so they did. ... Mr Cox states that ... never did he see greater enthusiasm displayed or more patriotic fervour shown than at his meeting in the little township of Pekina.

The meeting raised £70.[74] Before the crowd dispersed, a branch of the Irish National Federation (INF) was formed.[75] Figure 8 shows the response from Dublin in August 1890 when Pekina Irishmen sent £21 to Dublin.[76] Cox later spoke about his 'very curious' Pekina experience:

> The village consists of the sum total of five houses, including the inn. The surrounding district is entirely rural, and the houses are from 10 to 50 miles apart. ... [M]y meeting was fixed at 8. The secretary ... bade me be of good cheer, "that the people would roll up" – and sure enough, at 8 o'clock – the whole village was crowded, and the room in which the meeting was held crammed to suffocation, most of the visitors, to my certain knowledge, coming in buggies and on horseback across the plains distance of from 40 to 50 miles to attend; and it is worth noting that in this little hole-and-corner spot £80 was collected there and then for the relief of the evicted.[77]

Figure 8. INL letter from Ireland to Pekina, October 1890
(John Moten collection)

In 1893, the *Southern Cross* reported that 'the 'Pekina Irishmen have set a good example by starting a Home Rule fund'.[78] Research to date has not uncovered any Pekina reactions to Irish wartime events such as the Easter Rising or its violent aftermath. Orroroo's paper published the names of those who enlisted in the council area – there were seven names from Pekina.[79] Later reports of more pro- than anti-conscription meetings in 1916 did not fully clarify the Orroroo and district vote of 488 votes against and 398 votes in favour of conscription.[80] The following year when voters were again asked about conscription, one Orroroo meeting was described as one of the biggest crowds seen for many a day at the hall. People had to stand away back in the passage and some outside on the road. There were many visitors from Pekina, Euralia, Morchard, Walloway and Erskine.[81]

At a previous meeting a 'small number gathered to hear [speakers] on conscription'.[82] In 1921, building on the reputation that Pekina 'has always "rung true" for Irish nationality,' two Irish-born priests, Frs Morrissey and Nesdale ensured a branch of the Self Determination for Ireland League of Australia was founded in Pekina.[83] Another feature evident from the 1920s was the alignment of both the region and its inhabitants with the poetry of *Around the Boree Log*. First published in 1921, by 1929 over 32,000 copies had been published, and individual poems were often part of local performances.

Unsurprisingly, for many years the St Patrick's Day Sports continued as an important event. In 1897 for example, that day's recreation was judged as necessary 'to drive off the melancholy condition ... [the people] have fallen into through the bad season'.[84] In 1905 the 'Annual St Patrick's Day Sports and Bazaar' netted £17 for Pekina's school.[85] After an unexplained lapse of 13 years, the day was revived in 1921 – at this 'splendid meeting',[86] the comment that '[c]ars were in evidence from all over the district' showed changing times.[87] That gathering's success ensured the event's repetition in 1922.[88]

In December 1929, reporting that a 'Holy Hour' had been held in Pekina every week for two years,[89] the *Southern Cross* reminded readers that:

> Pekina has always been famous for its great loyal Irish Catholic citizens, and for the fact that it is the only town of any note that has no public school or any religious buildings of any other denomination. Its Catholic buildings are commodious, up-to-date, and a credit to the district. The children from the Convent, under the control of the good Sisters of St Joseph, have more than held their own with the outside world ....[90]

This judgement about Pekina's Catholicism and its 'Irishness' at the end of the 1920s provided a powerful base for the township's extraordinary history during the 1930s.

The 1930s and the 1940s

In the 1930s the combination of Pekina's 'Irishness' and its Catholicism had substantial impact during the state's centenary celebrations. Inevitably, the concentrated Irish nature of the area's early residents and their demonstrated commitment to Ireland had changed in a hundred years.[91] So, when Pekina attracted widespread publicity about its various centenary events in the 1930s, much of this was generated by Fr Michael Vincent Prendergast, its visionary Irish-born, Irish-speaking parish priest. He had reached the state in 1913 and been at the forefront of Irish-focused activity from the outset. Indeed, his commitment to Ireland, especially in relation to his founding role in the 1918 emergence of the radical Irish National Association (INA), had security authorities alarmed about his wartime loyalty.[92] He was Pekina's priest from April 1933 to September 1937. The era also reveals numerous Pekina allusions to sentiments expressed in *Around the Boree Log*, the book of poetry characterising Irish-Australians, by 'John O'Brien', alias Fr Patrick Hartigan. This pattern suggests those Irish-Australians saw themselves in the characters of the poetry.[93] Also significant in that decade, in addition to the impact of the Depression (which was felt in South Australia from 1927), were the consequences of drought in the late 1920s – many farmers relied on receiving seed, superphosphate and food for their families from the State Bank which then owned their crop. In his 1999 book, *No Place like Pekina*, John Mannion's comment reveals the outcome: 'This was possibly the bleakest period yet in the history of the Pekina district, and the region's population began a slow decline as farmers were forced off the land'.[94] The years of population decline, followed almost immediately by World War II, produced some unexpected consequences for the Pekina district.

The visible presence of the Church remained in parish operation, the contribution of the Josephites and their school, and, especially under Fr Prendergast in the middle of the 1930s, in a range of significant community events usually attended by the local bishop and large crowds. Fr Prendergast was closely focused on both the state's centenary and Pekina's diamond jubilee in 1936. In 1935 a 'representative vigilance committee' was formed with Fr Prendergast as chairman. *Southern Cross* reporting of planning makes interesting reading with its reference to the Sinn Fein policy, that is, 'Ourselves alone' or managing without outside help:

It is felt that as Pekina is such an old settlement it can expect some assistance from Centenary funds towards the planting of Centenary groves or other improvements. If the money is for Adelaide only, of course Pekina must adopt the Sinn Fein policy and see what can be done locally, with the assistance of the local district council.[95]

In a letter to the *Southern Cross* in March 1936, Fr Prendergast's major point related to trees. He hoped that readers would 'interest themselves … in the matter of tree planting in South Australia' because he recognised that 'Australia is gradually being denuded of trees'. In addition to ongoing spiritual links between Australia and Ireland, he also proposed establishing trade connections in the way of a 'goodwill ship' to transport 'suitable gifts to the Emerald Isle during this Centenary year'. Although he suggested the INA could make the arrangements – and he was a vice-president – nothing developed.[96]

The picnic meeting of 15 August 1935 was intended to allow 'some of the old glory of Pekina … [to] come back' as well as 'solv[ing] the financial difficulties of Pekina Parish'.[97] The revival of the 'well-known Pekina race meeting', alongside the greatest 'Wheelbarrow Race in the world's history', and a race ball was seemingly a prelude for 1936.[98] According to the *Southern Cross*, the day's 'success exceeded all expectations'.[99] Thus in 1936 the 'picnic races, sports and carnival on August 15 … [were planned as] the first official Centenary and Jubilee celebrations in the district'.[100] Many 'ex-residents of Pekina … said … [the big] picnic surpassed all their expectations'. And what was seen as the town was approached, led to numbers describing 'Pekina as the Oakbank of the North'.[101] The attendance of Bishop Gilroy in both 1935 and 1936 was of great symbolic importance for Pekina. In 1936 he 'cut the streamers at the entrance to the … Jubilee Oval and cycle track'. Fr Prendergast stated the bishop's presence at the 1936 ceremony 'was fitting … because it was as an ecclesiastical centre that Pekina was put on the map'. The estimated crowd of 2000 also heard George Frederick Jenkins MP congratulate the committee on their achievements, especially given their receipt of only £25 from the Centenary Committee. Thus, the Sinn Fein solution was activated – voluntary labour from 'the men of the parish' and 'splendid meals' provided by the women.[102] After Bishop Gilroy's elevation to Sydney, his successor, Bishop McCabe,

Figure 9. Pekina Institute 1906 (Postcard, courtesy John Mannion)

made Pekina his first official parish visit. At his welcome, Pekina's concert programme maintained the Irish focus in the choice of several items.[103]

Fr Prendergast publicised 'Pekina's unique achievements' in the *Southern Cross* of January 1937. Of greatest significance was his clarification that some months earlier a deputation had asked Bishop Gilroy about 'the Church tak[ing] over the Pekina Institute and run[ning] it as a parish hall'. This was accepted; 'His Excellency was very interested when informed that Pekina township is now a completely Catholic settlement'. Fr Prendergast further explained that proceeds from both the upcoming centenary ball (when the hall's floor renovation would be complete), and the 'Back to Pekina Centenary carnival and aerial display' would help defray 'the debt on the new parish hall'.[104] Further advance notice, with a clever aside to John O'Brien and his poetry, highlighted the planning for a transport display, with many old vehicles being located and prepared: 'Pekina will resound again to the rumble of the old Shandrydan as well as to the hum of the aeroplane on February 20.'[105]

Mention of the aeroplane referred to 'the air race or aerial derby from Parafield to Pekina' something which would give 'Pekina ... the distinction of being the first inland town in Australia to become the terminus of an air race'.[106] Although only three pilots participated, the event attracted much district attention.[107] The centenary ball, a fancy dress and 'a very bright affair', drew 29 couples in costume.[108] A further major event in the 1937 life of Pekina was the official opening of the Pekina centenary tennis courts in August. Archbishop Gilroy (now of Sydney), was the main performer, with Bishop Collins (Geraldton), Bishop Fox (Wilcannia-Forbes), and Monsignor Hartigan of Wagga (alias John O'Brien) also in attendance. As one reporter wrote:

> This must be the only day in the history of Pekina, that such a large congregation of learned prelates assembled together in one body, had been seen, and, coming from such far distances for the opening, could be appreciated by all.[109]

The object of their interest, the tennis courts, seemed disproportionate to the level of Church attention. At the September farewell to Fr Prendergast, the 200 who crowded Pekina's parish hall heard Martin Redden's 'sincere regrets' and statements that:

> Dr Prendergast had done a lot for Pekina during his stay there, and he was responsible for the very successful sports that were conducted ... [there] each August. He was the prime mover in the establishment of the very beautiful recreation grounds, and the trees which he had had planted in the streets of Pekina which will serve as a glowing tribute to his very great interest in the well-being of the town.[110]

The Irish priest's transfer to Jamestown (noted as a 'promotion to such an important parish') and the return of Australian-born Fr Kain seemed to represent some negative type of turning point in terms of Pekina's 'Irishness'. The two clerics represented opposite poles in terms of promoting the township, and whereas Fr Prendergast utilised everything available in his efforts, Fr Kain's approach, both before 1933 and after 1937, was far more passive.

From the 1930s parish balls provided both a social occasion and a financial source. Debutante balls were popular in Pekina from 1934 to at least 1945. Debutante numbers varied – 27 young women were presented to Monsignor O'Rourke in 1934. The girls were named and their gowns described; the stage was decorated in 'papal colours'.[111] In 1939 there were only eight but a crowd of 250 attended, in 1940 Bishop McCabe received 10, the 1941 attendance was over 250.[112] Dr McCabe returned in 1945 when seven young women were presented; the correspondent claimed these events were always popular because 'the public ... seems to regain its lost youth when they [sic] see the assembled debutantes'.[113] As indicated earlier, the Great Northern Picnic Carnival also included an evening ball; a local report of the 1937 event where 'the scene ... was one of brilliant splendour' – noted Fr Prendergast's transfer to Jamestown, mentioning his 'farewell speech'.[114] But the tradition of the carnival and race ball continued in 1938 when, despite wintry conditions, about 1000 attended what was seen as 'one of the most important [shows] in the North, for people journey from all parts to participate in this popular carnival'.[115] A very small item in 1940 reported 'a record crowd' attended the ball, the proceeds of which went 'to two worthy causes ... patriotic funds and reduction of the parish debt'.[116]

In 1933 the annual school concert presented by the Pekina students attracted a number of the parish's former priests. Their comments, and those of Fr Prendergast, endorsed the 'self-sacrifice and untiring interest' of the sisters, and suggested 'the concert [was] worth going a long way to see'. The programme included both Ireland- and Australia-focused items, with a recitation of 'St Patrick's Day', described as a 'typically Irish piece, ... [which] must have stirred up within the breasts of Pekina's Irishmen [sic] memories of the grand old days that are gone'. The proceeds were £25.[117] Details in the November 1935 *Southern Cross* revealed that the 'whole parish co-operat[ed]' in raising the £60 guaranteed annually to the sisters at Pekina; that year socials were held at Yatina, Tarcowie, Hornsdale and a collection made at Appila-Yarrowie, with the last event at Pekina. The financial burden was shared because '[t]hey all realise what a blessing it is to have a Convent and the good Sisters in their midst'.[118] In 1941 the Pekina boarding school was mentioned as one of a number in the diocese.[119] In the absence of certainty about when the Sisters of St Joseph decided the Pekina school was no longer viable, the combined impact of the already-mentioned population decline and the war helps explain the sisters' withdrawal.[120] A June 1945 letter to the children's page in the *Southern Cross* alluded to the change, writing about when 'the Sisters were taken away' as a 'big loss to the Catholics'.[121]

There were, however, several other facets of life in Pekina that were unusual and reinforced the township's uniqueness. One that closely involved the Sisters of St Joseph was the Pekina Hotel. It opened in 1878, but by early 1936 was found by the North East Licensing Authority 'to be in need of extensive repairs and renovations'.[122] It was bequeathed on 1 August 1936 to the sisters by a Thomas Ryan. He had been living in Adelaide prior to his death in 1935.[123] Although John Mannion's 1999 book acknowledges this unusual bequest,[124] in 2018 the sisters' archives had no record of the transfer.[125] Documents from the Lands Titles Office verified the situation showing the building was mortgaged until 1945 to 'The Congregation of the Sisters of St Joseph of the Sacred Heart, South Australia'. The publican at the time was a Mrs Gladys Phillips. The second feature involved the town's cemetery, the site of which was declared in December 1880.[126] Previously, in 1879, according to Mannion, the Church attempted to assert ongoing control of the area used as Pekina's burial ground. The then state superintendent of cemeteries proposed that Catholics use a specific area but without either fencing or any legal rights being applied. From July 1882 until April 1890 part of Sections 211 and 221, Pekina's public cemetery, was managed by five trustees – four Irish Catholics and one non-Catholic. Then, following some negotiation with the District Council of Ororoo (established in 1888), the administration of the site was regulated.[127] However, complete control of the ground did not pass to the council until the 1960s.[128]

The final unique element was the 'Pekina accent'. Information about this aspect was provided by the current bishop of the Port Pirie Catholic Diocese, Greg O'Kelly SJ AM DD. Both sides of his family have their origin in the northern areas of the state. In the 1950s, his mother Eileen (née Carter), identified that 'you can tell the people from Pekina by the way they speak'. The bishop attributes the retention of the Irish brogue to the fact of this strong Irish-Catholic community being largely isolated from outside influences until after World War II. Children attending St Joseph's School grew up in an atmosphere where they were exposed to the brogue, not only from many sisters and most clergy, but also from their peers' families.[129] The Pekina brogue, according to John Mannion, was still evident during the 1974 centenary in speeches delivered by three former local students, Jim Crocker, Len Duffy and Joe McNamara.[130]

Figure 10. Daly Grave, Pekina cemetery. (Photo courtesy John Mannion)
Patrick Daly died at Pekina on 30 November, aged 100 years

Conclusion

Examining Pekina's 'Irishness' and its nature as a distinctive Irish-Catholic township highlights the role played by the clergy, most of whom were Irish (see Appendix One), and in a different, less explicit, way the actions and involvement of the Sisters of St Joseph. Operating above and within a regional population with a largely Irish-born first generation which assumed 'critical mass' proportions, and which had mostly benefitted from colonial experience elsewhere, it seems these elements fused into a most unusual rural centre. Pekina's claim to be a centre of the Irish and Catholicism was established early with church, presbytery and school reinforcing its status in the 1870s. The subsequent absence from the township of either any other denomination's church or a government school strengthened this initial template. While the Irish background of three early sisters of St Joseph is known, it is likely that others were also Irish-born or of Irish descent. (See Appendix Two.) Local commitment to Irish issues was strong, and the focus on Irish-related items was very evident at school concerts. Inevitably, all these features diminished over time as second- and third-generation residents either moved away or became less committed to Ireland. The possibilities of regenerating Pekina's focus were ably demonstrated under Fr Prendergast's multi-directional energies, but the momentum could not be sustained under the triple weight of a very different cleric, the Depression of the 1930s with all its consequences in terms of population, and World War II. But for more than 60 years Pekina deserved its title as 'the most thoroughly Irish centre in South Australia'.

Appendix One

Priests serving in Pekina

Name of priest	Years in Pekina	Place of birth	Life dates	Place of burial
James Bieronski	1899–c. 1901, c. 1920	Pieterkopf, Russian Poland	1864–1944	West Terrace Cemetery
Nicholas Canny	1971–1990	Carrieton, SA	1928–1997	Crystal Brook
Patrick J. Carroll	1896	Ireland		New Norcia, WA
Joseph Maurice Casey	1931–1934, 1936	County Kerry	1882–1936	Died in Adelaide
Patrick Cleary	1902	Ireland		
Philip Cleary	1882–1885	County Kilkenny	1847–1896	Quorn Cemetery
Arthur J. Conway	1927–1931	County Offaly	1899–1975	Carrieton Catholic churchyard
Mark Delahunty	1880–?	County Kilkenny	1846–1927	West Terrace Cemetery
Richard Doyle*		County Kilkenny	1859–1900	Carrieton Catholic churchyard
William Doyle*	1898, 1929	County Kilkenny	1862–1929	Jamestown Cemetery
William T. Dunphy	?1891, 1898–?	County Kilkenny	c. 1865–1904	Died in Ireland
F or J. Dunne	1929			
Fr Dyer				
William Protase Kain	1922–1933, 1937–1964	Warnertown, SA	1891–1964	Pekina Cemetery
Mathew Kennedy	?–1883	Ireland	1833–1903	Died at Laura
William Joseph Kett	1907–1910, 1919	Ireland	1880–1952	Centennial Park Cemetery
Richard Kirby	1903–?	Ireland	1870–1916	West Terrace Cemetery
Philip Landy	1880–1881	County Tipperary	1858–1918	Mount Barker Catholic Cemetery
James Lecky	1904–1906	Ireland		
Patrick Edward McCabe	1910–1911, 1921–1925	Jamestown, SA	1886–1925	Pekina Cemetery
Michael McCurtin	1931–1933, 1965–1970	County Clare	c. 1904–1984	California, America
Hugh McEvoy	1911	County Kilkenny		
Timothy Joseph McEvoy	1908, 1911–1917	County Kilkenny	1887–1922	Port Pirie Cemetery
Patrick Joseph McKenna	1936	Ireland	1910–1955	Died in Adelaide
James Maher	1881–1905	County Tipperary	1849–1905	Pekina Catholic churchyard
Patrick Michael Molloy	1935–1936	Ireland	1908–1970	Died at Spalding
Francis Bernard Morrissey	1921–1925, 1928–1930	Ireland	1895–1954	Georgetown Cemetery

continued

'The most thoroughly Irish centre in South Australia': Pekina from the 1870s to the 1940s

Name of priest	Years in Pekina	Place of birth	Life dates	Place of burial
Edmund Mulcahy	1894–1900, 1904	County Waterford	1863–1937	Georgetown Cemetery
Bernard Nevin	1877–1881	County Roscommon	1837–1920	West Terrace Cemetery
William H. Nesdale	1920–1922	County Cork	?1896–?	
John Norton		Ballarat, Victoria	1857–1923	Peterborough Cemetery
Thomas O'Connor	1906–1928	County Kilkenny	1849–1928	Pekina Cemetery
Michael J. O'Flynn	1903–1904, 1905	County Waterford	1866–1909	Died at Hammond
John O'Mahoney	1897–?	Adelaide, SA	1872–1922	West Terrace Cemetery
James Grey O'Rourke	1905–1906,	County Leitrim or Cavan	1869–1941	Georgetown Cemetery
James Joseph Prendergast	?–1918	Ireland	1890–1967	Jamestown Cemetery
Michael Vincent Prendergast	1933–1937	County Waterford	1884–1952	Jamestown Cemetery
Edmund Ryan	1913, 1929–1932	County Tipperary	1866–1932	West Terrace Cemetery
Mathew Smith				
William T. Unsworth	1878–1880	England	?–1904	Returned to Plymouth, worked there 1894–1903
Francis Walsh	1931–1933	Ireland	?–1973	
Michael Ward	1892–?	Ireland	?–1922	

* The Doyles were brothers

Appendix Two

Sisters of St Joseph known to have taught at Pekina between 1878 and 1944

Christian name	Surname	Name in religion	Teaching role/s	Teaching details	From	To
Margaret	Casey	Benizi	Primary teacher	Teaching	10/05/1878	Unknown
Catherine	O'Loghlin*	Margaret		Unknown	10/05/1878	Unknown
Veronica Cecelia	O'Brien	Laurence	Primary teacher	Teaching	01/01/1879	Unknown
Mary Jane	Wilson*	Columba		Unknown	01/01/1883	19/08/1883
Bridget	Cosgrove	Laurentia		Unknown	01/01/1883	Unknown
Mary	Cox*	Berchmans		Unknown	01/01/1883	Unknown
	Hogan	Winifred			?/?/1889	?/?/1891
	Howley	Andrea			?/?/1891	?/?/1891
	Doherty	Flora			?/?/1892	?/?/1895
	Hiney	Paulina			?/?/1896	?/?/1896
	Schmidt	Leonard			?/?/1897	?/?/1897
	Duffy	Dolores			?/?/1898	?/?/1899
	Frost	Pius			?/?/1900	?/?/1900
	O'Loughlin	Reginald			?/?/1901	?/?/1904
Ellen Ada	Coles	Uriel Mary	Primary teacher/music	Teaching/music	01/01/1905	31/12/1908
	O'Loughlin	Winifred			?/?/1905	?/?/1909
Ellen Ada	Coles	Uriel Mary	Primary teacher/music	Teaching/music	01/01/1909	31/12/1914
	Gough	Peter			?/?/1910	?/?/1915
Mary Harietta	Vivash	Aquinas	Community ministry	House duties	06/10/1913	31/12/1914
	O'Loughlin	Winifred			?/?/1916	?/?/1918
Bridget	McMahon	Josephine	Music teacher	Teaching/music	01/01/1919	31/12/1920
	Clifford	Dominic			?/?/1919	?/?/1924
Ellen Ada	Coles	Uriel Mary	Primary teacher/music	Teaching/music	01/01/1920	31/12/1928
Bridget	McMahon	Josephine	Music teacher	Teaching/music	01/01/1924	31/12/1929
Annie Mary	Hansberry	Benedict	Primary teacher	Teaching/infants	01/01/1924	31/12/1924
Miriam Teresa	Godfrey	Helen	Primary teacher	Teaching/middle grades	01/01/1929	31/12/1933

continued

Christian name	Surname	Name in religion	Teaching role/s	Teaching details	From	To
Mary Agnes	Moroney	Mel	Primary/ secondary teacher	Teaching grades 5–7	01/01/1934	31/12/1937
Brigid Margaret Teresa	Fitzpatrick	Patrick	Primary teacher	Teaching grades 1–4	01/01/1935	31/12/1935
Miriam Rose Estelle	Boyle	John Vianney	Music teacher	Teaching/ music	20/03/1936	31/12/1936
Catherine Josephine	Wall	Ursula	Primary teacher	Teaching/ middle grades	01/01/1937	31/12/1937
Bridget Rose	Gleeson	Cecily	Music teacher	Teaching/ music	01/01/1938	30/09/1938
Ruth Monica	Case	Agneta	Primary/ secondary teacher	Teaching grades 4–7	01/01/1938	31/12/1941
Brigid Margaret Teresa	Fitzpatrick	Patrick	Primary teacher	Teaching grades 1–4	01/01/1939	31/12/1939
Elizabeth	Maher	Liam	Primary teacher	Teaching grades 1–4	01/02/1941	31/12/1942
Irene Hannah	Gapper	Angela	Primary/ secondary teacher	Teaching grades 4–7	01/01/1943	31/12/1943
Ruth Monica	Case	Agneta	Primary/ secondary teacher	Teaching grades 4–7	01/01/1944	31/12/1944

* Known to be of Irish birth

1889–1891 (2 sisters); 1891–1897 (3 sisters); 1898–1899 (4 sisters); 1900–1903 (3 sisters); 1904 (4 sisters); 1905–1924 (3 sisters).

Source: Sisters of St Joseph South Australian Archives, Kensington, Series 24, 'Pekina School'.

Appendix Three

Pekina Poem

McNamara was ready and with him stood
McCarthy and McMahon
Old John Daly, Maloney and Devitt
With Kenny, Keough and Kinnane.

Ryan, Raftery and Travers were eager
With Berry, Hoare, Burke and Rynne
A new life opened before them
But something was holding these men.

With Callaghan, and Hehir they waited
Caulfield, Clark, Lyons and Lee
Tierney, Clancy, Crocker and Redden
And Duffy and Marron you see.

Burns, Hogan and Shannon considered
Just how they would conquer the scrub
But all voices arose in a chorus
Won't somebody open the pub?

Then spoke the blacksmith Hinton
An Englishman was he
If Ireland will not break the drought
Then England your friend will be.

The dreaded drought was broken
When Hinton changed his trade
The scourge of the North was beaten
And Pekina could then be made.

Irish women in early South Australia

CHERRIE DE LEIUEN

From the outset of European colonisation, Irish women had substantial economic, social and political impacts in a variety of roles. Female Irish first and second generations were powerful constructors of South Australian society. However, despite their numbers, influence, and centrality to the success of the colony, their stories are overlooked. They are hardly seen or known in standard historical narratives, and when they are, it is primarily through the lens of emigration schemes, as a burden rather than an asset, and often typecast. This chapter seeks to fill some of the significant gaps in what is known about Irish women in the South Australian context. It is an alternative narrative, providing vignettes of four very different women's lives to shine a light on the diversity of experiences and challenges that they, and their contemporaries, faced. These form part of the mosaic of Irish women's stories, taken from small and often fragmentary pieces of information that when seen together form a much more extraordinary picture.

Research on female Irish

There is a lack of historical information and first-hand accounts of Irish women in South Australia. This is not a revelation, nor is it the first time it has been claimed. Internationally, writers on Irish history have argued the need for studies on female Irish since the 1980s. The seminal studies by Hasia Diner (1983) and Janet Nolan (1989)[1] prompted a number of important publications around the world, particularly in terms of the North American experience.[2] In Australia, most research has focused on women in the eastern states, and is framed by convict history.[3] The migration experience and particularly the cohort of over 4000 women who were sponsored under the Earl Grey Scheme to migrate from 1848 to 1850 have also been the focus of interest.[4] The stories of female Irish are also woven into a number of studies on colonial prostitution, institutions, the destitute, or women religious.[5] The 1998 edited volume *Irish Women in Colonial Australia* remains the only explicit work on this subject to date. For the most part, the topic remains a narrow area of specialty, valued by descendants, but not yet central to discussions on nation building. Patrick O'Farrell's *The Irish in Australia*, for example, limited discussion on women to a few pages. Further, Irish-Australian identity has principally been theorised through male experiences and perspectives, with women's value measured only in terms of reproductive or financial success.

For South Australia, the major studies on Irish women are by Cherry Parkin and Trevor McClaughlin.[6] These both focus on assisted migration in the 1840s and 1850s. Books by Margaret Barbarlet on state wards, Brian Dickey on social welfare, and Marie Steiner on servant depots also provide invaluable insights, though are not specifically on female Irish.[7] There is no major body of theory, no published diaries or memoirs in the public domain. Irish women are neither seen nor known in standard narratives of the state. This is likely a legacy of two main factors: a lack of documentation and the impact of bias. Histories are composed of the facets and facts of people's lives that an author deems important or interesting, and typically exclude the bulk of women's experiences. Further, the absence of Irish women's histories specifically may be a result of the deep-rooted prejudices and complex layers of power particular to South Australia. As this colony aimed to essentially re-create an idealised British colony, the transplanting of gender, class, and racial hierarchies was central. In this model, Irish women were very close to the bottom rung of the social ladder. Single females in particular were pitted against a colonial reconstruction of idealised British feminine gentility; their independence was translated into rhetoric on ineptitude, their difference as immorality and vulgarity.[8] In light of the paucity of information available about the lived experiences of Irish women in the colony, it is essential to locate and investigate their stories from multiple sources and standpoints. The information on women discussed in this chapter is thus found in their official records, snippets from newspapers, occasionally their own writing, and the material traces of their lives. Their stories are included because each of their stories emerged (as opposed to being sought out), while researching the site of St John's, near Kapunda. Each woman was connected, either directly or indirectly by physical location and by way of working for social justice. These women also demonstrate the diversity of life experiences, and the range of physical, economic and social situations of Irish women living in South Australia.

The storekeeper: Bridget Maria Donelly

Bridget Donelly (also recorded as Donnelly and Donoly) is likely to have arrived in Port Adelaide on 27 August 1850. There is no information about her prior to the information recorded on the passenger list for the *Tory*. She was one of the 31 needlewomen aboard whose voyage was sponsored through the Female Emigration Fund.[9] The document lists her as 16 years, a servant, and 'good character from last employers'. In this sense, Bridget differed from the many women and orphan girls who arrived at Adelaide in the 1850s who had no experience in domestic service as they were not afforded education, training or care in Irish workhouses. Perhaps this was the basis for her sponsorship, as a young marriageable woman able to address the perceived gender and labour imbalance in the colony. Perhaps as a single Irish female, she was also immediately judged. Perhaps she was herself embarrassed by her heavy boots and the dark shawl worn over her head or shoulders, which visually clashed with the slippers and bonnets of the Adelaide English girls. Perhaps the incredulous gaze of the male officials betrayed their belief that she and her peers were 'not equal to the English females whom we have been hitherto able to select ... wanting in that orderly and tidy appearance which characterize many of the female emigrants from Great Britain ... and are generally short and not at all well-looking'.[10] Perhaps she had heard of the Melbourne newspaper articles published earlier that year that labelled her cohort 'a set of ignorant creatures whose whole knowledge of household duties barely reaches to distinguishing the inside from the outside of a potato', whose skills were 'trotting across a bog to fetch back a runaway pig', and 'so stupid they are fit for nothing'.[11] Bridget and her generation were seen as outside the colonial notion of respectability.

It is not known whether Bridget went into service after arrival, but on 29 November 1855 she married Richard Haimes at St John's Catholic Church, just outside Kapunda. Richard was born in Queen's County (now County Laois), Ireland, and came to Van Diemen's Land as a young child around 1826. His parents Richard and Margaret Haimes owned the military canteen and the Waterloo Hotel in George Town (Van Diemen's Land), his mother taking over the licence on his father's death.[12] Richard became an architect,[13] and left for Victoria with his brother John before moving to South Australia around 1846. Bridget and Richard lived at Allen's Creek near Kapunda, and in 1851 he and John were licensees of the Sir John Franklin Hotel, Richard then being a cordial manufacturer. Bridget and Richard had three children: their son, John David, was born in 1859, but died aged six months; a daughter, Margaret Anne, was born in 1861 but died before her third birthday in 1864; Susannah Bridget was born in 1863. John David and Margaret Anne were both buried at the St John's cemetery.

St John's was the site of one of the earliest Catholic parishes in the state, established in 1849. Parishioners are said to have numbered in the hundreds, with many coming from the nearby Baker's Flat (see chapter by Arthure). It was perhaps a desire to be close to St John's, or an opportunity to capitalise on the location, that led to the Haimes family purchasing three acres there from John Rogers in 1865. Directly opposite the church they built a substantial four-roomed home with an adjoining two rooms for use as a general store and cellar, a barn, shed and forge. The premises also operated as a post office from 1867 to 1879. Oral histories recall that on Sundays the fences outside the store would be lined with horses and buggies, and, after mass, parishioners would purchase goods from the Haimes' store, such as books and newspapers including the *Irish Harp*. It was a place to congregate and socialise, and men often made a competition of trying to lift a heavy boulder that was on the side of the road.[14] This was at the centre of a thriving Irish-South Australian Catholic community.

The year 1871 was a difficult one for Bridget Haimes. Newspapers report that on 14 June[15] at about seven o'clock she trimmed the kerosene lamp, as usual, and left it burning safely while she and Richard went in to have tea in the adjoining room, from which the store cannot be seen. Directly after tea, Richard went out the front, and found the room on fire. All contents were destroyed, including the post office supplies; they were uninsured. Only a few weeks later, on 25 July, Richard died suddenly at home, aged 45 years.

Bridget deposed at the inquest that she had seen him that morning. He had gone outside to chop wood for the fire when he collapsed, blood streaming from his mouth. Their employee, Joseph Leahan, ran to alert her. She let out a scream, and ran to him to check he was breathing. Hearing her cries, their neighbour John McCormack came down and helped her carry him inside, but he died about a quarter of an hour later. Dr Blood attributed his death to the rupture of a blood vessel in his lungs.[16]

Now a widow and mother to a five-year-old daughter, Bridget took on the role of running the general store, post office and property; staff included Joseph Leahan, John Kelly and his brother, and Sarah Ann Sherwin.[17] She then became the holder of a colonial wine licence, and in 1875 applied for and was granted the contract by the Destitute Board to supply rations to the destitute in the district. In 1863, St Rose's Catholic church had opened in the main Kapunda township, and rather than walk the three miles to St John's, most parishioners attended that church. This, combined with a downturn of works at the copper mine, led to an exodus of people from the local area, and would have resulted in a significant decline in business. In December 1875, Bridget put the store, house and land up for sale;[18] however, she was unable to find a purchaser and continued to live there for a number of years.

Bridget Maria Haimes was a respected member of the community. In 1876, when Corporal Mallon charged her for selling wine on a Sunday (to Martin Costello after he had attended a funeral at St John's), the *Express and Telegraph* noted her as being 'a widow, very widely known, and much respected'. When she was fined £10 by the magistrate, her neighbours, 'praying for a remission of the fine', set up a memorial in her name. The same newspaper later noted 'so strong was public feeling in the matter that the amount of the fine, £10, was subscribed by neighbours and placed in Mr Mallon's hands to pay the fine ... and further that a brother of the informant's, who lived near Georgetown, was so annoyed when he read of the conviction that he rode down the whole distance to Kapunda to pay the fine.'[19] The magistrate did indeed rescind that fine, but Bridget was before the courts on two further occasions, as a witness to fire in the area, and then on 6 January 1877 as a victim of assault and robbery.[20] The *Kapunda Herald* reported that neighbours Philip Rodgers (born 1830 in County Westmeath) and Catherine Rodgers (née Gurry born 1837 in County Meath) made a forcible entrance onto her property, and Bridget was beaten with a fence rail. Though she was still the owner of Section 1452, the Rodgers claimed to have been let the property. Bridget testified she would not have done this without communicating with her brother-in-law, John Haimes, in Melbourne. It is not known when Bridget moved away from St John's, but her daughter Susannah worked as a teacher at Watt's Range school in 1887 and 1888 (near present-day Gulnare), and perhaps they moved to the Jamestown area together. She died in Caltowie on 22 September 1888, aged 58, the death notice posted by her daughter.

The schoolteacher: Susannah Bridget Haimes

At 24 years, Susannah (Susan) Haimes, began working as a teacher at Watt's Range school, established by Irish teacher John O'Connell in 1881.[21] Susan grew up at St John's, and was educated in the original slab hut used first for a church and then as the schoolroom on the site opposite her home, her teacher being Mrs Moore.[22] In 1869 the Sisters of St Joseph ran a school from the buildings on the site until 1874, as well as a number of others in the area. The education was sound, with annual examinations managed by an accredited agent of the Catholic University of Ireland and Father Julian Tenison Woods. For the examinations, the girls, including Susan, wore white dresses with ribbons distinguishing the monitors, as well as those with merits, coloured according to the system of regulations prevailing in the Catholic school system. The examination results for 11 November 1869, conducted by the sisters, lists the young second class results: 1st Susan Haimes, 2nd Kate Cash, 3rd Martin O'Neir. Susan likely valued education, as she became a teacher as a young adult, an occupation that contributed to her and her mother's economic and social status.

State Education Department records show that Susan resigned from teaching on 31 March 1888, likely due to her marriage two days later to Alfred Knowling at St Joseph's Catholic Church at Willunga. It was only five months later that her mother Bridget Haimes died, on 22 September 1888. Susan gave birth to a son the following day in Adelaide, and called him Clarence Richard Haimes Knowling. At this stage, the Knowling family was living on Sturt Street. On 26 May 1890, Susan's uncle, John Haimes, died in London. Wealthy, unmarried, and childless, he left more than £92,000 to friends, earned from hotels, breweries (including a partnership in the

Waverley Brewery at Mitcham), mail coaches and racehorses. His will dated 12 July 1887[23] names Susan as next of kin, and bequeaths her £500 and the property known as Mrs Joyce's at St John's.[24] The sum of £500 was also to be left to Bridget Haimes, who had died subsequent to the will being drawn up.

In 1891, following in her mother and grandmother's footsteps, Susan obtained a colonial wine licence and ran a store on King William Street. In 1892 Susan challenged her uncle's will and the bequeathing of £12,000 to the Colac Benevolent Society on the grounds that the society was not in existence at the time of his death. She was successful in receiving £6000. However, the following year she attended court to ward off creditors who accused her husband of defrauding them, as her husband 'had settled household furniture on his wife, being at that time, alleged, able to pay his liabilities'.[25] Though she won this trial, sadly her daughter, Eileen Rosa, died at eight months old on 17 December 1893. Susan passed away less than two years later, aged 32 years.

The sister: Mary Cox

Mary Cox was born in Dublin on 15 August 1848, a time of unprecedented change in Ireland. Young women who had survived the famine years had little choice of occupation in the following decades. Some were able to take the decision to train for service, or try to emigrate. Some chose to stay in Ireland, to marry and have a family, or to stay single. Some could try to find work in newly emerging industries, as farm work was declining, and many were in workhouses. Most young women probably had very limited choices, if any at all. With the intensification of the 'devotional revolution', one of the most valued occupations for women in 19th century Ireland was to become a nun (female religious), and it was the largest professional class of women, increasing ninefold from 1841 to 1901.[26] The attraction is clear: it offered a permanent home outside the constraints of marriage and motherhood, an education, the chance to teach, study, travel and to work in social welfare. It is not surprising then that the middle and upper classes viewed their daughters entering a convent as a respectable situation.

There is no information about Mary Cox's life in Dublin. It is not known how she, and her parents, crossed paths with Mary MacKillop. But in 1874, MacKillop was visiting a number of congregations and schools in Ireland, speaking about the Josephites and her work in Australia, aiming to recruit postulants. Mary became one such recruit, and entered the institute on 28 October 1874. It was a requirement that the postulant's parents pay the passage to Australia. This financial restriction meant that only half could make the trip, and MacKillop agreed to escort the 15 postulants to Adelaide. It also meant that those who became women religious were also from relatively affluent backgrounds. The day before departure, the first 15 Irish Josephites met at the Chapel of the Carmelite Convent in Ranelagh, Dublin, to make their final choice and say goodbye to their loved ones. Patrick and Henrietta Cox were likely there to farewell their daughter. On 31 October, Mary and the 14 other postulants, dressed in large black hats and veils, each with a blue linen kit bag, emerged one by one from the Mercy convent on Blandford Square at Marylebone in London, to enter the eight waiting cabs. A crowd had gathered to see the spectacle.[27] They travelled to London and then Melbourne, on the *St Osyth*, arriving at Port Adelaide on 4 January 1875.

Mary Cox became Sister Berchmans of the Assumption. She lived at Kensington in Adelaide, and then worked as a schoolteacher in Pekina, Caltowie, and Mintaro. In 1885, Mary MacKillop wrote to Archbishop Moran from Sydney, 'Sister Mary Berchmans (Cox) is the latter I referred to when speaking to Your Grace … Sister Mary Berchmans is one of the eight surviving postulants I brought out from Ireland, not one of whom cost the diocese of Adelaide one penny. If Your Grace will allow me to tell her to come over here, I shall be very grateful, for I know her disposition well and cannot answer for the consequences if she is tried beyond her strength, as I very much fear she now is'.[28] Presumably, Mary then went to Sydney and from 1895 to 1905 she taught at Temuka, New Zealand. On returning to South Australia, she was placed at St John's, Kapunda, which was now a Catholic girls reformatory, and was matron from 1908 to 1909. Sister Helena (Mary O'Brien), also from Dublin, had been matron from 1897. Susan O'Reilly from Cavan (Gaetano of the Presentation) and Mary Hayes (Wilfrid of the Scourging), who were also part of the first 15 from Ireland, also lived and worked at St John's. Mary MacKillop had managed the conversion of the St John's site into a reformatory in 1897, and the Irish connection was perhaps part of the reason that these four were sent there together.

During the 12 years of its existence a total of 125 girls were detained at St John's, with between 12 and 21 girls, and at least five sisters, resident at any one time. The girls were all aged between 12 and 18 years. There are no comprehensive records, but the scant existing documentation indicates that most had no official sentences or mandated release dates. The majority of girls were charged with being uncontrollable, or homeless, accusations that were almost always couched in terms of real or imagined sexual promiscuity.[29] Barbarlet observed that half of all reformatory girls in the South Australian system between 1887 and 1892 were of Irish descent, although the Irish made up only 14% of the total population.[30] The environment of the reformatory system was actively used to produce the desirable outcomes of cleaning up the streets, not only because these girls were perceived as 'bad', but also because they were poor, Catholic, Irish, and female. Dickey clarifies the ethos of the system, South Australian middle class, which used a 'deployment of state power' to 'rescue and reform' Irish working-class children, who were considered vulnerable to the corrupting influences of their disreputable families and associates, and place them within the 'preferred pattern of social order'.[31]

The girls undertook a variety of tasks during their detention. This included gardening, laundering, corset- and shirt-making for sale in town, sewing – both plain and fancy work, making their own clothes, cleaning, cooking, wood chopping, the laying of garden beds, and tending cows, a horse and poultry. They were instructed in domestic service, and had a daily prayer, mass, choir, and lessons.[32] A small number of girls were placed in service. Families who accepted them into their homes as domestic servants did not always prove to be suitable, or indeed, did not think the girls were suitable, so they were returned to the reformatory. The Catholic Church acknowledged this problem in a report on the St John's Reformatory for 1907 published in the *Southern Cross*, admitting that not a single girl had been placed in service during the year because of the shortage of suitable homes, but also perhaps from the reticence of non-Catholics to take Catholic girls in as domestics.[33] Just as the girls suffered from discrimination, Sister Berchmans was also saddled with stereotypes of identity from the wider community, good and bad. She also was subjected to paternal instruction from the church hierarchy, classification, observation, and discipline and lived within a strict hierarchy with no privacy and restricted outside contact; 'the nuns shared, even if on a voluntary or semi-voluntary basis, some of the conditions of the inmates, such as the bad food, the hard work, the confinement and the long periods of silence'.[34] Letters sent by Sister Berchmans to the State Children's Council demonstrate her role as disciplinarian, servant, carer and manager.[35] Her connection with her students and the wider community gave her a substantial, but largely unacknowledged, influence within South Australian society. Mary Cox, Sister Berchmans, died at Kensington on 29 September 1919.

The suffragist: Mary Lee

Mary Agnes Walsh was born in County Monaghan, Ireland, on 14 February 1821, and lived there until 1844 when she married George Lee. They probably lived in County Armagh, and they had seven children, although only a son, Charles, and daughter, Evelyn, survived Mary. Like most female Irish, there is scarce information about her life prior to her arrival in the colony. Where her story differs from other women is that she became a key figure in the political and social landscape of late 19th-century South Australia, and a leader for women's rights internationally. Despite a remarkable career, there is still a lack of well-researched biographical information or academic study on her life or work. The few available sources restate information from Mary's obituary, printed in the South Australian newspapers in 1909, and work by Helen Jones.[36] What is most problematic is the uncritical recycling of these sources, which perpetuate half-truths and stereotypes. Most biographies, for example, say that she grew up on Kilknock Estate where her father, John Walsh, was master of the Orange Lodge. There is, however, no evidence of such an estate in Monaghan, nor her father's affiliations.

Mary Lee was 58 and a widow when she arrived in Adelaide with daughter Evelyn on the *Orient* on 15 December 1879. In this sense she differed from many of her contemporaries, and also because the purpose of her voyage was not to emigrate, but to see her son Jonathan Benjamin Steadham (Ben) Lee who was living in Adelaide. Ben had tuberculosis, and died on 2 November 1880, aged 21. Mary and her daughter remained living in North Adelaide after Ben's death. They had rented 152 Barnard Street, which Mary also ran as a boarding house, and this was most likely her source of income. She befriended Harriet Searle, whose son Richard had worked with Ben at the Adelaide City Council. Harriet was active with the female refuge and local mission, and likely introduced Mary to charity and reform work in the colony. Both attended the Primitive Methodist Church in Wellington Square, though Mary Lee was Anglican and described herself as 'once the slip of an old red-hot Tory stem'.[37] Mary was likely well educated and from a relatively affluent background, which fitted her for the respectable 'ruling class' of female reform and charity workers. But whatever her position or faith, in Ireland Mary would have been exposed to death, hunger, demographic and political change, which likely garnered her to agitate for change and for women to have equal voting rights to be free of sexual and economic exploitation.

By 1883 Mary had become secretary of the Social Purity Society. In this role she lobbied successfully to raise the legal age of consent from 13 to 16 years, and began working for legal changes in women's social and sexual status.[38] In July 1888 she inaugurated the Women's Suffrage League, becoming the secretary, spokesperson and director of the campaign for women to have the vote. She steered their campaign and travelled around the colony speaking publicly about franchise. She collected subscriptions and organised petitions and deputations.[39] Mary also acted to change the poor conditions and wages of one of the largest category of women workers – seamstresses, tailoresses and milliners.[40] This campaign became the focus of major labour movement activity at the turn of the century in the fight to ensure legislative protection for female factory workers subject to abuse. At a public meeting in December 1889, Mary Lee suggested the Adelaide Council 'take immediate steps to form female trade unions in all branches of industry where the sweating exists'.[41] She proposed the formation of the Working Women's Trades Union (WWTU), South Australia, which was founded in 1890, and she became its secretary. By 1893 she was union vice-president,[42] and served on a number of social welfare committees, including that of the destitute asylum, the women's refuge and the 'lunatic' asylum (another of her concerns was with mentally ill patients).[43] In 1896 the South Australian government appointed Mary as the first female official visitor to the lunatic asylum and she performed this task with courage and compassion for 12 years. She also worked for the Women's Christian Temperance Union, Distressed Women's and

Children's Committee and the United Trades and Labour Council.[44] She is probably best known for organising the suffrage petition, whereby she travelled across the colony to collect 11,600 signatures. The 120-metre long document was presented to parliament in August 1894, and soon after on 18 December the Constitution Amendment Act was passed. Due in large part to the work of Mary Lee, South Australian women were the first in Australia, and second globally, to gain the vote, and the first in the world to have the right to postal votes and to stand for parliament.[45]

Her own words and the reports of her work recorded in newspapers of the day remain the best testament to her achievements.[46] The letters published by her antagonists also offer an insight into the patriarchy and hostile climate she faced. Often she is represented as having a minority view, ridiculed and publicly denigrated. Her strong opinions on women's rights and her intelligent arguments for change had clearly not endeared her to many. After the vote was won she was gradually forgotten in the public domain. In 1896, on her 75th birthday, the premier delivered her a modest amount of publicly donated money, after a call in the *Advertiser* for years of unpaid work, and as 'Mrs. Lee … is in destitute circumstances'.[47] She died in North Adelaide on 18 September 1909, and is buried with her son in a modest grave in Walkerville. Helen Jones claims that most of Mary Lee's documentation, including from the Women's Suffrage League, was buried at the Brompton dump by family members after her death.

Conclusion

This chapter merely sketches out a number of themes related to Irish women in South Australia (though there are hundreds more women integral to the fabric of the state whose stories have disappeared from collective memory). These themes are not those usually associated with historical perspectives of female Irishness. In O'Farrell's version, for example, Irish women were primarily seen as being devoted to the household in an idealisation of motherhood, or else as the rebellious but fun-loving heroine dancing her way through life.[48] In contrast, Eric Richards has contended that the Irish were largely indistinguishable from their British counterparts except in religious terms.[49] Yet in looking over pages and pages of research, what emerges is not only Irish women as virtuous wives and mothers, nor as seamlessly blending into colonial life, nor even as victims. The common thread of Bridget Donelly, Mary Lee, Mary Cox and their peers is their agency, their resilience and respectability. All transitioned to colonial life by creating and sustaining social networks and by moving beyond their gender strictures. All adapted to challenges in their lives and were respected, in contrast to the commentaries about Irish women in the colonial media. While these are not specifically Irish characteristics, what makes them particular to the Irish story is that these women adapted their cultural, religious and gender heritage to reweave and reinvent their social and cultural fabric in South Australia. What is also observable is that when successful, their Irishness disappeared. Mary Lee for example, wrote about 'dear London'; this is then speculated to mean she lived in London before she came to Australia,[50] (and so she is not really Irish). Similarly the successful Donelly's family members' Irishness is completely overlooked. But when women are unsuccessful, their Irishness is emphasised, such as with the girls who were sent to St John's reformatory.[51] A common thread that emerged was that all faced discrimination along the lines of their gender, class, religion, age, appearance, sexuality, marital status, occupation, language, traditions, lack of education, manners, domesticity, and so on and so on.

The stories of the four Irish women presented all highlight the different forms of nation building. Mary Cox (Sister Berchmans) was needed as a nun and as unpaid labour to carry out the various social and education policies the government wished to implement. Irish nuns were integral to Australian Catholicism but also to teaching, nursing and social work. Convents and schools were incorporated into local communities and provided a sound education, based in Irish tradition. Mary Cox showed leadership in education, and courage in travelling alone and into the unknown. Mary Lee was a worldwide pioneer in her work for women's suffrage, and throughout her 60s, 70s and 80s she worked in social welfare in a number of leadership positions. Similarly, Bridget Donelly (Haimes) was independent, and as a widow adapted to working in the male domain of business ventures, in addition to her unpaid labour in the home and as a mother. Beginning in domestic service, she became a respected member of the community. Susannah Haimes, her daughter, studied to become a teacher, working in a small community as an educator, then becoming a mother and also a business owner. She adapted to her changing, difficult circumstances to have economic success. Reclaiming and writing the role of these ordinary yet extraordinary women into South Australian history is an important step toward acknowledging the part played by Irish women in building and sustaining our community.

The 'wrong kind of immigrant': How existing prejudice on class, gender and ethnicity affected the reception of female Irish Famine orphans in South Australia under the Earl Grey Scheme

JADE HASTINGS

The Earl Grey Scheme operated as an assisted immigration scheme between Ireland and the Australian colonies from 1848 to 1850. One of the participating Australian colonies was the newly established South Australia, where the scheme faced opposition from the predominantly Anglo-Scottish colonists from its first proposal. Eric Richards estimated that the effects of Irish orphan immigration 'were temporary and became virtually unidentifiable after a few years.'[1] More recent scholarship, such as Mark Staniforth's 'The *Inconstant* Girls', investigated the long-term contribution of these migrants to the colony. This chapter examines the specific gender, ethnicity and class prejudices operating in 19th-century South Australia, and the role that these prejudices played in the termination of the Earl Grey Scheme less than three years after it began. It considers whether the issues that ended the scheme were legitimate, or if they were largely imagined by a population that was predisposed to dislike the Irish orphan girls before their arrival in the colony.

The sources used in this chapter provide a crucial insight into the attitudes of South Australian colonists and media, both before and during the Earl Grey Scheme. They also demonstrate the extent to which colonial attitudes and opinions toward the Irish orphan girls evolved as the scheme progressed. Furthermore, when the information presented in newspaper sources is compared with statistics and reports published in secondary sources and government documents, it is possible to determine the level of accuracy that the South Australian media was presenting regarding the Earl Grey Scheme.

Although their contributions can often be overlooked, the Irish orphan girls represent a significant aspect of the colony's history. It is estimated that approximately 30 per cent of Australians have some Irish heritage, and Staniforth asserts that the Irish orphan girls are the 'ancestors of a significant number of [them]'.[2] Despite this, many Australians are unaware of the Earl Grey Scheme, and the obstacles that the Irish orphan girls who participated in it faced upon their arrival in the unfamiliar Australian colonies.

Origins of the Earl Grey Scheme

The Great Irish Famine was the most devastating famine in Ireland's history. It ravaged Ireland for five years, from 1845 to 1850, and caused unparalleled social and economic disaster, the effects of which continued to be felt for generations afterwards. It is estimated that, during the Great Famine, approximately one million Irish people died of starvation and other famine-related illnesses, while a further million people escaped the disaster by emigrating elsewhere in the United Kingdom, the United States of America, and the British colonies in Africa, Australia, Canada and New Zealand.[3] Mass emigration was a cause for worry among a number of British politicians, including the Third Earl Grey. They were concerned that Irish emigration to the independent United States of America would cause 'political problems for Britain'.[4] Australia was firmly under British rule, which made it the preferred, if more expensive, option. In one attempt to circumnavigate the issue of expense, and therefore entice poorer Irish emigrants to Australia, the Irish orphan immigration scheme, or Earl Grey Scheme, was created.

The Earl Grey Scheme was an assisted emigration scheme created in the mid 19th century through the combined efforts of the British Colonial Land and Emigration Commission (CLEC), the Irish Boards of Guardians, and the Australian colonies of New South Wales, South Australia and Victoria. It was named for one of the strongest proponents of Irish orphan emigration, Henry George Grey (the Third Earl Grey), who was British Secretary of State for the Colonies from 1846 to 1852. The primary aim of the Earl Grey Scheme was to assist the migration of female orphans from Irish Poor Law workhouses to the participating Australian colonies.[5]

It aimed to simultaneously assist famine-riddled Ireland and the labour-hungry Australian colonies by relieving the burden placed on severely overcrowded famine workhouses, while also answering colonial demands for domestic servants and single female immigrants. The Earl Grey Scheme operated for less than three years. It ceased because of increasingly vocal opposition from Australian colonists and media, who widely objected to the suitability of the Irish orphan girls who were selected to participate in the scheme.

The Earl Grey Scheme in South Australia
The colonial government in South Australia agreed to participate in the Earl Grey Scheme to solve the shortage of domestic servants in the colony. According to Richards and Herraman, the colony's 'preferred type of utility domestic servant was only available in useful numbers in Ireland', because in the eyes of the Labour Office, poorly educated Irish orphans were preferable to 'highly educated poor women unaccustomed to manual labour'.[6] Three ships transported Irish orphan girls to South Australia under the Earl Grey Scheme: the *Roman Emperor* (arrived 23 October 1848), the *Inconstant* (arrived 7 June 1849), and the *Elgin* (arrived 12 September 1849).[7] In 1850, the *Tenth General Report of the CLEC* listed the total number of orphan girls who had arrived on board these ships as 621.[8] Of the colonies participating in the Earl Grey Scheme, South Australia received the smallest number of orphan immigrants, with 17 Earl Grey orphan ships despatched to New South Wales and Victoria during the same period.[9] Robins argues that the reason this colony received a comparatively small number of orphan immigrants was because 'there were influential circles in England which were anxious to protect the new settlement at Adelaide from pauper and convict immigration and to set it aside for a socially superior type of colonist'.[10] The idea of South Australia's 'social superiority' would affect the way the colony perceived the Irish orphan girls, even before the first ship arrived in Port Adelaide. Despite accepting the smallest number of orphan immigrants under the scheme, settlers in Adelaide reacted with similar levels of trepidation and dissatisfaction as those colonies that received a far greater number of orphan immigrants.

The experiences of the Irish orphan girls in South Australia differed from their counterparts in New South Wales and Victoria, and Trevor

McClaughlin believes that 'least of all is known about the female orphans who came to South Australia'.[11] Kay Caball, who studied some of the girls who arrived on the *Elgin*, believes that 'very little care [was] taken of any of the Irish orphan girls who arrived in Adelaide', which caused these girls to have more trouble in gaining and keeping employment, or in behaving in a 'seemly manner', than their counterparts who travelled to New South Wales or Victoria.[12] The circumstances surrounding South Australia's establishment as a purportedly socially superior colony in 1836 produced a distinct set of social conditions and attitudes within its population that influenced the way the Irish orphan girls would be received in the colony more than 20 years later. There have been significant contributions to the study of Irish orphan immigrants in South Australia since McClaughlin made his claim in 1991, most notably Eric Richards and Ann Herraman's *Irish Women in Colonial South Australia* and Staniforth's book chapter 'The *Inconstant* Girls'; however, there remain aspects of the Earl Grey Scheme in South Australia that are yet to be fully examined.

Pre-existing prejudice in South Australia

By 1846, some 22,390 immigrants had made South Australia their home.[13] Despite the colony's growing population, few of these early immigrants, assisted or otherwise, were from Ireland. According to Richards, it was the 'least Irish part of 19th-century Australia', with fewer Irish immigrants arriving in Port Adelaide than in any of the other significant Australian ports, and with Irish colonists consistently making up less than a third of the colony's population.[14] This is supported by information from the St Patrick's Society of South Australia, which declared that the disparity between English and Irish settlers in the colony, which should have been no more than 2-to-1, was 20-to-1 in 1847, with 5033 English immigrants arriving in Adelaide, compared to only 264 from Ireland in that year.[15] Additionally, an article published in the *South Australian Gazette and Mining Journal* in December 1848 detailed the exact number of German immigrants who had arrived in Adelaide, but of their Irish counterparts it only mentioned that, 'until lately there were no Irish in the colony'.[16] This was patently untrue, even if the numbers of Irish in South Australia were comparably small, but it does demonstrate a lack of awareness about, or care for, Irish immigrants in the colonial media during the first half of the 19th century.

There were also suggestions of a bias against Irish emigrants travelling to Australia before they had the chance to leave Britain. In 1849, the St Patrick's Society of South Australia accused English emigration agents of refusing passage to Australia to prospective migrants who were 'qualified in all other respects as candidates, *save for their being Irish*'.[17] A publication from the South Australian Migration Museum states that 'British South Australians were hostile towards Irish immigrants' Catholic heritage, their lack of capital and education, and their limited potential as employees [and] Irish arrivals were more restricted in their opportunities for advancement than immigrants of Protestant English and Scottish backgrounds'.[18] As a result of this deliberate creation of a predominantly English and Protestant colony, Richards has labelled South Australia as 'the most alien quarter of the new continent' for Irish immigrants in the 19th century.[19] Whether it was because of their religion, ethnicity, or some other unspoken reason, it is clear that, even before the Earl Grey Scheme was created, Irish immigrants were not among South Australia's first preference for settlers.

In his chapter on Irish workhouse children in Australia, Joseph Robins reports that, in England, protests had been submitted to the Colonial Office asking that South Australia be exempted from the Earl Grey Scheme.[20] Perhaps these protestors were the same people who had wanted to reserve the colony for a 'socially superior' kind of colonist, as Robins also declares that 'Irish settlers in particular were discouraged [from emigrating to South Australia]' from the colony's inception.[21] However, by 1847 the need for female servants in the colony had become so desperate that the colonists agreed to the immigration of the Irish orphan girls, all of whom came from pauper backgrounds. In October 1848, the *South Australian Gazette and Mining Journal* published an article in firm opposition to the Earl Grey Scheme, stating that 'we object to South Australia being mixed up with any wholesale or pauper schemes of emigration' and that 'the sooner the colonists meet to protest against [Irish orphan immigration] the better'.[22] Robins believes that the reason many South Australians were so opposed to pauper immigration is because they had 'developed an *amour propre* which rejected the idea that their developing state should be built up on the unwanted produce of the workhouses and gaols of Britain and Ireland'.[23] Another article from October 1848 described the assisted immigration of Irish famine orphans as 'a fraud upon the colonists' and as being against the 'social and moral interests of the community'.[24] Both of these articles were published within a week of the *Roman Emperor*'s arrival in Port Adelaide, which suggests that their opinions were not based on the actions of the girls themselves, but on preconceived ideas of single women, Irish people and pauper immigrants that existed in the colony before the Earl Grey Scheme was created.

As a respectable colony, South Australia also considered young, single women travelling alone as being generally unsuitable candidates for immigration. According to McClaughlin, single female immigrants were 'looked down upon' by religious figures and by the upper and middle class in Britain and Australia during the 19th century.[25] The negative reputation of single female immigrants often stemmed from the reports of captains and surgeons aboard emigrant ships rather than from the genuine actions of the women after their arrival in Australia; however, gossip could be just as damaging to a woman's reputation as genuine fact. McClaughlin suggests that, in the 19th century, Australian colonists believed that 'virtuous single women just did not emigrate to such a distant country as Australia' unaccompanied by a family member or guardian.[26] In the eyes of respectable settlers, it stood to reason that single women who did choose to emigrate alone must not have been particularly virtuous. Excluding other forms of prejudice against the orphan girls, McClaughlin believes that '[19th century] attitudes towards females were inimical to any easy acceptance of the orphans'.[27] One article, published before the *Roman Emperor* arrived in Adelaide, feared that the Irish orphan girls would make South Australia a receptacle for 'juvenile bastards, and incipient prostitutes'.[28] This idea that the Irish orphan girls would be easily enticed into prostitution demonstrates the early misgivings about the orphan girls' suitability for employment in the colony.

The prejudice surrounding Irish immigrants, single women and pauper immigrants in South Australia meant that, even before they arrived, some of the settlers had been predisposed to dislike the Irish orphan girls. McClaughlin believes that their arrival was 'a signal for anti-Irish and anti-Roman Catholic elements in the community to give free reign to their prejudice'.[29] Researchers from the South Australian Migration Museum support this belief, suggesting that, although most Irish Catholics who arrived in South Australia in the 19th century would have experienced discrimination as a result of anti-Catholic sentiment in the colony at this time, 'much of this hostility was vented at the young female immigrants [of the Earl Grey Scheme]'.[30] This suggests that these girls were seen as easy targets for prejudice, probably because, without families or the protection of a large Irish community, it would have been difficult for the orphan girls to defend themselves against hostile opinions, especially in the media.

Reception in South Australia

Even among the early protests, the colonial press did express some limited support for Irish orphan immigration. Any public support for the Earl Grey girls stemmed from pity garnered by their orphan status. After the arrival of Irish orphan girls in Adelaide, Sydney, and Port Phillip, one article in the *Goulburn Herald and County of Argyle Advertiser* declared that 'orphans are entitled to our sympathies'.[31] Another article, published in the *South Australian*, declared that, because the Irish girls were only pauperised by the deaths of their parents, they should be considered 'acceptable' immigrants.[32] It is unlikely that the Earl Grey girls would have been more financially secure had their parents been alive; however, these publications demonstrate that there was some sympathy for Irish orphans in the colony. This sympathy becomes somewhat lost in the face of multiple suggestions that the orphan immigration scheme should include an equal number of English and Scottish orphan girls. An article published in the *South Australian Register* wondered why Irish orphans alone were being sent to Australia, and asked if there were 'no orphan children in English workhouses? None in Scotland? None in the Principality of Wales?'[33] In 1849, the *Ninth General Report of the CLEC* included a despatch from Henry Young, the Governor of South Australia, to Earl Grey, which asked for 300 to 400 orphan girls to be despatched to the colony as soon as possible, on the proviso that a 'due proportion' of them were of English and Scottish heritage. Suggestions like this demonstrate the conflict that existed between the colonists' sympathy for orphaned children and their disdain for Irish immigrants.

The eagerness of colonists in Adelaide to distance themselves from the other Australian colonies is highlighted by an article published in the *South Australian Gazette and Mining Journal*, which discussed the idea that, due to strict immigration requirements, the colony 'to this hour had nothing in common' with New South Wales, Van Diemen's Land, Port Philip, and Western Australia, which had 'never shown much squeamishness as to [their labour's] quality'.[34] This article also suggested that the arrival of the first shipload of Irish orphan girls on the *Roman Emperor* would 'serve as an illustration of the mischief which an incautious and indiscriminate emigration would inflict upon [South Australia]', and that it was 'not likely to be productive of anything but injury to the future welfare of the colony'.[35] This negative opinion, expressed only a month after the arrival of the first Irish orphan girls, suggests that there was a faction of the public who were expecting the Earl Grey Scheme to fail and that this expectation was based solely on the orphans' pauper backgrounds. For some, the orphan girls' lower-class status rendered them too similar to convicts to be accepted as settlers in South Australia.

Irish orphans in the media
Media bias played a role in the negativity that surrounded the Irish orphan girls and the supposedly detrimental effect their immigration had on the budding colony. As the average colonist was unlikely to be reading official police reports or statistics from the Children's Apprenticeship Board, they would have relied on newspaper reports to provide them with information on subjects of criminality. The fact that the colonial newspapers often presented exaggerated, and even falsified, information regarding the Earl Grey immigrants would certainly have affected the way the orphan girls were perceived. This is supported by the publication of letters submitted by so-called concerned citizens. One claimed that colonial newspapers 'literally teem[ed]' with reports that the streets of Adelaide, as well as Sydney and Melbourne, were swamped by 'strumpets [prostitutes] who have been brought from the workhouses, under the most heart-winning name of orphans'.[36] Another, published in the *South Australian Register*, blamed a lack of supervision at the Native Location depot where the girls were housed for the fact that the streets of Adelaide were 'swarming with prostitutes'.[37] It is likely that such reports were the only way that many colonists heard about the alleged deeds of the Irish orphan girls, and these negative reports, no matter how loosely they were based in fact, probably affected the way the orphan girls were viewed in South Australia.

In early 1850, the *South Australian Register* published a series of interconnected articles on the lewd behaviour that had been witnessed at the Native Location depot where the unemployed Irish orphan girls were housed. It began in January, when an anonymous letter was submitted by a person using the pseudonym 'Aliquis'. It accused the Native Location depot of being a government-funded brothel, at which '[drunken] orgies' and other 'most disgusting scenes are nightly enacted'.[38] Three days later, a letter from the secretary of the Children's Apprenticeship Board was published, stating that they had conducted a 'careful enquiry' into the allegations made by 'Aliquis' and concluded that the claims were 'unfounded and false'.[39] However, below this letter was a comment from the editor, who called the board's report 'extremely flippant and contradictory', and said that the 'lewd conduct of many of the [Irish orphan girls] is notorious and has never been denied'.[40] This was followed by an article that declared the Native Location depot had never been seriously investigated for suspicions of prostitution because members of the police force had been 'suspected of nocturnal visits' to the girls who lived there, and did not want to see it closed down.[41] A final follow-up article was published in February, confirming that the allegations of 'Aliquis' had been satisfactorily proven to be false.[42] However, this reluctant retraction may have done little to convince readers that the previous accusations had been untrue, given that colonists and editors had previously supported accusations of bad behaviour.

It becomes clear that media reports about the Irish orphan girls were exaggerated when the statistics reported in colonial newspapers are compared with those published in government documents and peer-reviewed secondary sources. By the end of the Earl Grey Scheme, 87 Irish orphan girls could be labelled as having had a detrimental effect on the colony. According to statistics from the Children's Apprenticeship Board referenced by Robins, by November 1850, 32 Irish orphan girls had been prosecuted for various crimes, six had mothered illegitimate children, six were living with partners outside of wedlock, and 43 were known prostitutes.[43] However, even if these 87 girls had earned a poor reputation, that leaves some 513, or 83 per cent, of the 621 Earl Grey girls who travelled to South Australia that did not. Using this evidence, it is clear that the statistics presented in the media were, more often than not, heavily exaggerated. One newspaper article claimed that 'upwards of 150' Irish orphan girls were reported prostitutes in Adelaide in January 1851, which is an inflation of the 43 reported Irish orphan prostitutes suggested by the Children's Apprenticeship Board in the later months of 1850.[44] This example demonstrates that, where the Earl Grey girls were concerned, the colonial media had no issues with fabricating statistics to create a more dramatic story.

By 1850, there were no longer letters from the public suggesting that the Irish orphan girls were entitled to public sympathy. Instead, increasingly vocal protests from colonists were being published in the local press. A letter from the chairman (Jacob Hagen) and the treasurer (Samuel Stocks) of the Labour Office, published in early 1850, claimed that sending a large number of Irish orphan girls to South Australia had been a 'great mistake' that would lead to the 'regret of all right-minded citizens', because the orphan girls had married and subsequently left their employment in large numbers, and would presumably continue to do so.[45] Another letter, published in the *South Australian* in October 1850 from a man named E.L. Grundy, complained that the immigration commissioners were sending Irish orphan girls, 'whom we do not want', rather than 'handy and hardy' rural Irish labourers, whom he considered would be more practical for the growth of a new colony.[46] More than half of the orphan girls had successfully found and kept employment in the colony by this time, suggesting they were not as useless as critics would insinuate. One could be forgiven for thinking that the colonial press only published correspondence that supported their argument that the Earl Grey Scheme was detrimental to the colony. This refusal to examine the positive outcomes of the Earl Grey Scheme demonstrates a clear bias against the immigration of Irish orphan girls to South Australia in the media, probably because bad news has the propensity to sell more newspapers. This is supported by Richards and Herraman, who say that, during the years the scheme operated, it was cases of prostitution and destitution that 'caught the headlines' of colonial newspapers.[47] Although negative reports may have been exaggerated to improve newspaper sales, the opinions expressed in media sources could have influenced colonists' perceptions of the Earl Grey Scheme.

Conclusion

Mounting protests against the scheme came at a time when the need for female domestic servants in South Australia was less desperate than it had been in the late 1840s. It is probable that as the necessity of accepting Irish orphan girls into the colony lessened, the colonists felt more comfortable in expressing their displeasure for the scheme. In October 1849, Immigration Agent Charles Brewer wrote to the *South Australian Register* to say that, although the Irish orphans arriving on the *Elgin* seemed to have been more carefully selected than their predecessors on the *Roman Emperor* and the *Inconstant*, there had been difficulty in finding them employment due to the fact that the colony was 'now much better supplied with a more generally useful class of female servants'.[48] It is not clear who these more 'useful' servants were, but Brewer quoted the Orphan Board, which reported that selecting immigrants in family groups was 'the best and safest method of introducing a moral and industrious community to our shores'.[49] It is possible that, having stymied the shortage of female servants in the colony, South Australian colonists were eager to end their participation in the Earl Grey Scheme and focus their attention on attracting a more socially acceptable kind of immigrant.

Increasing discontent in the colonial media appeared to have a profound effect on the colony's overall willingness to participate in the Earl Grey Scheme. In 1849, the *Ninth General Report of the CLEC* had reported that the Earl Grey Scheme was operating as successfully as had been expected. An excerpt of the report read that, 'although in the first instance a prejudice had been conceived against [the Irish orphan girls], this feeling had given way before the good conduct of those who were first engaged – that all the remainder had immediately been taken off, and that the colony would willingly receive more of the same description'.[50] However, by the time the *Tenth General Report of the CLEC* was recorded, it was clear that the Earl Grey Scheme would not last past its third year. The commissioners reported that the public in South Australia wished for the emigration of female Irish famine orphans to cease immediately, until a relative proportion of English and Scottish orphan women could be despatched to the colony.[51]

Despite multiple accusations surrounding their respectability, and suitability for work, by the time the Earl Grey Scheme ended in 1850, most of the Irish orphan girls had successfully integrated into the colony. According to Richards and Herraman, by March 1850 approximately 430 Irish orphan girls had gained employment as domestic servants in South Australia, and 100 of them had entered reputable marriages.[52] Their lives may not have been particularly notable, with McClaughlin reporting that 'early marriage, large families and years of widowhood was the lot of most of the orphans'.[53] These unremarkable experiences suggest that reports of law breaking and prostitution were probably exaggerated in the media that both pre-empted their arrival and subsequently focused on the negative aspects of orphan immigration, while largely ignoring the positive experiences. While there was a small amount of sympathy expressed for the girls at the beginning of the scheme, instances of support were outnumbered by reports denouncing the scheme and its assisted immigrants. Exaggerated media reports contributed to complaints about Irish orphan immigration becoming louder and more persistent over time, and may have hastened the conclusion of the Earl Grey Scheme after less than three years in operation.

Irish lawyers and judges in South Australia, 1836-1914

PETER MOORE

The reputation of Irish lawyers in colonial Australia stands high for leadership as judges and politicians.[1] So high that they have been credited with 'undermining British Australia' and 'transforming English law' in Australia and contributing to 'Irish Supremacy' down under.[2] More phlegmatic luminaries like Sir Gerard Brennan described the Irish contribution to Australian law as 'significant yet indefinable' and Professor Alex Castles concluded that it 'cannot really be quantified'.[3] To meet their challenges, and to define and quantify the achievements of Irish lawyers as legal practitioners rather than as judges and legislators, scholars Tony Earls and Diane Campbell have investigated the lives and careers of Irish lawyers in the Australian colonies with the largest Irish populations.[4] This chapter takes that approach in 'the least Irish destination', South Australia.[5] It draws on profiles of all legal practitioners admitted between 1837 and 1914 to identify lawyers who were either Irish by birth or parentage, surveying each group separately in order to understand them as lawyers in Ireland, and to assess the lawyers they became in the colony-state. Considering their professional and other contributions to the colony-state,[6] it shows they were significant participants in the colony-state's legal life and that some proved to be major leaders in wider spheres.[7]

South Australia's Irish legal cohort

Irish legal men in South Australia to 1914 consisted of two out of 16 Supreme Court judges (12.5 per cent), and 60 practitioners out of a total of 591 admissions. Twenty-six were born in Ireland out of 255 born in the

United Kingdom. Eighteen of the Irish-born qualified in Ireland compared with 170 practitioners who first qualified in the United Kingdom. The other eight first qualified elsewhere. Qualifying elsewhere, too, were 34 fellows born outside Ireland to at least one Irish-born parent compared to 336 born outside the United Kingdom. By each measure Irishmen formed barely 10 per cent of the profession. Small numbers and limited proportions left the group well short of the critical mass to act as a potent minority, let alone be seen as a threat.

Numeric invisibility aside,[8] South Australia's legal system was always going to prevent the Irishmen from standing out as *Irish* lawyers. Promoted as a 'British Province', the colony was an exclusively English place of law.[9] No statute for Ireland could operate unless it was invoked by a local statute; the only known attempt failed.[10] Likewise, no Irish judgment would bind the Supreme Court; none is known to have been argued.

Rather than impeding the Irishmen, however, the transition proved relatively easy. Irish lawyers were cultural hybrids. They practised at one remove from Westminster's courts of Common Pleas, King's Bench, Exchequer and Chancery and repeated the performance in the colony. Dublin's Four Courts of the same names emulated Westminster's as did the Supreme Court in Adelaide. Moreover, lawyers in Ireland functioned like English lawyers and would do so again in South Australia. Irish barristers trained at King's Inns[11] as well as one of the Inns of Court in London, on which King's Inns was modelled.[12] Irish solicitors[13] trained under contractual articles of clerkship with an admitted solicitor, just like their English counterparts, and organised in law societies like England's. The intended result was that Irish lawyers worked and thought like English ones. In the colony, practitioners who behaved like Westminster lawyers would do fine. After all, even Englishmen had to adjust to practice in the colony, on the job.

Most importantly, oaths to the Crown and the court, English in content and context, identified lawyers with the admitting jurisdiction.[14] Formation in Ireland made an *Irish* man into an *Irish lawyer* while training in England turned an *Irish* man into an *English lawyer*. Admitted in Adelaide, however, Irish and English alike became South Australian *lawyers*. Irish-qualified men abandoned not their *national*, but their *professional* ethnicity.[15] Colonial trainees, of course, gave up nothing, being only ever colonial lawyers.

The judges

Two Irish judges, in no position to change the situation, did everything to reinforce it. Playing no part in constructing the court, and bringing dissimilar experiences of bar and bench, they presided only briefly, a dozen years apart.[16] The first, John Jeffcott (Figure 1) from Kerry, qualified for the English rather than the Irish bar, practised scarcely at all, and brought a few years' experience as a judge in Africa. His knighthood contrasted starkly with reputations as a duellist and a debtor. Jeffcott sat for just six days during 1837, died in December, and has no monument. George Crawford (Figure 2) from Longford, who sat from 1850 to 1852, brought nine years' practice and a solid reputation for complex equity work, although none as a judge. He lasted two years and enjoyed a state funeral. Both men came from a long line of imperial judges appointed from the Irish bar. They were also alike as products of the Protestant Ascendancy. Jeffcott's father was a Tralee merchant, Crawford's a pluralist parson.[17] Both graduated from Trinity College Dublin, although only Crawford trained at King's Inns. Their contributions in the colony were essentially English in legal character. Jeffcott made rudimentary rules that invoked all of Westminster's and instituted the English offices of barrister and solicitor. Crawford drove

Figure 1. Sir John William Jeffcott Kt, portrait in profile, possibly done in Van Diemen's Land on one of the judge's visits during 1837. (Private collection; artist unknown)

Figure 2. George John Crawford, 'strikingly handsome' with 'personality and charm' to match, according to Ralph Hague, Vol 2 pp. 179–80 (see note 10). (Private collection; artist unknown)

the abolition of the antiquated grand jury and revised the court's equity procedures. All survive in spirit and in terms to the present day.

The Irish-born practitioners
The 18 Irish-born practitioners who qualified in Ireland and were admitted in Adelaide were as constrained as the judges. Seven were King's Inn barristers, and 11 signed the solicitor's roll at the Four Courts. They ranged socially from the lower nobility to the upper trades. Barristers exhibited higher social caste, their fathers more noble or landed than professional or commercial. The highest ranking sat in both camps. Robert Molesworth, distantly descended from several peers, was the son of a Dublin solicitor.[18] John Bagot and Matthew Martyn were younger sons of landed squires in Laois and Galway respectively. Robert Bernard's father was a Dublin solicitor; William Barlow's and Frederick Pennefather's were both senior barristers. By contrast, Patrick Glynn's pater was a hardware merchant.[19] Solicitors hailed from a narrower social range. Landholding contributed only Thomas Lucas of Poyntzpass and James FitzGerald from Youghal. More fathers had professions: a vicar (Charles Johnston), doctors (Sidney Bernard,[20] James Kennedy and George Labatt), solicitors (William Bernard and Luke Cullen) and a tax collector (William Ma'guire). Two came from commerce: Edward Fitzgerald was a Galway brewer's son and Daniel O'Brien's a Clonmel shopkeeper. Next to nothing is known about the last to arrive, Charles O'Brien, admitted in Dublin in 1900 and Adelaide in 1913. Their family resources could sustain long years of formation, the bar being more expensive than solicitor training.

Dublin featured heavily in the emigrant lawyers' lives. Half were born and more were educated in its environs and almost all qualified there. Most bar students attended Trinity College, not to study law,[21] but because taking an arts degree reduced their pupillage from five to three years. Better educated than their English counterparts, solicitors Bernard, Kennedy and Labatt graduated and Johnston and Lucas enrolled for a year or two. Professional lives were Dublin-centred, too. All emigrant barristers and most solicitors gained their practical experience there. Two thirds had 10 or more years' standing, indicating that their emigrations were not about failing to make a start or sustaining a practice. Only two, Luke Cullen and Glynn, left within four years of admission.

Legal practitioners showed some mobility before 'taking the emigration'. Barristers had studied in London and most went the circuits at home. Some solicitors maintained professional contacts with their provincial roots as well as keeping a Dublin office. All but Molesworth, who was 47, left before they turned 40, giving themselves time to build careers abroad. They took the drastic step steadily rather than responding to national crisis.

Reasons to leave remain elusive. Molesworth, Protestant, better-connected and with twice the experience, emigrated six months ahead of Martyn, confessing himself as keen on pastoralism as practice.[22] All expected to improve their prospects or their health, and to avoid the effects of professional overcrowding, scant patronage, and commonplace sectarianism. Catholic Martyn's testimonials show all three, his success 'certain' yet so 'distant' in the 'crowded state of our Bar' that 'advancement' could occur only in a 'distant land'. Catholic and Protestant supporters alike used similar terms to explain why 'few opportunities' opened for young men 'unaided by strong connection', hinting that a Catholic from Connaught's small gentry passed little muster across the way at the Four Courts.[23] Thirty years later, fellow Catholic Glynn left in response to similar problems.[24] Overcrowding applied to solicitors too. Admissions surged between 1838 and 1850, as two thirds of the emigrant cohort entered the profession at home, set sail, or both. Cullen trained with his father's firm, yet inexplicably departed within a year of admission. Irish prospects, of course, related not only to legal practice. Barrister Bagot, a second son, looked unlikely to inherit his father's Kilcoursey estate and emigrated in 1850 to 'try his fortune' (his own words[25]). When he inherited unexpectedly, he went 'home' to take possession but returned to busy careers in both law and politics. Famine tumults upset Daniel O'Brien's arrangement to conduct the legal business for Clonmel's town council.

Leaving Ireland was one thing, choosing South Australia another. Some responded to the colony's promotion by Dr John Bernard, Sidney's father and Robert's and William's cousin. Its provincial character, free market and assured labour force fed middle-class aspiration while their subtext, land speculation, attracted eager investors – and conveyancers. Others joined relatives and friends already in the colony. In a chain of migration, Robert Bernard, expecting to practise under cousin John Jeffcott, set sail before hearing he was dead; William expected Robert to greet him but he too had died; and Sidney expected to join them both, found only William, and saw him into his grave before heading home himself. Bagot followed a cousin, Charles Harvey Bagot, a wealthy legislative councillor,[26] and his brother-in-law George Labatt joined him five years later. O'Brien caught up with his brother, Fr Michael O'Brien, Mount Barker's parish priest. John Brady joined his enterprising uncle Daniel, and Richard Cullen came to train with his brother Luke. A few were not jurisdiction-hopping for professional gain, but climate-changing for their health. Most won at least a few years' respite.[27] The three Bernards were all consumptive. Robert and William arrived at 29 and were dead at 32. Sidney, admitted at 21, left the colony soon afterwards, and died in Dublin, aged 28. Ponsonby Moore, barely 31, did not live to see his admission day. Martyn, too, had been ill prior to leaving home.

Missing motives may be deduced from prompt admission, office holding and practice duration. Most applied for admission soon after arriving, indicating that they expected to practise law. William Barlow, called in Dublin in 1858 and admitted in Adelaide in 1870, was so keen to practise he wrote ahead to Luke Cullen to give the court notice even before he arrived. Thomas Lucas, nearly 40 in 1838 when he left Armagh without (in his own words) 'any idea of following [his] profession', farmed at Reynella until the colony's economic collapse induced him to return to legal work.[28] A stopgap, apparently, Lucas practised for barely a year, in partnership with fellow Irishman James Kennedy.

A quarter of the Irish-born advanced their careers through legal office-holding. For barristers, the 'rule' that selected judges from the Irish and English bars, turn-about, offered good prospects.[29] Being on the spot for positions to open up worked for some, but proved more a matter of timing than talent. After holding a string of legal offices over two years, Robert Bernard sat as acting judge for three months in 1840, subsequently stepping into the lighter duties of registrar-general, before sinking into his grave in October. Molesworth and Martyn were admitted amid discussion in late 1852 about replacing Justice Crawford from the local profession. Neither succeeded. With 24 years' practice at the Irish bar under his wig, Molesworth did not seek the vacant seat but set up in practice until, a year later, he launched a distinguished Victorian career starting at the top with a stint as acting chief justice.[30] By contrast, Martyn applied on the strength of seven years' experience and a sheaf of high-powered testimonials solicited from senior Irish barristers and Catholic bishops. Admitted in June 1853, months after he knew he would not fill the vacancy, even temporarily, he took the next ship home.[31] Bagot and Glynn became attorneys-general. Pennefather, admitted when he was appointed Adelaide University's first professor of law without intending to practise, became a judge in New Zealand. Solicitors had fewer opportunities for public appointments although three held lower offices early, indicating their value as launching pads rather than career paths. Johnston was clerk to the magistrates from 1837 to 1838. William Bernard served as assistant crown solicitor from 1842 to 1843, and cousin Sidney assisted him for a time.

Only five of the 18 Irish-born-and-qualified stayed to practise. Thirteen, through short lives, low profiles and short stays contributed little to the development of South Australia's legal profession or its wider community. The Bernards died young. James Fitzgerald applied a decade's Dublin experience to 30 years as a humble clerk at the Registry of Deeds. Half of the cohort moved on. Edward Fitzgerald, who arrived in Adelaide in 1850 eight years after his Dublin admission, stayed only 18 months before joining the rush to the Victorian goldfields. He then practised in Castlemaine where, following his father's line, he started the famous brewery with his younger brother Nicholas, a Dublin barrister.[32] Molesworth shifted to Melbourne and Johnston (and Lucas possibly) to Hobart, while Ma'guire chose Sydney and Kennedy tried Auckland and then Dunedin. Remarkably, three lived the emigrant's dream of returning home. Martyn, without practising, and O'Brien after 20 years, returned to practise in Dublin, and Pennefather retired to the County Wicklow estate he inherited in 1904.[33]

Luke Cullen, John Bagot, George Labatt, William Barlow and Patrick Glynn, spared to lead long lives, committed themselves to the colony-state. All prospered. Brothers-in-law Bagot and Labatt developed a major practice. Cullen's firm, Belt, Cullen & Wigley, was among the strongest and most lucrative in the colony for decades. If an ethno-religious division loomed, Catholic Cullen bridged it, his partners both English, both Anglicans.

The majority took up the kind of legal work they had done at home, especially lucrative conveyancing. Johnston plunged in conspicuously during the spree from 1837 to 1840 and the rest followed. Few solicitors crossed over to barrister's work as they might in the blended colonial profession, although barristers did not deny themselves a slice of the conveyancing pie.

The Irish proved as Adelaide-centred as they had been Dublin-centred, with two exceptions. Daniel O'Brien, formerly decentralised at Clonmel, decentralised to Mount Barker once a local court opened there in mid 1850.[34] Patrick Glynn found getting legal work in Melbourne as difficult as 'attacking the devil with an icicle' and opened a Kapunda office for an Adelaide law firm in 1882. He bought the practice in 1883 and conducted it for five years before opening an Adelaide office.[35]

The Irish by parentage

Compared to 18 Irish-born-and-qualified, 42 fellows of Irish heritage made greater impacts as lawyers and as South Australians. Eight were born in Ireland but first qualified elsewhere: one each in England and Victoria, six in South Australia. Thirty-four with at least one Irish-born parent were both born and first qualified outside Ireland: 31 in South Australia, one in Montreal and two in England.

Most of this cadre sprang from the same middle-class spectrum as the Irish-qualified, although, as the century turned, the social and vocational range widened and Catholic numbers increased. From the Irish and English gentry came William Leader, with considerable estates in both Kerry and Cheshire, and the father of Gordon Cavenagh (later Cavenagh-Mainwaring) from Wexford. Three fathers had been minor Irish land-holders (James Casey, Nathaniel Knox, John Brady). Nearly half were sons of Irish professional men, with more engineers, military officers and civil servants than the Irish-born lawyers: clergy (d'Arenberg), retired military officers (Edward O'Halloran and Frederick and Spencer Rowley), doctors (Sidney Bernard, Henry Ayliffe, William and Frederick Lewis, and William and George Gunson), engineers (Charles and Strickland Kingston and Charles Hargrave), surveyor (George Hardy), and lawyers (Richard Cullen, Percy Whitby and Francis Villeneuve Smith). A few fathers came to take up public offices: as governor (John Daly) and as civil servants (Richard Beresford and James Hackett). Others took on public service as a magistrate (the Muirheads) and North Adelaide's stationmaster (Florence O'Sullivan). A quarter were sons of assisted immigrants who became shopkeepers

(Robert Bertram and Richard Hourigan), publicans (John Fox, Richard Dempsey, Charles Supple, William Denny and James Regan) and small farmers (Francis Kelly and Albert Hannan).

The three who qualified outside both Ireland and South Australia made little impact. Corkman Leader qualified in England and gave South Australia barely two years.[36] Clare-born Casey stayed two weeks. Admitted to the Melbourne bar in 1865, he was Victoria's minister for justice when he made a political visit in 1876 and was admitted in a show of intercolonial reciprocity.[37] Canadian-born Daly, his parents Irish-born, qualified as a French-style advocate in Montreal. He came to Adelaide in 1862 as private secretary to his father, Governor Sir Dominick Daly, and practised for eight years (as well as producing the colony's first lawbook) before undertaking legal offices in Mauritius and Africa.[38]

Their identity and impact

This group's Irish identity was affected by their parental ethnicity and South Australia's 'professional ethnicity'. Half had two Irish parents, nine an Irish father, eight an Irish mother. Fellows who first qualified in South Australia and with two Irish-born parents strongly identified culturally as Irish-South Australian. Lawyers with one Irish parent were more open to elect an identity. Irish fathers usually led to stronger Irish identity, while Irish mothers manifested weaker Irish identity. Most of the non-Irish parents were English or Scottish, within the bounds of 'British', and included the Kingstons' exotic Scottish-Portuguese mother. Regan's German mother complicated things during World War I, stereotyping him as both 'disloyal' and 'alien'.

Parental Irishness displayed different senses of 'home' while deferring to South Australia's English-style profession. When Dublin jeweller-magistrate Henry Muirhead and his Irish wife sent their Glenelg-born sons Charles and John 'home', it was to Dublin for secondary schooling, but not to qualify as lawyers. They returned to 'finish' at St Peter's College before Charles entered articles on his 16th birthday, the earliest possible date, while John waited until he was 20 to sign his indenture with his newly admitted brother. By contrast, 'home' meant England for three colonial-born lads with Irish mothers, Edward Hawker, George Hardy and Thomas O'Halloran Giles, and their goal was to qualify as English barristers.

South Australian qualification did not make for a cultural clash for the Irish by birth or by parentage. Sidney Bernard started his articles in Dublin and completed them in the colony in 1841 or 1842. He might be thought professionally bi-cultural yet admission to the English-style colonial court and early departure gave him little chance to show it. If Frederick d'Arenberg showed any bi-culturalism it was *English*-Australian. Dublin-born to an Irish mother and German father (professor of modern languages at Trinity College and beneficed Wicklow clergyman), Frederick studied for the English bar in London but emigrated without being admitted and had to train all over again to qualify in the colony.

Different backgrounds bred a variety of political hues. Frederick and Spencer Rowley were sons of a retired Indian Army captain who, as a proud scion of the Meath and Tipperary gentry, revived by royal licence the additional surname of Toler due to his descent from the father of John Toler, Lord Norbury, Ireland's 'Hanging Judge'.[39] Florence O'Sullivan's father from Kenmare was of another stamp. He wrote trenchant letters to the newspapers in support of Home Rule under the evocative pen-name 'Robert Emmett Fitzgerald'.[40]

If *being* Irish could be political, politics as such did not attract lawyers with Irish heritage. Three Irish-born and three colonial-born practitioners sat in the legislatures. Bernard sat ex officio from 1838 to 1840 in the Council of Government, but only two other Irish-born practitioners undertook political careers, both leading to legal and other ministries. Elected to the old council in 1853 and the new assembly in 1857, John Bagot was solicitor-general for 11 days in 1857 and attorney-general for 19 days in 1868 amid a stormy political career that included terms as Crown lands commissioner and chief secretary.[41] Patrick Glynn branched out of law into journalism as editor of the *Kapunda Herald* and then into colonial and federal politics. He was both attorney-general in the colony (briefly, in 1899) and federally (1910 to 1911) before longer ministries in external (1913 to 1914) and home affairs (1917 to 1919).

Of the colonial-born who sat in parliament, Edward Hawker represented Stanley, which included his family's Bungaree station, but showed little ambition and less Irishness. By contrast, the other two held political sway for decades with strong but different senses of being Irish. Charles Kingston (Figure 3) and William Denny (Figure 4) hailed from the social extremes and Denny contested Kingston's city seat in 1899, taking it when Kingston left it for the new federal parliament. Kingston's liberalism presaged the policies of the nascent Australian Labor Party, which he never joined, while Denny became the state's first Labor lawyer. Kingston, attorney-general in four ministries from 1884 to 1899, was also premier from 1893 to 1899. A dominating federationist, he saw the Constitution Act through the Westminster parliament in 1900 and held the first federal trade and customs ministry. Denny was attorney-general both before and after the Great War (in which he served) and spearheaded numerous social and legal reforms. Kingston, patrician and Protestant, made much of being Irish, or half Irish – 'the better half', he quipped.[42] He deployed this Hibernian rhetoric

Figure 3. 'The Right Honourable Charles Cameron Kingston, Patriot and Statesman' by English sculptor Alfred Drury RA. Adelaide's only statue to a self-identifying Irishman was erected in Victoria Square in 1916, eight years after his death, and unveiled by the governor-general. Kingston wears the dress uniform of a privy councillor, an office to which he was appointed in 1897 for his advocacy of Federation. According to 'An Old Friend', the statue was sculpted from a photograph which Kingston regretted he had ever permitted to be taken. *Register* 11 July 1916, p. 7. (Photo courtesy Peter Moore)

to largely Irish audiences for political effect, complete with contradictions and ambiguities that only a full biography will unravel.⁴³ Denny, workingman's son and Catholic, wore his Irishness without trying, as a Christian Brothers' graduate, editor of the Catholic newspaper *Southern Cross*, St Patrick's Literary Society pundit, and working-class politician.⁴⁴

Figure 4. William Joseph Denny MP, Attorney General in the State's first Labor Government under John Verran, 1910–1912.
(SLSA B6233; photographer not known)

The political arena witnessed a clash of cadres when colonial-born 'Charlie' Kingston and Irish-born 'Paddy' Glynn (Figure 5) locked horns in the assembly in both 1895 and 1898 over the very character of the legal profession. Kingston held the five-subject Final Certificate in Law rather than the 13-subject Bachelor of Laws degree. He completed his training on the job as a five-year articled clerk while degree-holders served only three. Kingston wanted to open the profession up to a broader spectrum of candidates by enabling practical over academic education and dropping Latin altogether. His most eloquent opponent, Glynn, a Trinity honourman, recommended the degree and insisted on Latin. Kingston's opposition succeeded and the profession changed hardly at all. Partly a clash about intellectual culture between an older man and a younger, it was also a clash between conservative and radical, Old World with New World. Neither gave any sign of Protestant-Catholic tension, however, let alone Irish nationalism in conflict with Australian democracy.[45]

Figure 5. Patrick McMahon Glynn. (SLSA B3683; photographer not known)

The colony-state might not support Irishmen as a distinctive professional group, yet at least one instance occurred of them associating in an Irish manner. All had trained under King's Inns[46] and almost a third attended Trinity College, helping to objectify and unify social and professional relationships at home in ways that survived individual emigrations. Outside Trinity College and King's Inn, solicitors associated in the Law Club since the 1790s and the Law Society since the 1830s. When an English-style Law Society failed in Adelaide in 1850 to 1851, an Irish-style Law Club replaced it. The club owed its origins to Justice Crawford's urgings to lawyers to form a law society. Dubliner William Ma'guire, the club's sole Irish member, became its honorary secretary. Their Irish experience probably contributed to its name and its program of dining together on the Thursday before term.[47] The Law Club lost its best patron with Crawford's decline during 1852 and any chance of reviving when Ma'guire left the colony the following year. Indeed, the Irish showed little clannishness within the profession. Barely a dozen Irishmen trained with other Irishmen; almost half of them with their brothers.

Lawyers showed other marks of Irish origins. 'Clanfergeal' was home to two O'Halloran lawyers, the Kingstons spent time at Marino (possibly named after an Irish seaside mansion), and George Cowan grew up at Erindale. The Gunsons were born at Hibernian 'Erina House' (formerly 'Emerald Cottage') and moved to 'The Acacias', a more Antipodean choice. Conversely, William Lewis passed his boyhood at Indigenous 'Yenda' and Irish 'Lisnamona', both at Gawler. John Daly's 'Benmore' at Hackney recalled his father's childhood home in Connemara. Hawker's maternal grandparents held 'Killanoola' near Naracoorte. Daniel O'Brien's seal for legal papers bore the three lions of the *clann* coat of arms.

Nicknames, too, pointed up Irish heritage, not always positively. Glynn's 'Paddy' was predictable, but son Charles was ambivalent about it.[48] The elder, shorter of two brothers, Charles copped 'Little Pat' and the younger, taller Strickland wore 'Big Pat', forms that parodied the Irish convention by reversing it.[49] Moreover, in one of Irish South Australia's enduring mysteries, Charles chaired the meeting that welcomed the Irish Redmond brothers in 1883, declaring his pride in being Irish so energetically that when the Irish National League formed a week later under John Redmond, Charles was offered its presidency – yet declined, for a 'reason best known to himself', stunning the Irish community as much as outsiders.[50] Frank Villeneuve Smith played down his maternal Irish heredity, played along with putative descent from the French admiral of Trafalgar fame, and played down his *mulaitresse* grandmother. Educated at Christian Brothers' College, he was a stalwart of Hibernian societies, an associate of Supple and Denny, and his first wife an English Catholic, yet Frank named his house and his children after British law lords.[51]

Like the Irish-qualified, most of the locally qualified stuck to the City of Adelaide, with three Irish-born fellows making the exceptions. William Lewis gave Gumeracha a go before returning to Gawler where he had grown up. John Brady hung his shingle at Kapunda but, in financial crisis before long, disappeared from record. Richard Cullen set up in Penola for the barely two years left to him.

Measures of success varied. Charles Kingston and Villeneuve Smith were appointed Queen's Counsel, yet no Irish lawyer after the 1840s held significant legal offices until Glynn and Kingston became attorneys-general in the 1890s. Irishmen avoided other offices, too, with the exception of

William Barlow's three decades as university registrar and vice-chancellor. Similarly, lawyers' fortunes came from investments rather than fees; few left more than their primary residence. Frank Villeneuve Smith's success as an investor was launched by the 1910 bequest of £2500 from his namesake uncle, a retired chief justice of Tasmania. Frederick Pennefather's estate of £41,000 by 1921 was due to inheritance rather than salaries as an Adelaide law professor and New Zealand judge. Glynn's £30,000 in 1932 consisted largely of luck with mining shares. On the other hand, Leader's Victorian estate of £760 in 1907 is misleading, as his executors were not required to declare real property in Australia, England or Ireland.

Despite acting as English-style lawyers, the professional capacity of the Irishmen could be cast in blatantly 'national' terms. Robert Bernard discharged the duties of advocate general amid criticism that mounted over 18 months, some of it sheeted home to being Irish. When all 35 accused were acquitted at the March sessions in 1839, the blame was laid at Bernard's failure to study 'criminal jurisprudence' in Dublin. That report was flawed in numerous ways: there was demonstrably more to it than Bernard's Irish legal skills, and the paper knew it. The session's cause-list was three times longer than any preceding gaol delivery sitting. A previous advocate general, an English solicitor, had been expressly engaged to assist and fared no better. Witnesses did not answer their subpoenas, stranding the prosecutors without essential evidence. Bernard very properly moved to estreat every recognisance.[52] What is more, he did very well at the next sessions in some tricky trials. Nevertheless, when he retired, the governor's praise of his 'honour, integrity and judgement' as a legislative councillor omitted to mention his professional abilities. His posterity was to be headlined as a 'Crown Solicitor in a Hole', recalling his fall into a crater left from an uprooted gum tree on a dark night en route to Government House for dinner.[53] Even an Englishman acting as advocate general, being legalistically convoluted, was chided for speaking 'clear and classic Milesian'.[54] Decades later, the Dublin barrister called on to defend Justice Boothby, though completely unknown in South Australia, was decried as 'briefless', his opinion derided as mere 'sintiments'.[55] The ethnic slur is nothing if not a cheap shot.

Conclusion

Whether qualified in Ireland, in South Australia, or elsewhere, Irish lawyers in South Australia contributed to the law's administration rather than its making. Local trainees rather than the Irish-born helped assure the perpetuation of the profession and its development as a distinctly 'South Australian' cadre. They offered Irish-South Australians an Irish alternative for legal services, although it is next to impossible to measure its scale. Anecdotally, O'Brien at Mount Barker and Glynn at Kapunda acted for their local Irish communities, as did the Muirheads on Adelaide's west side in the later 19th century and, in the early 20th, Supple and Denny throughout the inner western suburbs.[56] None, however, made their livings from Irish clients alone, just as many Irish clients consulted non-Irish lawyers.

The South Australian cohort was fairly representative of United Kingdom lawyers in Australian colonies, although how representative they were of 19th-century Irish lawyers is less clear. All were next to invisible as *Irish lawyers* because of the English character of the legal system, and as South Australian lawyers because two thirds practised briefly or not at all, dying young or leaving the colony-state for fresh pastures. Those who practised extensively proved to be more alike than different from their English and even their Scottish counterparts.[57] The Irish, along with the Scots, provided a point of comparison with English lawyers but not an 'other' to contradict them. Rather, lawyers of Irish heritage complemented the English within the practice regime. Neither the immigrants nor the locally trained undermined or transformed the law – not as individuals, not as a group, not even for a while. Audible brogues and burrs and demonstrable Milesian manners made these 'learned Patlanders'[58] observable as men, but not as lawyers. The surprise would be if they did.

South Australia's Irish colonial surgeons: The first 30 years, 1836-1866

BRONTE GOULD

This chapter examines four Irish-born doctors in their roles as colonial surgeons or assistant colonial surgeons during the first 30 years of South Australia's British settlement. In 1834, Robert Torrens, chairman of the Colonisation Commission, wrote to Lord Glenelg, secretary of state for the colonies, notifying him of the appointment of officials for the new colony of South Australia.[1] After much competition, Irish-born Thomas Young Cotter was appointed as the first official colonial surgeon in July 1835, 17 months before the proclamation of the new colony in December 1836.[2] Cotter, however, was not the only Irish-born medical practitioner who undertook this role. Robert Waters Moore followed later as a colonial surgeon. And subsequently both George Tallis and John Benson were assistant colonial surgeons. The early years of the fledgling colony were challenging socially and economically, but many settlers were encouraged to emigrate thousands of miles away with the promise of land ownership or employment. It was the colonial surgeon or their assistant to whom settlers turned in times of accident or illness in these early years. Examining these four Irish-born doctors in their roles as colonial surgeon, the chapter goes beyond the medical careers of these Irishmen and explores aspects of their wider contributions to colonial society. It seeks to clarify whether these men made further contributions to the South Australian colony once they completed their terms as colonial surgeon or assistant colonial surgeon. Furthermore, it looks for evidence of their integration within South Australia's Irish community or their confinement to an elite medical circle.

There has been limited research into South Australia's colonial medical history and none about the contribution of Irishmen to that history. The historiography has been limited to the work of medical historians. A.A. Lendon's unpublished research, titled 'Papers of Dr Alfred Austin Lendon 1854–1935', presents a broad and largely biographical history of early South Australian physicians.[3] This includes material relating to Thomas Young Cotter and Robert Waters Moore. Ian Forbes's *From Colonial Surgeon to Health Commission: The government provision of health services in South Australia 1836–1995* utilises more extensive archival sources, and his scrutiny encompasses a broader context of colonial medical history.[4] The study of these four Irishmen will add to an understanding of 19th-century South Australia as well as highlighting aspects of the early colonial medical system.

South Australia's first appointed colonial surgeon

Thomas Young Cotter was born at Bantry, County Cork, in 1805. His father was a purser in the Royal Navy. It is likely that he spent time as a naval cadet in the West Indies with his father. Cotter obtained his medical qualifications after he returned to London.[5] He married Jane Nicholson at Christ Church, Marylebone in Middlesex, on 9 August 1834.[6] South Australian medical registration did not commence until 1844; registration records show Cotter as holding a licentiate of the Company of Apothecaries on 24 January 1833.[7] His medical background was judged sufficient for him to be selected as South Australia's first official colonial surgeon.

The term colonial surgeon suggests that this was an important official position, but this was not necessarily reflected by the salary. As the first official colonial surgeon, Cotter only received £100 per annum for his services in 1835.[8] While this salary matched that of the official storekeeper, it was much less than both the governor at £800 per annum and the £400 paid to the Colonial Secretary.[9] In Western Australia, however, the colonial surgeon was paid just over £68 for the quarter ending 31 December 1834 – a much higher sum than that paid in South Australia.[10] The reason for this intercolonial discrepancy is unclear. Precise requirements of the South Australian colonial surgeon are also unknown because written schedules have not been found. Cotter finally left England in September 1836 aboard the *Coromandel* (as ship's surgeon) and arrived in Adelaide in January 1837 after the colony's proclamation.

The role of the colonial surgeon

Writing on behalf of Governor Hindmarsh on 28 January 1837, Robert Gouger, the Colonial Secretary, instructed Cotter that his primary role was to care for the poor. Brian Dickey suggests the new colony was not expected to have 'social dependents', firstly because the colonists were carefully selected, and secondly because the balance between 'land, labour, and capital' was intended to be closely monitored.[11] However, it is clear from Governor Hindmarsh's communiqué of January 1837 that poverty did exist in the colony. Part of the governor's instructions plainly stated that Cotter should 'consider your attention upon the Officers of the Government and their families as a secondary instead of primary part of your duties'. Cotter was instructed to extend his attention 'particularly to those poor persons whose funds may not enable them to pay for medical advice'.[12] According to Forbes, preparations for the voyage to South Australia included Cotter's examination of 'the officers who were to make the voyage'.[13] He believes this initial focus on officers and their families may have triggered concerns among colonial authorities that Cotter might neglect the poor. This communiqué signalled the beginning of tensions between Cotter and early government officials which culminated in later press allegations that he had neglected his duties toward the poor.

Suggestions that Cotter was neglecting the poor should have been allayed by a letter he penned to the working classes of South Australia in May 1838 through the *Southern Australian* newspaper. In this, Cotter encouraged members of the working class to form an Independent Medical Club to relieve their financial stress in times of illness, injury or destitution.[14] This followed the example set by the Poor Law Amendments of 1836 in Britain which had proposed the establishment of an Independent Medical Club. The subscriptions were to act as a form of medical insurance to alleviate parish expense of treating the poor.[15] However, the Independent Medical Club in South Australia did not eventuate, possibly because the general consensus was that such a club was not needed. It was not until 1840 that Adelaide's first friendly society was formed, but this was administered by Manchester Unity, not the British government.[16] This aside, the proposed Independent Medical Club demonstrates Cotter's foresight about the poor and working classes' need for some form of insurance in times of illness or injury. Conditions at the infirmary also worried Cotter.

The infirmary: Allegations of neglect and suspension

Built sometime in 1837 west of the present-day railway station, the infirmary was of a poor standard.[17] Cotter described it as 'ill constructed and badly ventilated, and in every respect totally unfit for the reception of sick persons'.[18] Writing to the press in August 1838, Cotter drew further attention to its poor conditions. He included copies of letters he had sent to authorities in the hope that the incoming governor, George Gawler, would address the situation, preferably by allocating more money for improvements. Cotter referred to a lack of fuel, light, soap, and vegetables; and the need for the laundering of blankets and shirts. He reported patients had even pooled their money to buy one candle.[19] Furthermore, he added the bedding 'consists of a few dirty blankets, great coats, and sacks sewn together and filled with shavings'.[20] Three iron double bedsteads had been borrowed from an unknown source. While the government was prepared to pay for a colonial surgeon, funding for the establishment and administration of an infirmary or hospital was clearly inadequate. However, while the *South Australian Gazette and Colonial Register* (hereafter the *Gazette and Register*) agreed that the infirmary was in poor condition, the newspaper also accused Cotter of neglecting his patients.

The *Gazette and Register*, referring to the infirmary, stated 'A man of common feeling would be ashamed to see his dog-kennel in the filth in which human beings, some of them in the last stage of disease, are allowed to remain'.[21] Accusations of neglect by the colonial surgeon included several patients he had treated but been unable to follow-up for some days. Authorities were called upon to 'punish' the colonial surgeon whose conduct was deemed 'unjustifiable'.[22] Rather than receiving support from the colony's earliest newspaper, Cotter was condemned for his perceived neglect, as well as the poor condition of the infirmary.

Cotter responded in the rival newspaper, the *Southern Australian*, in a letter to the 'Editor of the South Australian Gazette and Colonial Register' in which he stated his case. He believed the complaint was a 'fabrication' by George Stevenson (the *Gazette and Register*'s editor), who was friendly with members of the board of enquiry formed to investigate both conditions at the infirmary and Cotter's alleged neglect.[23] The colonial surgeon accused Stevenson of possessing an 'overacted cunningness which characterised [his] demeanour'.[24] The pressures facing Cotter are revealed in his statement about the expectations of his role as colonial surgeon. His duties required him:

> to attend in every case in which a medical practitioner is required, *midwifery included*, all persons connected with the public service and their families, as well as emigrants for three months after their arrival in the colony, together with the jail, infirmary, and every case of destitution, making upwards of 1400 persons entitled to gratuitous medical attendance, many of them scattered over the country for a distance of several miles, and in addition until very recently, to dispense the medicines and visit the shipping – all for the salary lately increased to £200 per annum, with an allowance of three shillings per day for a horse.[25]

Defending the charge of patient neglect, Cotter argued he had arranged for other medical practitioners to care for these individuals in the short term. He added that in one case the patient was dying with little more that could be done for him.[26]

Support for Cotter came from Charles Mann, the editor of the *Southern Australian*. He commented on his situation in January 1839 stating:

> We understand that this officer, one of the remnant of the Commissioners appointments, has been subjected for some time to a series of annoyances from the government officials of a most unfair and insulting nature.[27]

Attention was also drawn to Cotter's poor pay and the fact that he was 'insulted like an apprentice'.[28] Not surprisingly, the *Gazette and Register* published a letter from someone calling himself 'Detector' who refuted these claims and placed the blame solely on Cotter. The editor added that 'the charges made by Mr Cotter are so absurd as to carry exaggeration on the face of them'.[29] In July 1839, the Colonial Secretary, Robert Gouger, announced Cotter had been suspended and replaced by James Nash.[30]

Cotter responded that he had 'long felt a conviction it was his Excellency's determination to remove [him] from office'.[31] Unsurprisingly, Stevenson supported Cotter's removal. Although the *Southern Australian* remained loyal to Cotter, this was to no avail.[32]

The press

The editor and part-owner of the *Gazette and Register*, George Stevenson, a journalist, was also secretary to Governor Hindmarsh.[33] Archivist, librarian and historian George Pitt describes Stevenson as 'possessing an unusual literary style' and his newspaper as having unique qualities. Pitt also refers to Stevenson as an 'unofficial governor'.[34] The *Gazette* section of his newspaper published the governor's 'official acts and orders of the Colonial Government', while the *Register* portion printed any non-official item, such as general news either within the colony, in the other Australian colonies or from overseas.[35] At the time, he was 'probably the cleverest man in South Australia,' writing 'devastating invective' against the governor's opponents which included the resident commissioner, James Hurtle Fisher.[36] The *Gazette and Register* was a conduit through which Stevenson was able to wield power as someone closely associated with the governor. Stevenson was therefore highly influential during Hindmarsh's term as governor from 1836 to 1838.

The *Southern Australian* was founded by opponents of Governor Hindmarsh, including Resident Commissioner Fisher.[37] Pitt notes that the roles of governor and resident commissioner clashed due to overlapping duties.[38] Editor Charles Mann and Stevenson often exchanged literary blows. During 1837 and 1838 these two newspapers became 'deeply involved' in all disputes which proved problematic in such a small, young colony.[39] Within this toxic environment, the colonial surgeon dispute emerges as an example of that destructive press engagement which was so detrimental to Cotter and his reputation.

In July 1838 Governor Hindmarsh was recalled to Britain. His replacement, George Gawler, did not take up his position until October of that year. The new governor ensured the *Gazette and Register* became separate entities – the *South Australian Gazette* (*SAG*) and the *South Australian Register* (*SAR*) – from 20 June 1839. This distanced government issues from other matters. The first edition of the *SAR* indicates that this arrangement was inevitable when it stated:

> It was ... distinctly arranged that whenever the Colonial Government might deem it expedient that the *Gazette* should be published apart from the *Register*, we should be obliged to do so.[40]

While Stevenson lost much of his influence from this point forward, this came too late for Cotter.[41] Despite the public controversy, ex-Colonial

Surgeon Cotter remained in South Australia, working in private as a medical practitioner. He died at Port Augusta in January 1882.[42] In the years before his death, Cotter pursued both medical and wider interests. Significantly, he retained links to Ireland as well as to the small but growing Irish community in South Australia.

Cotter's years post-colonial surgeon

Cotter was secretary of the Mechanics' Institute in South Australia at its inception in June 1838; he edited both the *South Australian Magazine* in 1842 and the *South Australian Almanack*.[43] In 1849 he became secretary of the newly formed St Patrick's Society of South Australia, an early important network of colonial Irishmen (see chapters by O'Reilley and James). This society offered Irish immigrants information about the colony; acted as a contact in the colony; and gave assistance and collegiality as required. As well, the society promised to 'remonstrate with Earl Grey strongly against the injustice to the Irish', that is their non-selection of the Irish as emigrants to the colony.[44] In a memorial sent to Earl Grey, secretary of state for the colonies, the society stated:

> That your Memorialists are prepared to prove that the Irish immigrants of South Australia are as orderly, industrious, and thrifty as their brethren of England and Scotland, and make equally good colonists.[45]

The society made it clear that the Irish were an equally valuable source of emigrants as those from England and Scotland, yet authorities continued to ignore their selection.

In addition to his work for the St Patrick's Society, Cotter's interests in medicine and its advancements continued to be demonstrated. Later in 1849, his letter regarding the use of colchicum to treat cholera was published in various Irish and British newspapers, including Dublin's *Freeman's Journal*.[46] He referred to his experiences visiting Ireland and London, but his failure to provide any dates means the timing of the visits unfortunately remains unknown. In January 1854 Cotter stood successfully for Grey Ward in the Adelaide Council elections.[47] However, he did not remain long in Adelaide, instead moving within the colony, working variously at Mount Barker, Queenstown, Robe and Angaston before being appointed as surgeon to the Great Northern Mining Company at Nuccaleena near Blinman in South Australia's north, possibly in early 1862.[48] After the mine failed in 1864 he moved briefly to Port Augusta before relocating to Glenelg. In 1870 Cotter finally returned to Port Augusta. He was also noted as 'one of the founders of the Masonic Lodge' in Port Augusta, and 'an honorary life-member of the Oddfellows' Society, and a member of the Foresters' Society'.[49] His other interests included membership of the Port Augusta Literary Society, and president of the local chess club, thus demonstrating his broad interests. At the first annual St Patrick's Society dinner, Cotter admitted 'his tongue was tipped with a bit of the brogue' of the Irish despite the years spent away from his homeland.[50] In his first year in Adelaide he subscribed one pound one shilling toward the building of the Anglican Trinity Church.[51] His obituary records him as a 'kind and considerate benefactor'.[52] These examples suggest Cotter not only worked within his community, but also joined in its local activities. While he retained links to Ireland and the Irish, it appears this did not influence his choice of where to live or work, nor did he seek to confine himself socially within the medical fraternity. Cotter was later followed by another Irishman, Robert Waters Moore, in the colonial surgeon position.

Robert Waters Moore
In the years before the appointment of Irishman Robert Waters Moore as colonial surgeon, there were two English appointees, James George Nash and William Gosse. English-born Nash served in the position until March 1857, a total of just over 17 years. Newfoundland-born Gosse, raised in England and trained in London, followed Nash.[53] He acted briefly as colonial surgeon when Nash returned to England owing to ill-health. Gosse was then appointed colonial surgeon on £400 per annum, plus a forage allowance for his horse. He resigned after 12 months. In March 1858 Robert Waters Moore was appointed as colonial surgeon.[54]

Born in 1819 in Cork, Ireland, Moore trained in 1835 at the Cork South Infirmary, then moved to Charing Cross Hospital in London in 1840. He became a member of the Royal College of Surgeons in August 1842.[55] It was not unusual to have qualifications from outside Ireland. An oversubscription of medical schools in Ireland led to many potential Irish medical students moving to England or Scotland for their training, or after graduating in Ireland looking for work opportunities outside the country.[56]

In 1847 Moore arrived in New South Wales as a ship's surgeon. The reasons for his travel to South Australia are unclear, but he registered with the local medical board there on 13 July 1847.[57] He was soon appointed medical officer at the Burra mine, resigning this position in July 1849.[58] Lendon states he went to the Victorian goldfields for a short period.[59] In December 1851 he married Luduvina Dutton in Adelaide. She was the daughter of William Hampton Dutton, an early landholder, merchant and brother of Francis Stacker Dutton who was later premier of South Australia.[60]

Moore was appointed colonial surgeon on 12 March 1858 on a salary of £700 plus allowances and held this position until his resignation in late December 1869.[61] Like Nash, he was also appointed president of the medical board in 1858.[62] The duties of the colonial surgeon had expanded since Cotter's time. Moore's role was:

> To advise the Government in all matters affecting the public health and the sanitary conditions of the colony; to exercise the entire charge and control over the Public Hospital; to act as Superintendent of the Lunatic Asylum, and Medical Superintendent of the Convict Stockade; to take medical charge of the Gaol; of sick and destitute persons receiving Government aid, within the city boundaries of North and South Adelaide; of the Sappers and Miners, with their wives and families; of the Mounted and Foot Police; to give evidence at the Supreme and Local Courts; and to attend Inquests, whenever called upon by the Coroner; to examine and give certificates to all candidates for admission into the Police Force; also to be President of the Medical Board and Central Vaccine Board, and Member of the Destitute Board.[63]

While the duties of the colonial surgeon were more comprehensively defined, they were no less burdensome. Lendon, however, suggests the list may not be accurate, because for example, the gaol was supervised by the medical officer for the destitute, and the British military no longer had a presence in the colony.[64]

The Adelaide Lunatic Asylum opened in 1852 near the present-day Botanic Gardens.[65] Evelyn Shlomowitz explains that Moore received his mental health training from a 'leading English authority, Dr John Conolly, of the Hanwell Asylum' near London.[66] She states that during his term as superintendent of the asylum, Moore introduced some progressive practices, for example, the abolition of 'mechanical restraints,' and the construction of a padded room. In his role as superintendent of the lunatic asylum, Moore was considered as positive and kindly.[67]

Despite this, Moore was the subject of at least two enquiries. In January 1852 a complaint was lodged with the colonial surgeon, James Nash, regarding a prescription. It was alleged that Moore, then house surgeon at the Adelaide Hospital, had written the prescription incorrectly, but he laid the blame for the error on the dispenser, Henry Briggs. In turn Briggs blamed Moore. Briggs appealed for protection as he believed he was receiving 'ungentlemanly treatment and aspersions' from Moore.[68]

There was a further complaint about Moore's treatment on 26 January 1852, in a letter from a patient Hellen [sic] Haynes. Moore challenged Haynes's letter. He believed the letter was the 'disguised' handwriting of the hospital's clerk Alexander Henry May, adding that the charges were 'concocted'.[69] May later admitted he had written the letter on behalf of the patient.[70] Although the matter was referred to the medical board Lendon suggests it was treated as a 'storm in a tea cup'.[71] Both Briggs and Moore retained their positions at the Adelaide Hospital, with Moore later appointed colonial surgeon. This confirms there were no major ramifications either from this incident or the prescription error.

Despite these accusations, Moore appears to have been kindly in relation to the case of an alleged assault on him. In February 1861 the press reported that Edward Egan, 29 years old, had pleaded guilty to the assault of Moore. Moore asked that the court show mercy to the prisoner, adding: 'When he committed the assault he was under the influence of drink.' The court decided as the prisoner had already spent two months in gaol, was of previous good character and had attracted mercy from Moore, he would only be fined one shilling.[72]

In his role assisting the coroner, Moore was called to testify at many inquests. In one notable case in February 1862, Moore was called upon to examine the body of police Inspector Richard Palmer Pettinger following his shooting at Government House.[73] The scene involved the sale of outgoing Governor Richard MacDonnell's furniture and effects prior to his departure from the colony. Pettinger and George Tallis (assistant colonial surgeon), were both present at the sale. Tallis testified he was going upstairs and heard the gunshot – he found Pettinger 'lying on his face with his hands under his body; he was bleeding profusely from a wound in the side of his head; he was still breathing, but was not conscious'.[74] A disgruntled policeman, dismissed by Pettinger for his 'drunkenness and neglect of duty', was found guilty of the shooting and subsequent murder. Because the weapon was concealed behind the apron the murderer was wearing, this later became known as the 'Black Apron Murder'.[75]

By September 1862, Moore had been appointed a justice of the peace, indicating his integration within Adelaide's community.[76] This allowed him to sit on the bench of Adelaide's Police Court with a presiding magistrate.[77] However, it appears Moore did not remain a justice of the peace for long.

In 1864 Moore was also required to appear as a witness at an enquiry into the management of the Lunatic Asylum and the Adelaide Hospital.[78] He appeared controlled and informative in his answers although Forbes suggests he had been a 'veritable dictator' during his term at the hospital.[79] The enquiry was intended to ascertain the state of the Adelaide Hospital. Recommendations were made to remediate identifiable issues such as those involving nurses and night duty, medication dispensing and the need for an assistant dispenser. However, the treatment of the patients, according to witnesses, 'was both attentive and humane', confirming that the colonial surgeon and house surgeon had performed their duties well.[80] Yet in February 1867, following the publication of the minutes of the select committee that enquired into the Adelaide Hospital management, the press published a letter from John Benson, a former Adelaide Hospital house surgeon, who expressed dissatisfaction with evidence from George Tallis during the enquiry.[81] Benson's letter made it clear Tallis had fallen out with Moore, and that the letter writer supported Moore. Benson's letter caused some angst among the medical fraternity. Letters to the press of varying opinions included those from medical practitioners Lawrence Healey and Frederick Spicer, as well as someone calling themselves 'Vidette'.[82]

In the following month, an M. Thomas (probably Morgan Thomas who obtained his medical qualifications in England and first registered in South Australia in July 1852), chose to reply in the press. He stated first that he did not 'endorse any other man's evidence, and especially any Irishman's – the Irish are too imaginative for me'.[83] Needless to say, he did not support Moore as colonial surgeon, believing Benson's letter read like a 'certificate of character', and that Moore ought to take a copy to Melbourne, in other words leave the colony and move to Victoria. These exchanges between and about other doctors highlight the passions and some of the issues faced by Irish doctors, let alone those in the position of colonial surgeon or assistant colonial surgeon. Tallis and Benson, both of whom served periods as assistant colonial surgeons, were obviously in disagreement. Their shared Irish backgrounds and medical practitioner roles did not prevent such occurrences.

George Tallis

Tallis was born circa 1804 in Ireland. His qualifications included a certificate of the Apothecaries Company of Dublin on 5 July 1839, and sometime later, a licentiate from the Royal College of Surgeons of Ireland (RCSI) dated 30 March 1854. His birthplace is unclear, but the RCSI noted his address as Rossmore, County Kilkenny.[84] In 1846 he was listed as an apothecary at the Sir Patrick Dun Hospital in Dublin.[85] At the parliamentary enquiry into the Adelaide Hospital, Tallis confirmed he had worked there for eight years prior to arriving in the colonies. In both 1854 and 1855 Tallis had sailed to Portland, Victoria, as a ship's surgeon. He eventually settled there for a time as the Portland district coroner. In 1860 he moved to Penola in the South East of South Australia. By December 1860 he was appointed as assistant colonial surgeon and house surgeon to the Adelaide Hospital, and remained in the latter role for slightly less than two years.[86]

Tallis moved a great deal within South Australia as a doctor. In late February 1862, he went to Kapunda where he entered into practice as assistant to Irishman Dr James Alexander Greer Hamilton. In mid August 1865 Tallis was appointed as the resident medical officer at the Adelaide Lunatic Asylum. By October 1866, however, he was practising in Moonta before returning to Kapunda in April 1867. There Tallis chaired a meeting of the Friends of Ireland, organised to assist the widows and children of state prisoners in Ireland. Adding that he was willing to do what he could 'for his country', Tallis explicitly demonstrated his ongoing commitment to and continued ties with Ireland.[87] The state prisoners were Fenians, members of an early, secret organisation, ready to use violence against Britain to attract attention to Ireland's problems. Because the Kapunda meeting coincided with great international and Australian alarm about the Fenian threat,

Tallis's public actions in a relatively small country town were courageous. His role as chairman of that meeting in April 1868 had him placed on an official police 'List of those who are suspected of having Sympathy with the object of Fenianism and are otherwise disloyally disposed'.[88] Yet, in March 1868, following the assassination attempt on the Duke of Edinburgh during his visit to Australia, Tallis was among those at a meeting who attested his loyalty to the Queen. He described the perpetrator, an Irish Catholic, as a 'wretched miscreant'.[89]

Tallis never married. Like Moore, he had also been appointed as a justice of the peace but had taken a more active role in this position in Kapunda's local courts.[90] Just before his death at Kapunda in December 1868, Tallis converted to Catholicism.[91] He is buried at Kapunda, next to the Irish priest who guided his conversion, Father John Smyth. Tallis's successor to the role of assistant colonial surgeon, John Benson, was also Irish but far less about him is known.[92]

John Benson

Benson was born circa 1838 in Ireland, son of John Benson from Castlecomer, County Kilkenny, also a medical practitioner. His brother Charles was a minister of the Church of Ireland and in 1855 opened a school at Rathmines near Dublin. Benson qualified with a licentiate of the RCSI on 1 April 1863. His address then was 24 Rathmines Road, the school's address.[93] He married Charlotte Deborah Fitzgibbon on 2 November 1862 at Bray, Wicklow, Ireland.[94] Benson arrived in Melbourne, Victoria, some time in 1863 and may be the medical practitioner who was listed as of Brunswick near Melbourne.[95] The press noted in November 1864 he had 'recently arrived from Melbourne' to take up his position as assistant colonial surgeon and house surgeon at the Adelaide Hospital.[96] After leaving the hospital, Benson practised at Kensington near Adelaide, and it was noted he showed 'deeds of kindness and charity to the poor'.[97] He died prematurely in 1877, and money was raised by public subscription for both a memorial fountain at Norwood, and his widow who was left with eight children including one that was born after his death. Ten years previously Benson had indicated in a letter to the press that he was proud to be an Irishman, but there is little else known about his connections to Ireland or the wider Irish colonial community.[98]

Conclusion

This chapter has examined four Irish-born doctors in their roles as colonial surgeons or assistant colonial surgeons. The research has revealed that the position of colonial surgeon brought with it potential exposure to tensions between government and hospital authorities as was clear in Cotter's story. His predicament was probably intensified because he was the first colonial surgeon, and neither clear limits for the job nor processes for resolving disputes had been developed. By 1858, when Robert Waters Moore took on the role, both the delineation of the position and the salary showed progress.

The lives of these Irish doctors reveal a developing colonial medical framework, and their local careers demonstrate much mobility, suggesting that moving between city and country medical positions was very common. Their social contribution to the various communities in which they lived points to their interest in becoming integrated rather than remaining aloof. While little is known about Robert Waters Moore in this context, his innovations to the care of the mentally ill patients in the asylum were very beneficial. All four remained in South Australia once they relinquished the role of colonial surgeon or assistant colonial surgeon, and most appeared to have maintained some links with Ireland.

Assessing the extent to which these men attempted to integrate with the Irish community presents a challenge. Cotter's early membership of and role within the St Patrick's Society demonstrates his interest in being part of that Irish network but no evidence of a similar affiliation has been located for the other Irishmen. It is apparent that Moore, Tallis and Benson were known to each other, but this may have been more because of their roles as medical practitioners rather than the importance of them sharing an Irish background and interest in Ireland or Irish affairs in the colony. Further research into their social and professional lives may reveal other reasons for their connections. As shown in other chapters in this volume, it should be noted too that there was little evidence of public Irish activity during the period of study here, a factor affecting opportunities to demonstrate 'Irishness' in the colony.

St Patrick's Day in South Australia, 1836–1945

SIMON O'REILLEY

The Irish, as a founding people in South Australia, formed strong social and community networks, while maintaining bonds of kinship with their homeland. Given this attachment, it is only natural that the feast of St Patrick, Ireland's patron saint, would be commemorated with as much importance in South Australia as in any other place around the world where Irish migrants settled. From the beginning of European settlement, St Patrick's Day in South Australia has been commemorated annually as a rallying call to express Irish identity in a new land. By observing the public expression of St Patrick's Day over time, an insight into Irish aspirations can be examined through succeeding generations in South Australia.

The intention and form of St Patrick's Day has varied over the decades. This chapter seeks to highlight these changes in a chronological overview and analysis, exploring the public expression of St Patrick's Day in two parts. The first section (1836–1917) looks at the growing sense of Irish identity in South Australia, from its infancy in seeking acceptance within the new society, toward a more cohesive and confident expression that threw its support behind Irish national aspirations. The second section (1917–1945) looks at the maturing of St Patrick's Day as an annual event that reached its peak expression at a time when local, Irish and world events forced the celebration to evolve. Eventually, St Patrick's Day celebrations became less dynamic, as South Australians of Irish descent became woven into the fabric of the state, leaving new Irish migrants to continue the tradition.

From 1836 to 1916

It is more than likely that St Patrick's Day would have been celebrated among the first Irish-Catholic families that came to South Australia in the early years of settlement, either privately or in clusters, through religious devotion or as a small celebration. However, a number of the colony's prominent early citizens were Irish Protestants who were proud of the land of their birth. It was one of these, George Kingston, who organised the first publicly announced celebration of St Patrick's Day, advertised in 1840. Just four years after the colony's founding it was proclaimed that, 'The Sons of Erin will celebrate the festival of their Patron Saint by dining together at Fordham's hotel'.[1] Since the cost of attendance was 30 shillings, this event was probably not intended for the general Irish community. By 1843, a celebration for the wider community was organised:

> Colonists from the Emerald Isle intend this day enjoying themselves in honor of their Saint WITH A GAME OF FOOT-BALL After which, with their friends, they hope to regale themselves with a portion of an ox roasted whole opposite the market house Thebarton.[2]

Incidentally, this is 'the first reference to a game of football being played in South Australia ... probably a variety of Gaelic Football'.[3] The following year it was advertised that 'a few of the ancient games of our forefathers will be revived on the green'.[4] By 1845, three separate festivities for St Patrick's Day were advertised,[5] with Kingston's dinner at the Freemason's Tavern; football and a roasted ox at Thebarton; and publican, Edward McEllister of the Irish Harp, Rundle Street, supplying tickets for a supper at 2s 6d each, a much cheaper ticket compared with Kingston's dinner.

By 1849, the St Patrick's Society of South Australia was formed. Its founding members include prominent Irish Protestants such as Major Thomas O'Halloran, George Kingston, and Robert Torrens, as well as Catholics including Edward McEllister and Fr Michael Ryan. The society was essentially a lobby group with a clear agenda to revive old associations, communicate information to Ireland, assist new immigrants on their arrival, and pressure government for a fairer proportion of Irish immigrants granted passage to South Australia from Irish ports. The society also emphasised the suitability of Irish migrants for life in the colony.[6] The following year the society had erected St Patrick's Hall in

Leigh Street adjoining the Wellington Inn, with a well-attended meeting on St Patrick's Day. In a speech at the formation of the society Robert Torrens declared: 'The Thames alone should not supply the fertilising stream of emigration; equally valuable labour abounded on the banks of the Shannon, which had an equal right to share in the abundance with which we are blessed'.[7] Composed of such prominent citizens, the society had some effect, as Irish migration to South Australia began to pick up into the mid 1850s. By 1857, Bishop Murphy reported a population of 14,000 Catholics in South Australia, the majority being Irish.[8]

The 1850s saw races at Thebarton, the main event being St Patrick's Purse, with the course encircling the township. In 1853, Patrick McCarron, proprietor of the Foresters and Squatters Hotel, catered for the day with two bullocks roasted whole, one for St Patrick and the other for Prince Patrick, son of Queen Victoria.[9] When Patrick Boyce Coglin's horse, United Irishman, won the purse that year, 'the delight of the multitude knew no bounds. The animal was decorated with green ribbons, and went into Adelaide literally with flying colours.'[10]

St Patrick's Day was by now accepted as a holiday for most Irish residents with many happy gatherings occurring in various parts of the city.[11] It was noted in 1856 that Governor MacDonnell, the first Irishman to be appointed governor of South Australia, attended the annual St Patrick's Day dinner.[12] The foundation stone of St Francis Xavier Cathedral was also laid on St Patrick's Day, 1856, by the 'Very Rev. Michael Ryan Vicar-General, in the presence of a very numerous assemblage of spectators'.[13] In contrast to these august occasions, the following day a dozen people fronted the Adelaide Police Court to answer for their 'outrageous merriment' due to a 'liberal consumption of excisable liquors on St Patrick's Day', with each being fined 5s. Another was fined for 'thrashing a constable'.[14]

During the early to mid 1860s, the organisation of St Patrick's Day in Adelaide seemed to wane, while the country areas picked up the theme. In a letter to the editor of the *South Australian Advertiser* in 1864, 'Erinensis' stated that he had 'only experienced one St Patrick's Day here, and as far as he observed or knew, no emblem was hoisted, no shamrock drowned, no dinner, supper or ball given publicly to celebrate that anniversary'.[15] This is curious, as the 1860s was a time of large-scale Irish migration to South Australia. Perhaps the Church hierarchy had taken a dim view of such celebrations, in light of Irish Cardinal Paul Cullen's[16] far-reaching efforts to 'Romanise the Irish Church',[17] creating a 'devotional revolution'.[18] St Patrick's Day always falls during the season of Lent and perhaps an attempt to stifle pre-famine Irish folk traditions had seen the public celebration cease in Adelaide, leaving only the celebration of mass on the day.

As previously stated, however, the 1860s saw many country areas conducting their own St Patrick's Day races, including Gawler, Virginia, Kapunda, Marrabel and Rhynie. Port MacDonnell was organising a regatta and sports event by 1862.[19] These events were popular affairs with large attendances, and in the case of Kapunda they would continue strongly for a century. Virginia, by the late 1860s, was conducting a formal procession through the town, one of the first to do so.[20]

The attempted assassination of Prince Alfred in New South Wales on 12 March 1868 by self-proclaimed Fenian Henry O'Farrell placed much suspicion on Irish communities all over Australia. A few days later, just before St Patrick's Day, two soldiers of the 50th Regiment compelled a tradesman in Adelaide to haul down a 'Fenian flag' outside his premises.[21] Another incident some years later during a Catholic procession in Kadina had some parallels, when a police officer attempted to seize an Irish flag, provoking a defiant response.[22] In the late 1860s, Fr Julian Tenison Woods used St Patrick's Day to lecture on the evils of drunkenness, forming a temperance association that night in 1868, which became known as the St Patrick's Temperance Association.[23] Despite the lull in celebration earlier in the decade, by the late 1860s and early 1870s the celebration of mass and a lecture followed by a concert in the town hall was the norm for St Patrick's Day in Adelaide, with the first mention of a procession being made in 1870.[24]

However, it was not until 1878 that an imposing formal procession through the principal streets of Adelaide was organised by a committee headed by the Hibernian Australasian Catholic Benefit Society (HACBS). Taking part too were the Australasian Catholic Benefit Society (ACBS), the Labourers' Branch of the Labor League and the United Cabmen's Society of Adelaide. General interest from the public was shown by the fact that five to six thousand people were present to witness the start of the procession. Along the whole route, the inhabitants turned out en masse to witness the procession, from St Francis Xavier's Hall down Grote Street, along West Terrace and down Hindley Street, where the balconies and windows of the different shops and houses were thronged with spectators, to North Terrace and through to the grounds of Government House, where they were received by Governor William Jervois. The HACBS carried a splendid banner bearing the motto 'United we stand, divided we fall, we unite to protect, not to injure', an interesting statement, no doubt to allay the fears of non-Irish Catholics. An Irish national concert was held that evening in the town hall, which Charles Gavan Duffy was invited to chair. He was unable to attend due to parliamentary duties, but sent a congratulatory message. George Kingston was invited to chair the evening instead, a link with Adelaide's first public St Patrick's Day celebration 38 years previously.[25]

The following year a hurling match was played on St Patrick's Day between Irishmen and colonials,[26] and from 1880 St Patrick's Day grew from strength to strength, as more societies and bands joined the procession (Figure 1a). Proceeds from St Patrick's Day 1880 were used to aid the Irish Relief Fund, and an impressive £8000 was sent direct to Ireland.[27] The exhibition grounds were now used for amusements and athletic sports. In 1882, 11,000 people paid admission to the grounds on St Patrick's Day. The procession that year saw some thousands of spectators line the streets and it required the utmost diligence on the part of the mounted troopers to preserve the route. Various banners were held aloft with pride, the most noticeable being one belonging to the HACBS, which was obtained from Limerick at a cost of 100 guineas.[28] The increased intensity of celebration, combined with the heightened interest in political tensions in Ireland, prompted the vicar-general, Fredrick Byrne, to advocate a cessation of such demonstrations on the grounds that it would stir up strife and 'counter demonstrations which may cause ill-feeling and hatred among the citizens of this hereto peaceful land'.[29] He appears to have been ignored by the majority of his flock. A notice was inserted by the Committee of the St Patrick's Day Demonstration requesting that:

> IRISHMEN ASSEMBLE and celebrate in a fitting manner the National Festival. It is not held to glorify the triumph of sect or party. It is the memory of our mother country, and to show our enduring love for her. Show that you can be law abiding citizens and good Irishmen; show by your numbers your emphatic disapproval of any movement which would give even the appearance of sectarianism to a wholly Irish reunion.[30]

From 1883, the proceeds of the St Patrick's Day festivities were in the hands of the Irish National League; the funds were used to support Irish Home Rule candidates in the House of Commons (see Figure 1b) and evicted tenants. In this year at the conclusion of the concert in the Adelaide Town Hall it was reported that 'a large number of those present seemed to forget the common act of courtesy usually displayed by loyal citizens whilst the National Anthem is being performed' – by refusing to stand.[31] In the ensuing years 'God Save the Queen' was to be dropped from the concert programme and replaced by 'God Save Ireland'. In 1884 it was reported that 'since the mission of the Redmond brothers to South Australia, the demonstrations on St Patrick's Day have assumed a political aspect'.[32]

By 1890, the South Australian government had proclaimed a 'half-holiday throughout the Civil Service in honour of the day, and members and would-be members of parliament vied with each other in laudable desire to express sympathy with Ireland in her trials and struggles'.[33] Home Rule was beginning to gain a respectable air by this time. The celebration in Adelaide in this year was made more special by the Home Rule delegates John Deasy and J.R. Cox delivering orations on the day.[34] The political aspect of St Patrick's Day was to persist for a number of years until 1896 when Archbishop O'Reily argued that the profits of the day should be devoted to the liquidation of the heavy debt on the archdiocese.[35] This was not given over without lengthy deliberations and a good deal of sparring with nationalist supporters. Eventually the archbishop won his point and the church took a stronger grip on proceedings, although the day still retained a strong national flavour. In 1897, the archbishop was invited by the committee to lead the toasts at the luncheon. In typical good humour he said:

> A subject on which there was much divergence of opinion was Home Rule. In South Australia they went in largely for politics, but with due respect to the members of the Ministry and other political gentlemen present he thought it would be better to leave politics alone because if they once got into the arena of politics it might interfere with their digestion (laughter).[36]

However, politics was never far from the surface. During the 1898 St Patrick's Day banquet, held under the auspices of the Irish National

Federation, the memories of the 'Men of '98' were toasted.³⁷ South Australian politician Patrick McMahon Glynn, president of the South Australian branch of the Irish National Federation, was unable to attend, and sent the following telegram from the Australian Federation Convention in Melbourne, where he played such an important part in framing Australia's Constitution:

> I join in your toasts to the memories of the Men of '98, and your celebration of the anniversary of our patron saint. The convention is just finishing its great work. May it be a happy augury of the success of the constitution that its Godspeed was uttered on St Patrick's Day.³⁸

The new century ushered in new enthusiasm and sympathy for St Patrick's Day from the wider community as reports of the bravery of Irish soldiers in the Transvaal filtered back to Australia. Queen Victoria was soon to visit Ireland and the royal order that Irish soldiers wear a sprig of shamrock in their headdress to commemorate the day was followed by many civilians in Adelaide.³⁹ A military Irish rifle corps was formed in Adelaide at this time, led by Capt. James V. O'Loghlin, a prominent politician who championed Ireland's cause in South Australia over many years. The Irish corps would give military displays at Adelaide Oval during St Patrick's Day the following year.⁴⁰ In 1901, following Federation, renewed calls were made on St Patrick's Day by the United Irish League for self-government for Ireland. Charles Kingston, Laurence O'Loughlin and James V. O'Loghlin, prominent South Australian politicians of Irish parentage, all made connections between the predominance of Irish-Australian politicians in the creation of Australian nationhood and the capacity of Irishmen to self-govern in Ireland. Charles Kingston, son of George, stated:

> the history of each State showed that Irishmen were ever in the van, showing a capacity to govern second to none, and indicating there were none who had greater pre-eminence in the ability required for the development and equipment of Ireland as a nation (Hear. Hear). The Commissioner of Crown Lands, Hon. L. O'Loughlin in acknowledging the sentiment, said it was apparent to all of them Ireland should have Home Rule. All the Australian states had their own parliaments and they were none the less loyal for it.⁴¹

Irish South Australia

Figure 1a
Figure 1b
Figure 2a
Figure 2b
Figure 2c
Figure 3a
Figure 4a
Figure 4b
Figure 4c
Figure 4d
Figure 5b
Figure 6a
Figure 6b
Figure 7a
Figure 7b
Figure 7c
Figure 7d

St Patrick's Day and political badges. For details see key, pages 188–191.

Figure 8a

Figure 8b

Figure 9

Figure 10

Figure 11a

Figure 11b

Figure 11c

Figure 12

Figure 13a

Figure 13b

Figure 14

Figure 15a

Figure 15b

Figure 15c

Figure 16a

Figure 16b

From the turn of the century, with the Catholic Church's stronger control of the St Patrick's Day procession, local Catholic schools began to take a more noticeable part, with a great number of children in the column. Every school from the city and suburbs was involved. The procession at this time was half a mile in length and proceeded to Adelaide Oval for sports and dancing competitions.[42] By the turn of the century large St Patrick's Day demonstrations were well established in Mount Gambier, Port Pirie, Kadina and many towns and areas across the state (see Figure 2a, 2b and 2c).[43] By 1912, a feature of the procession in Adelaide was the newly formed Irish Pipe Band. The band would be at the head of the column for many years and indeed still is to the present day. The recently formed Irish National Foresters (see Figure 3a) also appeared for the first time this year.[44] By 1914, St Patrick's Day speeches from the United Irish League echoed sentiments that fully anticipated Home Rule to be granted following the passing of the Westminster Bill, after decades of careful political lobbying, mostly by the same people who were lobbying in the 1880s.[45] Little did they know, while on the cusp of success, that everything would change utterly: the Great War, the subsequent Easter Rising in Dublin, and the psychological shift of Irish sentiment from cautious Home Rule politics to outright militant demands for an Irish Republic. The Great War seemed not to dampen the enthusiasm for St Patrick's Day in Adelaide; a feature of the parade in 1916 was the voluntary inclusion of soldiers from training camps around Adelaide, the total muster being 1431 officers and men.[46] The sectarian division caused by the conscription debate and the Irish Rising of April 1916 did not seem to have an adverse effect on the St Patrick's Day demonstration itself in the ensuing years; indeed, they gave the day further emphasis (Figure 3b), although resentful loyalist voices were to become louder.

From 1917 to 1945

The turbulent period from 1917 to the close of World War II proved to be formative for both Irish nationhood and Australian identity. In the context of South Australia, changing attitudes and interests can be observed through a pictorial collection of South Australian St Patrick's Day badges. The badges range from 1917 to 1941 and are unique to South Australia.[47] Their design was open to the public in the form of a competition.[48] Each

Figure 3b. St Patrick's Day, King William Street, Adelaide, 1916

year, the winning design was approved by the St Patrick's Day Committee, with proceeds from the sale given to a different cause.

The badges portray the symbolism of St Patrick's Day as an outward expression of the South Australian form of Catholicism and support for Irish Nationalism, still a force to be reckoned with in the early-to-mid 20th century. Spanning the period in which they were produced, a shift in sentiment can be seen in their design. Initially, subtle emanations of Irish symbolism are displayed, leading into strong support for Irish nationalism from the Irish War of Independence to the mid 1920s, followed by a shift away from politics after this period and a return to religious sentiment.

The height of sectarian division and the conscription referendum in Australia coincided with the beginning of mass-produced St Patrick's Day badges in 1917. During these years, when loyalty to Empire was being demanded and 'accusations against the Irish, whether they were Australian or Irish born, were wide spread',[49] the badges (see Figure 4a, 4b, 4c and 4d) defiantly use Irish symbolism only, and never feature the Union Jack. In a further show of defiance, the procession for 1917 was reported as being 'imposing ... almost a mile in length'.[50]

The 1918 death of John Redmond (following that of his brother William in 1917) cast a shadow on St Patrick's Day proceedings for that year. The cause of Home Rule died with them. The Redmonds were idolised by nationalists in South Australia following their visits. Despite this cloud,

St Patrick's Day celebrations proceeded unabated, with the use of tableau displays in the procession being mentioned for the first time in 1918.[51] The inclusion of tableaux persisted for many years, with the various Catholic schools displaying elaborate designs and sets, portraying Irish nationalistic or religious themes (Figure 5a). The archbishop presented a shield for the best tableau each year, to be kept for 12 months by the winning school.[52]

Figure 5a. A Dominican convent tableau

The following year, 1919, saw the commencement of the Irish War of Independence. Atrocities committed in Ireland by auxiliary forces such as the Black and Tans forced previously moderate Home Rule supporters in South Australia to support moves to secure an Irish Republic, in defence of their beleaguered compatriots. On St Patrick's Day, Fr F.A. Connell S.J. gave a fully reported speech on 'The Cause of Ireland,' which concluded: 'They call us Rebels. Well now, if we are rebels in weeping over the sorrows of our sires, in exalting over the glorious struggles against devilish oppression ... we will be rebels to the end'.[53]

In 1920, there was mounting vocal opposition from loyalist Protestant groups such as the South Australian Protestant Federation, the League of Loyal Women and the Unley Ministers Fraternal on the 'disloyal sentiments expressed in the speeches of Roman Catholic priests' as well as questioning the noticeable absence of the Union Jack or the Australian

Flag at the head of St Patrick's Day processions.[54] The mayor of Adelaide, Frank Moulden, was lambasted by sections of the loyalist community for not leaving during the speeches at the St Patrick's Day banquet held under the auspices of the Irish National Society.[55] Following a welcome by the chairman 'on behalf of the 60,000 Irish exiles and descendants of the Irish race in South Australia' the speeches, by Fr R. Hyland, RSA, and Bro. D.G. Purton, MA, spoke of the great wrongs committed in Ireland by Britain. Fr Hyland commented: 'Never had the English Government of Ireland rested on anything but naked force and unabashed corruption. England stood before the world branded by her own acts the colossal hypocrite of all time (Applause)'.[56] The murderous actions of the British government at the height of the Irish War of Independence in 1921 prompted calls for the usual celebrations of St Patrick's Day to be cancelled:

> Would it not appear inconsistent – to put it mildly – for us Irishmen, or Irish-Australians, who grieve for Ireland's sufferings, to join in the proposed joyous celebrations on the Irish national festival at the very moment when Ireland is being tortured by her centuries old oppressor?[57]

Archbishop Spence had been on a tour of Ireland in late 1920, receiving the keys to the city of Cork, his native town.[58] He caused a stir back in Adelaide when it was reported that he had saluted the Irish tricolour during his tour.[59] On his return in February 1921, Archbishop Spence spoke of the atrocities occurring in Ireland at the hands of the Black and Tans, commenting that 'the state of Ireland was awful; beyond description'[60] (Figure 5b). The lord mayor of Cork, Terence MacSwiney, had died on hunger strike the previous October. This caused worldwide outrage, including in Australia. The Adelaide branch of the Irish National Association was named in his honour (Figures 6a, 6b). The association fostered a yearning for Irish independence; they also held St Patrick's Day banquets and ceilidhs (Ir. *céilí*) for many years. Loyalist South Australians were unable to silence the call for Irish nationhood. Even in 1922, with the Anglo-Irish agreement, Prior Hogan, OP, gave a speech at the St Patrick's Day banquet of the Irish National Association (Terence MacSwiney branch). He stated, when referring to the Irish Free State:

> It is not for me to say, whether the title is a fully satisfactory title or not ... No man can be asked whether he is satisfied if, when a debt of 100 Pounds is

owing to him, he receives 75 Pound. He has a right to the remainder. Ireland has a right to independence (Applause).[61]

In response to the rising sentiment, from 1922 to 1925 (Figures 7a, 7b, 7c and 7d) the badges became very political in design, with the inclusion of the Irish tricolour, reflecting South Australia's strong ties with Irish nationalism during this time. In subsequent years the badges become less political. In 1928 (Figure 9) the badge design indicated that sentiment was moving away from Ireland and toward Australia, as religion rather than nationalism became the focus of the celebration. This may be a reflection of Irish-Australia's opinion of the Irish Civil War and broad acceptance of the Anglo-Irish Treaty and subsequent Irish Free State,[62] although some would still foster the hope of a united Irish Republic.

The following year, 1929, was a special year for the celebration of St Patrick's Day, being the centenary of the granting of Catholic emancipation (Figure 10). This was celebrated in Adelaide with all due reverence. However, by the 1930s, the Great Depression was apparently taking its toll on celebrations, as the badges were made using cheaper materials (Figures 11a, 11b and 11c). Despite this, 1932 marked 1500 years since the landing of St Patrick on the Irish coast in 432 AD and a few made the pilgrimage from the archdiocese of Adelaide to the International Eucharistic Congress in Dublin.[63] Coinciding with the congress, 25,000 people were present at the Jubilee Oval in Adelaide at a solemn celebration in honour of the Holy Eucharist.[64] The following year marked 50 years of ordination for Archbishop Spence (Figure 12), who always saluted the St Patrick's Day parade from the balcony of the Adelaide Town Hall. He passed away the following year.

In 1935, given the continued effects of the Great Depression, it was decided that, instead of a procession involving the expensive exercise of making tableaux, a demonstration at the Wayville showgrounds would be held. This decision caused one local, 'Irish-Australian', to write in a letter to the paper, 'As one of the thousands who, from early childhood, has taken part in the celebration of "This Great Day", I am deeply grieved for I consider that our annual procession compared favourably with that of any other state'.[65]

The following year, 1936, saw the resumption of a procession, in what was a special year for South Australia, being the centenary of European settlement. The badge of that year harked back to the foundation of Catholicism in South Australia, featuring an image of Adelaide's first bishop, Francis Murphy (Figure 14). The year was also special for South Australian Catholics as Adelaide hosted the Australian Catholic Education Congress, a triumph for the archdiocese.

Despite the success of the previous year, 1937 appears to be the last formal procession through the streets of Adelaide. The following year Archbishop Killian passed away, and 1938 was also the year of an infantile paralysis outbreak. St Patrick's Day processions had involved children for many years. Fear of spreading this disease forced the archbishop to cancel the usual parade and sports.[66] The badge for this year (Figure 15b) featured the Australian flag for the first time, including the Union Jack. It is intriguing that the St Patrick's Day committee was able to exclude both the Australian flag and the Union Jack on the badge for so many years, given the ties of the wider community to Empire at the time. Sections of the South Australian community, particularly Protestant associations, had pushed for the inclusion of the Union Jack and the Australian flag at the head of the Adelaide St Patrick's Day parades for some time.[67] To its credit it appears that the Adelaide City Council did not enforce this provision. The St Patrick's Day Committee in Melbourne, on the other hand, did have this provision forced upon them.[68] The Adelaide stance demonstrates a boycotting of British imperialism among Irish-South Australians at a time when such a thing was not easy.

In 1939, St Patrick's Day was celebrated with a concert instead of a parade or sports, and the badge for that year included the South Australian emblem of the piping shrike for the first time, suggesting an inward focus (Figure 15c). In 1940, Matthew Beovich was installed archbishop of Adelaide, the first non-Irish-born prelate in the history of the archdiocese. The badge for this year (Figure 16a) is the shape of an ecclesiastical vestment from Dalmatia, being a nod to the new archbishop's 'Yugo-Slav ancestry',[69] an augury of approaching change. Also represented in the amalgam are the Irish Cross of Cong and the piping shrike. The following year, 1941, is the final badge in the collection (Figure 16b), designed by the Rev. Fr K. O'Hannan, OP.[70] The Australian flag is again included, not surprisingly, given the ongoing conflict of World War II, but the Irish tricolour is still a feature. In 1942 a ceilidh social for the celebration of St Patrick's Day was held by the Irish National Association, but it was advertised that 'no procession, sports, or concert will be held this year because of war time conditions'.[71] The subdued St Patrick's Day celebrations continued through the war years, but it was the migration of many different nationalities and cultures, with differing faith traditions, after World War II that changed the face of South Australian Catholicism, and along with it the domination of the Irish form of Catholicism in South Australia. Through all this upheaval, the glory days of triumphant Irish-Catholic expression on St Patrick's Day had passed. Nevertheless, the arrival of new Irish migrants in the postwar period and the establishment of the Australian-Patrician Association in Adelaide ensured the continuation of the public celebration of St Patrick's Day.[72] Some country areas also continued with events into the 1960s.

Conclusion

The continuity of St Patrick's Day speaks of a strong sense of community and identity among Irish migrants and their descendants over generations in South Australia. Domestic, Irish and global events combined with religious constraints, folk traditions and external community expectations formed the evolution of this expression. Initially, St Patrick's Day was used to express loyal sentiments, but political events in Ireland provoked notions of solidarity. This connection to Ireland would last well into the 20th century, as a strong sense of Irish identity was passed on from Irish migrants to the next generations. At the moment when notions of Irish identity in South Australia were confidently at their peak, tumultuous political events in Ireland, the Great Depression and World War II forced Irish-South Australians to re-evaluate their focus. After generations of looking to Ireland, the close connection could no longer be sustained and their focus would turn to local issues of politics, religion and society in Australia.[73]

Key to illustrations on pages 180-181

Figure 1a. St Patrick's Day medalet, 22 mm diameter (no maker's mark). Inscribed on one side – REMEMBRANCE MARCH 17th, with an Irish harp and shamrocks. The reverse side has the Advance Australia coat of arms, dated 1880. From the collection of Miss Nora Mary Supple (see endnote 47). Photo: P. Moore.

Figure 1b. Celluloid/metal pin back button badge, 23 mm diameter (no maker's mark or date). Image: Irish nationalist flag with Irish harp. Inscribed: HOME RULE FOR IRELAND. From the collection of the author, purchased in Kapunda (see endnote 47). Photo: P. Fleig.

Figure 2a. Celluloid/metal pin back button badge, 33 mm diameter (Maker I.R. Cartwright, Byron St, Moonee Ponds). Image: Portrait of Fr John O'Mahony surrounded by shamrocks. Inscribed: St PATRICK'S DAY – PORT PIRIE 1922. Note: Fr O'Mahony was born in Adelaide in 1872, stationed at Port Augusta and Port Pirie, where he died in 1922. A keen spectator on St Patrick's Day in Port Pirie (*Southern Cross*, Friday 24 February 1922). From the collection of the author. Photo: P. Fleig.

Figure 2b. Celluloid/metal pin back button badge, 33 mm diameter (no maker's mark). Image: Irish harp with shamrocks. Inscribed: St PATRICK'S DAY – KADINA 1918. From the collection of the author. Photo: P. Fleig

Figure 2c. Celluloid/metal pin back button badge, 23 mm diameter (no maker's mark). Image: A shamrock. Inscribed: ST. PATRICK'S DAY SPORTS PETERSBURG – MARCH 17 1917. From the collection of the author. Photo: P. Fleig.

Figure 3a. Celluloid/metal pin back button badge, 33 mm diameter (maker's mark – A.W. Patrick 3 Unley Rd Adelaide). Image: Irish National Foresters emblem of three seated maidens. The central figure is holding an Irish harp and an Irish nationalist flag containing the sun rising over an Irish scene. An Irish wolfhound is standing in front of the figures. Inscribed: UNITY – NATIONALITY – BENEVOLENCE – IRISH NATIONAL FORESTERS – FIRST ANNUAL PICNIC DEC. '25 '26. From the collection of the author. Photo: P. Fleig.

Figure 3b. 'ST PATRICK'S DAY ADELAIDE – THE PROCESSION HEADED BY THE IRISH PIPE BAND PASSING ALONG KING WILLIAM STREET ON ITS WAY TO THE ADELAIDE OVAL. (Krischock photo)'. *Adelaide Chronicle* Saturday, 25 March 1916, p. 25.

Figure 4a. Celluloid/metal pin back button badge, 33 mm diameter (no maker's mark). Image: A shamrock. Inscribed: St PATRICK'S DAY 1917. Note: The proceeds from the sale of this badge went to St Mary's hostel for Catholic girls. From the collection of Miss Nora Mary Supple. Photo: P. Moore.

Figure 4b. Celluloid/metal pin back button badge, 33 mm diameter (no maker's mark). Image: An Irish harp, wreath of shamrocks below. Inscribed: St PATRICK'S DAY 1918 – ERIN GO BRAGH. From the collection of Miss Nora Mary Supple. Photo: P. Moore.

Figure 4c. Celluloid/metal pin back button badge, 33 mm diameter (maker's mark – A.W. Patrick 3 Unley Rd Adelaide). Image: St Patrick flanked by shamrocks. Inscribed: ADELAIDE 1919. Note: The image of St Patrick is the same as that used on the banner at the head of the parade for many years. From the collection of Miss Nora Mary Supple. Photo: P. Moore.

Figure 4d. Celluloid/metal pin back button badge, 33 mm diameter (maker's mark – A.W. Patrick 3 Unley Rd Adelaide). Image: An Irish harp flanked by shamrocks. Inscribed: St PATRICK'S DAY – ADELAIDE 1920. Note: This badge was designed by Mr E.G. Walsh of Royston Park. From the collection of Miss Nora Mary Supple. Photo: P. Moore.

Figure 5a. Dominican Convent (Franklin St) Adelaide, St Patrick's Day tableau circa 1920s. Photo: With kind permission from St Mary's College Archives, Adelaide.

Figure 5b. Celluloid/metal pin back button badge, 33 mm diameter (maker's mark – A.W. Patrick 3 Unley Rd Adelaide). Image: Archbishop of Adelaide Robert Spence, surrounded by shamrocks. Inscribed: CEAD MILLE FAILTHE – ST PATRICK'S DAY 1921. From the collection of Miss Nora Mary Supple. Photo: P. Moore.

Figure 6a. Celluloid/metal pin back button badge, 33 mm diameter, circa 1921 (maker's mark – A.W. Patrick 3 Unley Rd Adelaide). Image: Portrait of Terence MacSwiney. Inscribed: THE LORD MAYOR OF CORK – ALDERMAN McSWINEY. From the collection of the author. Photo: P. Fleig.

Figure 6b. Celluloid/metal pin back button badge, 33 mm diameter, circa 1921 (no maker's mark or date). Image: Portrait of Terence MacSwiney, surrounded by shamrocks. Inscribed: LATE ALDERMAN McSWINEY – St PATRICK'S DAY – GOD SAVE IRELAND. From the collection of the author, purchased in Kapunda. Photo: P. Fleig.

Figure 7a. Celluloid/metal pin back button badge, 33 mm diameter (maker's mark – A.W. Patrick 3 Unley Rd Adelaide). Image: Large shamrock surrounded by Irish national colours. Inscribed: St PATRICK'S DAY – ADELAIDE – 1922. From the collection of Miss Nora Mary Supple. Photo: P. Moore.

Figure 7b. Celluloid/metal pin back button badge, 33 mm diameter (maker's mark – A.W. Patrick 3 Unley Rd Adelaide). Image: An Irish harp with shamrocks, surrounded by a heart shape on a stylised banner edged with wattle, flanked by two Irish tricolour flags, topped with a Milesian crown. Inscribed: O ERIN – THOU ART SHRINED IN ALL TRUE HEARTS – FAITH – FREEDOM – St PATRICK'S DAY 1923. From the collection of Miss Nora Mary Supple. Photo: P. Moore.

Figure 7c. Celluloid/metal pin back button badge, 33 mm diameter (maker's mark – A.W. Patrick 3 Unley Rd Adelaide). Image: An Irish harp, flanked by two kookaburras, surrounding the harp is an Irish High Cross, Irish round-tower, shamrocks and a pair of crossed Irish tricolour flags. Inscribed: St PATRICK'S DAY 1924. Note: This badge was designed by Sister Dominica of the Dominican Convent, Adelaide. From the collection of Miss Nora Mary Supple. Photo: P. Moore.

Figure 7d. Celluloid/metal pin back button badge, 33 mm diameter (maker's mark – A.W. Patrick 3 Unley Rd Adelaide). Image: A large shamrock, each leaf contains a separate image of an Irish High Cross, a map of Ireland and the Southern Cross constellation. This is flanked by two Irish tricolour flags with shamrocks below. Inscribed: FAITH – MY COUNTRY – BROTHERHOOD – ERIN GO BRAGH – ST PATRICK'S DAY 1925. From the collection of Miss Nora Mary Supple. Photo: P. Moore.

Figure 8a. Celluloid/metal pin back button badge, 33 mm diameter (maker's mark – A.W. Patrick 3 Unley Rd Adelaide). Image identical to 1919 badge (Figure 4c). Inscribed: ST PATRICK'S DAY 1926. From the collection of Miss Nora Mary Supple. Photo: P. Moore.

Figure 8b. Celluloid/cardboard thin badge cut out in the shape of a shamrock, 33 mm x 31mm (no maker's mark). Image: Irish harp, above shamrocks. Inscribed: St PATRICK'S DAY 1927. From the collection of Miss Nora Mary Supple. Photo: P. Moore.

Figure 9. Celluloid/metal pin back button badge, 33 mm diameter (no maker's mark). Image: A map of Australia with shamrocks below. In the centre is a radiant Irish High Cross and the Southern Cross constellation. Inscribed: ST PATRICK'S DAY 1928. From the collection of Miss Nora Mary Supple. Photo: P. Moore.

Figure 10. Celluloid/metal pin back button badge, 33 mm diameter (maker's mark – A.W. Patrick Maker Unley). Image: Statue of Daniel O'Connell. Inscribed: CATHOLIC EMANCIPATION CENTENARY 1829–1929, ST PATRICK'S DAY 1929. From the collection of Miss Nora Mary Supple. Photo: P. Moore.

Figure 11a. Celluloid/cardboard thin badge in the shape of a shield, 41 mm x 28 mm (no maker's mark). Image: Radiant Irish High Cross with shamrocks. Inscribed: St PATRICK'S DAY ADELAIDE 1930. Inscribed: ST PATRICK'S DAY 1928. From the collection of Miss Nora Mary Supple. Photo: P. Moore.

Figure 11b. Celluloid/cardboard thin badge in the shape of a shield, 35 mm x 25 mm (no maker's mark). Image: Illustration of St Patrick, flanked by shamrocks. Inscribed: St PATRICK'S DAY 1931. From the collection of Miss Nora Mary Supple. Photo: P. Moore.

Figure 11c. Celluloid/cardboard thin badge cut out in the shape of a shamrock, 33 mm x 30 mm (no maker's mark). Image: A Radiant Irish High Cross above shamrocks. Inscribed: St PATRICK'S DAY 1932. From the collection of Miss Nora Mary Supple. Photo: P. Moore.

Figure 12. Celluloid/metal pin back button badge, 33 mm diameter (maker's mark – A.W. Patrick 3 Unley Rd Adelaide). Image: Portrait of Archbishop Robert Spence identical to 1921 badge (see Figure 5). Inscribed: GOLDEN JUBILEE – ST PATRICK'S DAY 1933. From the collection of Miss Nora Mary Supple. Photo: P. Moore.

Figure 13a. Celluloid/cardboard thin badge in the shape of a shield, 47 mm x 31 mm (no maker's mark). Image: An Irish High Cross with the Southern Cross constellation. Inscribed: St PATRICK'S DAY 1934. From the collection of Miss Nora Mary Supple. Photo: P. Moore.

Figure 13b. Celluloid/cardboard thin badge in the shape of a shield, 42 mm x 29 mm (no maker's mark). Image: Coat of arms of Archbishop Andrew Killian. Inscribed: St PATRICK'S DAY 1935. Note: This was Archbishop Killian's first St Patrick's Day as archbishop of Adelaide. He was the last Irish-born archbishop of Adelaide, there being a succession of seven Irish-born bishops and archbishops in the archdiocese. From the collection of Miss Nora Mary Supple. Photo: P. Moore.

Figure 14. Celluloid/metal pin back button badge, 33 mm diameter (no maker's mark). Image: Portrait of Bishop Francis Murphy, flanked by shamrocks. Inscribed: DR. MURPHY – FIRST BISHOP OF ADELAIDE – ST PATRICK'S DAY 1936. From the collection of Miss Nora Mary Supple. Photo: P. Moore.

Figure 15a. Celluloid/cardboard thin circular badge, 30 mm diameter (no maker's mark). Image: Identical to 1928 badge (see Figure 9). Inscribed: ST PATRICK'S DAY 1937. From the collection of Miss Nora Mary Supple. Photo: P. Moore.

Figure 15b. Celluloid/cardboard thin badge in the shape of a shield, 35 mm x 25 mm (no maker's mark). Image: An Irish High Cross flanked by the Irish tricolour flag and the Australian flag and shamrocks below. In the middle is a banner, inscribed: ST PATRICK'S DAY 1938. From the collection of Miss Nora Mary Supple. Photo: P. Moore.

Figure 15c. Celluloid/cardboard thin badge in the shape of a shield, 35 mm x 26 mm (no maker's mark). Image: A piping shrike with an Irish High Cross above and shamrocks below. The background is the Irish tricolour. A banner carries the inscription: ST PATRICK'S DAY 1939. From the collection of Miss Nora Mary Supple. Photo: P. Moore.

Figure 16a. Celluloid/cardboard thin badge in the shape of a 'conventionalised dalmatic, an ecclesiastical vestment introduced at an early date from Dalmatia. This has been adopted as a token of welcome to the Archbishop-Elect, who is of Yugo-Slav ancestry' (*Southern Cross*, 1 March 1940), 40 mm x 30 mm (no maker's mark). Image: A representation of the Irish Cross of Cong, flanked by shamrock and wattle. Behind stands the piping shrike bordered by the Irish national colours. Inscribed: St PATRICK'S DAY 1940. From the collection of Miss Nora Mary Supple. Photo: P. Moore.

Figure 16b. Celluloid/cardboard thin badge in the shape of a shield, 35 mm x 25 mm (no maker's mark). Image: An Irish High Cross flanked by the Irish tricolour and the Australian flag and surrounded by shamrock and wattle. Inscribed: SAINT PATRICK'S DAY 1941. Note: Designed by the Rev. Kevin O'Hannon, OP. From the collection of Miss Nora Mary Supple. Photo: P. Moore.

Varieties of Irish nationalism in South Australia, 1839–1950: Changing terms of engagement

STEPHANIE JAMES

South Australia's Irish supported a continuous lineage of Irish nationalist groups for almost 80 years, from the late 1870s until the early 1950s. Such a record is unparalleled elsewhere in Australia, a slightly anomalous outcome for a colony/state perceived as the 'least Irish'. While this chapter will chart the course negotiated in those decades, examining the factors and individuals that shaped changing interactions between Irish South Australians and Ireland, it will be argued that for the first 40 years most Irish-South Australians did not display a developed sense of Irish nationalism – that is, the policy of asserting the interests of their nation, viewed as separate from the interests of Britain.[1] Instead, utilising language from the 1851 St Patrick's Society report, most Irish colonists

> united to testify their love for the green isle of their fathers, by cultivating the social virtues, the benevolent principles, and the patriotic spirit which has ever characterised the land of their birth.[2]

Importantly, this approach was neither divisive in terms of denominational differences, nor on the potentially more problematic level of challenging imperial patriotism. As Ireland changed from the late 1870s, with increasing numbers of organisations and individuals moving toward both the articulation of Ireland's 700 years as a nation, and demands for independence from Britain, so too many across the diaspora shifted in terms of expectations for Ireland, and attitudes toward Britain.

Using the framework of the (unwritten) terms of engagement or the scope and limitations of the local relationship to Ireland provides insight into its evolution: the shift from a constitutional focus (which was associated with financial demands/obligations); to a more radical post-Rising emphasis; to, ultimately, a cultural emphasis emerging from the 1920s. Within the engagement process there were a number of important variables: the visibility of dominant individuals commanding respect (based on position or prestige; in other words, their social capital); acute sensitivity to local politico-social nuances; resilience in terms of new stimuli (Irish visitors, news or Irish events, but also events in Australia); and, in the background, changes in Catholic Church participation.[3] The chapter will survey the context of colonial Irish organisations from the 1830s to the 1870s as important background for examining the profile of local commitment to Irish nationalism. The focus will then move to different eras: the years between 1879 and 1883 during which the Home Rule Association (HRA), the Irish Land League (ILL) and the United Irish Association emerged (UIA); discussion of the Irish National League (INL) (1883–1890), the Irish National Federation (INF) (1890–1900), and the United Irish League (UIL) (1900–1920) will follow; and, finally, the Irish National Association (INA) (1920–1951) will be examined.[4] The fading of the direct lineage in the 1950s is consistent with the arrival of the post-World War II immigrants who changed South Australia's social landscape.

Inter-denominational cooperation among Irish immigrants was a consistent feature of most of the colonial era. As other chapters in this collection have shown, not only were Protestant Irish of great significance in the colony's first decades, but some early Irish organisations included both Protestant and Catholic members. Some evidence of this formal interaction persisted until at least the Great War. But one of the many challenges confronting contemporary researchers of the Irish in South Australia is the absolute dearth of any official records of local organisations. The consequent reliance on newspapers is enormous. Before the *Southern Cross* was launched in mid 1889, there had been eight short-lived Catholic newspapers in the colony since 1867.[5] When there was no local Catholic paper, news or details about Irish-South Australians appeared inconsistently either in the local secular press, or interstate Catholic newspapers, like Melbourne's *Advocate*. Thus, some sections of the history remain sketchy.

From 1836 to 1878

The South Australian landscape was designed to be different from other Australian colonies: planned, no convicts, no established church, and 'few Irish'.[6] The colonial Irish were deliberately constructed as a minority group. The significant and public contribution of Irish Protestants to early colonial history suggests that it was the Catholic Irish who were unwanted. As is discussed elsewhere in this collection, St Patrick's Day was celebrated in various ways from at least 1839. In 1840 the impetus for the Sons of Erin seems to have come from the more establishment Irish, while the 1849 focus on increasing Irish immigration, accompanied by the establishment of the St Patrick's Society, reflected Irishmen celebrating their 'Irishness' in the colony's first decades without any sense of distance from, much less critique of, Britain. Reasons for the subsequent gap in development of Ireland-focused organisations are not clear. While St Patrick's Day continued to be significant for Irish across the denominations, from the mid 1850s until the late 1870s the colony was without any Ireland-focused body. But, in these decades, glimpses of fervent local honouring of Ireland were revealed, for example in the 1875 centenary of Daniel O'Connell's birth.

The earliest Irish organisation, the 'Sons of Erin', seemed to confine its attention to St Patrick's Day. References in 1840, 1841 and 1845 suggest it was small, possibly consisting only of Protestants – G.S. Kingston was the sole person consistently mentioned.[7] Reports in 1849, 1850, 1851 and 1856 about the more enduring St Patrick's Society reveal the names of 21 Irishmen, mostly known and prominent Protestant Irishmen, but including at least six known Catholics.[8] This body's initial achievement was its 1849 memorial to the Colonial Secretary, Lord Grey, arguing strongly that what the colony needed was more Irish immigrants.[9] The Colonial Office's formal response challenged whether their proposals 'would be acceptable to the majority of settlers',[10] a statement redolent of the unfavourable English to Irish ratio, and inherent prejudice.[11]

The famine-related events in Ireland, and the inability of Irish immigrant dispatch to be successfully aligned with colonial workforce demands (due to impossible time and distance issues), created lasting problems hinging on prejudice and bigotry. The large numbers arriving post-famine included all shades of Irish families: those who worked and prospered, those unable to do so, and some who became a burden to the colony. For many,

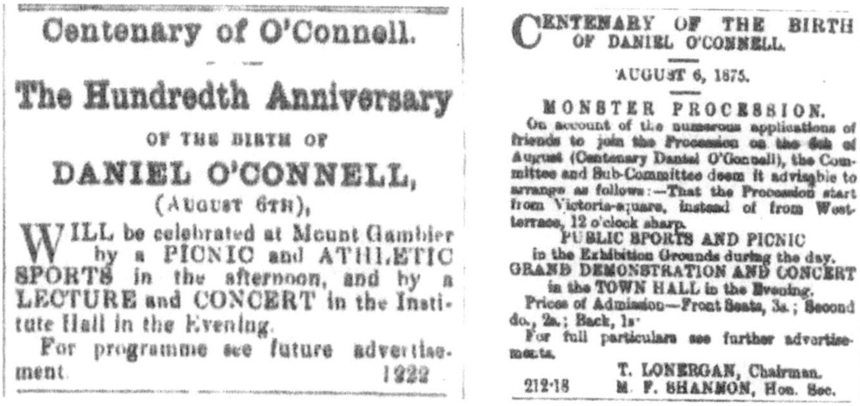

> **Centenary of O'Connell.**
>
> **The Hundredth Anniversary**
> OF THE BIRTH OF
> **DANIEL O'CONNELL,**
> (AUGUST 6TH),
>
> WILL be celebrated at Mount Gambier by a PICNIC and ATHLETIC SPORTS in the afternoon, and by a LECTURE and CONCERT in the Institute Hall in the Evening.
> For programme see future advertisement. 1222

> **CENTENARY OF THE BIRTH OF DANIEL O'CONNELL.**
>
> AUGUST 6, 1875.
>
> **MONSTER PROCESSION.**
> On account of the numerous applications of friends to join the Procession on the 6th of August (Centenary Daniel O'Connell), the Committee and Sub-Committee deem it advisable to arrange as follows:—That the Procession start from Victoria-square, instead of from West-terrace, 12 o'clock sharp.
> **PUBLIC SPORTS AND PICNIC**
> in the Exhibition Grounds during the day.
> **GRAND DEMONSTRATION AND CONCERT**
> in the TOWN HALL in the Evening.
> Prices of Admission—Front Seats, 3s.; Second do., 2s.; Back, 1s.
> For full particulars see further advertisements.
> T. LONERGAN, Chairman.
> 212-18   M. F. SHANNON, Hon. Sec.

Figure 1. (left) *Border Watch*, 28 July 1875, p. 3; (right). *South Australian Register*, 6 August 1875, p. 1

Ireland became a distant dream: families were not always able to remain connected across the distance, many lacked literacy, and local reporting of Ireland was invariably tinged with English bias. The net effect was an Irish minority focusing on struggles toward survival in an English-dominated environment, one purportedly not interested in Irish affairs.[12]

However, examining the way Irish-South Australians responded to the August 1875 centenary of the birth of Daniel O'Connell, 'the Liberator', provides an important example of changing interaction. It shows both deep attachment to Ireland, and the process of this community coming together without a formal organisation. In June 1875, a clerically sponsored meeting was called to 'consider the best means of celebrating' the day: the vicar-general, Fr Byrne (chairman) suggested a 'soiree', including a lecture on O'Connell and 'national songs', would be most appropriate.[13] The appointed committee of laymen called a public meeting for 5 July. On that occasion (again chaired by Fr Byrne), the platform presence of Bishop Reynolds, plus three more priests, suggested ongoing clerical interest or control. The bishop promoted the notion of diocese-wide collections to fund a monument – promising £20 with another £13 offered by his colleagues. He wanted a pontifical high mass in the morning and agreed to lecture on O'Connell at the evening concert. Supporting the concert over a banquet, Timothy Lonergan commented that the latter would be limited to males, 'whereas if they had a concert wives and families could attend'.[14] Tickets for the concert at between one and three shillings were later advertised, and in a procedural lapse bypassing the high mass, a 'Monster Procession' at 10 o'clock from West Terrace 'for public sports and a picnic' at the North Terrace 'Exhibition [Building] Grounds', on 6 August was also publicised.[15] No doubt responding to clerical pressure, Lonergan and Secretary M.F. Shannon adroitly extricated themselves by stating that 'numerous applications from Friends to join the Procession' had resulted in plans for it to leave the Cathedral at 12, in other words, after mass.[16] Advance publication of the concert programme showed that G.S. Kingston would speak on 'The Memory of Daniel O'Connell'; the advertisement also urged those intending to join the procession 'to wear a green ribbon'.[17] As it happened, Bishop Reynolds was unwell after the demands of the high mass, so Kingston both chaired the meeting and entertained the audience with his thoughts and experience of O'Connell. While Mount Gambier organised its own celebration,[18] the Adelaide organisers ensured that 'all the townships easy [sic] of access to Adelaide ... [were] invited to join in the "gala"'.[19] Contemporary coverage from Kapunda's newspaper provided something of objective comment on the day:

> The Daniel O'Connell centenary has been the chief topic of talk among other folk than those who hail from the fair land of the shamrock and thistle. Among the latter it is not using the language of hyperbole to say that it has not only been the chief, but the absorbing subject of thought as well as of conversation. If the great Liberator could have seen the demonstration of Friday last, and could have interpreted the feelings of those who took part in it, he would have been abundantly satisfied with the place he still retains in the memory and affection of his countrymen.[20]

This celebration, then, did more than engage the Irish-born; their fellow colonists also showed interest in and appreciation of O'Connell's wider achievements. Numerous editorials were devoted to his role in bringing about change,[21] and reports of the day mentioned that:

> attendance at the celebration ... was not by any means confined to Roman Catholic citizens, numbers of others taking part in the proceedings, and

notwithstanding the crowded attendance at the Town hall, the greatest order and good humour prevailed throughout.[22]

From 1879 to 1883: Home Rule Association, Irish National Land League, and United Irish Association

In Adelaide, the years between 1879 and 1883 represent a fertile turning point for Irish nationalism in South Australia with three different organisations emerging. This pattern of local groups dedicated to action on Ireland's behalf reflected an important change to the terms of engagement, and some of the names associated with these developments recurred throughout following decades. The individuals include Patrick Whelan, Patrick Healy (both first-generation men from County Clare), and second-generation Irishmen J.V. O'Loghlin and F.B. Keogh.

Figure 2. Patrick Whelan. (J.S. Battye, *Cyclopedia of Western Australia*, Cyclopedia Co, Perth, 1912, p. 904)

From 1879, Irish colonists responded to events in Ireland associated with a serious agricultural downturn. The agrarian protest of that year involved Irish tenants firstly demanding rent reductions, then Michael Davitt's October promotion of the Irish National Land League, which transformed the protest into a generalised plan of campaign, emanating from County Mayo (where distress was extreme), against landlordism. When landlords refused tenant demands, rent refusal followed, and the ensuing eviction processes – opposed legally and physically – resulted in diminished control over tenants. Thus, landlord legitimacy was challenged, and significantly, Land League rhetoric 'identified it with the British connection'.[23] The consequences of such drastic socio-political shifts in Ireland were reflected in the formation of the Home Rule Association in Adelaide, a foundational, overtly Irish nationalist organisation.[24] Thus the change to the terms of engagement involved Irish colonists responding to Irish issues. It is only from F.B. Keogh's 1901 account that names of the three founding individuals emerge – J.A. Hewitt, M.M. Ryan and John Bradley.[25]

Figure 3. F.B. Keogh, *Southern Cross*, 15 July 1927, p. 8

Adelaide was again preeminent in its response to the 'Irish Distress', publicised in late 1879 after three years of crop failure.[26] There were a number of important consequences of a public meeting in December: in addition to effective local fundraising tactics (collecting almost £9000), a nation-wide appeal gathered at least £95,000 for Ireland. Speaker of the House of Assembly, G.S. Kingston, was treasurer, and Patrick Healy and M.T. Montgomery were joint secretaries.[27] In addition, the close colonial Irish connection around this issue facilitated the formation of the Land League involving numbers from the Home Rule Association.[28] But Keogh also credited J.V. O'Loghlin and his letters to the press on the question of Home Rule as helping influence many in the community toward favouring Irish autonomy.[29] Keogh explained:

The league grew in strength, and by means of subscriptions and the celebration of St Patrick's Day, a substantial sum was forwarded every year to Dublin to aid the evicted tenants.[30]

Direct contact between Ireland and Australia from mid 1881 was critical for colonial focus on Irish nationalist politics. J.W. Walshe, an Irish Parliamentary Party (IPP) delegate arrived in Melbourne, tasked with both setting up the Land League in Victoria and raising funds to send to Ireland.[31] In a letter to the Irish League treasurer of 1 August 1881, Walshe stated that '[m]ost of our people were altogether ignorant of the objects of the Land League until my arrival', something unsurprising in view of the consistently negative, colonial London-filtered press.[32] The IPP's intervention in sending Walshe instituted important changes to the terms of engagement, redefining the relationship between Irish-Australians and Ireland. Walshe was a founding member of Davitt's National Land League,[33] and quickly established an Australian central committee and league branches in Victoria and New South Wales. And antipodean generosity raised the profile of Irish-Australians in Ireland.[34]

The mid-1882 visit of Walshe's colleague Pierce Healey[35] eventually resulted in an enthusiastic Adelaide public meeting about the problems in Ireland. Some years later J.A. Hewitt, mentioned above as involved in the early Home Rule Association, spoke about the beginnings of the Land League just before his first return to Ireland.[36] He stated:

> The Land League in South Australia resulted from a little society formed for the celebration of St Patrick's Day in 1881. Then Mr Pierce Healy [sic] arrived in the colony, and the members of this society took up the cause and arranged a meeting for him at a time when he had almost despaired of doing anything in Adelaide, and thought of leaving in disgust.[37]

A nine-person committee was set up to 'receive funds to assist the Land League of Ireland'.[38] The *Register* warned that potential subscribers needed to ensure their funds were not going 'to maintain the accursed system of terrorism which has brought things to such a fearful pass in Ireland'.[39] This tacitly acknowledged change in the local relationship with Ireland. J.A. Hewitt and others formed a branch of the league and about £600 was collected for Ireland.[40] Between June 1882 and May 1883, Healey spoke at Norwood, Port Adelaide, Kapunda, Georgetown, Clare, Petersburg, Wilmington and Hammond. Audience size varied, but there were 200 at Pekina.[41] The resulting committees collected funds to assist the Irish Land League.

Virtually coinciding with Healey's arrival, the United Irish Association formed in Adelaide. Details about this group are very thin; its brief survival suggests Adelaide was unable to support two Irish-focused organisations. Forty attended a mid-July 1882 founding meeting called by two men prominent in early INL discussions.[42] The association planned to be educative, 'politics and literature' its focus, along with religion, without any influence; an initial committee was formed. After some difficulties about purpose, meetings in August attempted to clarify its role, and the first of the promised papers about Irish history was presented.[43] But by mid October there had been three secretaries and no more was heard of the association.[44] So little is known of this group that any assessment of its position vis-a-vis the terms of engagement with Ireland must be qualified. It seems to have been contesting the stance reflected in the Irish National League.[45]

From 1883 to 1890: Progress and Development of the Irish National League (INL)

Walshe's labours prepared the ground for the 1883 visit of John and William Redmond. They spoke first at Adelaide's town hall, and then in rural centres, raising the needed funds for Ireland.[46] It was at their February meeting that the resolution to disband the indigenous league was passed and the Irish National League formally instituted, a change with long-term significance for colonial engagement with Irish nationalism.[47] The link to the IPP dominated the next three-plus decades through variously titled local organisations, Irish parliamentary delegations and strong financial commitment.[48] And consistent with the Ireland-generated terms of engagement, Redmond proposed a convention of the Australian Irish to appoint 'a Federal Council to establish and maintain the Irish National League in Australia'.[49] First-generation Irishmen, INL president and secretary, William Dixon and Patrick Whelan, and second-generation men F.B. Keogh and J.V. O'Loghlin represented the colony in Melbourne. The INL organised welcomes and addresses for distinguished visitors – for example in 1886 when Dr Kevin Izod O'Doherty, one of the Irishmen of 1848 transported to Tasmania and subsequently a successful Brisbane doctor and MP, was travelling to take his seat at Westminster, his ship called at Adelaide, and he was feted.[50] And in 1887 the INL presented Ireland's previous viceroy Lord Aberdeen and his wife with an illustrated address.[51]

Figure 4. J.V. O'Loghlin (SLSA, B4997)

The late 1880s resulted in a series of highs and lows for the INL. Accusations against Ireland's IPP leader C.S. Parnell led to fundraising across the diaspora for his defence.[52] The advertisement (in Secretary Whelan's name) for a public meeting in October 1888 to discuss plans was expressed strongly, suggesting the local emergence of more explicit nationalism:

> Irishmen living in the City and Suburbs who will absent themselves from this Meeting without a reasonable excuse will be looked upon as Renegades and Enemies to their Country.[53]

Given that the colony's total was £350, and the Irish-born population somewhere between 18,246 (1881) and 14,369 (1891), the INL might have been disappointed.[54] In April 1889 when another IPP delegation visited, a reception committee of 400 friends (including 25 clerics) met John Dillon.[55] His public speaking drew large crowds and William Dixon represented the colony at another convention in Melbourne.[56] But when members learned of the 'disruption of the Irish Party' after Parnell was cited in a widely publicised divorce case, this raised leadership issues locally.[57] The decade thus ended with conflict across the diaspora, conflict emanating from events in Ireland and London. All overseas communities were confronted in terms of personal allegiance to Parnell, a major challenge to the previously accepted terms of engagement.

From 1890 to 1900: Irish National Federation (INF)

Adelaide's INL members were alarmed about the impact of IPP divisions – Irish members diverged over Parnell's future – on the future of Home Rule.[58] Furthermore, the heated local debates over the right to comment on Irish affairs indicated further destabilisation of previous terms of engagement.[59] But ultimately Adelaide followed the majority IPP decision in 1891[60] – Parnell refused to resign and the IPP split. All INL branches dissolved, replaced immediately by branches of the Irish National Federation.[61] A decade of distasteful conflict followed with two groups claiming to speak for Ireland.[62] Financial contributions, that critical dimension of engagement, subsided. Visits from Irish delegates declined and attracted opposition. For example, those collecting for evicted tenants in April 1891 were more successful in South Australia than in the eastern colonies.[63] An Adelaide letter to Dublin late in June 1891 clarified the issues:

> The disruption in the National ranks over the question of the leadership has sadly disheartened Irish men everywhere, and has materially affected the subscriptions to the fund. ... [W]e may mention that in South Australia we almost unanimously support the majority of the party who have remained true to their pledges [to the leadership.][64]

Monthly INF meetings in Adelaide and some country areas continued into the 1890s.[65] The INF organised Michael Davitt's 1895 visit, which drew large and enthusiastic crowds.[66] His interaction with INF leadership contributed to Irish understanding of how damaging IPP divisions were for the diaspora. Davitt's subsequently published book about his sojourn in the colonies acknowledged the numbers of former INL members he met in South Australian country towns.[67] Comments in Brisbane reflected his delight about what he generally found:

> I have been surprised at the intensity of [our Irish people's] feeling, though I have been aware for some time that they have been our most generous

supporters. In proportion to population there is more active sympathy from the Irish in Australia than from the Irish in America.⁶⁸

Such a popular Irishman's endorsement totally reinforced the terms of engagement. However, in 1896 major and unprecedented changes to these terms followed newly appointed Archbishop of Adelaide O'Reily's insistence that he take control of St Patrick's Day. Decreeing that the proceeds, usually between £150 and £200, must be assigned to defray diocesan debt, and thus not sent to Ireland for the cause, his edict elevated local financial demands above those of Ireland's future.⁶⁹ Quickly recognising that his demand also totally altered the non-sectarian character of the day, *Southern Cross* accounts reported outrage from some INF members. A series of meetings debated the issues, and, eventually, the INF reluctantly supported the archbishop's decision.⁷⁰

This was a difficult decade for the INF. In addition to the intra-IPP complexities, more immediately, the 1899 South Australian decision to join other colonies in sending troops to support Britain's imperial adventure in South Africa revealed local INF friction points.⁷¹ As president, Irish-born Patrick McMahon Glynn, a former state MP and lawyer, did not always perceive issues in the way other INF colleagues did.⁷² In 1900 when some wanted to send a message to Queen Victoria during her wartime visit to Dublin, hoping 'that God may spare her to open an Irish Parliament,'⁷³ he wrote to his mother:

Figure 5. Patrick McMahon Glynn (SLSA B11254)

> My blessed countrymen here insisted on importing into a telegram to the Lord Mayor of Dublin welcoming the Queen, a Reference [sic] to Home Rule. I told them it was bad taste and useless, but they insisted. However, in a changed form I sent it to the Lord Mayor instead of the Queen & am glad he appears to have ignored it.[74]

McMahon Glynn thus reflected more conservative terms of engagement at the beginning of an era when this differentiated him from those INF colleagues shifting in their perceptions (partly in response to British treatment of the Boers as a small nation) about the route toward Home Rule.[75]

From 1900 to 1920: United Irish League (UIL)

In 1900, under enormous pressure from across the diaspora and within Ireland, the two wings of Irish constitutional nationalism reunited as the United Irish League (UIL) under John Redmond's leadership.[76] South Australia's Irish adhered to the established pattern: the INF cautiously followed other states in becoming the United Irish League in January 1901.[77] In 1901 writing to Dublin, Secretary M.J. McAllister's relief and pleasure, as well as a slight retrospective rebuke, were clear:

> It is with great pleasure we see the Irish Party united and active once more, and as strong as ever.
>
> We are sending you £25 towards your fund. The amount no doubt would have been larger but for the unsatisfactory state of affairs at home during the last few years. But it gives us renewed hope and ... confidence to see the party again united and demonstrative in their demand for justice in the old land. I feel certain that before long we will be able to send you another donation.[78]

Significantly, the earlier terms of engagement were fully reinstated. Visits from IPP delegates in 1906 and 1911 did much to revive and re-focus local commitment.[79] Reforms to the House of Lords and the passage of the third Home Rule Bill through Westminster in 1912 reinforced the constitutional underpinning of the terms of engagement.[80] Most Irish-Australians then felt assured that Home Rule was guaranteed. From Table 1, some approximation of Australia's financial engagement with Ireland between 1880 and 1912 becomes clear.

Table 1. Famine relief, IPP delegates, tours, and amounts raised[81]

Year/s	Names	Dates	Amounts
1879/80	Irish Distress	December 1879 to 1880	£95,000
1881	John W. Walshe	June	£14,000 by early 1883[82]
1883	John and William Redmond	February to November	£15,000 to £40,000
1889	John Dillon, John Deasy and Sir Thos Esmonde	March to September	£35,000 to £40,000, £1000 in SA
1891	J.R. Cox	April to November	£3000
1906	Joseph Devlin and John T. Donovan	April to August	£22,000
1911/12	Wm A.K. Redmond, John T. Donovan and Richard Hazelton	October to August	£30,000
TOTAL			**£225,000**[83]

In June 1914, Adelaide's huge demonstration – 10,000 at the Exhibition Building when the city's population was around 190,000 – marking the Home Rule Bill's third parliamentary circuit in London represented local jubilation at the milestone.[84] The UIL, led by Patrick Healy since 1909, generated the idea, combining with other Irish organisations to plan the event. Rather than requesting cables of support for Home Rule to go to London, politicians across the parties were invited to attend. This would 'force [MPs] to declare their views, and show on which side they were'.[85] Many, mostly from the Liberal faction, neither responded nor expressed their views, but their Labor colleagues, both state and federal, attended in significant numbers, and spoke to resolutions.

Figure 6. Patrick Healy, *Southern Cross*, 27 August 1920, p. 7

The UIL then struggled to deal with the impact of war. UIL treasurer, F.M. Koerner, was also editor of the *Southern Cross*. This was the most trusted vehicle for transmission of news about Ireland, but its early wartime message was at best confused and at worst misguided in promoting the safety of Home Rule, and recognising British disinterest in Irish issues beyond the provision of troop supplies.[86] Thus when news of the Dublin Easter Rising in April 1916 was confirmed, the UIL, bolstered by national and international reports in the *Southern Cross*, roundly condemned the proclamation of the Republic and the immediate results.[87] An interview with UIL President, Patrick Healy was front page news in the *Advertiser*.[88] Amidst all the confusion of the weeks after the Rising, by mid May Koerner commented that

> If there is now a certain amount of sympathy with the rebels, it is on account of the hastily carried out military executions and the severe treatment accorded them ...[89]

This somewhat tortured attitude to wartime Ireland encompassing consistent disorder, the IPP decline and Sinn Fein's concomitant rise, was evident in UIL decisions and statements. The death of John Redmond in March 1918 and John Dillon's role as his replacement were insufficient to reverse the momentum. Although invited to participate in 1918 meetings about a new Irish nationalist body, Patrick Healy could not even face attending. When Britain's election of December 1918 resulted in a virtual annihilation, with Sinn Fein gaining 73 seats to the IPP's six, local members rejected Patrick Healy's January 1919 proposal that the UIL should dissolve itself in favour of the recently formed Irish National Association.[90] That shift took another year of agonising discussion.[91] The group's struggle about its demise related directly to its decades-long promotion of terms of engagement centred on the IPP and Home Rule; these were now totally irrelevant.

From 1918 to c. 1951: Irish National Association (INA)

In the longer term, Dublin's Easter Rising of April 1916 initiated the most radical challenge to local ideas about Irish nationalism, utterly changing the terms of engagement. The Rising also created major concerns about Irish-Australian loyalty, especially when the Special Intelligence Bureau

(SIB), already primed for the local existence of Sinn Fein,[92] discovered in early 1918 that some UIL members were planning an alternative body. This move represented the reversal of the preceding terms of engagement, with Irish-Australians responding to the changed stimuli from Ireland and determining the shape and nature of their reaction. Recognising that Home Rule had been bypassed and alert to a new Irish future, individuals such as Irish-born Fr M.V. Prendergast (Burra) and second-generation Irishmen, Brother D.G. Purton (Christian Brothers College), P.E. O'Leary and Frank Doherty (UIL), were under surveillance, and their correspondence was monitored.[93] Although it is unclear how or when they met, comments made retrospectively explained they acknowledged the need for 'a society that would acclaim and support the ideals of the Sinn Fein Party'.[94] An enthusiastic public meeting in May (chaired by J.V. O'Loghlin), preceded the development of a constitution based on the Irish National Associations of New South Wales, Victoria and Queensland. SIB attitudes toward the new group combined suspicion and alarm, particularly after seven interstate INA members were arrested soon after Adelaide's first meeting.[95] Files in the National Archives of Australia (NAA) document the measures taken to outwit the disloyal Irishmen, for example: sending an undercover agent to the 5 August launch of the Irish National Society (INS), placing named meeting attendees under 'secret censorship', accessing back copies of the *Southern Cross* for further names, and noting all INS members working in government departments, especially the GPO where censors were located.[96]

Known INS strategies such as avoiding the postal service, and circulating banned books, frustrated the SIB.[97] Equally, INA dedication to Irish cultural nationalism was consistently interpreted as disloyal in the light of the deterioration of the postwar situation in Ireland into open warfare.[98] Whereas previous Irish nationalist organisations, although increasingly critical of British refusal to accord any form of self-government to Ireland, had never been judged as treacherous, from its inception that was how the INS/INA was perceived.[99] Thus the January 1920 UIL and INS amalgamation as the INA opened a totally new phase of engagement where the existing constitutional terms were publicly contested by the INA.

From 1920 until its slow fading away of the early 1950s, the INA both informed its members about Ireland via public lectures, and provided

Figure 7. (left) P.E. O'Leary, *Adelaide News*, 7 February 1927, p. 6; (right) P.A. Greene, *Southern Cross*, 24 March 1939, p. 9

an impressive range of cultural activities.[100] Lectures organised in the early 1920s reveal speakers in a two-to-one ratio of clerics and laymen.[101] The association struggled during the 1920s when the combination of competition from the Self Determination for Ireland League (SDIL), and the damaging impact of Ireland's civil war drastically affected the membership base.[102] However, the dedication of two second-generation men, long-term Irish nationalists – P.E. O'Leary and P.A. Greene – led to the INA resurrection of 1927.[103] Two decades of creatively presenting Irish culture to Adelaide audiences, through various classes, and more publicly through both the Aeridheacht (outdoor day in the hills) and the wireless nights, ensured a visible and audible footprint. The Aeridheacht ran from 1927 until at least 1963,[104] while live studio broadcasts of Irish vocal, instrumental and spoken items operated from 1928 to 1935.[105] It is, however, important to acknowledge that in this iteration, the ecclesiastical presence and role in the INA was highly visible.[106] The impact of World War II on an organisation where key second-generation members were ageing, and the third generation either involved in war activities, or less interested in Ireland, resulted in a weakened INA facing the postwar world.[107] The organisation does not seem to have had an official end; reports in the *Southern Cross*, having become fewer in the 1940s, just stopped.[108] In correspondence relating to the de Valera-sponsored 1948 Australian League for an Undivided Ireland (ALUI), there was reference to attempts to revive the INA, but the contact between P.E. O'Leary and Albert Dryer of the Sydney INA dwindled to nothing by 1954.[109]

Conclusion

South Australia's unique contribution to the record of Irish nationalism in Australia has not been fully acknowledged. The early decades of articulated yearning for Ireland and inter-denominational cooperation among Irishmen helped construct a solid base for the years of more focused interaction with Ireland's political affairs. Fidelma Breen suggests a constellation of factors explains the history between the 1870s and 1918. In her study of support for Home Rule between 1883 and 1912, Breen draws out particular characteristics, including the absence both of antagonistic political figures and of strong Catholic and/or nationalist figures such as Archbishop Mannix and Nicholas O'Donnell in Melbourne. She argues that the size and nature of the Irish community allowed for the development of networks that worked both within this group and across the non-Irish sector, and that the general moderation of the Irish leadership (and its longevity) in conjunction with group unity reduced wider community fears of this minority.[110] So as F.B. Keogh's turn-of-century precis highlights, the various nationalist organisations continued to attract Irishmen other than Catholics.[111]

Moving to look at the terms of engagement beyond the early decades when colonial Irishmen gathered to celebrate their remote homeland, the pace and nature changed from the 1870s. Events in Ireland, largely connected with land, both motivated local Irishmen and convinced parliamentary leaders that Irish exiles could now serve a role in Ireland's progress. This template was one in which the directions were set in Ireland, diaspora organisations operated within their guidelines, and the finances flowed back to Dublin. Supporting the 'old country' by raising money in an atmosphere where showing gratitude to Ireland was seen as a priority, and alongside the constant additional appeals for money to build local churches and/or schools, often created tensions. But this template officially persisted until the UIL voted to disband in 1920. During the early decades of these nationalist organisations, there was little specific cultural emphasis – Irish music and dance were clearly valued, but accepted as a given component of events, not something actively needing transmission. The INA, however, had Ireland at its centre and drew its inspiration from this source, but it also operated independently and without financial or other obligation to that country. Among its major motivations was the responsibility for facilitating the provision of Ireland's cultural legacy to younger generations and the wider community.

The other variables mentioned at the outset included the visibility of dominant individuals in the various organisations. Leadership remained remarkably stable, and some men achieved incredible records; Patrick Healy a member of the executive of every Ireland-focused body from the Irish Distress Fund of 1879 until the end of the UIL in 1920;[112] Patrick McMahon Glynn was involved in all groups from 1889 until 1921.[113] In addition to these two first-generation Irishmen, the role of second-generation individuals was critical: J.V. O'Loghlin was a constant between 1883 and 1925 when he was the INA's second president,[114] P.E. O'Leary had been a vice-president of the UIL from 1914 before becoming a foundation INA member,[115] and, from 1919 until the late 1940s, P.A. Greene was INA treasurer and assistant secretary.[116] Place of birth was clearly not a factor determining commitment. Neither Healy nor the latter two individuals shared the social capital of McMahon Glynn and O'Loughlin as parliamentary representatives; however, they clearly possessed extraordinary organisational and leadership skills unrelated to their employment profiles. The guiding (or perhaps interfering) arm of the Church was a constant, but there were peaks of increased clerical intervention – Archbishop O'Reily's 1896 intervention into the dispersal of St Patrick's Day funds, and aspects of INA progress after 'The Year of Reorganisation' in 1927, clearly showed this trait.[117]

The terms of engagement between South Australia's Irish community and Ireland were modified over time. The earliest version was probably activated by yearning for homeland, while the more active connection with Irish affairs which dominated the next four decades reflected pressure from Ireland in terms of supporting Irish Home Rule. During the years of Irish Party division from 1891, colonial Irishmen faced different challenges, and although Ireland went into the Great War with a reunited party, this was totally incapable of managing the shape and demands of a post-Rising nation. The local formation of the INA in 1918 heralded a new era for South Australia's Irish community. There were many struggles and hurdles encountered in its early years, but a confident cultural platform became visible from the late 1920s. Meanwhile the world was changing, and by the late 1940s, with the arrival of many 'new Australians', it became clear that for the old Irish-Australians belonging to what had been an Irish minority, the terms of engagement were again re-drawn, and the need for the INA no longer existed.

Ireland, Home Rule and the Orange Order in South Australia

FIDELMA BREEN

The Orange Order was formed as a Protestant defence organisation in County Armagh, Ireland, in 1795. It subsequently spread throughout the British Empire and in many places was the foremost opponent to the quest for Irish self-determination represented by the Home Rule movement from the 1870s, led by the Irish Parliamentary Party (IPP). This chapter presents an insight into the 'false start' the Loyal Orange Order of Ireland had in establishing itself in South Australia as the Loyal Orange Institution of South Australia (LOISA) and its subsequent slow growth. It looks at its members' interaction with South Australian society as seen through the lens of the colonial press, and explores why the Order failed to establish a vociferous anti-Catholic and anti-Irish Home Rule lobby group such as existed along Australia's eastern seaboard.

Irish Home Rule

In colonial times Irish identity in Australia generally had two facets: the nationalist and invariably Catholic group, often termed the Green; and the loyalist, unionist and usually Protestant cohort sometimes entwined with membership of the Orange Order, hence the name Orange. While Irish nationalists sought the return of an Irish parliament to Dublin, loyalists, particularly concentrated in the northern province of Ulster, sought to maintain a strong connection to England. Excepting a brief flirtation with militant republicanism in 1879, the Home Rule movement was largely constitutionalist and moderate in its demands. While the English Liberal leader, Gladstone, committed to the idea of Home Rule and facilitated the introduction of the first Home Rule Bill in 1886, subsequent conservative governments attempted to 'kill Home Rule with kindness' passing a number of Acts designed to conciliate Irish demands without weakening the connection to England. Also known as 'constructive unionism', this policy excluded the possibility of a Dublin parliament. A constant theme of speeches made in South Australia in support of Irish Home Rule was the happiness of the people of the colonies where self-government had been granted. The leadership and good example shown by the colony's Irishmen, whether in business, political or social circles, assisted the notion that the Irish would prosper under the governmental conditions sought for Ireland by the new breed of constitutional nationalists in the IPP. The move away from militancy toward constitutionality in the last quarter of the 19th century allowed high-profile, non-Irish South Australian men to lend the local Home Rule movement credence, their presence inducing confidence, credibility and respectability for the wider population.

Why did colonial South Australians support the Irish Home Rule movement? How did that support manifest itself? The answers to these questions are multifaceted and vary over time. Fundamentally, support was given in cash to a number of visiting Irish parliamentary delegations[1] as well as to South Australian Irish organisations, but the fundraising was aided by other elements of South Australia's socio-political nature: the colony was relatively young and had a natural affinity with the issue of self-government; the press was rather more liberal than that in other colonies and provided an intellectual and generally even-handed treatment of Irish political and social issues; South Australian Irish organisations and their committeemen were steady, industrious, sober types far removed from the Irish stereotype, thus posing little of its perceived threat; and finally, the colony's Orange Order was less concerned with Home Rule than its Victorian and New South Wales counterparts and offered little resistance to either the hype created by each Irish envoy visit or the long-term nationalist organisations. The Orange Order's response to the Home Rule campaign, evidenced by occasional letters to the press from individual members, rather than an official organisational doctrine, was to highlight the points of religious danger it envisaged in a Home Rule settlement of Ireland. Other voices occasionally appear in opposition, but these were defined by aspects of a class division rather than anything else – the long-running antagonism between the Hon. Samuel Tomkinson and well-established Irishman Michael Kenny is perhaps the best example of this.[2] The colonial response to each IPP delegation differed and, in the main, improved over time. This was partly to do with the developing sophistication of the Home Rule argument and the fortunes of the IPP in Britain, but the reputation and behaviour of Irishmen in the colony also played an integral part to the movement's success in the local context.

Built on sand

A partial explanation for the unequal prominence of the two Irish sides in the public arena may be present in the secretive nature of the Orange Order, which hinders an investigation of its impact. Speakers at LOISA meetings often claimed that most Protestants in the colony were unaware of the aims of the organisation, and that many more would have been members if this were not the case.

The late development of the Orange Order in the colony should be considered also as one explanatory factor in the lack of an anti-Home Rule movement in South Australia; another was the colony's inherent religious liberalism. The appearance of the Order was not welcomed in South Australia. The first reports of Orangeism in South Australia appeared in a Tasmanian paper in 1847. Hobart's *Colonial Times*, in responding to a letter penned by 'Spartan' supporting the formation of a lodge there, wrote:

> Our objection to the formation of an Orange Lodge is based ... upon the mischievous tendency of such an institution – a tendency decidedly proved by the inevitable and indisputable truth of history ... We can refer confidently to Ireland, poor Ireland! to Sydney, to Port Phillip, and, if we recollect rightly, to Adelaide, for a confirmation of the disastrous effects of Orangeism, discord, ill-will, with polemical and political strife, being invariably attendant upon its organisation.[3]

Yet there is no mention of the Order in the Adelaide papers until 1849. In July of that year, the *Register* reported:

> We regret to announce the formation of an Orange Lodge in Adelaide. We had hoped, when we came to South Australia, that religious and political acerbities, perpetuated in the United Kingdom for unholy purposes, would have been allowed to subside here; but seeing there are spirits whose

insatiate purpose cannot be accomplished without some demon of discord, we denounce their purpose, and solemnly warn our fellow colonists against the possibility of being trammelled by connection with a society which can answer no good end.[4]

The same column gave evidence of South Australia's general commitment to religious harmony and tolerance when it expressed happiness at news that a synagogue was to be built in Rundle Street, and urged readers to contribute to the building, 'more especially since as many Hebrews have pecuniarily helped to rear some of our Christian places of worship'.[5]

The development of the Orange Order in South Australia was reported briefly in the *Moreton Bay Courier* which stated simply, 'An Orange Lodge has been established in Adelaide'.[6] Richard Davis's 'Orangeism in Tasmania, 1832–1967' shows the formation of a lodge in Tasmania in August 1848. Davis tracks newspaper reports of celebratory banquets until April 1851 when the movement appears to have petered out, not to be revived again until the Fenian scare in 1868 precipitated by the attempted shooting of Prince Alfred, the Duke of Edinburgh, by Henry James O'Farrell.[7] It is not unlikely that a similar chain of events took place in South Australia. That the earliest lodges did not survive is supported by the Adelaide press itself, which in 1871 expresses surprise and, clearly, regret, at the announcement of the existence of the Orange Order in the colony:

> We learned to our surprise, from an announcement appearing in our advertising columns a day or two ago, that a Society calling itself the 'Loyal Orange Institution' is in existence in South Australia ... we simply record the fact in order to express our regret that such a Society should be formed in a land where perfect religious freedom has always prevailed ... If Protestants desire to oppose what they deem the errors of the Roman Catholic faith, the means of argument and persuasion are abundantly open to them without their assuming a name which has been the badge of faction and oppression for centuries, and which can serve no purpose save that of arousing the angry feelings of our Irish Catholic fellow colonists. We are sorry to see a Christian minister lending himself to such a demonstration.[8]

The Order's grand chaplain, Reverend James Pollitt, in responding, described this meeting of the Order as the second anniversary tea of

Figure 1. Members of an Orange Lodge with their families at 'Drumcalpin', Auburn c.1890. (SLSA, Auburn Collection, B37092)

LOISA, implying, as was the case in Tasmania, that the initial founding reported in the 1840s had been a false start. Yet one writer, calling himself 'A True Protestant', wrote that the *Register* must have been 'napping, as this Society it deems so pernicious has existed at its very door for years'.[9] In 1889 an Orangeman wrote a reply to a letter which deemed the Order to be a poisonous upas tree taking root in the colonies. As 'one of that noble band, who are banded together for God's right and man's liberty', he stated that:

> previous to the attempt of the assassination of the Duke of Edinburgh, the Orange Lodge, although in existence then, was dormant, and it was through the action of that Fenian who shot the Duke that the Orange Lodges in the Southern Hemisphere number 100 in New Zealand, 100 in Victoria, 50 in Adelaide, 50 in Queensland, and 225 in New South Wales, and wherever Popery is rampant the orange and purple will and must take root – not as an upas tree, but as an antidote to Popery.[10]

Ill-informed he may have been as to the strength of the Order as even at its strongest point records indicate that the Order did not have 50 lodges in South Australia, but his explanation for the impetus for the society's revival makes sense. Despite the far geographical spread of the early lodges in the colony, that impetus appears to have been relatively weak, since it would be another three decades before the Order would achieve a dramatic increase in membership.[11] One must assume the number of people involved at this point to have been small given the development attracted no comment in the preceding two years. Between the years 1871 and 1875 there is little public evidence of activity in Orange circles. The *Adelaide Observer* of 2 December 1871 carried an advertisement for Loyal Orange Lodge No. 1 Derby lodge which showed William III on horseback, stating that the meeting will be held 'Tuesday next at 7:30 in the lodge room of Freemason's Tavern, Pirie St'.

The Order seems to have also suffered an inauspicious second start since some of the first public reports of its members were court reports involving both murder and unseemly marriages. The newspaper report describing the anniversary of LOISA provides some detail of those who occupied its upper echelons, naming as worshipful grand master John Stokes Bagshaw, pioneer colonist, businessman and one of the founders of Adelaide's Holy Trinity Church where a plaque commemorating his contribution to the community can be found.[12] His entry in the *Australian Dictionary of Biography* states that he was a city councillor from 1870 to 1874 and his engineering expertise made him a prominent member of the Health and Public Works Committee. While the entry states that he was a founder of the Ancient London Order of Oddfellows in South Australia, it omits his position as worshipful grand master of LOISA. Bagshaw garners his fair share of attention in the coverage of business news. The innovative development of farming implements secured the future of Horwood Bagshaw Ltd well into the 20th century, and J.S. Bagshaw & Sons remained a family affair long after the merger with the J.A. Horwood business. Also noted in the article describing the Order's anniversary celebrations are Mr Lugg, deputy grand master; Mr Newell, treasurer; Mr Potter, worshipful master of Lodge No. 2; Mr Cowan, MP; Mr Spinks; Rev. James Pollitt and Mr Mudge, grand secretary. The colonial press, as well as publications such as Boothby's almanacs, proved the best source of further information on some of these individuals due to their positions as chaplains, businessmen, councillors and politicians.

The Reverend James Pollitt was born in Lancashire in 1813 and arrived in the colony in 1846 on board the *Emu*. He and his first wife had seven children, one of whom followed in his father's footsteps as a minister. The Rev. Pollitt and his son Canon Pollitt feature regularly in the reporting of church business. In 1857 the reverend was the recipient of the colony's kindness after the destruction of St Luke's Parsonage by fire. In 1876 he was maligned in the press for having 'banded together with other mischief makers to drag religion into the mire of politics in forming the No. 1 Pioneer Lodge of the Protestant Political and Benefit Association of South Australia'.[13] Advertisements for various church events, sermons and lectures frequently feature the Pollitts. However, it is the press associated with James Lugg, deputy grand master and Burnett Patch Mudge, grand secretary, which sparks the most immediate interest in these Orange brethren.

James Nicholls Lugg, importer and upholsterer, was born in Penzance in 1824 and arrived on the *Calabar* in 1853 with his wife, Mary. In 1883, he was the target of an attempted murder. William James Painter, former Orangeman, shot at Lugg at the rear of his business in Grenfell St, accusing him and the Orange Order of having ruined his life. At his trial, the prisoner, in defence, said that he had joined the Orange Order in 1870, and shortly afterwards his brother-in-law had also wanted to join but was refused on the grounds that he had married a Catholic. From that point on, Painter maintained he was persecuted by the Order, and by Mr Lugg in particular. He stated that he then left the Order and, in fact, left the city, moving to Yorke Peninsula, but the 'secret influence of the Society' had followed him there and caused further unemployment.[14] Apart from the human-interest aspect of this story, the incident belies Fitzpatrick's assertion that the Order was no harbinger of hate toward Catholics. Painter stated in his testimony that the Orange Order was responsible for all his misery. He asserted that Lugg had visited his workplace and over the course of three days had spread the story of his papist connections with the result that Painter could no longer gain employment and was almost destitute. It is worth noting that the press and, one assumes, the judge in the case deemed Painter to be of unsound mind. The report of the Supreme

Court trial states that the prisoner's conduct throughout made it appear as though his mind was slightly deranged. The jury found the prisoner guilty, but the sentence of life imprisonment was spent in Parkside Mental Hospital where Painter remained for 39 years before his death in 1922.[15]

The grand secretary, Rev. Burnett Patch Mudge, 'attained some notoriety in the colony'[16] due to his propensity to perform 'suspect' marriage ceremonies, one of the most outrageous being that 'between a fair South Australian girl, whose appearance indicated she was in her teens, and a man of color'.[17] In this instance, Rev. Mudge was accused of failing to assure that the bride-to-be, Edith Sawtell, was at least 21 years of age or to speak with her parents, even though her family was 'well known in Adelaide'. She was, in fact, the granddaughter of the colony's first watchmaker, Edwin Sawtell. During the trial it was also implied that Mudge charged much more than the standard £3 10s marriage fee when the prosecution asked if he had, on occasion, secured fees of up to £25.

In the almanacs of 1872 to 1878 Mudge is listed as a schoolmaster working at Crowther St, and in 1877 he is listed as B.P. Mudge, M.A., district deputy ruler of the Independent Order of Rechabites (IOR), and a year later he was district chief ruler of same. In the press report of the 1876 annual meeting of the IOR he is listed simply as Mr B.P. Mudge – DDR; district secretary and district trustee. The newspaper reports of the trial revealed that he was not, in fact, a Master of Arts and further ridicule ensued. The *Advertiser* was particularly harsh:

> It is a puzzle ... the fact that for a long time the letters M.A. were attached to his name is mysterious. He was never a Master of Arts; and in reply to Mr. Smith's questions in the Supreme Court yesterday he first denied on his oath that he had ever signed himself B.P. Mudge, M.A.; then successively stated that he had never so signed himself to his knowledge; that he never remembered doing so; and lastly, that he might have done so "inadvertently." ... it is not surprising that the jury preferred the testimony on the other side, and acquitted Momphlait ... It is evident that Mr. Mudge is not a person who can safely be trusted with the responsibilities attaching to an officiating minister authorised to perform the ceremony of marriage, and justice to parents and the community demands that his enrolment should be cancelled ...[18]

Figure 2. Members of an Orange Lodge, *c.* 1910.
(SLSA, Minlaton Collection, B472082)

Mudge may well have lost his licence to perform marriage ceremonies because, after April 1884, there are no further reports of him as celebrant in the family notices of the Adelaide press. He continues to be named alongside Bagshaw in connection with the Orange Order into the late 1880s.

During the anniversary tea the vice-chairman gave a toast to:

> The Parliament of South Australia remarking that there was one Orangeman in the House of Assembly. In consequence of the unavoidable absence of Mr Cowan MP, Mr Spinks responded to the toast. In doing so he said that although there was only one Orangeman at present at the House of Assembly he knew of four other members who he believed would be numbered amongst them within the next twelve months.[19]

Thomas Cowan, MP, was born in County Tyrone, Ireland, in 1839, and was the first son of Belfast-born John Cowan, a wheelwright, farmer, storekeeper, publican and resident of Two Wells. Thomas came to Adelaide with his parents, John and Margaret, on the *Epaminondas* in 1852 along with his sisters, Sarah Anne and Mary Jane, and brothers, John and James. He appears to be the only named Orangeman to have had any connection with Ireland. Reported as absent from the anniversary meeting, there are no further reports of Thomas Cowan in connection with the Orange Order. Neither is there any press coverage of the four parliamentarians Mr Spinks considered prospective Orangemen.

Little is to be found of the other Grand Lodge officers. Newell may well be one of 30 gentlemen by that surname listed in the resources.[20] A 'Brother Newell' is listed as foreman of committee in Balaklava Loyal Orange Lodge No. 56 in 1911. A John Potter appears on the electoral lists, which may connect Newell and Lugg, but there is no way of further identifying this individual in order to determine which of the resource entries he may be. Aside from the 1875 article there is no mention of Mr Spinks in the colonial press.

Some of Adelaide's first publicly named Orangemen were the epitome of respectability, but others appear to have been slightly maverick and less conventional. Some occupied offices in other societies, supporting Sweetman and Fitzpatrick's assertion that the Orange Order, along with Freemasonry, fulfilled a fraternal need and an escape from the mundane with their secrecy, ritual and mystery.[21] These individuals appear to have been politically aware and active as demonstrated by their support of candidates and participation in municipal and state elections. They were also active in the colony's business and religious life. The scandal attached to the Lugg and Mudge affairs may well have discouraged public engagement by respectable colonists with LOISA, a fact that hindered its growth at a time when Irish nationalists in the colony were attracting significant non-Irish support to their cause.

In 1903 Grand Master James Johns revealed that LOISA was organising a number of new lodges:

> The order is progressing by leaps and bounds. When I took office four years ago the membership totalled 379; today we muster about 2,000 active members, and many new lodges have been opened.[22]

Johns's evidence offers some explanation for the lack of an Orange voice in the colony in the last quarter of the 19th century. But despite a large and well-dispersed organisational network of an eventual total of 36 lodges, the Order continued to do little to oppose later delegations or hamper colonial support for the Irish nationalist movement, which had, by this time, a well-established support base.

In South Australia, Orange activity concerned itself primarily with religious and not political issues in the wider sense. Although there was localised concern about Catholic dominance of the civil service, and the organisational power of that Church when it came to elections in the colony, there were few demonstrations of a deep concern regarding Home Rule by South Australian Orangemen. The only protest given at the time of the Redmonds' visit in 1883 was a lecture delivered by a young man on a pleasure tour of the colonies. Mr E. Riley claimed to be both an Irishman and a Catholic, but doubts were expressed as to the former given the lack of a traceable Irish accent. The resolution of Riley's meeting was not to denounce colonial Irishmen or even condemn the formation of the Irish National League in South Australia, but 'to record its want of confidence in the proposed National Land League, and withhold its countenance and support from that organization until its objects are more clearly defined, and some guarantee is given that the money collected will be applied to the furtherance of some legitimate object'.[23] The meeting, held the same day the Redmonds departed town, attracted about 300 people but 'excepting the presence of two members of the Adelaide Club and the Chairman (G.W. Cotton, MLC), Mr Riley had not any support on the platform'.[24] There was no mention of the Orange Order as an opponent.

David Fitzpatrick asserts that the Order existed in South Australia as a fraternal and social organisation rather than one concerned with Ireland's, and particularly Ulster's, continued relationship with England.[25] Irish nationalist fundraising was hugely successful but there was no corresponding structured anti-Home Rule movement dedicated to hosting Irish unionists or raising money for the Ulster loyalists. Sydney MP Francis Abigail appeared to be a lone voice when, in June 1890, he called for an Irish Unionist delegation to visit Australia as a counter action to the Dillon delegation, not having the support of Orange leaders in Ulster and no echo in Adelaide.[26] The Protestant Defence Association was interested in the bogey effect of Home Rule as Rome Rule. The Orange Order as an organisation devoted no time or energy to protesting the delegations of Irish nationalists, although individual Orangemen wrote to the press denouncing the Home Rulers and their local Irish and non-Irish supporters. There are no public records of donations being made to the Ulster Volunteer Force, which pledged to fight Home Rule, apart from the small sums mentioned in the minutes of Lodge No. 7 detailed below. And yet, this could not have been due to pecuniary difficulties as some Orangemen could lend their own lodges substantial amounts for various reasons.[27] The variation in economic status among Orangemen is indicated by the fact that while some had substantial reserves, many members were struck off the books for non-payment of dues, others were placed on 'Grand Lodge dues only' because of financial hardship, and more still had money donated *to* them. In stark contrast to some brethren's generosity to their own lodges, and to the generosity of South Australians to the various Irish appeals, the only reference to a donation by a local lodge in the minute books available refers to the sum of 4d which was donated from lodge funds to make up to £2.2.0 the members' voluntary donation to the anti-Home Rule forces in July 1914.[28] The amount given to the Ulster Defence Fund, a force setting itself up to fight both Irish nationalism and the British parliament, appears all the more paltry when one considers that it represents merely twice what most lodges contributed to a down-at-heel brother.

Given that lodge records report little concern over the advancement of Home Rule, one might assume that the members were removed from events in Ireland. While most meetings record the presence of intra- and interstate brethren, there are only a few reports of international visitors. In 1903, the year of Johns's claims of increased membership, Orangemen from interstate, America and Ireland were noted as being present at the reopening of the Sir Colin Campbell lodge in Hindmarsh. In this year also, the North Adelaide lodge, William Johnston, reopened, and the South Australian Protestant Defence Association was formed at a meeting in the Tivoli Theatre on the motion of Rev. Dill Macky of Sydney.[29] At a 1910 meeting the worshipful master of Loyal Orange Lodge No. 7 welcomed Brother Currie from Tasmania and Brother Tasker of 'Belfast in Ireland'.[30] The differences in support of and interest in events in Ireland between the Orange and Green Irish in South Australia were great.

While the 'Irish Question' certainly caused verbal clashes, there were few instances of physical or mass confrontation around Irish issues in South Australia. A public meeting held on Wakefield St in June 1887 against Salisbury's Irish Crimes Bill led by MPs Solomon, Glynn, Nash, and Cohen attracted almost 600 people, but passed peacefully.[31] An anti-Home

Rule meeting was held in Adelaide in April 1906, but the lectures of the ex-priest Slattery and his wife, the 'Escaped Nun', occasioned the only incidence of a sectarian riot recorded in Adelaide up to 1900, and one of the first quasi-official appearances by the Orange Order. In June 1900, the Slatterys ran a series of public lectures on Catholicism. Orange support of the controversial lectures can be seen both by the presence of leading Orangemen on the Slattery platform and through a letter condemning an upsurge of 'larrikinism' in the city and rule by a 'mob ... composed of a single nationality' signed by 'Orange'.[32] One can safely infer that the Irish were the nationality referred to if similar occurrences interstate are taken account of: in Kalgoorlie the Slattery lecture was disrupted by 'hurleyites' and in Brisbane, Slattery himself named the Irish as the unruly crowd outside the hall.[33] The *Barrier Miner* reported the Adelaide events stating that 'there was a large attendance, among whom were a number of Orangemen, who were avowedly present to help in keeping order'.[34]

The incident was quite a spectacular one for Adelaide. A crowd of 3000 people gathered in the narrow thoroughfare of Gawler Place in the city centre to view events at Victoria Hall where the Slatterys were to appear. Adelaide's entire police force was called into attendance after the invasion of the hall on the first night of the lecture series, which resulted in the cancellation of the advertised address. The sensationalism of the occasion may be concluded from the fact that 11 magistrates sat to hear the case against two citizens on a charge of riotous behaviour.[35] Both cases were dismissed but the proceedings drew spectacular public attention with over 200 people cramming into the 'public freezing chamber' as the *Register* described the City Police Court.[36]

Reports of the lectures, letters from the public and the coverage of the court proceedings show that the Slattery affair was a major topic of public conversation at the time. While it was not about Home Rule, it involved the Irish since they formed a significant portion of the Catholic community that was the subject of the Slattery attack. The greatest danger the episode presented was its potential to affect colonial perception of the Irish at a time when the Home Rule movement in Ireland was unstable. Some letters, though not outspokenly supportive of the Slatterys, objected to the ruination of Adelaide's reputation as a fair place where freedom of speech was respected. The majority of letters to the press condemned the lecturers for calumniating the priest and nuns from whom a great portion of the community had received an education.[37] Others argued that the lectures had awakened sectarianism and caused sentiments of bigotry to be aired in the city such as had never before been witnessed. The Slattery incident caused sectarian feeling to manifest in Adelaide, and although the Irish were identified as the main stakeholders in the protest, the real division shown was that between Catholic and Protestant, with less regard for the nationalities involved. The next non-nationalist demonstration in Adelaide to be concerned with the Irish Question, at least on the surface, occurred six years later.

Adelaide's anti-Home Rule demonstration
In 1905 the Commonwealth parliament passed a resolution in favour of Irish Home Rule. In doing so it imitated the actions of the Canadian parliament which, between 1886 and 1903, issued no less than four resolutions supporting modified self-government for Ireland.[38] Through savvy political manoeuvring, Hugh Mahon, the member for Coolgardie, former Land Leaguer and one of the organisers of the 1883 IPP mission, managed to guide a Home Rule resolution through 12 hours of parliamentary debate although private bills were only allotted two hours discussion time. The motion had been sponsored by Henry Bourne Higgins, a Belfast-born Protestant, who had already proven himself a true friend of the movement having been one of the few prominent men to stand on a platform with the Redmonds in 1883 when they were unpopular in the eyes of the electorate. Reaction to the resolution was fierce – by July 1906 over 75,000 signatures had been collected on the counter address. In general, the resolution was opposed because the Australian parliament had dared interfere in what was seen by some as a domestic affair of Britain's. The fact that the resolution concerned Irish Home Rule was not the central matter. Higgins described the Orange anti-Home Rule petition meeting in Melbourne as a 'ticket mutiny' in a letter to John Redmond; 'every precaution was raised that there should be no dissenting voice'. It was 'noteworthy that they lay stress on interference in imperial matters rather than in the point that it is not expedient to grant Ireland Home Rule – have had definite reports of children signing and tricks in getting signatures from adults'.[39]

South Australian participation in the anti-Home Rule protest took the form of a town hall meeting on 10 April 1906 led by Victorian Orangemen.[40] The 'large and enthusiastic attendance' included W.H. Wilks, MHR, from the Loyal Orange Institution of Victoria, who along with Grand Master O.B. Snowball had initiated the counter-resolution that aimed to gather signatures on an address to the King condemning the actions of the federal parliament. Also in attendance were Dr Barlow (vice-chancellor of the university), Rev. Henry Gainsford, A.J. Clarke, A.T. Magarey and W.A. Magarey. It was clear that a portion of the audience, albeit small, were supporters of Home Rule judging from the interjections made against claims that Home Rule meant separation from England. When Wilks asked, 'Was an army of Home Rulers in Australia desirable?' there were cried of 'Yes' and 'No'. When he said, 'Another point to be remembered was that a third of the population of Ireland did not want Home Rule', a voice replied, 'Your sort'. Wilks moved that the meeting protest against the 'action of the Federal Legislature in passing a resolution in favour of granting Home Rule to Ireland and wishes to place upon public record its disapproval of the resolution as being outside the scope of Federal politics'. This was seconded by Gainsford, chaplain of the Order, who 'ventured to say the federal parliament had not Australia behind it when it passed the resolution in favour of Home Rule. Ireland today was a seething centre of sedition and rebellion'. The mayor requested that such a sentiment not be expressed as it 'was not fair to Ireland', and Gainsford acquiesced although 'he had not said a word that was not absolute fact' and resumed his seat to prolonged cheers. The motion was carried with six dissentients who were probably the interjectors. When A.T. Magarey proposed that the work of obtaining signatures for the address to the King be carried out energetically throughout South Australia, his motion was seconded by Brother J.M. Lambert, worshipful master of Duke of York Loyal Orange Lodge No. 7.

The groundwork for Magarey's proposal had, in fact, already been laid. In February, a committee had been formed to distribute the petition, consisting of Sir John Downer, MLC, Rev. A.J. Clarke, Dr W. Barlow, C.H. Angas and a number of Orangemen. In July the *Register* reported that over 20,000 signatures had been obtained in South Australia.[41] Jeff Kildea states that when Wilks's petition was presented to the governor-general in July 1906 it contained 75,832 signatures.[42] As the Adelaide meeting took place in April most South Australians must have signed the petition started by the Victorian Orangemen and not the one initiated in Sydney on Empire Day, 24 May 1906, which contained 35,900 signatures and was presented in March 1907. Patrick O'Farrell claimed that:

> the pressures to be Irish did not come only from the Irish delegates ... Their visits provoked loyalist counter-demonstrations ... provided a recurring stimulus and focal point for anti-Home Rule and anti-Irish Catholic forces. Each delegation had the effect of reviving moribund Irish Unionism and Orange energies within Australia and of providing them with the materials and occasions necessary for them to sustain their sense of outrage and the vigour of their attack ...

Yet it was the actions of the Australian parliament that prompted the most vigorous anti-Home Rule demonstration in South Australia.[43]

Few political figures are recognisable as supporters or members of the Orange Order. At a meeting in 1906 the grand master himself admitted that few public men would stand on an Orange platform:

> The Orange Institution was not so fortunate in South Australia as in some of the States of getting public men to be present on the platform at its gatherings, the reason being that public men were afraid of the influence of the Roman Catholic vote. There were ministers of the Gospel in South Australia who feared to be seen on the platform.[44]

Adelaide, then, sits in striking contrast with the position of the Orange Order in Canada, for example, where, 'by the 1880s, over a fifth of state parliamentarians were brethren of the Orange Order'.[45]

Conclusion

The appearance of the Orange Order in South Australia in the 1870s was not welcomed by the majority of colonists. Though it experienced significant growth in the early 1900s, the Order never channelled its energies into anti-Home Rule activity. Numerous occasions that could have been used to publicise the cause of their fellow brethren in Ulster were not availed of even when Irish nationalism was not fashionable. The Order demonstrated a higher concern with religious matters than with political ones. While it bemoaned the electoral organisation and reach of Catholics in the civil service, it did little to contest them other than exhort its members to be true to Protestantism and do their best to further membership of the order among fellow Protestants. The Order, viewed as having introduced sectarianism into an argument widely considered in the colonies to be one about democracy and freedom of colonial attachment to the Empire, only became popular in South Australia in the early years of the 20th century. By this time, it had shown itself either incapable or unwilling to engage in an anti-Home Rule movement and was largely seen to be a fraternal organisation, with developing ladies' lodges and juvenile branches. By the time the Orange Order had gained a credible membership in the state, support of Irish nationalism was well entrenched there.

Cultural capital and Irish place names

DYMPHNA LONERGAN

'When you emigrate, you fracture your belonging to the language of your homeland.'[1]

If we think of place names as being part of a homeland's language, we can imagine the importance of homeland place names in a new setting. The state of South Australia began as a colony, grew into a province, and under Federation became a state. Before all that, it was the home of Indigenous people who named its geographical features and places; for example, the Kaurna people called the flat Adelaide plains Tandanya.

Although the 1836 British 'Letters Patent' for South Australia said that the 'Natives' and their descendants must still be able to enjoy and occupy the land,[2] one of the first occupying acts of the South Australian colonists was to rename places and geographical features and to paper over Indigenous names that reflected local history and culture. Although some Indigenous names were kept, many of these were to change over time; for example, the 1843 place name Curry-kalina[3] was written as Curracalinga in 1860,[4] in 1866 as Carracalunga,[5] and is now spelt Carrickalinga. In this name change alone we can see Irish or Scottish settler influence (carrick=*carrig* Irish and Scots Gaelic word for 'a rock'; also note the Northern Ireland town Carrickalina). We must acknowledge, then, that every Irish place name discussed here has replaced an Indigenous one, and that the Irish stories below are being told at the expense of Indigenous stories. We wish it had been otherwise.

> We may select that quality of land in the best situation, call it Loughrea, and there might be a handsome lake, too, attached to it, and thus these settlers

might fancy themselves still in their old Loughrea with their associations and friends about them.⁶

Nearly a hundred years after Robert Torrens promoted the name Loughrea to Irish landlords, Irish place names in Australia were seen to be a panacea for the pain of exile in Australia, exemplified in the chorus of a popular mid-20th-century song, 'If We Only Had Old Ireland Over Here' whose first verse is:

> If the Blarney stone stood out on Sydney Harbour / If Dublin town to Melbourne came to stay / If the Shannon river joined the Brisbane waters / And Killarney's lakes flowed into Botany Bay / If the Shandon Bells rang out in Old Fremantle / And County Cork in Adelaide did appear / Erin's sons would never roam; all the boys would stay at home / If we only had old Ireland over here.

While the song imagines a utopian transfer of Irish towns to Australia, naming a place after your home town might go some way to minimising the felt distance between home and a new home. Names as items of a moving culture are often visible in house names. South Australia's colonial elite included the O'Halloran brothers, Thomas and William, whose houses were named after words on their family crest. Edward Burton Gleeson named his house in South Australia Inchiquin in memory of his home town in Ireland. Charles Harvey Bagot's house in North Adelaide was named Nurney House after his family estate in Kildare.

While anyone can name a private house, not everyone can name a public place. Public place naming is very much controlled. In Australia today, local government and state government committees oversee the naming of places and public buildings. There are guidelines for these committees to follow that reflect a variety of interests such as heritage, history, and Indigenous culture and language.

Irish place names in Australia have many stories to tell about Irish Australian history and heritage. In the new settlement of South Australia in the 19th century, an opportunity was afforded some Irish migrants to leave their mark in a visible and permanent way. As mentioned, Charles Bagot moved his family estate name to Australia, but he had even more to offer. His family coat of arms became the coat of arms for the Kapunda council.

This grant was agreed to by the Bagot family who remained in Ireland, and it was recorded in the Irish Heraldry Register. The new Kapunda council added mining symbols to the crest to represent its South Australian provenance, and retained the Bagot motto *Antiquum Obtines*, 'In the best tradition'.[7]

Beyond their role as geographical markers or as part of local history, place names may carry with them significant cultural and social capital. French theorist Pierre Bourdieu[8] proposed that these kinds of capital lead to advantage: at graduation, for example, an individual recognised by an institution acquires the cultural capital of a university degree. A university degree may, in turn, lead to economic capital in terms of a better paid job. Some Irish place names in Australia show evidence of Bourdieu's theory of capital. An example is South Australia's Clare district, which has been twinned with County Clare in Ireland for over 30 years with Irish and Australian delegations making reciprocal visits. As a result of the increased social networking, the individuals involved in the twinning of Clare have increased their social capital. Delegates are selected by local government to represent their area in Ireland. The idea of town twinning includes a desire to maximise the economic potential in such an arrangement and so the economic capital of having a place named Clare in South Australia is assured. South Australia, however, has a range of other Irish-related place names with unexplored cultural capital. Developing the cultural capital of South Australian names with an Irish connection may reveal opportunities for acquiring further economic capital. It would be a sound investment, especially given that Irish ancestry was the third highest reported ancestry nationally in the 2016 Australian census.

Historically, the term 'Irish' has not been a term associated with wealth, and other Irish related place names in South Australia are not always connected to an Irish person. Sometimes an Irish place name has stand-alone cultural value. Dublin is one such name. In 1840, the *Register* reported that the map showing the allotments for a proposed village of Dublin was on display at the Emu Inn, Morphett Vale.[9] While local history shows a small Irish community in this area in the 19th century, the place name did not eventuate at that time. In 1876, however, the name Dublin appeared in the Hundred of Dublin: named for the Irish and Dublin-born Governor MacDonnell. Before that, Dublin town, north of Gawler, was settled in the

1870s. The founding of Dublin town in South Australia was not prompted by the existence of a local Irish or Catholic community. Nevertheless, the name is linked nominally with Ireland, and individuals and communities occasionally exploit the connection: in 1970, the South Australian Dublin Progress Association invited Richard O'Brien, the Irish ambassador, to open its centennial celebrations.[10]

Certainly, there was little economic, social, or cultural capital to be gained by the recognition of Irish origin in 19th-century Adelaide. The term 'Irish' often had different connotations then, judging by the name Irishtown being applied unofficially to a section of North Adelaide.[11] Australia-wide there are many places with 'Irish' in their title, some official and some unofficial. While we may guess at the origin of some of these as places where the Irish congregated in discernible numbers for a short time, as with the goldfield era, the perpetuation of these terms must give us pause. Who names a place Irishtown? Irishtown, as a place name that marginalised the Irish, began in 12th-century Ireland when the English expelled Irish rebels from the walled town of Waterford as punishment for their opposition to the English invasion.[12] The rebels' new home was on low-lying and marshy ground and was known as Irishtown. Later, New Ross, Wexford, also had a designated Irishtown that was physically separate from the main town. Overall, around nine Irishtowns were named in Norman- and English-controlled Ireland in the 12th and 13th centuries. North Adelaide was designed by Colonel Light as part of his plan for the city of Adelaide. The south-east corner of North Adelaide village was designated as a business section. South of this is Lower North East Adelaide, which was developed as housing for labourers and their families under the Wakefield plan: a tiered city would comprise a ruling class, merchant class, and a labouring class. Land prices were kept high to make sure that the labouring classes remained so, for the good of the fledgling colony. From the very beginning, this social divide manifested itself in the big houses of North Adelaide that contrasted with the small cottages in Irishtown. The earliest mention of North Adelaide's 'Irish Town' appears to be in the *South Australian Register*, when on 10 March 1849 there was a skit about a fictional meeting between Irish-born Richard Torrens, collector of customs, and Mr Cassell of London, who had been sent to Adelaide to investigate alleged impropriety.[13] The skit has Torrens offering

Cassell hospitality in 'Irish Town' in return for a favourable report. The next recorded example is in the Destitute Asylum register in 1855. While Irish migrants had arrived from the first years of settlement, the 1840s saw significant numbers through assisted immigration. In 1849, the *Inconstant* brought hundreds of Irish female famine orphans. Although the Irish were not proportionally numerous in Adelaide, they were sometimes present in sufficient numbers so as to attract attention. When the name Irishtown was first recorded in Adelaide, the Irish population had increased substantially: 15,447 Irish arrived in the decade 1848 to 1858.[14] We do not know whether a concentration of Irish in Irishtown, North Adelaide, led to the place name or whether the name evolved from a need to distinguish those North Adelaide residents who owned big houses from those labourers who occupied the cottages. However, the 1850s and the gold rushes brought great changes. With newfound wealth, servants could become masters, and many did. In turn, they built the type of homes previously unavailable to them. These changes heralded an end to the building of the big house in North Adelaide and eventually[15] an end to the place name Irishtown.

South Australia has many Irish place names, some that have passed out of living memory such as Irish Row, and others that are still used on a daily basis such as the suburbs of Erindale and O'Halloran Hill. These names are listed below. Many of the place names discussed here appear in *The Manning Index of South Australian History* (2002), an initiative of Geoffrey Manning now available online courtesy of the State Library of South Australia. These names are indicated with an asterisk. The Irish place names list that follows provides geographical information (the hundred) and, where relevant, the spelling and explanation for the original Irish place name. Extra information such as a comment on the Irish-language basis to a name is also provided. Where possible, the date of official naming is included; however, it is worth noting that a place name may have been in use for many years before it was named officially, and some places were never named officially. Incorporated are homesteads in South Australia that have Irish language names. These can be found using the interactive map Mapcarta.com.

Rodney Cockburn's *What's in a Name?* (1908) is another key source for place names in South Australia, as are almanacks, local histories and newspapers. The aim of this collection is to highlight the importance of

Irish place names to Irish settlers, and to recognise the contribution made to South Australian settlement by the Irish, whether rich or not so rich, and regardless of religious allegiance. Expanded explanations for many of the place names below can be found in the Flinders University work-in-progress database: http://irishplaces.flinders.edu.au.

A

*Adare (1925) Hundred of Goolwa

The name Adare is associated with the pastoral pioneer family, the Cudmores, from Limerick. Adare House in Victor Harbor is now a conference centre. The name Adare is the anglicised form of Irish *Áth Dara*, 'ford of the oak grove'. Manning gives 1889 as the founding year.

Anderson's Creek

This creek in Morphett Vale no longer has this as its official name. It was named in *Balliere's South Australian Gazetteer and Road Guide* (1866) as honouring 'a gentleman named Anderson'. It is likely that this is Alexander Anderson, mentioned in chapter one.

*Armagh (1859); **Armagh North; Armagh South; Armagh Creek** Hundred of Clare

North-west of the town of Clare in South Australia is the beautiful Valley of Armagh. The South Australian Armagh was named by either Patrick Butler (Wicklow), E.B. Gleeson (Clare, Ireland), or William Henry Clark. Armagh in Irish is *Árd Mhaca*, 'Macha's Height', named after Macha, an Irish queen.

*Arno Vale Hundred of Gawler

Manning states that John Reid may have named this place after a spot in Ireland. (See also **Clonlea**.)

*Auburn (1841) Hundred of Upper Wakefield

Seven miles from Athlone, Ireland, is Lissoy, Westmeath, where the poet Oliver Goldsmith grew up. It took on the name Auburn after the place was immortalised in Goldsmith's 'The Deserted Village' (1770). Oliver Goldsmith was Roscommon-born and raised.

B

Bagot (1860) Hundred of Bagot

Bagot's Gap; Bagot's Head Station; Bagot Range; Bagot's Well (1855) Hundred of Belvidere

Captain Bagot, an Irish emigration agent for Clare, was born and raised in County Kildare. He arrived in 1840 on the *Birman* with hundreds of immigrants mostly from County Clare.

*Baker's Flat Hundred of Kapunda

This flat piece of ground next to the Kapunda mine was occupied for over 70 years by hundreds of Irish squatters who defied many attempts to evict them. Today there is little to see of this once vibrant settlement, but a replica thatched 'Irish' cottage may be seen in the Bagot's Mine museum in Kapunda.

Balla Mckenny (1876) Hundred of Colton

County Clare-born Michael Kenny arrived in Adelaide in 1842. The Kennys ended up in Colton on a wheat and sheep property they named Balla Mckenny (Ir. *baile*, 'home'). They exported wheat from Port Kenny.

Ballnahinch House (homestead)

Ballnahinch is Irish, *Baile na hInse*, 'homestead of the island'. The place name is found in counties Down, Galway, Tipperary and Wicklow.

Ballard Road; Ballards Corner Hundred of Gilbert

Ballards Corner was never an official name but marked the spot of the Ballard family in Riverton. William Ballard of Tipperary arrived in 1851, married Catherine Lynch (Cavan), and they had 14 children. The name Ballard is of Norman origin.

Bandon (1898) Hundred of Bandon

This hundred was named for the County Cork Irish town by Governor Buxton in honour of Sir George Strickland Kingston who arrived aged 29 as deputy surveyor to Colonel Light. The Irish town Bandon is named after the river Bann, which in turn is named after the Celtic goddess, and possibly *bean*, the Irish word for 'woman'.

Bates (railway station) Hundred of Ooldea
Daisy Bates is known for her work with Indigenous people in Western and South Australia. She migrated to Australia in 1884. Daisy Bates was born Margaret Dwyer in Roscrea, County Tipperary, in 1859, and named after her godmother. She is buried in the Anglican cemetery in Walkerville. Her gravestone is inscribed with the word *Kabbarli*, the Indigenous name for 'grandmother'.

Behanville Hundred of Adelaide
Once part of Port Adelaide, it was named by Philip and Honora Mary (Behan) Brady. Philip (Cavan) arrived on the *Northumberland* in 1864 as a labourer. He married Honora Mary Behan from Clare in 1878.

Brady Hill Hundred of Pandie
Brady Hill is named after Cavan-born Thomas Brady, who discovered gold at Teetulpa.

C

Cabra (1909) Hundred of Adelaide
Now part of Cumberland Park, Cabra was named for the Dominican nuns who arrived in 1868 and whose headquarters are in Cabra, Dublin. The name *cabrach* in Irish means 'poor land'.

Cape Torrens (1857) Hundred of Kingscote
The cape is named for Robert Richard Torrens of County Cork, who invented the Torrens Title system of land transfer.

Carey Gully (1865) Hundred of Onkaparinga
According to the South Australian online gazetteer, Carey Gully was named by 'Young' in 1849 after a Patrick Carey.

Cash Hill Hundred of Rounsevell
Thomas Patrick Cash's mother was Mary Cash of Kerry who came with her parents on the *Mary Dugdale*. (See also O'Sullivan Beach.) His father was Patrick Cash from Wexford.

Catherine Hundred of Noarlunga
This is now a subdivision of Morphett Vale. In 1855, it included the Emu Inn licensed by Alexander Anderson from Northern Ireland. His wife's name was Catherine.

Cavan (1855) Hundred of Yatala
This area is named after the Cavan Arms hotel whose first licensee was Bernard Gillick from Cavan, Ireland, who arrived in 1850 on the *Joseph Somes*. The Irish place name *An Cabhán* means a hollow surrounded by a round grassy hill.

Cavandale (homestead) Hundred of Stanley
Patrick Dowd came from Cavan in 1857. He served on the council of Hanson and was a justice of the peace.

Clanfergil/Clan Feargal Hundred of Adelaide
The name of the house, Clanfergil, was taken from the O'Halloran family crest. It means 'Fergal's family'.

*****Clare** Hundred of Clare
Edward Burton Gleeson settled in Clare circa 1842. He arrived from Calcutta on the *Emerald Isle* with his wife, Harriet, their children and his brother Hampton Carroll and family. Clare in Irish comes from *clár*, 'a level place'.

Claredale Farm (near Auburn)
Patrick McNamara arrived from County Clare in 1846 on the *Hooghly* and farmed on the Wakefield. He served on the Upper Wakefield council and was a justice of the peace.

*****Claremont** Hundred of Adelaide
Daniel Cudmore from Limerick named this property in Glen Osmond in 1862. It was never an official name. (See also Adare and Cudmore Hill.)

Claremont (Manoora homestead)
Michael Buckley from Clare arrived on the *Coromandel* in 1855. He worked as a bullock teamster to the Burra mines at first. He died in 1931.

Clarke Hill Hundred of Encounter Bay
Clarke Hill was named by John Clarke from Killarney who arrived in 1836 on the *Tam O'Shanter*. His house Wattleville is still standing.

Clonagh (homestead)
There are towns named Clonagh in Kildare, Laois, Offaly, Limerick and Westmeath. The name comes from Ir. *cluain* 'a meadow' and *each* 'a horse'.

Clonlea (1839) Hundred of Mudla Wirra
John Reid and his family were the first settlers in Gawler in 1839 and named their property Clonlea after a family property in Newry, County Down. The Irish *Cluain Lao*, 'meadow of the calves', is the origin of Clonlea.

Coglin Creek (1815–1892) Hundred of Apoinga
Coglin Hundred of Coglin
Patrick Boyce (Paddy or P.B.) Coglin from Ballymote, County Sligo arrived in 1836 on the *Lady Liverpool*. He was a timber merchant, a pastoralist, a publican, a town mayor and a member of the South Australian parliament.

Coolangatta (homestead)
This may be named after the townland in Kerry. The name is Irish *Cúl an Geata*, 'back of the gate'. The Queensland Coolangatta is apparently named either for a schooner that was wrecked there or for an Indigenous word.

Connemara (homestead)
Connemara is the heart of Gaelic Ireland. The Irish name is *Cuain na Mara*, 'harbours of the sea'.

Cork Hill Hundred of Jellicoe
This is most likely named for Cork city or the County of Cork. The name comes from Ir. *corcaigh*, 'marsh'.

Cross Keys (1849) Hundred of Yatala
Daniel Brady from Cross Keys, County Cavan, Ireland, was the first licensee in the area. The 'keys' in the place name is for a keystone or cornerstone.

Cudmore Hill Hundred of Woolundunga
Cudmore Park Hundred of Adelaide
The Cudmores, Daniel and Mary (Nihill), arrived in Adelaide from Hobart in 1837 having emigrated from Tory Hill, County Limerick. Daniel Cudmore started out as a schoolmaster, built pisé houses, founded breweries and, with money from an inheritance, took up pastoral leases in South Australia, Queensland and New South Wales. (See also Adare and Claremont.)

Curraghmore (homestead)
This name means 'great marsh'. There are Curraghmores all over Ireland.

D

Dalkey (1856); **Dalkey Hill** (1866) Hundred of Dalkey
Dublin-born Governor MacDonnell named this hundred after the wealthy Dublin seaside suburb. A school, post office, and a mine are also named for Dalkey. The Irish name is *Deilginis*, and this matches the meaning of the English/Viking Dalkey, 'thorn island'.

*Daly County (1862) Hundred of Kadina
Daly Head Hundred of Carribie
Daly Waters (1861) Northern Territory
These places were named after Governor Sir Dominick Daly from County Galway, South Australia's first Catholic governor.

Derry Bore Hundred of Copley
This may be named for the city or county of Derry. The word *doire* means 'oakwood'.

Derrymore (homestead) Hundred of Grey
The name means 'big oak wood' and typically there are Derrymores all over Ireland.

*Dismal Swamp (1851) Hundred of Young
Anthony Sutton of County Wicklow named this place near Tarpeena. He arrived from Victoria in 1845 and died in Mount Gambier in 1879. The name Dismal Swamp also occurs in Tasmania and Victoria.

Donnybrook (1855) Hundred of Clare
Donnybrook Hundred of Talia
Donnybrook (homestead) Hundred of Encounter Bay
Donnybrook Hundred of Encounter Bay
Donnybrook is a suburb of Dublin. The name was given to this section of Clare, South Australia, by William Paxton. The name is from the Irish *Domhnach Broc*, 'church of Saint Broc'.

Dublin (1876) Hundred of Dublin
Hundred of Dublin
In 1840 plans for a 'Dublin' were on view at the Emu Hotel in Morphett Vale, but that place name did not eventuate as an official name. In 1846, a place named 'little Dublin' was recorded on the outskirts of Mount Barker. The

town of Dublin near Mallala north of Adelaide is named after Governor MacDonnell. The name is made up of Irish *dubh*, 'black', and *linn*, 'pool', although the Irish name for Dublin city is *Baile Átha Cliath* 'the town of the ford of the hurdles'.

Dunluce Estate Hundred of Noarlunga
Now part of the suburb of Brighton, Dunluce Estate was named by Alex and Will McCully after the place name near the Giant's Causeway in County Antrim. The Irish *Dún Libhse* means 'palace'.

Dunmore (homesteads) Hundred of McNamara; Hundred of Dublin
A *dún mór* is a 'big fort' and naturally there are many places in Ireland named after these defensive structures.

E

Eastview Hundred of Adelaide
This section (868) Hundred of Adelaide was named by the Doolette family. In 1855 George Doolette, his wife Eliza and son George emigrated from Dublin to South Australia aboard the *Nashwauk* that foundered off Moana.

Egan Hut Hundred of Nangwarry
Laurence Egan from Clare arrived in 1849 and purchased Tarpeena Station in 1861. He contributed greatly to the development of that town by opening a blacksmith's shop, hotel and store. The name in Irish is *Mac Aodhagáin*, 'son of Egan'.

Ennis (1871); **Ennis Park** Hundred of Stanley
Ennis Hill (1851) Mount Lofty Ranges
Thomas John and Michael Cunneen from Clare, Ireland named Ennis after their home town. The name is from *Inis*, the word for an island. The Irish town is on the river Fergus that has a number of islands.

Ennisfree (homestead) Hundred of Barunga
This is likely a coined name evocative of the Inishfree made famous by W.B. Yeats and the County Clare town Ennis. Both Inish and Ennis derive from Irish *inis*, 'island'. The 'free' is Irish *fraoi*, the word for 'heather'.

Enniskillen Lodge (homestead) Hundred of Clare
A John Spratt lived in this homestead. The 1901 Irish census shows a John Spratt, farmer, aged 22 living in Enniskillen, County Fermanagh.

*Erindale Hundred of Adelaide
Erindale (homesteads) Hundred of MacDonnell; Hundred of Mobilong; Hundred of Mayura; Hundred of Mudla Wirra; Hundred of Bright; Hundred of Tungkillo
The name includes the word 'Erin', from *Éireann*, the Irish word for Ireland.

F

Farrell Flat Hundred of Hanson
Two Irishmen may have initiated the naming of this place: James Farrell was a shepherd employed in nearby Koonunga; Rodney Cockburn suggests Longford-born Reverend James Farrell who was the second colonial chaplain as being associated with the name. He bequeathed money to St Peter's College and is acknowledged in Farrell House, one of the 10 houses in the school system.

Ferns District Hundred of Hawker
This town was closed in 1901. The town Ferns in County Wexford is from the Irish word *Fearna*, 'elder trees'.

Flaherty's Corner Hundred of Maroowie
The Flaherty family lived here from 1878. Flaherty is a distinctive west Connaught name prevalent in Galway. The Irish *Ó Flaithbheartaigh* means 'bright ruler'.

G

Galway (homestead) Hundred of Encounter Bay
Galway Range (homestead) Hundred of Parsons
Galway is a popular holiday spot in Ireland for its scenery, music and Irish language culture. The Irish *Gaillimh* means 'stony' (river).

Galway Bay Hundred of Maitland
While the famous Irish Galway Bay comes to mind, from 1914 to 1920 South Australia's governor was an Englishman named Galway.

Garrymore (homestead) Hundred of Joanna
The Irish *garraí* or 'garden' was for crop growing rather than for growing flowers and vegetables. There are numerous *garraí mór*, 'big garden', place names in the country.

Gillentown Hundred of Clare
Thomas and Bridget Gillen (née McCann) arrived from Cavan, Ireland in 1855. The surname in Irish is *Ó Giolláin* (*giolla*, 'a lad'). The town is named after their son, Peter Paul, an MP who died in 1896 aged 38.

*Glandore (1882) Hundred of Adelaide
The O'Deas arrived in 1840 on the *Birman*. Glandore in Irish is *Cuan Dor*, 'Dor's harbour'.

Gleeson Creek Hundred of Copley
Gleeson's Hill (1841) Hundred of Adelaide
Gleeson Well Hundred of Blyth
This 'hill' was the name given to the start of the rise behind Gleeson's property in south-east Adelaide. (See also Clare and Gleeville.) The name in Irish is Ó Gliasáin, a leading sept in Lower Ormond.

Gleeville-under-the-hills Hundred of Adelaide
Edward Burton Gleeson from Ennis, County Clare, arrived in the province in 1838 on the *Emerald Isle* from Calcutta with his brother, John Hampton, and their families. The house succumbed to white ants, but the barn still stands on Dashwood Drive, Beaumont.

Glen Kenny (homestead ruin) Hundred of Colton
This was the name of one of the farms on Michael Kenny's selection near Colton. (See also Balla McKenny.)

Glenroe (homestead) Hundred of Macgillivray
There are red glens in Clare, Limerick, Wicklow and Tyrone.

*Glynn Hundred of Glynn
Patrick (Paddy) McMahon Glynn from Gort, County Galway, was a late arrival to South Australia in 1883. He became co-editor of the *Kapunda Herald* and a state politician, becoming attorney-general in 1899.

Gortmore (homestead) Hundred of Kilkerran
Place names for the 'big field' or *gort mór* are to be found in almost every county in Ireland, but there are gortmores in Scotland too.

H–I

Higginsbrook (homestead) Currency Creek

This property was named after Higginsbrook in County Meath, Ireland, the family home of Thomas Walker Higgins, who arrived in Adelaide in 1839. After a short time working in the post office he moved south to Currency Creek. (See also Middleton.)

Inchiquin (homestead) (c. 1843) Hundred of Clare

The land, and later big house, of E.B. Gleeson outside Clare township was named after the barony in Ireland.

Innisfail (homestead) Hundred of Bremer

This homestead is now known as East of Eden. In Ireland the name Innisfail is pronounced *inishfawl*. The historical name *Inis Fáil*, 'the island of destiny', is not a place name, however, but a mythical name for the island of Ireland.

Irish Harp Road (Regency Road) Hundred of Adelaide

Named after the Irish Harp inn whose licensee in 1844, Thomas Edward McEllister, was from Kerry. (See also Norahville.) The road is now known as Regency Road. The name Irish Harp is also preserved in the name of a Prospect reserve and one of the rooms in the council chambers.

Irish Row Hundred of Adelaide

In 1869 tenders were called for building the Adelaide Club on North Terrace on a site once known as Irish Row. We can presume that Irish Row was named for the number of residents who were Irish, perhaps passengers from the ships carrying the Irish orphans.

Irishtown Hundred of Adelaide

A section of lower north-east North Adelaide bounded by Melbourne and Stanley streets was unofficially named Irishtown from at least 1849 through to the 1870s. By the time the Sisters of St Joseph opened a school there in 1869, the name was well known enough for the Catholic Church to use it as the locality name.

K

*Kainton Hundred of Clinton
Kainton post office is named after Patrick Kain from Limerick who bought land here in 1877.

Kells Dam Hundred of Port Augusta
Kells in County Meath may be the reference here. The famous *Book of Kells* now in Trinity College Dublin is thought to have been written in a Kells monastery. The word comes from Ir. *na cealla*, 'the cells', referring to monks' cells.

Kelly Flat
Patrick Kelly from Kinnegad, County Westmeath, took up a pastoral lease here in 1851. Sponsored by Montague Fetherstonaugh, he arrived in 1848 aged 19.

Kenihans Road and the Braes Reynella Hundred of Noarlunga
Hugh Kenihan was a landowner here in the early 19th century. Most of his land is under the Happy Valley Reservoir.

*Kevin (1894) Hundred of Kevin
This hundred was named after Kevin Kingston, the adopted son of C.C. Kingston and adopted grandson of Sir George Strickland Kingston of Bandon, County Cork.

Kildare; Kildare (homestead) Hundred of Mount Gambier
Cill Dara, the church of the oak, in Ireland is historical, said to be where Saint Brigid established a nunnery that had separate houses for women and for men.

Kilkenny (1849); **Kilkenny East** (1885) Hundred of Yatala
This suburb to the west of the city may have been named after Most Reverend Dr O'Reily's birthplace. Reverend John O'Reily was Adelaide's first Catholic bishop. St Cainneach's church is the translation of *Cill Ceannaigh*.

Killanoola (homestead) Hundred of Wattle Range
This was the home of magistrate Henry Conway Seymour from Cork who arrived in 1841 on the *Siam* having worked as a barrister in Dublin and

Cork. The name may be Indigenous: *killen oorla*, 'black jay (magpie) nest', but there is a Killanully in Cork: *Cill an ealaigh*, 'the wood of the cattle'. Nomenclature practice is to favour the Indigenous name.

Killarney (homesteads) Hundred of Baker; Hundred of Killanoola; Hundred of Willaooka; Hundred of Conmurra
Killarney Park Hundred of Kanmantoo
Killarney is a popular name for a homestead in Australia. The name Killarney Park as a variant is only found in South Australia.

Killarney (1880) Hundred of Caltowie
Killarney Dam Hundred of Chowilla
Twenty-year-old James Kildea from Galway who arrived on the *Confiance* named this subdivision in Caltowie. *Cill Airne* means 'church of the sloes'. There are a number of Killarneys in Ireland; the most famous is in Kerry.

Kingston Park (1845) Hundred of Noarlunga
Kingston SE (1858) Hundred of Lacepede
Kingston on Murray (1895) Hundred of Moorook
Kingston East (1900) Hundred of Port Adelaide
Sir George Kingston arrived in 1836 on the *Cygnet* as South Australia's deputy surveyor, and later set up as an architect. He was trained as an engineer, possibly in his birthplace of County Cork, but certainly in Birmingham, England. Kingston Park is named for his wife, Lucy. Kingston on Murray is named after his son, Charles, who became premier of South Australia.

Knoxville (now part of the suburb of Glenside) Hundred of Adelaide
Nathaniel Alexander Knox named sections 272 and 273 Knoxville. He was born either in Aghclowy, Derry, or in County Antrim, and arrived aged 13 in 1850 with his father N.A. Knox Snr. Their ship, the *Grecian*, was wrecked near the Port River with the loss of one life.

L

Lake Newry and Lake Newry (homestead) Hundred of Wells
This was named by Professor D. Williams, professor of zoology at Adelaide University. *Newry* is in Irish *an tIúr*, 'the yew tree'.

Lake Torrens
This was discovered by Edward Eyre in 1839 and named after Colonel Robert Torrens.

Little Dublin Hundred of Macclesfield
Near Blakiston and Mount Barker was a small settlement of Irish people in the 19th century that was unofficially called Little Dublin. Nearby was the Dublin Castle Hotel. The name remains as Little Dublin Road.

Little Ireland
This was an unofficial name given to the Macclesfield area in the 19th century.

Lizard Lodge O'Halloran Hill
Major Thomas Shuldham O'Halloran named his house at O'Halloran Hill Lizard Lodge after the animal depicted in the O'Halloran family crest. The O'Hallorans were a Limerick family.

Lynch's Corner
Never an official name, this place east of Hawker was the home of the Lynch family. Bernard Lynch and Eileen Smith from County Cavan emigrated and settled in Mintaro in 1858 where they were married. They had 13 children.

M

MacDonnell County (1857) Hundred of Glenroy
Hundred of MacDonnell (1858)
MacDonnell Bay; Port MacDonnell Hundred of MacDonnell
Governor Sir Richard Graves MacDonnell from Dublin named all of these places. He arrived in 1855 and in his seven years as governor he was involved in the literary arts, education, the volunteer defence movement, and exploration of the northern parts of the province.

Magarey Park Hundred of Naracoorte
Thomas Magarey from County Down who arrived with his brother in 1845 owned land here in 1861. His great-nephew William Ashley Magarey was the initiator of the Magarey Medal awarded each year by the South Australian National Football League for the 'best and fairest' player.

Mahoney's Paddock Hundred of Nuriootpa
Dr David Mahoney from County Kerry settled in Gawler in the 1840s and married the daughter of John Reid. Mahoney's Paddock encompassed most of Gawler East. (See also Clonlea.)

Manning Well Hundred of Eurelia
The large Manning family from Six Mile Bridge, County Clare, Ireland, was sponsored by Alexander Anderson in 1848.

Marybank Farm (homestead)
Near Magill and Morialta, the Marybank house was bought by the Fox family in 1852 and is still in the family. Arthur Fox trained as an apothecary in Dublin and arrived in Adelaide in 1845; he set up in business at 7 Rundle Street. His daughter, Mary, married Daniel Cudmore. (See also Adare.)

McBride Dam Hundred of Curnamona
James Martin McBride from Newry, County Down, arrived in 1874 as a seaman and went on to become a pastoralist in the Mid North.

McConville Track north of Farina
Henry McConville from Belfast arrived in 1855 on the *Bucephalus*. He was an early pioneer in the Flinders Ranges, buying property and stations, and prospecting for gold.

Middleton Hundred of Goolwa
This was supposedly named by Thomas Higgins for an Irish town of the same name. His family home was in County Meath. There is a Middleton in Westmeath.

Monaghan Bore Hundred of Ororoo
Monaghan is one of the counties of Ulster and also a surname. It is from Ir. *Muineacháin*, 'place of little thickets'.

Monalena (1870s) (lagoon and homestead ruin) Hundred of Torrens
There is a Monalena in County Limerick, Ireland. It is two Irish words: *Móin*, the word for bogland, and *an lín*, which may refer to 'flax'. It was named by J.G. Moseley in the 1870s.

Moncrieff Bay Hundred of Barker
This bay is named after Alexander Moncrieff from Dublin who arrived in 1875. He became the railway engineer for the Port Augusta to Oodnadatta project, president of the Institute of Surveyors in 1901, and in 1909 engineer-in-chief for the South Australian Railways.

*Moody Hundred of Moody
This hundred is named for Derry-born David Moody MP who arrived from Victoria in 1858 and took up land at Kapunda. He was the first president of Kapunda's Liberal Union political party and served as a member of the South Australian parliament from 1878 to 1899.

Mount Bates
On the border of South Australia and Western Australia, Mount Bates is named after Daisy Bates.

Mount Benson (homestead) Hundred of Waterhouse
This was the last home of Henry Conway Seymour from Cork. (See also Killanoola.) He arrived in 1841 and died at Mount Benson on 12 December 1869.

*Mount Gunson (1875) Hundred of Torrens
North-west of Port Augusta, Mount Gunson is named after Limerick-born Dr John Michael Gunson who arrived in the *Grasmere* in 1852.

Mount Jeffcott Hundred of Myponga
Judge John Jeffcott from Tralee, County Kerry, served South Australia for less than a year but was not forgotten after his untimely death in 1837. He named three of Adelaide's Streets: Jeffcott, Kermode and O'Connell.

Mount Kingston Hundred of Warrina
This mountain was named by the explorer John McDouall Stuart in honour of George Strickland Kingston.

Mount Shanahan Hundred of Frome
John Shanahan discovered copper here in 1890.

Mount Sullivan Hundred of Gason
This mountain is named for Richard Forbes Sullivan who had lease of the Kanowna run in 1882.

Mount Torrens (1849) Hundred of Talunga
This is named after Derry-born Colonel Robert Torrens, chairman of the South Australian Commission.

Moy Farm (homestead)
In district 'C' lived Irish farmers John and Matthew Colville. There is a Moy in County Tyrone: Irish *Maigh*, 'a plain'.

N–O

Native Valley Hundred of Kanmantoo
Patrick Mullins, his wife and four children arrived in 1846 on the *Lady Bruce* along with brothers John and Michael, and named this place east of Nairne.

Navan (1856) Hundred of Gilbert
Father Francis Murphy was Adelaide's first Catholic bishop. He arrived on the *Mary White* in October 1844. He was born in Navan, County Meath, Ireland.

Neagles Rock Hundred of Clare
George Neagle from County Kerry settled in Clare with his brothers in the 1840s; this look-out point is named after him.

*Ned's Corner
Edward Meade Bagot, third son of Captain Bagot, named this run along the river Murray in 1854. He stocked his properties with horses and cattle and was considered to be an excellent judge of stock and a fine racehorse breeder. The place was named for one of his shepherds.

Newry (homesteads) Hundred of Monbulla, Hundred of Duffield
The name comes from Irish *an tIúr*, 'the yew tree'. Legend has it that St Patrick planted a yew tree at the head of Carlingford Lough and founded a monastery there. (See also Lake Newry.)

Nora Creina Bay Hundred of Lake George
This name's Irish connection is in the Thomas Moore melody 'Lesbia Hath a Beaming Eye', with the reference to 'Oh, my Nora Creina, dear / My gentle, bashful Nora Creina'. The Irish word *crionna* means 'wise'. Nora Creina Bay was named after the brig *Nora Creina*, which was wrecked near Robe in 1859.

Norahville (1880) Hundred of Port Adelaide
Thomas Edward McEllister named this section after his wife Nora(h) O'Leary.

*O'Halloran Hill (1848) Hundred of Noarlunga
The O'Hallorans of Limerick were a military family who served in the Indian army. Both Thomas and his brother William sold their commissions and emigrated to Australia. (See also Lizard Lodge.)

O'Loughlin (1890) Hundred of O'Loughlin
Cornelius O'Loughlin from Ennistymon in County Clare arrived in South Australia circa 1844. He was a carrier, farmhand, and later a successful farmer. His eldest son, Laurence, was born in Virginia and he too became a farmer, and later took up the farmers' cause as a representative in local and state politics.

O'Sullivan Beach Hundred of Noarlunga
Ignatius O'Sullivan from Kerry arrived on the *Mary Dugdale* in 1840 with his family. Stone from his property was used to build St Mary's Help of Christians Catholic Church in Morphett Vale. His daughter Mary, who was eight when they arrived, married Patrick Cash from Wexford. (See also Cash Hill.)

P–Q

Paddy (various)
A nickname often attributed to an Irishman in general or as a shortened form of Patrick, there are a number of names with Paddy in them: Macclesfield was known once as Paddystown; the hill near the Mount Barker Catholic cemetery was known as Paddy's Hill; and Paddys Bridge School was in Port Gawler. Manning's *Index* has Paddys Plain and Paddys Stack.

Phil Ma Cool Mine Hundred of Copley
This is a possible corruption of the name Finn Mac Cumhal, the mythological Irish giant and leader of the Fianna band of warriors.

Port Kenny Hundred of Wright
Michael Kenny from Six Mile Bridge in County Clare moved from Morphett Vale to the goldfields where he made his money, and then to the Venus Bay

area where, as the first European settler, he established a wheat exporting industry. Kenny was one of the first farmers to attempt to grow grain rather than raising sheep. (See also Balla McKenny.)

Port Rickaby Hundred of Koolywudle
This port on the Yorke Peninsula was named after Irishman Thomas Rickaby in 1876. Thomas Rickaby arrived in 1858 and joined the South Australian Mounted Police. He was first president of the Minlaton Agricultural show.

*Quin Rock Hundred of Kersaint
This rock off Kangaroo Island is named for Hugh Quin who arrived in 1836 on the *Cygnet,* the fifth vessel to arrive in Holdfast Bay. He became ship's pilot and later harbour master at Port Adelaide.

R–S

Rathmines (1856) Hundred of Yatala
Rathmines was an early name for what is now known as Parafield. The Irish name is *Ráth Maoinis*, 'the ringfort of de Moenes' a 14th-century family. A ringfort was a circular dwelling place sometimes surrounded by an earthen bank.

Rostrevor Hundred of Adelaide
Ross Thompson Reid from Newry, Ireland, arrived in 1839 on the *Orleana* aged six with his parents, brothers and sisters. (See also Clonlea.) Ross married Lucy Reynell at Christ Church O'Halloran Hill and became wealthy enough to buy a subdivision and build Rostrevor Hall which is now Rostrevor College. Rostrevor, Ireland, is a village about 10 miles from Newry.

Roscommon (homestead) Hundred of Curramulka, Hundred of Napperby
St Comán was an 8th-century monk. *Ros* is the name for a wood.

Roscrea (homestead); **Roscrea Hill** (homestead) Hundred of Minlacowie
Roscrea is in Tipperary. The name Roscrea is made up of *Ros*, 'a wood', and *Cré*, a name: we do not know who Cré was.

Shamrock (homestead) Hundred of Mongdata
Shamrock Mine Hundred of (O.H.) Copley
The various mines, pools and dams with the name Shamrock presumably have an Irish connection. The word shamrock is from Irish *seamróg*, the name of a trefoil plant and one of the national symbols of Ireland.

Shannon Dam Hundred of Stuart
The Shannon is Ireland's largest river. The word is an anglicised spelling of Irish *sionann* from the name of a Celtic goddess.

She-Oak Log Hundred of Nuriootpa
In 1844 it was here, north of Gawler, that Captain Bagot's plough that had been defining a road between Kapunda and Gawler broke down. Bagot improvised another plough from the forked branch of a she-oak tree and continued making his road. There has been some speculation that the Australian she-oak tree's name may have been influenced by Irish *síog*, 'a fairy' (pronounced *shee-oge*), because of the whispering sound the trees make in the breeze.

Skillogalee Creek Hundred of Upper Wakefield
The word 'skilly' or 'skillagolee' is a type of thin gruel. The origin of the word is unknown. One Irish connection with the South Australian place name Skillogalee is John Hope from Maghera, Derry, who with John Horrocks, stopped at this spot and shared a meal of 'skilly'.

Slaney Creek and Slaney Island Hundred of Chowilla
The Slaney River runs through Wicklow and Wexford.

***Sod Hut** Hundred of Kooringa
Daniel O'Leary from County Clare arrived in 1840 on the *Lysander*. He leased this spot from G.S. Kingston. O'Leary was a leather maker and he tanned the first hide in the province. He is best known for the large mill he established in Clare in 1855; it was later saved from fire because he had placed a 'holy relic' under the foundations.

***Somerton** (1856) Hundred of Noarlunga
Somerton is in the City of Holdfast Bay. It was named by James Walsh who purchased land there in 1854 and who hailed from this suburb in Dublin, Ireland.

T–W

Tara (homesteads) Hundred of Kuitpo; Hundred of Riddoch; Hundred of Tungkillo; Hundred of Joanna; Hundred of Palabie; Hundred of MacGilliviray; Hundred of Woolumbool
Mount Tara (homestead) Hundred of Myponga
The place name Tara is found in Offaly, Meath and Down, the Meath site being the traditional royal site of Irish kings. The Irish *Teamhair* means 'elevated hill' or 'assembly point', or it is named after the earth goddess Temair.

*Tarlee (1867) Hundred of Gilbert
Both Cockburn and Manning say that Tarlee is a misspelling of the name Tralee, County Kerry's largest town. In the *Northern Argus* of 7 June 1899, a report on the death of Robert McEllister misspells his ancestral home as 'Tarlee', Kerry, Ireland. The Irish name is *Trá Lí*, the strand of the Lee (though some argue it is *Trá Liath*, the grey strand).

Tipperary Dam Hundred of Chowilla
Tipperary (homestead) Hundred of Senior; Hundred of Yatala
Tipperary and Clare were the origins of the majority of 19th-century Irish migrants in South Australia. The river Ara in Ireland gave its name to the Irish place name, along with the word for a 'well', *tiobar*.

Tir-nan-og (homestead) Hundred of Jellicoe
Tír na nóg is the mythological 'land of youth' where Oisín, son of Finn Mac Cumhal, lived for 300 years. He remained young as long as he did not touch the earthly ground. Anxious to visit the land of mortals again, he rode a fairy horse, but on dismounting he forgot about the spell, and on touching the ground he was turned into an old blind man.

Torrens River (1836) Hundred of Adelaide
Torrens Island (1857) Hundred of Port Adelaide
Torrens Park Hundred of Adelaide
Torrens Vale (1860) Hundred of Yankalilla
Torrenside (1878) Hundred of Adelaide
These are named after Derry-born Colonel Torrens, chairman of the South Australian Colonisation Commission. He never visited South Australia, but did buy land here.

Torrensville
Named after Robert Richard Torrens who arrived on the *Brightman* in 1839 as collector of customs. He was treasurer in 1852 and premier for a short while in 1857.

Tullamore (homesteads) Hundred of Wannamana; Hundred of Onkaparinga
The *tulach mór*, or 'big hill', on County Offaly is where St Catherine's Church stands.

Tyrone (1899) Hundred of Pirie
James Cowan named this place after his mother's birthplace.

*Virginia (1858) Hundred of Munno Para
Daniel and Rose Brady from Cavan arrived in 1840 on the *Diadem*. They bought land north of Adelaide and named it Virginia after the place name in County Cavan that had been named for Queen Elizabeth 1.

Waterford (homesteads) Hundred of Para Wirra; Hundred of Kuitpo
Waterford is a 9th-century Viking town. The name is Norse, *Vadrefjord*.

Wexford (homestead) Hundred of Scott
This is another Viking name, from the words *esker fjord*.

Wicklow (1881) Hundred of Port Adelaide
Now incorporated under the Wingfield heading, Wicklow was one of the early small subdivisions of Port Adelaide. The Irish town is known in the Irish language as *Cill Mantáin*, 'St Mantan's Church'. *Wykynoelo* is the Viking origin of Wicklow.

*Wolta Wolta (1846) Hundred of Clare
John Hope from Maghera, Derry, gave this name to his home outside Clare. He arrived in 1839 and built Wolta Wolta in 1846. From a one-room cottage it developed into a substantial home.

Notes

Preface

1. Douglas Pike, *Paradise of Dissent: South Australia 1829–1857*, Melbourne University Press, Melbourne, 1967.
2. See J.B. Hirst, *Adelaide and the Country, 1870–1917: Their social and political relationship*. Melbourne University Press, Melbourne, 1973, pp. 42–45 for a description of life as an English country gentleman in Adelaide in the 1870s.
3. Eleanore Williams, *A Way of Life: The pastoral families of the Central Hill country of South Australia*, Adelaide University Union Press, Adelaide, 1980, p. 2.
4. Martin Shanahan, 'Personal Wealth in South Australia', *Journal of Interdisciplinary History*, vol. 32 no. 1, 2001, p. 79.
5. G.L. Fischer, 'Rounsevell, William Benjamin (1843–1923)', *Australian Dictionary of Biography*, National Centre of Biography, Australian National University, Canberra, http://adb.anu.edu.au/biography/rounsevell-william-benjamin-8281/text14511 accessed 20 October 2012.
6. David Fitzpatrick, 'Exporting Brotherhood: Orangeism in South Australia', *Immigrants & Minorities*, vol. 23, 2005, pp. 277–310.
7. Fidelma Breen, "'Yet We Are Told that Australians Do Not Sympathise with Ireland": A study of South Australian support for Irish Home Rule, 1883 to 1912', MPhil thesis, University of Adelaide, 2013, p. 45.
8. *South Australian Register (SAR)*, 30 June 1885, p. 4 and 9 July 1885, p. 4.; *Chronicle*, 12 June 1886, p. 7.
9. Stephanie James, 'Becoming South Australians?: The impact of the Irish on the County of Stanley, 1841–1871', MA thesis, Flinders University, 2009, p. 247; Paul Sendziuk and Robert Foster, *A History of South Australia*, Cambridge University Press, Cambridge, 2018, p. 42.
10. Breen, 'Yet We Are Told', p. 45.
11. T.A. Coghlan and New South Wales Statistician's Office, *A Statistical Account of the Seven Colonies of Australasia*, Charles Potter, Government Printer, Sydney, 1890, p. 15.
12. *SAR*, 3 May 1911, p. 6.
13. The South Australian Club was wound up just two days before the Adelaide Club was established on 2 July 1863: E. Morgan and the Adelaide Club, *The Adelaide Club, 1863–1963*, Adelaide Club, Adelaide, 1963, p. v.
14. Morgan, *The Adelaide Club*, p. iii.
15. John Tuthill Bagot (1818–1870) was a founding member, also John Hope (1808–1880), Robert Waters Moore (1819–1884), Nathaniel Alexander Knox (1837–1908), Henry

Seymour (1800–1869) and his son, Thomas Seymour (1823–1897). Two sets of brothers, Henry and Savile L'Estrange and Ross and William Reid, may also have been Irish. The list of members states that Savile returned to Ireland in 1867 and was ordained a priest, and that William retired to Ireland in 1880 but returned to the colony when he did not receive payment for his share of Tolarno Station. Morgan, *The Adelaide Club*, pp. 97, 104, 107.

16   See, for example, Eric Richards, 'Irish Life and Progress in Colonial South Australia', *Irish Historical Studies*, vol. 27 no. 17, 1991, pp. 216–236. See also Philip Payton (ed.), *Emigrants and Historians: Essays in honour of Eric Richards*, Wakefield Press, Adelaide, 2016, pp. 183–194 for complete 'Eric Richards Bibliography'.

17   Eric Richards, 'The Importance of Being Irish in Colonial South Australia', in John O'Brien and Pauric Travers (eds), *The Irish Emigrant Experience in Australia*, Poolbeg Press, Dublin, 1991, pp. 62–102.

18   Margaret Press, *From Our Broken Toil: South Australian Catholics 1836 to 1905*, Catholic Archdiocese of Adelaide, Adelaide, 1986; Margaret Press, *Colour and Shadow: South Australian Catholics 1906–1962*, Archdiocese of Adelaide, Adelaide, 1991.

19   David Fitzpatrick, 'Exporting Brotherhood', p. 283; David Fitzpatrick, 'Irish Immigration 1840–1914', in James Jupp, *The Australian People: An encyclopaedia of the nation, its people and their origins*, Angus and Robertson Publishers, Sydney, 1988, pp. 563–564.

20   Ann Herraman, '"A Certain Shade of Green": Aspects of Irish settlement in nineteenth-century colonial South Australia', in Jeff Brownrigg, Cheryl Mongan and Richard Reid (eds), *Echoes of Irish Australia: Rebellion to republic: A collection of essays*, St Clements Retreat and Conference Centre, Galong, NSW, 2007, pp. 135–144.

21   James, 'Becoming South Australians?'.

22   Susan Arthure, 'The Occupation of Baker's Flat: A study of Irishness and power in nineteenth century South Australia', MArch thesis, Flinders University, 2014; Susan Arthure, 'Being Irish: The nineteenth century South Australian community of Baker's Flat', *Archaeologies*, vol. 11 no. 2, 2015, pp. 169–188; Susan Arthure, 'Australia's First Clachan: Identifying a traditional Irish settlement system in nineteenth century South Australia', *Journal of the Historical Society of South Australia*, vol.. 45, 2017, pp. 19–30.

23   Breen, 'Yet We Are Told'.

24   Dymphna Lonergan, 'The Irish in South Australia: Names and naming', http://ehlt.flinders.edu.au/humanities/exchange/asri/migrate_pdf/migrate_ab_DLonergan.pdf accessed 8 August 2018.

25   Kingston Historic House, http://kingstonhouse.com.au/pages/history.html accessed 1 July 2018.

G.S. Kingston and other pioneer Irish in South Australia

1   Donald Langmead, *Accidental Architect*, Crossing Press, Sydney, 1994, p. 1.
2   Langmead, *Accidental Architect*, p. 3.
3   Langmead, *Accidental Architect*, p. 6.
4   *Adelaide Times (AT)*, 28 March 1851, p. 3.
5   *AT*, p. 6.
6   Langmead, *Accidental Architect*, p. 19.
7   Langmead, *Accidental Architect*, p. 58.
8   Langmead, *Accidental Architect*, p. 58.
9   www.slsa.sa.gov.au/manning/pn/t/torrens.htm accessed 5 January 2018.
10 Robert Torrens, *Systematic Colonisation: Ireland saved without cost to the Imperial Treasury*, T. Saunders, London, 1849.

11 Langmead, *Accidental Architect*, p. 59.
12 Langmead, *Accidental Architect*, p. 62.
13 Langmead, *Accidental Architect*, p. 28.
14 Langmead, *Accidental Architect* p. 116.
15 *South Australian Register* (*SAR*), 21 May 1877, p. 6.
16 *SAR*, 7 March 1840, p. 1.
17 *SAR*, 11 July 1849, p. 3.
18 Langmead, *Accidental Architect*, p. 165.
19 *SAR*, 11 December 1880, p. 1.
20 The Pioneers' Association of South Australia 1957, no. 89 Captain Hugh Quin, p. 5.
21 The Pioneers' Association of South Australia 1957, no. 89 Captain Hugh Quin, p. 5.
22 *SAR*, 2 May 1896, p. 6.
23 *SAR*, 30 April 1896, p. 7.
24 *AT*, 11 March 1856, p. 1.
25 Sir John William Jeffcott (1796–1837), *Australian Dictionary of Biography*, vol.. 5, Melbourne University Press, Melbourne, 1974.
26 *Journal of the Cork Historical and Archaeological Society*, Notes & Queries, vol.. 8, 1902, pp. 258–259.
27 See the *Tasmanian*, 26 December 1834, p. 6, for an account of the time leading up to the duel.
28 State Library of South Australia n.d. Nomenclature of the streets of Adelaide and North Adelaide, http://www.slsa.sa.gov.au/digitalpubs/placenamesofsouthaustralia/Streets_of_Adelaide_and_Nth_Adelaide.pdf accessed 25 February 2018.
29 State Library of South Australia n.d. Nomenclature of the streets of Adelaide and North Adelaide, http://www.slsa.sa.gov.au/digitalpubs/placenamesofsouthaustralia/Streets_of_Adelaide_and_Nth_Adelaide. pdf accessed online 25 February 2018.
30 *Parliamentary Papers Relevant to Emigration*, Colonial Secretary's Office, Adelaide, 1842, p. 252.
31 www.southaustralianhistory.com.au/coglin.htm accessed online 23 November 2017.
32 www.slsa.sa.gov.au/manning/pn/c/c8.htm#coglin, Rodney Cockburn, *Pastoral Pioneers of South Australia,* 1927, trove.nla.gov.au/work/8449221 accessed 5 January 2018.
33 R.F. Williams, *Early Settlers in the Yankalilla District*, Yankalilla and District Historical Society, Yankalilla, 1989, p. 241.
34 R.F. Williams *Early Settlers*, p. 241.
35 Information received from John Corbett, great-great-grandson of John Clarke, in May 2006 in the form of a letter and a copy of a 'resume' of the Clarke history written by James Clarke, John Clarke's son.
36 Charles Beaumont Howard (1807–1823), *Australian Dictionary of Biography,* vol. 5, Melbourne University Press, Melbourne, 1974.
37 Howard, Charles Beaumont (1807–1823), *Australian Dictionary of Biography,* vol. 5, Melbourne University Press, Melbourne, 1974.
38 H. Hussey, *Colonial Life and Christian Experience*, Hussey and Gillingham, Adelaide, 1897, p. 60.
39 Charles Beaumont Howard (1807–1823), *Australian Dictionary of Biography,* vol. 5, Melbourne University Press, Melbourne, 1974.
40 Daniel Michael Cudmore (1811–1891), *Australian Dictionary of Biography,* vol. 5, Melbourne University Press, Melbourne, 1974.
41 Maurice H. Ward, *Some Brief Records of Brewing in South Australia*, The Pioneers' Association of South Australia, Adelaide, 1950, p. 5.

42 Daniel Michael Cudmore (1811–1891), *Australian Dictionary of Biography,* vol. 5, Melbourne University Press, Melbourne, 1974.
43 David J. Towler, *A Fortunate Locality,* Peacock Publications, Adelaide, 1986, p. 14.
44 *Royal South Australian Almanack 1839,* Libraries Board of South Australia, Adelaide, 1969, p. 22.
45 Thomas Shuldham O'Halloran (1797–1870), *Australian Dictionary of Biography,* vol. 5, Melbourne University Press, Melbourne, 1974.
46 Alison Dolling, *The History of Marion on the Sturt,* Peacock Publications, Adelaide, 1981, pp. 16–17.
47 *SAR,* 18 March 1851, p. 3.
48 Rodney Cockburn, *What's in a Name? Nomenclature of South Australia,* Ferguson Publishers, Adelaide, 1984, p. 45.
49 'Mrs Mahony's Scrap-book', in *Proceedings of the Royal Geographical Society,* South Australia Branch, vol. 29, 1926–7, p. 43.
50 *SAR,* 4 July 1885, p. 7.
51 *Pastoral Pioneers of South Australia,* Publishers Limited Printers, vol. 2, Adelaide, p. 246.
52 Dudley Colmar (ed.), *The First Hundred Years,* Corporation of the City of Burnside, Adelaide, 1956, p. 27.
53 Elizabeth Warburton, *The Paddocks Beneath: A history of Burnside from the beginning,* Corporation of the City of Burnside, Adelaide, 1981, p. 152.
54 Daniel George Brock, *Recollections of D.G. Brock 1843,* Royal Geographical Society of Australasia, South Australian Branch Inc., Adelaide, 1981, p. 54.
55 Cockburn, *What's in a Name?* p. 164.
56 See Stephanie James, 'Becoming South Australians?: The impact of the Irish on the County of Stanley, 1841–1871', MA thesis, Flinders University, 2009, pp. 65–79 for a comprehensive profile of E.B. Gleeson.
57 Win Johnson, *Cottages and Cameos of Clare,* District Council of Clare, Clare, 1988, p. 5.
58 *Northern Argus (NA),* 6 June 1924, p. 8.
59 www.onkaparingacity.com/libraries/localstudies/view_details.asp?RefID=2302 accessed 25 February 2018 and Yvette Faria-Pronk, *Spirit of the Vale,* Morphett Vale Catholic Parish, Adelaide, 2005, pp. 13–15.
60 Towler, *A Fortunate Locality,* p. 3.
61 *SAR,* 19 March 1842, p. 2.
62 www.onkaparingacity.com/libraries/localstudies/view_details.asp?RefID=2302 accessed 25 February 2018.
63 It is usually reported that Anderson gave or 'presented' the land, but land title records show that he sold the land for 10 shillings.
64 *SAR,* 1 January 1846, p. 2.
65 'Mrs Mahony's Scrap-book', p. 34.
66 Margaret M. Press, *From Our Broken Toil: South Australian Catholics 1836–1906,* Catholic Archdiocese of Adelaide, Adelaide, 1986, p. 12.
67 *Parliamentary Papers Relevant to Emigration,* Adelaide, Colonial Secretary's Office, 1848, p. 288.
68 Press, *From Our Broken Toil,* p. 32.
69 E.H. Coombe, *History of Gawler 1837–1908,* Austaprint, Adelaide, 1978 (1910), p. 16.
70 See Stephanie James, 'Becoming South Australians?', for further discussion of John Hope.
71 This is an anglicised spelling of *Céad Míle Fáilte.*
72 *SAR,* 31 December 1844, p. 2.

73 See Wilfrid Prest (ed.), *The Wakefield Companion to South Australian History*, Wakefield Press, Adelaide, 2001, pp. 544–545 for detailed discussion of Torrens title.
74 Torrens, Sir Robert Richard (1814–1884), *Australian Dictionary of Biography*, vol. 5, Melbourne University Press, Melbourne, 1974.
75 www.marion.sa.gov.au/webdata/resources/files/Marion-Historical-Society-Newsletter-March-2016.pdf accessed 12 December 2017.
76 Faria-Pronk, *Spirit of the Vale*, p. 14.
77 oldcolonists.weebly.com/-1840-william-Nicol.html accessed 5 January 2018.
78 www.slsa.sa.gov.au/manning/pn/g/g4.htm accessed 23 November 2017.
79 Greg Drew and Joyce Jones, *Discovering Historic Kapunda*, Department of Mines and Energy and Kapunda Tourism Committee, Adelaide, 1988, p. 42.
80 David Fitzpatrick, *Oceans of Consolation*, Melbourne University Press, Melbourne, 1995, pp. 97–98.
81 Charles Harvey Bagot (1788–1880), *Australian Dictionary of Biography*, vol. 5, Melbourne University Press, Melbourne, 1974.
82 'Mrs Mahony's Scrap-book', p. 35.
83 H. John Lewis, *Salisbury South Australia: A history of town and district*, Investigator Press, Adelaide, 1980, p. 17.
84 *Parliamentary Papers Relevant to Emigration*, Adelaide, Colonial Secretary's Office, 1848, p. 294.
85 Eric Richards, 'The Importance of Being Irish in South Australia', in John O'Brien and Pauric Travers (eds), *The Irish Immigrant Experience in Australia*, Poolbeg Press, Dublin, 1991, p. 89.
86 *SAR*, 24 July 1860, p. 3.
87 Michael Kenny (1808–1892), *Australian Dictionary of Biography*, vol. 5, Melbourne University Press, Melbourne, 1974.
88 Towler, *A Fortunate Locality*, p. 129.
89 *SAR*, 5 August 1871, p. 7.
90 Fidelma Breen, '"Yet We Are Told Australians Do Not Sympathise with Ireland": A study of South Australian support for Irish Home Rule, 1883 to 1912', MPhil thesis, University of Adelaide, 2013, p. 65.
91 Michael Kenny (1808–1892), *Australian Dictionary of Biography*, vol. 5, Melbourne, Melbourne University Press, 1974.

Irish settlement in the Mount Barker region, 1836-1891

1 Special Survey 35 – In the period beset by delays in survey implementation and land distribution, the Mount Barker settlers were beneficiaries of the Special Survey provision, which enabled well-resourced investors to acquire extensive holdings on prime land. The Special Survey Clause 35 – a major deviation from the Wakefield 80-acre 'concentrated' model – was implemented by Governor Gawler in 1839 as a matter of urgency. The provision enabled investors to purchase 4000 acres selected from 15,000 acres of previously identified and surveyed land. Following intense criticism the Special Survey facility was withdrawn by a select committee in 1841. By this time 37 Special Surveys had been allocated in prime rural locations to the north and east of Adelaide. Eight of these adjoining Special Surveys were located on the eastern side of the Mount Lofty Ranges along the Onkaparinga and Angas Rivers, broadly defined as the Mount Barker Region.
2 The Census, 1841, State Library of South Australia (SLSA).
3 The Census Returns, South Australia, South Australian Parliamentary Papers, 1881.
4 The Census Returns, 1881.
5 J. Faull (ed.), *Macclesfield: Reflections along the Angas*, Macclesfield Historical Book Committee, Macclesfield, 1980, pp. 66–118.

6   For more detailed information see Eric Richards and Ann Herraman, '"If She Was to Be Hard Up She Would Sooner Be Hard Up in a Strange Land than Where She Would Be Known": Irish women in colonial South Australia', in Trevor McClaughlin (ed.), *Irish Women in Colonial Australia*, Allen & Unwin, Sydney, 1998, pp. 82–104; Ann Herraman, '"A Certain Shade of Green": Aspects of Irish settlement in nineteenth century colonial South Australia', in Jeff Brownrigg, Cheryl Mongan and Richard Reid (eds), *Echoes of Irish Australia, Rebellion to Republic*, St Clements Retreat and Conference Centre, Galong, NSW, 2009, pp. 135–145.
7   Ann Herraman, 'Patterns and Profiles: A study of the settlement population of the Mount Barker Region –1836–1841', BA(Hons) thesis, Flinders University, 1994, pp. 84–95.
8   Ann Herraman, 'Patterns and Profiles', pp. 84–95.
9   Kath Faulkner (ed.), *St James Blakiston, 1847–1997, a Journal of 150 years of Faith, Worship and Service*, Littlehampton, 1996, p. 29.
10 SA *Advertiser*, 13 June 1901, p. 4.
11 Faulkner, *St James Blakiston*, p. 29.
12 Faulkner, *St James Blakiston*, p. 29.
13 *Advertiser*, 13 June 1901, p. 4.
14 Trevor McClaughlin, *Barefoot and Pregnant?: Irish Famine orphans in Australia*, Genealogy Society of Victoria Inc., Melbourne, 1991.
15 Family research reported to the Mount Lofty Districts Historical Society in March 2018 indicated that 11 female passengers on the *Inconstant* were from England.
16 Faulkner, *St James Blakiston*, p. 166.
17 Richards and Herraman, 'Irish Women', pp. 82–104.
18 Richards and Herraman, 'Irish Women', pp. 82–104.
19 Marie Steiner, *Servants Depots in Colonial South Australia*, Wakefield Press, Adelaide, 2009, pp. 91, 151.
20 Marriage Register of the Mount Barker Catholic Mission, 1848–1883, Registry of Birth and Baptisms of Catholics of South Australia Mount Barker Mission, 1848–1880, Adelaide Catholic Archives, Adelaide, South Australia.
21 Marie Steiner, *Servants Depots*, pp. 91, 151.
22 Faull, *Macclesfield*, pp. 66–118.
23 Ann Herraman, 'The People of Mount Barker, a Demographic Study of the Settlement in Special Survey Selections on the Eastern Side of the Mount Lofty Ranges, 1830–1890', PhD Thesis, Flinders University, 2010. See Table 3.9, 'Births and Birth Rates in Five District Councils', p. 93.
24 Faull, *Macclesfield*, p. 63.
25 Agnes Craig, Beth Ritchie (née Anderson), Carlene Farmer (née Anderson) and Bruce Kelly between 1985 and 1995, 'Research Notes of the Anderson Family', Mount Barker Library Local History Centre, Mount Barker; Tom Dyster Family Papers, 2009.
26 Tom Dyster, Milligan and Anderson family papers, 2009.
27 Dyster, 2009.
28 Dyster, 2009.
29 Dyster, 2009.
30 Faull, *Macclesfield*, pp. 12, 31, 70.
31 South Australian Deaths, Index of Registration, 1842–1915, April 2004, vol. A-C, p. 25.
32 Craig, Ritchie, Farmer and Kelly, 'Research Notes of the Anderson Family', 2009.
33 Dyster, 2009.
34 Edward Gibbon Wakefield, *A Letter from Sydney*, 1829, pp. 164–165.
35 Craig, Ritchie, Farmer and Kelly, 'Research Notes of the Anderson Family', 2009.
36 Dyster, 2009.

37 W.B. Modystack, 'Historical Notes', Strathalbyn Parish, State Library of South Australia, quote from *Southern Cross*, 27 August 1897.
38 Herraman, 'A Certain Shade of Green', pp. 135–145.
39 Modystack, 'Historical Notes'.
40 Reverend Timothy Murphy prevented the Mount Barker parishioners from supporting the sisters who were found to be in such poor health that MacKillop withdrew them temporarily from the district. See Marie Foale, *The Josephite Story*, St Joseph's Generalate, Sydney, 1989, p. 80.
41 J.E.T. Woods, Directory and Order of Discipline, Adelaide, 1870, pp. 84–86 illustrated in Foale, *The Josephite Story*, pp. 200–201.
42 Modystack, 'Historical Notes', quote from *Southern Cross*, 27 August 1897; Herraman, 'A Certain Shade of Green', pp. 141–142.

Fortune and misfortune: Early Irish colonists in the Clare Valley

1 The data shows the colonial figure was 10.1 per cent. By 1871 some local council areas around Clare showed high Irish concentration, e.g. in the Mintaro-based Stanley Council, 20 per cent were Irish-born, at Saddleworth the figure was 13.2 per cent, and for the Clare Corporation, it was 12.5 per cent.
2 These six lives were chosen, not only because there was information available, but also because to some extent, they represent the different walks of life pursued by early Irish immigrants to the Clare Valley. While not claiming these lives are 'typical' or 'average', they do provide a social and historical 'snapshot' of the complex patchwork that comprised the Clare Valley community during the colonial years.
3 *Government Gazette*, 16 January 1840. Special Surveys, by which individuals or groups could finance the survey costs of land parcels beyond the surveyed districts and then be eligible to have the first choice of these blocks, formed part of the Wakefield plan to regulate settlement and land sales. See State Library of South Australia (SLSA) PRG 239/15/33 for details of planning on 30 June 1840, which included the process for allocation of land following the Special Survey.
4 Michael Williams, *The Making of the South Australian Landscape: A study in the historical geography of Australia*, Academic Press, London, 1974, pp. 6–7. The region is also known as the Central Hill District.
5 Gleeson was allocated Sections 40, 42, 43, 136, 138, 139 and 20 acres of Section 44.
6 *Southern Australian*, 29 September 1840, p. 3. Gleeson's flock was stated as 11,000 ewes and lambs. Two hundred of the displaced Indigenous – few women and children – were said to be surrounding his station.
7 Gerald A. Lally, *A Naulty Family History: 150 years in South Australia 1846–1996*, Gerald Lally, Clare Print, 1996, p. 8.
8 For information on John Hope's early landholdings in the Clare area, see *Diaries of George Charles Hawker*: 'Station life at Bungaree' SLSA D2620 (L) and D2619 (L); Colonial Secretaries Office Correspondence Transcript of a Record (GRG 24/6/1846/1482) dated 5 March 1846. Heading: John Hope of the River Broughton. License no. 143; Occupation licenses to John Hope, River Broughton: No. 113 (dated 1847) GRG 24/6/1846/1482, and no. 121 (dated March 1846) GRG 24/6/1847/731.
9 Dates of Hope's employment of Geary were included as evidence in the Geary v Hope Trial, see SA *Advertiser* of 17 September, p. 3, 16 September, p. 3, 19 September, p. 3 and 20 September 1869, p. 3 for report of Supreme Court – Civil Sittings.
10 See Eleanore Williams, *A Way of Life: The pastoral families of the Central Hill country of South Australia*, Adelaide University Union Press, Adelaide, 1980, for discussion of class and status in the Clare Valley region.
11 State Records of South Australia (SRSA) GRG 78/49, Special List, Royal Adelaide Hospital, Admission records 1840–1904, vol. 3, p. 125 of 719. Mary's religion is shown here as Protestant.

12 Certified search copies re. Mary Anne Geary: Will (signed 26th August 1863); Probate (signed 27th February 1865) – both from Supreme Court of South Australia Civil Registry; Death (signed 24th January 1865) from Births, Deaths and Marriages Registration Office, Adelaide.
13 The court case involving Mary and her employer, John Hope, involved her letters being read in court; although Coffy's literacy is less certain, she signed her marriage certificates, her daughters were well educated, one becoming a teacher, and contemporary family understanding supports her being literate.
14 Robert J. Noye, *Clare: A district history*, Investigator Press, Adelaide, 1980, p. 12. Unfortunately, without referencing, it is unclear on what this figure was based.
15 Peter Moore, 'Half-burnt Turf: Selling emigration from Ireland to South Australia 1836–1845' in Philip Bull, Chris McConville and Noel McLachlan (eds), *Irish Australian Studies: Papers delivered at the sixth Irish Australian Conference*, Latrobe University, 1991, p. 110. See Adelaide *Southern Cross* (*SC*) of 15 August 1911 p. 8 for obituary of Dubliner William O'Shaughnessy Brooke (born Calcutta in 1831) who came to South Australia with his brother 'to learn sheep farming. He was on Mr Gleeson's farm at Clare for a time …'.
16 Geoffrey H. Manning, *Manning's Place Names of South Australia: From Aaron Creek to Zion Hill*, (Revised Edition), Gould Books, Adelaide, 2006, p. 97.
17 See M. Stephanie James, 'Becoming South Australians?: The impact of the Irish on the County of Stanley, 1841–1871', MA thesis, Flinders University, 2009, p. 265, table 27 for details of 'Counties of Origin' for her Clare Valley research cohort; Clare, Cavan, Wicklow and Cork provided most immigrants, in contrast to Eric Richards, 'The Importance of Being Irish in Colonial South Australia' in John O'Brien and Pauric Travers (eds), *The Irish Immigrant Experience in Australia*, Poolbeg Press, Dublin 1991, p. 72, showing that the counties providing the greatest number of assisted immigrants to South Australia were Clare, Tipperary, Limerick and Cork.
18 Damian John Gleeson, 'A True Specimen of the Fine Old Irish Gentleman' in *Mining the Past: The history, people and places of Silvermines District*, vol. v, 2017, p. 157.
19 Gleeson, 'A True Specimen,' p. 157.
20 Gleeson, 'A True Specimen,' p. 158.
21 *South Australian*, 28 July 1838, p. 3. The item describes E.B. Gleeson with his wife and three children, John with his wife and son, they came with some £4500, 12 indentured servants, a house and a pure Arab horse. See *Southern Australian* of 28 July 1838, p. 3 for details of the Australian Association of Bengal. Founded in mid 1837, it brought together Calcutta's most affluent and aimed to support regular communication between India and the colonies. John Morphett was the Adelaide agent expected to foster men of 'superabundant capital' as their experience 'would give a maturity to our social institutions which we might otherwise despair of attaining for many years to come'.
22 See *South Australian Register* (*SAR*), 31 October 1840, p. 2 for Gleeson's unsuccessful attempt to be elected to the Community Council, a forerunner to the Adelaide City Council, and *Southern Australian*, 26 March 1841, p. 3 for Gleeson and Irish-born Major O'Halloran as horse judges at Noarlunga.
23 See SRSA, GRG 66/6/39 for details of Gleeson's 1842 financial situation.
24 Jean Schmaal, *The Inchiquin Story*, National Trust of South Australia, Clare and District Branch, Clare, nd, p. 6. He began to lay out the village on Section 40 and part of Section 42, and by 1843 had established a homestead.
25 See 'Government Gazette' in *Southern Australian*, 12 January 1847, p. 5 for reference to Gleeson's application for an occupation license 'West of the Hutt River', *Adelaide Observer*, 22 May 1852, p. 2 for his pasturage lease, no. 116, for 14 years, and James, 'Becoming South Australians?', pp. 75–7 and 82–4.
26 *Adelaide Observer* supplement, 14 July 1849, p. 1. John Hope was also a founding member.

27 See *Adelaide Observer* supplement of 4 May 1850, p. 2, *SAR*, 18 March 1851, p. 3 and *Adelaide Times, (AT)* 18 March 1856, p. 3.
28 *South Australian*, 8 February 1850, p. 3.
29 *SAR*, 3 August 1850, p. 3. See *SAR* of 11 July 1856, p. 3 for his appointment as a special magistrate.
30 Noye, *Clare*, p. 188.
31 E.B. joined other local notables on 27 February 1850 – Rev J.C. Bagshaw, C.H. Watts, G.C. Hawker and J. Maynard – in proposing the construction of a church on land given as a grant in 1848 to Bishop Short. Mrs Gleeson laid the cornerstone in late 1850, and construction began in early 1851, see https://data.environment.sa.gov.au/heritagesurveys/lower-north-eight-towns-survey-clare-1990.pdf accessed 19 February 2018.
32 See *SA Gazette and Mining Journal*, 26 December 1850, p. 2, *SAR*, 15 December 1856, p. 2, *SAR*, 24 December 1856, p. 3 and *SAR*, 27 December 1856, p. 3. At the final Gumeracha meeting, he was proposed and seconded. The two 1856 items mentioned his name as a possibility.
33 See James, 'Becoming South Australians?', pp. 238–240, table eight, 'Irish Female Immigrants at Clare Servant Depot 1855–56'.
34 *Adelaide Observer*, 12 April 1856, p. 3.
35 *SAR*, 29 October 1857, p. 3. See reference to this in Peter Brady's life below.
36 *SA Gazette and Mining Journal*, 9 January 1851, p. 3.
37 *AT*, 11 October 1854, p. 3.
38 *SAR*, 24 October 1859, p. 3.
39 *SAR*, 19 September 1865, p. 3.
40 See *SAR*, 10 October 1861, *Adelaide Observer*, 23 April 1859, p. 3 and 1 August 1864, p. 3.
41 See SA *Advertiser* of 28 February 1859, p. 3 and *SAR* of 6 September 1862, p. 3. The report shows Gleeson both signed and read the customary address to Daly, and the governor spoke of Gleeson as 'his friend the chairman'. MacDonnell was governor between June 1855 and March 1862; Daly (the first Catholic governor in any Australian colony), followed from March 1862 until his death in office on 19 February 1868.
42 *SAR* 1 March 1858, p. 3, *SA Weekly Chronicle*, 18 September 1858, p. 2.
43 *John Hope Diaries, 1853–1880 (JHD)*. These 11 diaries are among the private papers in the possession of Rory Hope. The diaries show numerous interactions between Gleeson and Hope, for example see entries for 12/6/1853, 4/4/1854, 5/5/1855, 16/12/1856, 4/7/1857, 10/10/1857.
44 See for example, *AT*, 18 March 1851, p. 3 and *SAR* of 24 October 1859, p. 3.
45 *SAR*, 22 August 1866, p. 3.
46 See *SAR* of 7 February 1870, p. 3 for report of funeral. See also *Northern Argus* (*NA*), 4 February 1870, p. 2 and *SAR*, 3 February 1870, p. 8 for obituaries neglecting mention of Gleeson's Irishness.
47 Hope's arrival in Australia was confirmed in a letter of 17 October 1902 from Robert Barr Smith to Hope's daughter, Frances Diana Christison (F.D.C.); he knew John Hope personally. For additional information about Hope's arrival and early South Australian experiences see letters, 28 November 1902, Eliza S. Mahony (England) to F.D.C. 28 November 1902, and 28 October 1902, J. Harris Browne (Surrey) to F.D.C. Letters in the possession of Rory Hope. For further information about the life of John Hope, see Rory Hope, 'John Hope of Clare: An under-recognised colonial achiever,' *Journal of the Historical Society of South Australia (JHSSA)*, Number 46 (2018), pp. 5–25.

48 Margaret and Alistair Macfarlane, *John Watts: Australia's forgotten architect 1814–1819 and South Australia's postmaster general 1841–1861*, SunBird Publications, New South Wales, 1992, pp. 85–90.
49 *JHD*, 12 May 1853.
50 SRSA GRG 24/6/1846/1482, Colonial Secretary's Office, Outwards Correspondence file, no.143 of 1846, no 1B, GRG 24/6/1846/1482 no. 113 (dated 1847), GRG 24/6/1847/731, no. 121 (dated 5th March 1846).
51 *SAR*, 15 April 1857, p. 3 and *Adelaide Observer*, 13 March 1858, p. 3.
52 *SAR*, 13 July 1860, p. 3.
53 Letter, 16 July 1903, E.S. Wadell (England) to F.D.C. Letter in the possession of, and transcribed by, Rory Hope.
54 *JHD*, 14 June 1853.
55 *JHD*, 9 August 1865. He described his photo being placed in a bottle under the stone, and £8.11.5 being donated 'on the stone' and £16 at the afternoon tea. See entry of 25 February 1863 for mention of his laying the courthouse foundation stone; he had provided stone for this building's quoins.
56 *JHD*, 28 May 1860.
57 *JHD*, 28 February 1860.
58 *JHD*, 28 April 1863. There is a further reference to different potential school sites on 11 July.
59 *JHD*, Tuesday 5 May 1863.
60 Some examples of Hope employing Indigenous men: *JHD*, 13 May 1853, 30 October 1853, 6 March 1856, 30 June 1856, 19 August 1874.
61 John Hope's ledger of 1863–1874, 185 pages (Rory Hope).
62 See Rory Hope, 'John Hope of Clare'.
63 John Hope's date of death is taken from a certified death certificate. See also *Adelaide Observer*, 26 June 1880, p. 38.
64 *NA*, 22 June 1880, p. 2.
65 See SRSA GRG 66/6/39 (1842) for the schedule that establishes Gleeson's debts totalled £9986 while his credits equalled only £3078. See also James, 'Becoming South Australians?', pp. 72–73 for further discussion of his bankruptcy profile.
66 Brian Condon (ed.), *The Journal of Francis Murphy First Catholic Bishop of Adelaide*, SACAE, Magill Campus, Adelaide, c. 1980, pp. 14–15.
67 *South Australian*, 19 January 1849, p. 3. See *JHD*, 7 July 1849.
68 See *AT*, 13, 14, 17 March 1849, pp. 2, 4, 2; and 11, 12, 14, 18 December 1850, pp. 3, 4, 2, 3; and *Register*, 11 March, p. 3 and 15 March 1851, p. 2.
69 *Government Gazette*, 5 April 1850, p. 3, *SAR*, 11 July, p. 3.
70 See *AT* of 8 September, p. 3 and 29 September 1855, p. 3. The pattern was similar in 1857.
71 See *SAR* of 13 December 1859, p. 3 for details of Clare committee. This item refers to SAPA's anti-immigration policy, perhaps an unexpected plank for Irish-born to accept.
72 See James, 'Becoming South Australians?', pp. 238–240, table eight, 'Irish Female Immigrants at Clare Servant Depot 1855–56'.
73 *SAR*, 13 September 1864, p. 3, *Chronicle*, 6 April 1867, p. 4.
74 *SAR*, 2 October 1857, p. 2. See also, *SAR*, 19 September 1865, p. 3 and *SAR*, 8 September 1866, p. 3.
75 SA *Advertiser*, 13 September 1864, p. 3.
76 See Ann McGrath, 'Shamrock Aborigines: The Irish, the Aboriginal Australians and their children,' in *Aboriginal History*, vol. 34, 2010, pp. 55–84 for discussion of connections between these two peoples.

77 *JHD*, 14 June 1853, Hope recorded asking Butler 'about buying Bullocks from the [Burra] Copper Company for me'; 4 June 1860, Hope noted that he 'Got P. Butler to assist me to Bring horses from Stanley'; 17 and 18 September 1866, Hope wrote of asking Butler's help in moving some horses, and 'Butler came today to assist me in regulating the horses'.
78 *JHD*, 24 August 1853, 'Went to Butlers'; 2 July 1855, '[c]alled at Butlers. Came home at night'; 14 March 1863, '[T]ook a parcel for Issie [Hope's wife] to Butlers'; 15 March 1867, '[C]alled at Butlers, not at home'.
79 *JHD*, 27 September 1853, 'Butler came with me and cut Jacob's colt'; 18 April 1863, 'Went to Butlers to ask him to take trough to new well'; 4 February 1867, 'Butler bled the mare'.
80 *JHD*, 14 July 1853, 'Paid off Charley Brock'; 1 October 1857, 'Paid off Sam Morgan'; 28 September 1866, one of many references to Cecil Webb.
81 *JHD*, throughout John Hope's diaries he mentions passing individuals; examples are 18 August 1853, 'Chas and Miss Chapman'; 1 April 1856, 'Thredgold with Miss Gleeson'; 25 May 1855 'Charles Hawker'.
82 *JHD*, 19 May 1856, 'George Hawker came with Beare for Dinner, stopped all night'; 26 September 1866, 'Went down to Clare, voted for Bagot, Hughes, Stow and Parker'; 12 June 1853, 'Mail did not come till after tea at Gleesons'.
83 See John Hope account book (Rory Hope), 18 August 1868. Hope lent Butler £317.16.0, and Butler made several repayments but the ledger suggests the debt was not fully honoured. See also letter from John Hope to Henry Burgess, 16 June 1869 (located in Diary 10), mentioning an interest rate of 8 per cent for Butler.
84 *JHD*, 8 February 1867. Unfortunately, there is no further mention of this matter.
85 *JHD*, 5 December 1855.
86 See *JHD*, 17 November 1857, Hope noted going to the Broughton with Sam Butler who helped lead horses; 14, 15 and 22 February 1860, Hope asked Butler if his son James could travel to locate a horse; 1 March 1867, Hope wrote of Mick Butler helping with horses.
87 *JHD*, 16 March 1867, Hope noted contact with three local pound-keepers 'desiring them to send Notice to Mr P. Butler of Armagh of any animals of mine that may be impounded'. Letter (copy) John Hope to Henry Burgess, 4 November 1869, deals with Butler's breaking in of Hope's horses while he is in Ireland, and with earlier conversations about the council and fencing areas affected by changes to roads.
88 *NA*, 18 April 1873, p. 2.
89 *NA*, 18 April 1873, p. 2.
90 *NA*, 23 April 1875, p. 2.
91 See SA *Advertiser* of 14 April 1876, p. 3 for coroner's report.
92 *NA*, 8 June 1877, p. 2.
93 See Condon, *The Journal of Francis Murphy*, pp. 109, 114, 145, 149, 174, 178, 186 and 204 for reference to monies paid to a Cavan bishop for Mr Smith's passage.
94 The 1841 census shows Brady in Stanley Street, North Adelaide, an area designated as 'Irishtown'. Birth records show the family at Mount Barker and Rapid Bay prior to choosing Mintaro.
95 Gerald Lally, *A Landmark of Faith: Church of the Immaculate Conception, Mintaro and its parishioners 1856–2006*, Gerald Lally, Clare Print, 2006, p. 8. For details of Brady's involvement in the building process, see Condon, *The Journal of Francis Murphy*, p. 375.
96 *AT*, 29 November 1856, p. 2.
97 *Adelaide Observer*, 16 October 1858, p. 4.
98 See *SAR* of 24 May 1856, p. 4, and *SAR* of 27 December 1859, p. 3. E.B. Gleeson was a judge.
99 *SAR*, 20 May 1865, p. 3.

100 SAR, 16 May 1867, p. 4.
101 AT, 10 January 1854, p. 4. Further evidence of his popularity was reflected in his consistent nomination as a founding member in Mintaro's attempts to secure its own council, 1858, 1859, 1861 and 1862.
102 In 1854 for example, Butler and Brady cooperated in questioning the treasurer's report (AT, 16 March 1854, p. 3), but in 1856, only Brady supported Gleeson in resolving a divisive rates issue (AT, 24 May 1856, p. 3). In 1857 council nominations, Gleeson proposed Brady while Hope and Wm Lennon (the Irish town clerk), nominated Butler, SAR, 9 March 1857, p. 3.
103 See AT of 19 September 1855, p. 2, and SA Advertiser, 21 November 1862, p. 3.
104 SAR, 29 October 1857, p. 3.
105 The challenger was Clare's district clerk Wm Lennon. Gleeson opposed this, but Butler welcomed the move; it would be the end of class misrule and mismanagement. Lennon's bankruptcy soon ended his parliamentary career. The new election was held in May 1861; Kingston's win was greeted by a petition questioning his victory. The Court of Disputed Returns endorsed his success, and a vindictive Kingston was subsequently a member of a select committee examining how petition signatures were obtained. When Kingston threatened forgery charges against signatories signing for others, the issue of self-incrimination was a concern. See James, 'Becoming South Australians?', pp. 182–187, 225–226. See SAPP, 1861, 2, no. 111. Report of the Select Committee of the House of Assembly appointed to report on petition against Return of G.S. Kingston Esq.
106 SA Advertiser, 18 April 1861, p. 3.
107 SAR, 18 May 1860, p. 3.
108 SAR, 14 September 1864, p. 3.
109 See Adelaide Observer, 30 July 1864, p. 2, SAR, 13 September 1864, p. 3, Adelaide Observer, 12 August 1865, p. 4, and SAR, 29 August 1868, p. 4. Five thousand were in attendance.
110 SA Advertiser, 21 June 1867, p. 3.
111 My thanks to Brian Brady and Sue Boyland for this information. See SA Government Gazette, 24 June 1869, and NA, 16 July 1869, p. 1.
112 According to the information received from the above researchers, Peter Brady was cash-poor when he died, having borrowed from his brother and others; his widow received a life interest in his valueless real and personal property. The liquidation of his debts resulted in his liabilities exceeding his assets by £3.15.6.
113 There is no known record of her birth, but the birth year can be estimated from: i) Certified copy of Mary Geary, Death Certificate 535, Registrar of Births, Deaths and Marriage, Adelaide, ii) Official assisted passage passenger lists (Special List) GRG 35/48/1, 1845 – 1886. 11/1850 Joseph Soames. SRSA; iii) SRSA GRG 78/49 Admission records, Adelaide Hospital.
114 SRSA GRG 35/48/1, 1845–1886, Official assisted passage passenger lists (Special List) 11/1850 Joseph Somes.
115 For further detail about the life of John Hope, see Rory Hope, 'John Hope of Clare'.
116 For information about the life of George Charles Hawker, see Frankie Hawker and Rob Linn, Bungaree: Land, stock and people, Turnbull Fox Phillips, South Australia, 1992. For Hawker's employment of Mary Geary, see Law and Criminal Courts-Supreme Court-Civil Side, SAR, 19 September 1861, p. 3 and SAR, 20 September 1861, p. 3.
117 See AT of 8 February, p. 4 and 8 March 1854, p. 3 for details of Mary taking Frederick Briggs to court over theft and his alleged damage to Hawker's fence. He was sentenced to three weeks in Redruth Jail; Hope, Hawker and Gleeson were the magistrates. Perhaps this court experience prepared Mary for her later case against Hope.

118 Examples of Mary's activities are found in the following *JHD* entries: 23 December 1853, 18 February 1854, 14 May 1856, 26 July 1857, 4 October 1857, 7 September 1857 and 6 November 1857.
119 *JHD*, 7 and 13 September 1857, interaction with Gleeson family; 6 November 1857, Mary had Mrs and Miss Hawker plus some of the Filgate family 'to lunch'.
120 William Pattullo, *The Land History of Polish Hill River 1842–1990*, Clare Regional History Group, Clare, 1961, p. 93, South Australian Land Titles Office, Certificate of Title, vol. CT507, folio 172.
121 *JHD*, 26 December 1855, 'gave him [Young] a cheque for £90 to pay for Mary's land'.
122 South Australian Land Titles Office, Certificate of Title, vol. 31, folio 77.
123 Certified search copies re Mary Anne Geary: Will (signed 26 August 1863); Probate (signed 27 February 1865) – both from Supreme Court of South Australia Civil Registry; Death Certificate (dated 24 January 1865) from Births, Deaths and Marriages Registration Office, Adelaide.
124 First Trial (aborted): Law and Criminal Courts, Supreme Court-Civil Side, 18 June 1861, Geary v. Hope, *SAR*, 19 June 1861, p. 3. Second Trial: Supreme Court-Civil Sittings, 17 September 1861, Geary v. Hope. See also SA *Advertiser*, 20 September 1861 p. 3. See also Law and Criminal Courts-Supreme Court-Civil Side, September 18 and September 19, *SAR*, 19 September 1861, p. 3, and 20 September 1861, p. 3.
125 Law and Criminal Courts. Supreme Court. – In Banco. Geary v. Hope. Monday 7 October 7. Motions for New Trials. Gearey [sic] v. Hope; *SAR*, 8 October 1861 p. 3.
126 Elizabeth M. Milburn, 'Clare 1840–1900: Changing elites within a South Australian community', MA thesis, University of Adelaide, 1982, pp. 130–133.
127 See note 11.
128 Although Catherine's surname is typically spelt Coffey, her marriage certificates show this as Coffy, including her signature. Catherine's spelling has been adopted in this chapter.
129 Neither Catherine's county of origin nor year of birth are certain. Her death certificate shows Westmeath as her place of birth, but see Marie Steiner, *Servants Depots in Colonial South Australia*, Wakefield Press, Adelaide, 2009, p. 133 for this as Kings County (Offaly), while Miller (Mueller) family history cites County Clare.
130 See Janet Callen, *What Really Happened to the* Nashwauk? *Moana, South Australia 1855*, Butterfly Press, Adelaide, 2004, for information about this incident.
131 See chapter by Jade Hastings in this volume.
132 See Steiner, *Servants Depots*, for general background of the country depots and their inhabitants.
133 SRSA GRG 24/6/1855/2095, 2155, 2259, colonial secretary's office.
134 See James, 'Becoming South Australians?', pp. 243–245, table 10, 'Known Details of Irish Female Immigrants sent in 1855 to Clare Servant Depot & Remaining in [County of] Stanley'.
135 See James, *Becoming South Australian*, pp. 238–240, table eight, 'Irish Female Immigrants at Clare Servant Depot 1855–56'.
136 *JHD*, 25 September 1855, Hope noted that 'P. Henry called for CLH,' Patrick was probably Robert Henry's brother, so John Hope may have had some contact with Catherine Coffy and her husband.
137 See Williams, *A Way of Life*, pp. 82–83 for discussion of Hope's interest in exploring ideas about moving to either Banda Oriental or Uruguay.

The unexpected Irishmen: How David Power and Anthony Sutton established an Irish colonial presence in the South East of South Australia

1 Leith G. Macgillivray, 'Land and People: European land settlement in the South East of South Australia, 1840–1870', PhD thesis, University of Adelaide, 1983 http://digital.library.adelaide.edu.au; Leith G. Macgillivray, "We Have Found Our Paradise':

The South-East squattocracy, 1840-1870', in *Journal of the Historical Society of South Australia*, No. 17, 1989, pp. 25-38.

2   Pam and Brian O'Connor, *Second to None: A story of the rural pioneers of Mount Gambier*, District Council of Mount Gambier, 1988.

3   Eric Richards, 'Irish Life and Progress in Colonial South Australia', *Irish Historical Studies*, vol. 27 no. 107, 1991, pp. 216-234; Eric Richards, 'The Importance of Being Irish in Colonial South Australia', in John O'Brien and Pauric Travers (eds), *The Irish Emigrant Experience in Australia*, Poolbeg Press, Dublin, 1991, pp. 62-102.

4   Anthony Sutton, Baptism Record, Callary, Delgany, Co. Wicklow Ireland, 28 February 1808 http://www.rootsireland.ie.

5   Anthony Sutton and Mary Kirwan, Marriage Record, Enniskerry, Co. Wicklow, Ireland, 24 October 1836 http://www.rootsireland.ie; John Sutton, Baptism Record, Aurora, Enniskerry, Co. Wicklow, Ireland, 27 August 1837 http://www.rootsireland.ie; James Sutton, Baptism Record, Enniskerry, Co. Wicklow, Ireland, 6 October 1839 http://www.rootsireland.ie.

6   Assisted Immigrants Shipping List, *Middlesex*, 30 September 1841, NRS 5316/4, State Records NSW.

7   *Port Phillip Gazette (PPG)*, 6 November 1841, p. 2, *Naracoorte Herald*, 7 February 1913, p. 3, J.C. Sutton, 'A South-Eastern Pioneer: Interesting experiences and reminiscences'.

8   O'Connor, *Second to None*, p. 85.

9   Macgillivray, *Land and People*, pp. 22-23, 52.

10 J.C. Sutton, *A South-Eastern Pioneer;* O'Connor, *Second to None*, p. 86.

11 David Power, Baptism Record, Carrick-on-Suir, Co. Tipperary, Ireland, 31 March 1813. Irish Roman Catholic Parish Registers, NLI http://www.findmypast.com.au *Waterford Mail*, 8 June 1831, p. 1 http://www.findmypast.com.au.

12 *Sydney Gazette and New South Wales Advertiser*, 14 July 1840, p. 2.

13 R.V. Billis and A.S. Kenyon, *Pastoral Pioneers of Port Phillip*, second edition, Stockland Press, Melbourne, 1874, p. 281, *Geelong Advertiser and Squatter's Advocate*, 8 November 1845, p. 6.

14 *Port Phillip Government Gazette* (Supplement), 23 February 1849, pp. 152-153.

15 *Adelaide Observer*, 8 August 1846, p. 8.

16 'An Act for Protecting the Waste Lands of the Crown in South Australia from Encroachment, Intrusion and Trespass', no. 8 of 1842 http://www.austlii.edu.au *Adelaide Observer*, 4 April 1846, p. 6. AO, 8 August 1846, p. 8.

17 Return of the Commissioner for Crown Lands 1848-1850, GRG 24/4/2844/1851, State Records of South Australia (SRSA).

18 *South Australian Government Gazette*, No. 46, 7 November 1850, pp. 629-631 http://www.austlii.edu.au.

19 The lease papers of Run No. 354 have not been able to be located. When the lease was being examined by George Goyder, the surveyor-general, in 1864, it was described as being taken out by Edward Crow, see Anne McCarthur (ed.), *Through the Eyes of the Surveyor-General's 1864-5 Valuations of 79 Pastoral Runs in the South East of South Australia*, Kanawinka Writers and Historians, 2007, p. 224.

20 Register of Pastoral Leases, GRS 3519, vol. 1, SRSA.

21 *Adelaide Times* (AT), 18 January 1851, p. 8. Memorial nos 270, 271, book 40, Old Systems Services, Land Service Group South Australia. The 'upset price' is the reserve price set by the government of the day on land blocks.

22 Richard Killeen, *A Short History of Ireland*, Gill and Macmillan, Dublin, 1994, pp. 24-25.

23 Killeen, *A Short History of Ireland*, pp. 25-31, 36-37.

24 *South Australian Register (SAR)*, 9 June, 1854, p. 2, Macgillivray, *Land and People*, pp. 95–96, 98, 100.
25 Memorial no. 332, book 116, memorial no. 422, book 89, and memorial no. 331, book 93, Old Systems Services, Land Service Group South Australia.
26 Memorial no. 226, book 53, Old Systems Services, Land Service Group South Australia. Billis and Kenyon, *Pastoral Pioneers of Port Phillip*, p. 281.
27 List of applications for survey, GRG 35/467/ 99/53, SRSA. Register of Pastoral Runs, GRS 3519, vol. 1, SRSA. Memorial no. 97, book 90 and memorial no. 497, book 75, Old Systems Services, Land Service Group South Australia.
28 Register of Pastoral Runs, GRS 3519, vol. 1 and Register of Pastoral Runs, GRS 3519, vol. 1, SRSA.
29 Pastoral Leases (surrendered) GRS 3570, SRSA.
30 Correspondence files, Surveyor-General's Office, GRG 35/2/385/1857, SRSA. List of applications for survey, GRG 35/467, vol. 3, 12 May 1857, SRSA. Memorial no. 105, book 218; Old Systems Services, Land Services Group South Australia. Folios 230 and 231, vol. 1; folios 11, 12, 109, 110, 112, 113, 138, book 2, Historic Titles, Land Services Group. www.SAILIS.sa.gov.au.
31 List of applications for survey, GRG 35/467, vol. 3, 11 March 1858, SRSA. Folio 209, vol. 1, Historic Titles, Land Services Group. www.SAILIS.sa.gov.au.
32 *Hobart Town Daily Mercury*, 18 October 1859, p. 3.
33 Memorial no. 206, book 174, Old Systems Services, Land Service Group South Australia. To place this sum in context, in 1863 the wages of a shepherd working on one of the stations in the district would have been £30–35 per annum with rations. A hut-keeper would have earned a little less, £25–30 per annum with rations, and a stock-keeper a little more, £45–70 per annum plus rations. A married couple working as domestic servants with board and lodging would have earned £50–70, less if they had children as these were considered extra mouths to feed without producing any effective income. Cattle were worth £3–10 each and sheep cost between 5 and 17 shillings and 6 pence, depending on age and condition. Horses could cost up to £30 for a saddle horse and £60 for a draught horse, a working animal. Meat could be purchased for 3–10 pence per pound, butter 11 pence to 2 shillings and 6 pence per pound and milk 6–10 pence per quart. For further details of the cost of living in Australia in the 1860s, see Henry Heylen Hayter, *Victorian Year Book: A digest of the statistics of the colony for the year 1873*, first edition, Melbourne, John Ferres,1874, pp. 25–28. http://babel.hathitrust.org.
34 SA *Advertiser*, 16 February 1859, p. 2.
35 Macgillivray, *Land and People*, p. 150.
36 Macgillivray, *Land and People*, pp. 139–141.
37 *SAR*, 12 March 1860, p. 3. *AO*, 22 December 180, p. 1, *Border Watch (BW)*, 28 June 1861, p. 2.
38 David Power, England Census, 1871, http://www.ancestry.com.au; SAR, 03 October 1871, p. 4, David H. Power, Obituary, 16 June 1924, http://www.oa.anu.edu.au; *Australasian*, 26 April 1884, p. 5. SA *Advertiser*, 8 May 1884, p. 6.
39 Anthony Sutton, Death Certificate, 20 June 1879, Births, Deaths and Marriages South Australia, book 96, p. 227; Anthony Sutton, Will, Probate Registry, Supreme Court of South Australia, 1879.
40 MacGillivray, *Land and People*, p. 44.
41 Due to the notorious difficulty of searching Irish land records, it is not possible to know with certainty if the Sutton family in Wicklow did actually own any land. Their use of the assisted migration scheme suggests they were certainly not as well off as the Power family members who could afford to fund their own journey to Australia. The Tithe Applotment Records for the parish of Upper Calary in Wicklow in 1824 show an Anthony Sutton, together with J. Fox and John Sutton, occupying 110 acres

of land, with a valuation of £106.13. 9. Baptism records for this parish support that he may be the father of the subject of this chapter. However, Tithe Applotment Books, which were kept for the purpose of determining the tax due to the Church of Ireland, only indicate occupation, not ownership of agricultural land in this case. These records may be accessed at http://titheapplotmentbooks.nationalarchives.ie.

42   David Power, Death Certificate 22 March 1884. Births Deaths and Marriages South Australia, book 137, p. 36. *Argus*, 16 May 1884, p. 7.
43   *Naracoorte Herald*, 24 June 1879, p. 3. Anthony Sutton, Will, Probate Registry, Supreme Court of South Australia, 1879.
44   Richards, 'The Importance of Being Irish', pp. 72–73.
45   Assisted Immigrants Shipping List, *Middlesex*, 30 September 1841, NRS 5316/4, State Records New South Wales.
46   O'Connor, *Second to None*, pp. 90–92. Folio 78, vol. 69; folio 26, vol. 7; folio 78, vol. 106; Historic Titles, Land Services Group. www.SAILIS.sa.gov.au.
47   O'Connor, *Second to None*, pp. 90–92. Folio 78, vol. 69; folio 26, vol. 7; folio 78, vol. 106; Historic Titles, Land Services Group. www.SAILIS.sa.gov.au.
48   *Sydney Gazette and New South Wales Advertiser*, 14 July 1840, p. 2. Thomas Herbert Power, Biography. http://www.parliament.vic.gov.au/about/people-in-parliament/re-member. Accessed 11 January 2018.
49   David Power and Anne Pile, Church of England Marriage Register, St George's Church, Gawler, 28 October 1851, SRG94/A34, State Library South Australia (SLSA).
50   *SAR*, 30 July 1852, p. 2. *Argus*, 24 August 1853, p. 4, *Portland Guardian and Normanby General Advertiser*, 28 August, 1854, p. 2, *Argus*, 10 December, 1855, p. 5, *Portland Guardian and Normanby General Advertiser*, 2 April 1857, p. 2, *Adelaide Observer*, 14 August 1858, p. 3. David Power, England Census, 1871.http://www.ancestry.com.au.
51   *Argus*, 26 March 1853, p. 7, *Argus*, 6 September 1856, p. 1.
52   Robin Haines, *Emigration and the Labouring Poor: Australian recruitment in Britain and Ireland, 1831–60*, Macmillan Press, London, 1997, p. 274.
53   Letters sent – Colonial Secretary's Office, GRG24/4/1854/2107, SRSA. Correspondence files – Colonial Secretary's Office, GRG 24/6/ 1854/687, SRSA.
54   Richards, 'The Importance of Being Irish', pp. 75–79, Marie Steiner, *Servants Depots in Colonial South Australia*, Wakefield Press, Adelaide, 2009, pp. 24–32.
55   Steiner, *Servants Depots*, pp. 57–63.
56   Letters sent – Colonial Secretary's Office, GRG 24/4/1855/2533, and GRG 24/4/1855/2531, SRSA.
57   *BW*, 25 June 1879, P.2.
58   O'Connor, *Second to None*, p. 89.
59   O'Connor, *Second to None*, pp. 89–90; Brian Condon, *The Journal of Francis Murphy, First Catholic Bishop of Adelaide*, SACAE Magill, 1983, p. 314.
60   Condon, *The Journal of Francis Murphy*, pp. 220–221, 224, 242, 250, 316, 385–386, 396, 407, 410, 418.
61   O'Connor, *Second to None*, pp. 92–93.
62   Father T. Murphy to Fr Frederick Byrne, 3 April 1880 in Brian Condon, *Letters and Documents in 19th Century Australian Catholic History*, Web edition, SACAE Magill, South Australia, 2000. http://www.library.unisa.edu.au accessed 21 January 2018.
63   *BW*, 6 March 1863, p. 3.
64   *BW*, 26 September 1866, p. 2 and *BW* 1 September 1869, p. 2, *Evening Journal*, 4 September 1869, p. 2.
65   *SAR*, 18 July 1850, p. 1 and SAR, 10 June 1851, p. 1.
66   *SAR*, 20 May 1853, p. 3.
67   Bishop Augustus Short, Diary, 1855, PRG 160, SLSA.
68   *SAR*, 27 February 1856, p. 2.

69 *AT*, 18 July 1856, p. 3.
70 Index to letters received – Colonial Secretary's Office, GRG 24/8/ 1858/1209, SRSA.
71 *SAR*, 18 February 1857, p. 3, AO, 28 February 1857, p. 7, *AO*, 13 March 1858, p. 2, *South Australian Weekly Chronicle (SAWC)*, 14 August 1858, p. 3, SAR, 25 January 1859, p. 3, *AO*, 5 February 1859, p. 3, *SAWC*, 5 February 1859, p. 8.
72 *SAWC*, 19 February 1859, p. 5, *Age*, 25 February 1859, p. 5.
73 *Portland Guardian and Normanby General Advertiser*, 9 August 1859, p. 1.
74 *SAR*, 18 August 1859, p. 6.
75 *SAWC*, 27 August 1859, p. 4. Register of letters received – Colonial Secretary's Office, GRG24/7/ 407/1859, p. 17, SRSA.
76 SA *Advertiser*, Tuesday 6 December 1959, p. 3.
77 Register of letters received – Colonial Secretary's Office, GRG 24/7/ 407/1859, p. 19, SRSA.
78 Register of letters received – Colonial Secretary's Office, GRG24/7/ 407/1859, Appendix, SRSA.
79 *SAR*, 6 July 1854, p. 3.
80 E.M. Yelland, *The Baron of the Frontier*, Hawthorne Press, Melbourne, 1870, p. 130.
81 Robert Rowland Leake to John Leake, 26 March 1859, Leake Papers, L1/B206, University of Tasmania Archives (UTA).
82 *Portland Guardian and Normanby General Advertiser*, 2 April, 1860, p. 2, *SAR*, 7 March 1860, p. 2.
83 Richards, 'Irish Life and Progress'; Richards, 'The Importance of Being Irish'.
84 David Power and Anne Pile, Church of England Marriage Register, St George's Church, Gawler, 28 October 1851, SRG94/A34, SLSA. David Power, Internment Record, Wesleyan Compartment B, Grave 0273, St Kilda Cemetery, Melbourne, 1884. http://www.stk.scmt.org.au accessed 1 February 2018.
85 Bishop Augustus Short, diary, 1855; Millicent Glen, diary, 1858. PRG 160, SLSA.
86 *SAR*, 5 October 1858, p. 1. O'Connor, *Second to None*, pp. 92–3.
87 Melbourne *Advocate*, Saturday 25 September 1880, p. 11.
88 *Church of England Messenger and Ecclesiastical Gazette for the Diocese of Melbourne and Ballarat*, 6 October 1880, p. 4.
89 Power's behaviour in regards to religion is in sharp contrast to that of his brother, Thomas Herbert, the Melbourne auctioneer. Although the latter engaged with others of different faiths, his Catholicism was publicly evident and he took an active part in Church affairs. See *Melbourne Times*, 7 January 1843, p. 3.
90 O'Connor, *Second to None*, pp. 55–57, 84–106.

Kapunda's Irish connections
1 Frederick Sinnett, *An Account of the Colony of South Australia Prepared for Distribution at the International Exhibition of 1862*, Bradbury and Evans, London, 1862, p. 60.
2 Bagot's name has been mostly seen in print as 'Charles Hervey Bagot', with the middle name pronounced as 'Harvey' although spelled with an 'e'. Research published by Greg Drew in 2017 (*Captain Bagot's Mine: Kapunda Mine 1844–1916*) examined signed documents held by the Bagot family and in the State Library of South Australia, and confirms the correct spelling as 'Charles Harvey Bagot'. This spelling has been used in this chapter.
3 Charles Hervey Bagot, *A Holograph Memoir of Capt. Charles Hervey Bagot of the 87th Regiment*, The Pioneers' Association of South Australia, Adelaide, 1942, p. 1.
4 Bagot, *A Holograph Memoir*, p. 2.
5 Bagot, *A Holograph Memoir*, p. 18.
6 Bagot, *A Holograph Memoir*, pp. 18–19.

7   Bagot, *A Holograph Memoir*, p. 19.
8   Bagot, *A Holograph Memoir*, p. 22.
9   Greg Drew, *Captain Bagot's Mine: Kapunda Mine 1844–1916*, Greg Drew, Adelaide, 2017, pp. 14, 19.
10 Charles Hervey Bagot, Draft Extracts From a Journal of a Voyage From Cork to Port Adelaide, South Australia, 1840–1841, unpublished manuscript held in the Borrow Collection, Flinders University Library, 1841, p. 1; Bagot, *A Holograph Memoir*, pp. 22–23.
11 Bagot, Draft Extracts, p. 1.
12 Bagot, Draft Extracts.
13 Bagot, *A Holograph Memoir*, p. 22.
14 Bagot, *A Holograph Memoir*, p. 23.
15 Peter Moore, 'Half-burnt Turf: Selling emigration from Ireland to South Australia, 1836–1845', in Philip Bull, Chris McConville and Noel McLachlan (eds), *Irish-Australian Studies: Papers Delivered at the Sixth Irish-Australian Conference July 1990*, La Trobe University, Melbourne, 1991, p. 112.
16 Eric Richards, 'Irish Life and Progress in Colonial South Australia', *Irish Historical Studies*, vol. 27 no. 107, 1991, pp. 220–221; Eric Richards, 'The Importance of Being Irish in Colonial South Australia', in John O'Brien and Pauric Travers (eds), *The Irish Emigrant Experience in Australia*, Poolbeg Press, Dublin, 1991, p. 69.
17 Drew, *Captain Bagot's Mine*, p. 14.
18 Moore, 'Half-burnt Turf', p. 110.
19 Bagot, Draft Extracts, p. 9.
20 Bagot, *A Holograph Memoir*, p. 38; Drew, *Captain Bagot's Mine*, p. 15; George E. Loyau, *Notable South Australians, or, Colonists – Past and Present*, George E. Loyau, Adelaide, 1885, p. 120.
21 Bagot, Draft Extracts, p. 13.
22 Bagot, *A Holograph Memoir*, pp. 24–25; Francis Stacker Dutton, *South Australia and Its Mines, with an Historical Sketch of the Colony, under its Several Administrations, to the Period of Captain Grey's Departure*, T. and W. Boone, London, 1846, pp. 266–267.
23 Dutton, *South Australia*, pp. 268–274.
24 *Adelaide Observer* (*AO*), 5 July 1845, p. 5; Rob Charlton, *The History of Kapunda*, The Hawthorn Press, Melbourne, 1971, p. 9.
25 Bagot, *A Holograph Memoir*, p. 38; Charlton, *History of Kapunda*, pp. 15, 156; Loyau, *Notable South Australians*, p. 120.
26 J.L. Symonds, 'The Making of Cadia Mine, Smelter and Village', unpublished paper prepared for the Cornish Association of NSW, Sydney, 2004, p. 10.
27 Charlton, *History of Kapunda*, pp. 15, 101.
28 Gordon J. Forth, 'The Anglo-Irish in Early Australia: Old world origins and colonial experiences', in Philip Bull, Chris McConville and Noel McLachlan (eds), *Irish-Australian Studies: Papers delivered at the Sixth Irish-Australian Conference July 1990*, La Trobe University, Melbourne, 1991, pp. 58–59.
29 Charlton, *History of Kapunda*, p. 64; John A. Daly, *Elysian Fields: Sport, class and community in colonial South Australia 1836–1890*, J.A. Daly, Adelaide, 1982, p. 162.
30 Sinnett, *Account of the Colony*, p. 62.
31 Sinnett, *Account of the Colony*, p. 62.
32 Charlton, *History of Kapunda*, p. 18; Rob Nicol, 'Racial Minorities and the Settlement of Kapunda, Part 1', *Historical Society of South Australia Newsletter*, vol. 48, 1983, p. 13.
33 Charlton, *History of Kapunda*, pp. 18, 64.
34 SA *Advertiser*, 31 October 1890, p. 4; SA *Advertiser*, 29 September 1904, p. 7; SA *Advertiser*, 17 July 1913, p. 8; Beth Robertson, 'Full Transcript of an Interview with

Anne Liddy on 19, 26 August 1985 by Beth Robertson for "SA speaks": An oral history of life in South Australia before 1930', State Library of South Australia, Adelaide, 1985; personal communication R. Dundon 11 June 2013, L. Heffernan 28 June 2013.

35 In the 19th century, assisted passage schemes supported emigration to the new colony of South Australia. From 1834 to about 1860, these schemes were financed primarily from the sale of Crown land, which then subsidised the passage of emigrants, usually labourers.
36 Richards, 'Irish Life and Progress', p. 221; Richards, 'The Importance of Being Irish', p. 72.
37 Drew, *Captain Bagot's Mine*, pp. 17–21.
38 Drew, *Captain Bagot's Mine*, pp. 19, 38.
39 Susan Arthure, 'The Occupation of Baker's Flat: A study of Irishness and power in nineteenth century South Australia', MArch thesis, Flinders University, 2014, p. 173.
40 Arthure, 'Occupation of Baker's Flat', p. 173.
41 Moore, 'Half-burnt Turf', p. 110.
42 *Southern Cross (SC)*, 10 June 1949, p. 8.
43 *SC*, 10 June 1949, p. 8.
44 A horse whim was used in mining to haul ore or water to the surface. The whim, worked by a horse, consisted of a large winding drum (capstan) with a vertical axle, rope and pulleys. As the horse pulled the rope round a circular platform, the drum turned, lowering the rope with an empty bucket and raising the rope with the full load.
45 Drew, *Captain Bagot's Mine*, p. 38.
46 Drew, *Captain Bagot's Mine*, p. 38.
47 Nicol, 'Racial Minorities', p. 13.
48 Leslie N. Tilbrook (ed.), *Memories of Kapunda and District by a Circle of Friends*, Kapunda Herald Print, Kapunda, 1929, p. 32.
49 Tilbrook, *Memories of Kapunda*, p. 31.
50 Charlton, *History of Kapunda*, p. 18; Nicol, 'Racial Minorities', p. 14.
51 Charlton, *History of Kapunda*, p. 18.
52 *South Australian Register (SAR)*, 2 June 1860, p. 3.
53 *Kapunda Herald and Northern Intelligencer (KHNI)*, 26 November 1864, p. 3.
54 *KHNI*, 23 February 1866, p. 3.
55 *AO*, 3 May 1873, p. 5.
56 *AO*, 15 December 1877, p. 11.
57 *SAR*, 5 December 1865, p. 3.
58 Patrick Fynes, which appears to be a variant spelling of both Flynes and Foynes, arrived in South Australia in 1854 and moved to Baker's Flat the same year. His death certificate records his occupation as school teacher, and the family history records him as having been a musician and headmaster; *SAR*, 24 May 1854, p. 2; *Kapunda Herald (KH)*, 24 April 1903, p. 3; personal communication I. Coverdale, May 2016.
59 *KHNI*, 21 September 1866, p. 3.
60 *KHNI*, 26 April 1867, p. 2.
61 *KHNI*, 23 July 1869, p. 3.
62 Rev. Fr T.J. Maloney, 'Early Days and Ways in Kapunda: Baker's Flat, No Man's Land – A Nursery of Catholicism in Australia', *SC*, 6 November 1936, p. 29.
63 Maloney, 'Early Days and Ways', p. 29.
64 H.I. Bettison, 'Transcript of Interviews with W.W.G. Townsend, M. O'Brien, E.E. Fuller and Mrs Beanland, Interviewed by H.I. Bettison, April 1975', in possession of South Australian Museum, Adelaide.

65 *Chronicle*, October 1899, p. 18.
66 Bettison, 'Transcript of Interviews'; George Hazel, 'Baker's Flat – Unpublished Account 1975', in possession of South Australian Museum, Adelaide.
67 Kevin Danaher, *Ireland's Vernacular Architecture*, Mercier Press, Cork, 1978, pp. 9–12; Alan Gailey, *Rural Houses of the North of Ireland*, John Donald, Edinburgh, 1984, p. 8; Barry O'Reilly, 'Hearth and Home: The vernacular house in Ireland from c. 1800', *Proceedings of the Royal Irish Academy, Section C: Archaeology, Celtic studies, history, linguistics, literature*, vol. 111C, 2011, pp. 193, 203.
68 Danaher, *Ireland's Vernacular Architecture*, p. 30; O'Reilly, 'Hearth and Home', p. 199.
69 *KHNI*, 9 February 1866, p. 3.
70 Susan Arthure, 'Australia's First Clachan: Identifying a traditional Irish settlement system in nineteenth century South Australia', *Journal of the Historical Society of South Australia*, vol. 45, 2017, pp. 19–30.
71 *SAR*, 2 June 1860, p. 3.
72 *KH*, 12 September 1902, p. 3.
73 Maloney, 'Early Days and Ways', p. 29.
74 *KH*, 12 September 1902, p. 3.
75 *KH*, 12 September 1902, p. 3.
76 *KH*, 20 May 1948, p. 2.
77 *KH*, 14 June 1945, p. 2; Hazel, 'Baker's Flat'.
78 *KH*, 18 July 1902, p. 3.
79 *KHNI*, 21 September 1875, p. 2.
80 *KHNI*, 21 September 1875, p. 2.
81 *KHNI*, 3 July 1877, p. 3.
82 *KH*, 7 May 1880, p. 2.
83 *KH*, 4 June 1880, p. 4.
84 *KH*, 9 March 1888, p. 3.
85 *KH*, 16 February 1892, p. 3.
86 *KH*, 14 June 1892, p. 3.
87 Arthure, 'Occupation of Baker's Flat', pp. 171–172.
88 Arthure, 'Occupation of Baker's Flat', pp. 171–172.
89 *KH*, 3 April 1894, p. 3.
90 'Forster et al. v. Fisher, Records of the Supreme Court of South Australia', GRG 36/54 File 47/1892, State Records of South Australia, Adelaide.
91 Charlton, *History of Kapunda*, p. 49; 'Forster et al. v. Fisher'.
92 'Forster et al. v. Fisher'; *KH*, 3 April 1894, p. 2; *KH*, 4 July 1902, p. 3.
93 Gerald O'Collins, *Patrick McMahon Glynn: A founder of Australian Federation*, Melbourne University Press, Melbourne, 1965, pp. 1–5.
94 O'Collins, *Patrick McMahon Glynn*, p. 21.
95 O'Collins, *Patrick McMahon Glynn*, p. 33.
96 O'Collins, *Patrick McMahon Glynn*, pp. 35–36.
97 O'Collins, *Patrick McMahon Glynn*, p. 39.
98 Charlton, *History of Kapunda*, p. 44; O'Collins, *Patrick McMahon Glynn*, p. 44.
99 Gerald O'Collins, *Patrick McMahon Glynn: Letters to his family (1874–1927)*, The Polding Press, Melbourne, 1974, p. 56.
100 O'Collins, *Patrick McMahon Glynn: Letters*, p. 49.
101 O'Collins, *Patrick McMahon Glynn*, p. 100.
102 O'Collins, *Patrick McMahon Glynn*, p. 12.
103 *KH*, 20 May 1893, p. 2.
104 'Forster et al. v. Fisher'.

105 *KH*, 3 April 1894, p. 2.
106 *KH*, 3 April 1894, p. 2.
107 *KH*, 3 April 1894, p. 3.
108 *KH*, 12 September 1902, p. 3; *KH*, 4 July 1902, p. 3.
109 *KH*, 12 September 1902, p. 3.
110 *KH*, 26 September 1902, p. 3.

Irish graves in Mid North South Australia, 1850-1899: An examination of cultural significance

1   Eric Richards, 'British Poverty and Australian Immigration in the Nineteenth Century,' in Eric Richards (ed.), *Poor Australian Immigrants in the Nineteenth Century, Visible Immigrants: Two*, Division of Historical Studies and Centre for Immigration and Multicultural Studies, Research School of Social Sciences, Australian National University, Canberra, 1991, p. 2.
2   Eric Richards, 'Irish Life and Progress in Colonial South Australia', *Irish Historical Studies*, vol. 27 no. 107, 1991, p. 222.
3   M. Stephanie James, 'Becoming South Australians?: The impact of the Irish on the County of Stanley, 1841–1871', MA thesis, Flinders University, 2009; Eric Richards and Ann Herraman, '"If She Was to Be Hard Up She Would Sooner Be Hard Up in a Strange Land than Where She Would Be Known": Irish women in colonial South Australia', in Trevor McClaughlin (ed.), *Irish Women in Colonial Australia*, Allen & Unwin, Sydney, 1998, pp. 82–104; Richards, 'Irish Life and Progress', pp. 216–236; Eric Richards, 'The Peopling of South Australia, 1836–1976', in Eric Richards (ed.), *The Flinders History of South Australia: Social history*, Wakefield Press, Adelaide, 1986, pp. 115–142; Eric Richards, 'The Importance of Being Irish in Colonial South Australia', in John O'Brien and Pauric Travers (eds), *The Irish Emigrant Experience in Australia*, Poolbeg Press, Dublin, 1991, pp. 62–102.
4   Susan Arthure, 'The Occupation of Baker's Flat: A study of Irishness and power in nineteenth century South Australia', MArch thesis, Flinders University, 2014.
5   See chapters by Herraman, Wratten, Arthure, Mannion, de Leuien, James and O'Reilley in this book for additional discussion of this topic.
6   James, 'Becoming South Australians', p. 7; Richards and Herraman, 'Irish Women', pp. 82–104; Richards, 'The Importance of Being Irish', pp. 62–102; Richards, 'British Poverty and Australian Immigration', pp. 1–30; Richards, 'The Peopling of South Australia', pp. 115–142; Peter Moore, 'Half-burnt Turf: Selling emigration from Ireland to South Australia, 1836–1845', in Philip Bull, Chris McConville and Noel McLachlan (eds), *Irish-Australian Studies: Papers delivered at the Sixth Irish-Australian Conference July 1990*, La Trobe University, Melbourne, 1991, pp. 103–119; Martin Greet, 'The Irish and Fenianism in South Australia during 1868', BA(Hons) thesis, Flinders University, 1987; Christopher Nance, 'The Irish in South Australia', *Journal of the Historical Society of South Australia,* vol. 5, 1978, pp. 66–73.
7   Sarah Tarlow, *Bereavement and Commemoration: An archaeology of mortality*, Blackwell Publishers, Oxford, 1999.
8   R.J. Noye, *Clare: A district history*, Lynton, Coromandel Valley, 1975, p. 20.
9   State Heritage Branch, Department of Environment and Natural Resources, *Mintaro: State Heritage Area,* 1990, www.environment.sa.gov.au accessed 14 April 2014.
10 Noye, *Clare*, p. 125.
11 Mary Burrows, *Riverton: Heart of the Gilbert Valley*, District Council, Riverton, 1965, p. 29.
12 H.S. Carroll (compiler), *The District Atlas of South Australia and Northern Territory, 1876,* E.S. Wigg & Son, Adelaide, 1876, p. 4.
13 Burrows, *Riverton*, pp. 29–30.

14 History SA, 'Saddleworth District', http://community.history.sa.gov.au/saddleworth-district-historical-society-museum accessed 9 March 2015.
15 Burrows, *Riverton,* p. 1.
16 Jean V. Moyle, *The Wakefield, Its Waters and Its Wealth: The story of a winding river,* Moyle, Riverton, 1982, p. 98.
17 Richards, 'Irish Life and Progress', p. 221.
18 D. Hilliard and A.D. Hunt, 'Religion', in Eric Richards (ed.), *The Flinders History of South Australia: Social history,* Wakefield Press, Adelaide, 1986, pp. 212–213.
19 Australian Data Archives, '1861 Census for South Australia', 2012, http://hccda.ada.edu.au/regions/SA accessed 15 June 2014; Australian Data Archives '1871 Census for South Australia', 2012, http://hccda.ada.edu.au/regions/SA accessed 15 June 2014.
20 Malcolm Campbell, 'Irish Nationalism and Immigrant Assimilation: Comparing the United States and Australia', *Australasian Journal of American Studies,* vol. 15 no. 2, 1996, p. 25.
21 Malcolm Campbell, *Ireland's New Worlds: Immigrants, politics, and society in the United States and Australia, 1815–1922,* University of Wisconsin Press, Wisconsin, 2008; Malcolm Campbell, 'Immigrants on the Land: Irish rural settlement in Minnesota and New South Wales, 1830–1890', *New Hibernia Review/Iris Éireannach Nua,* vol. 2 no. 1, 1998, pp. 43–61.
22 See chapters by O'Reilley and James for further discussion of St Patrick's Day.
23 Patrick O'Farrell, *The Irish in Australia,* New South Wales University, Sydney, 1987, p. 173.
24 Richards, 'Irish Life and Progress', pp. 233–234; Richards, 'The Importance of Being Irish', pp. 92–93.
25 James, 'Becoming South Australians?', pp. 94–95, 209–210.
26 Susan Arthure, 'Australia's First Clachan: Identifying a traditional Irish settlement system in nineteenth century South Australia', *Journal of the Historical Society of South Australia,* vol. 45, 2017, pp. 22–23.
27 James, 'Becoming South Australians?', p. 209.
28 James, 'Becoming South Australians?', pp. 21–22, 210, 221.
29 James, 'Becoming South Australians?', pp. 8, 211.
30 Sallie A. Marston, 'Neighborhood and Politics: Irish ethnicity in nineteenth century Lowell, Massachusetts', *Annals of the Association of American Geographers,* vol. 78 no. 3, 1988, pp. 414–432; Stephen A. Brighton, 'Symbols, Myth-making, and Identity: The red hand of Ulster in late nineteenth-century Paterson, New Jersey', *International Journal of Historical Archaeology,* vol. 8 no. 2, 2004, pp. 149–164; Stephen A. Brighton, 'Middle-class Ideologies and American Respectability: Archaeology and the Irish immigrant experience', *International Journal of Historical Archaeology,* vol. 15 no. 1, 2011, pp. 30–50; Paul E. Reckner, 'Negotiating Patriotism at the Five Points: Clay tobacco pipes and patriotic imagery among trade unionists and nativists in a nineteenth-century New York neighbourhood', *Historical Archaeology,* vol. 35 no. 3, 2001, pp. 104–114.
31 P. Frei, 'Cemeteries', 2014, http://www.canberrahistoryweb.com/cemeteries.htm accessed 2 October 2014; L.M. Schulze, 'Graven Images: Gravestone motifs and their meanings', 2014, http://www.olivetreegenealogy.com/misc/grave.shtml accessed 14 September 2014; Anon, 'Headstone Meanings', 2013, http://www.gravesecrets.net/headstone- meanings.html accessed 1 October 2014.
32 Edwin S. Dethlefsen, 'The Cemetery and Culture Change: Archaeological focus and ethnographic perspective', in Richard A. Gould and Michael B. Schiffer (eds), *Modern Material Culture,* Academic Press, New York, 1981, p. 140.
33 Tarlow, *Bereavement and Commemoration,* p. 66.
34 Harold Mytum, 'Faith in Action: Theology and practice in commemorative traditions', in James Symonds, Anna Badcock and Jeff Oliver (eds), *Historical*

Archaeologies of Cognition: Explorations into faith, hope and charity, Equinox Publishing, Sheffield, 2013, p. 162.
35   Ryan K. Smith, 'The Cross: Church symbol and contest in nineteenth-century America', *Church History* vol. 70 no. 4, 2001, pp. 705–734.
36   One explanation of this abbreviation is *Iesus Hominum Salvator* – Jesus Saviour of Mankind; Colm Donnelly, 'The IHS Monogram as a Symbol of Catholic Resistance in Seventeenth-century Ireland', *International Journal of Historical Archaeology,* vol. 9 no. 1, 2005, p. 39.
37   Mytum, 'Faith in Action', p. 167.
38   Jeanne Sheehy and George Mott, *The Rediscovery of Ireland's Past: The Celtic Revival, 1830–1930,* Thames & Hudson, London, 1980, p. 29.
39   O'Farrell, *The Irish,* p. 30, cited in Campbell, 'Irish Nationalism', p. 33.
40   T.N. Brown, *Irish-American Nationalism 1870–1890,* J.B. Lippincott Company, Philadelphia, 1966.
41   Kerby A. Miller, 'Emigrants and Exiles: Irish cultures and Irish emigration to North America, 1790–1922', *Irish Historical Studies,* vol. 22 no. 86, 1980, p. 104.
42   Fidelma E.M. Breen '"Yet We Are Told that Australians Do Not Sympathise With Ireland": A study of South Australian support for Irish Home Rule 1883–1912', MPhil thesis, University of Adelaide, 2013.
43   *Encarta World English Dictionary,* 2009, https://www.webcitation.org/5kwbrFM3c?url=http://encarta.msn.com/dictionary_1861689851/Erin_go_bragh.html accessed 6 April 2018.
44   Denis Gojak and Iain Stuart, 'The Potential for the Archaeological Study of Clay Tobacco Pipes from Australian Sites', *Australasian Historical Archaeology,* vol. 17, 1999, p. 45.
45   M. Stephanie James, 'Mobility Patterns of Irish Immigrants in the Clare Valley', in Margrette Kleinig and Eric Richards (eds), *On the Wing: Mobility before and after emigration to Australia, Visible Immigrants:7,* Anchor Books Australia, Sydney, 2012, p. 110.
46   O'Farrell, *The Irish,* p. 173.
47   Lizzie Deas, *Flower Favourites: Their legends, symbolism and significance,* Jarrold & Sons, London, 1898, p. 104.
48   Anon, 'The Shamrock', *Ulster Journal of Archaeology,* vol. 5, 1857, p. 12.
49   William Frazer, 'The Shamrock: Its history', *The Journal of the Royal Society of Antiquaries of Ireland,* vol. 4 no. 2, 1894, p. 133.
50   Liam Mac Mathúna, 'Irish Perceptions of the Cosmos', *Celtica,* vol. 23, 1999, pp. 174, 177.
51   Deas, *Flower Favourites,* p. 105.
52   John Hutchinson, 'Archaeology and the Irish Rediscovery of the Celtic Past', *Nations and Nationalism,* vol. 7 no. 4, 2001, p. 505.
53   Hutchinson, 'Archaeology and the Irish Rediscovery', p. 510.
54   Hutchinson, 'Archaeology and the Irish Rediscovery', p. 510.
55   Hutchinson, 'Archaeology and the Irish Rediscovery', pp. 513–514.
56   Derek Bryce, *Symbolism of the Celtic Cross,* Llanerch Enterprises, Felinfach, Wales, 1989, chapter 5.
57   Miller, 'Emigrants and Exiles', pp. 122–125.
58   James, 'Becoming South Australians?', pp. 198–199.
59   Arthure, 'The Occupation of Baker's Flat', p. 112.
60   Brighton, 'Symbols, Myth-making, and Identity', pp. 149–164.

'The most thoroughly Irish centre in South Australia':
Pekina from the 1870s to the 1940s

1. The agents are Wardle and Co, Port Pirie, and the asking price is $140,000.
2. *Harp and Southern Cross* (*H&SC*), 4 December 1874, p. 4.
3. See Janis Sheldrick, *Nature's Line: George Goyder, surveyor, environmentalist, visionary*, Wakefield Press, Adelaide, 2014 for details about Goyder's 'line of rainfall' dividing South Australia into sustainable and non-sustainable farming regions.
4. The authors acknowledge the assistance of Suzanne Ryan (archivist), Brian Daly of Pekina and Bishops Eugene Hurley and Greg O'Kelly SJ.
5. See *Southern Cross* (*SC*) of 5 June 1891, p. 8 for letter from Kapunda that stated: 'The best of the Kapunda Irishmen have gone to the North. ... [Pekina] is where the best of our Kapunda Irishmen have gone.' But the writer goes on to argue Pekina had as many from Tipperary as from Clare.
6. See Appendix One (p. 112) for known details of priests at Pekina.
7. See Appendix Two (p. 114).
8. Although the terms Irish and Catholic are not necessarily interchangeable, Pekina's Irish community was Catholic. John Mannion has not located any Protestant Irish residents in his Pekina research.
9. See D.W. Meinig, *On the Margins of the Good Earth*, Rigby Limited, Adelaide, 1976, pp. 26, 41, 43 and 119 for discussion of 1869 Strangways Act and its 1872 and 1877 amendments.
10. John Mannion and Malcolm McKinnon, *No Place like Pekina: A story of survival*, Pekina 125 Committee, Burra Community Print, 1999, p. 12.
11. *H&SC*, 26 June 1874, p. 6. See *South Australian Register* (*SAR*) of 1 January 1880, p. 1 for advertised sale of Pekina 'Blacksmith and Machinist's business' plus dwelling – 'owners going farming'.
12. South Australian *Chronicle* (*SAC*), 30 January 1875, p. 7.
13. *The South Australian Government Gazette*, 20 May 1875, pp. 926–928. The price for Sections 228, 229, 237, 238, 246, 247, 255 and 256 was £12.
14. *SAC*, 6 May 1876, p. 22. See NSW *Wingham Chronicle and Manning River Observer* of 9 October 1942, p. 2 for details of the post office then being in the Duffy family for 67 years, Michael Duffy Jr having taken over in 1914.
15. *Adelaide Observer* (*AO*), 23 September 1876, p. 4.
16. According to Marie Therese Foale, *The Josephite Story: The Sisters of St Joseph: Their foundation and early history 1866–1893*, St Joseph's Generalate, Sydney, 1989, pp. 226–227, the following foundations were made: Appila-Yarrowie, Caltowie (1877), Pekina (1878) and Ororoo (1880). In 1875 church foundation stones were laid at Melrose, Yarrowie and Yatina as well as Pekina.
17. The men were Patrick Redden, Jas Hoare, Joseph Travers, Peter Tierney, Peter Moroney, J.P. O'Loughlen, Jas Keogh and Patrick Leo.
18. *H&SC*, 4 December 1874, p. 4.
19. *SAC*, 9 October 1875, p. 10. The Pekina men were Michael Duffy, P. Dooley, J. Daly, B. Travers, M.E. Kenny and P. Leo.
20. *Express and Telegraph*, 12 October 1876, p. 2.
21. Mannion, *No Place like Pekina*, p. 69.
22. *SAR*, 19 August 1881, p. 2.
23. See Appendix Two (p. 114) for names of 'Sisters who have taught at Pekina'.
24. Mannion, *No Place like Pekina*, p. 93.
25. A copy of the letter of 21 August 1878 in possession of John Mannion. The letter also stated that one of the sisters needed to make bread as there was no local baker.

26 See *SAR* of 11 February 1882, p. 1 for report of the builder, O'Dea, facing court for payment of £23.14.10 'for material supplied for Pekina Convent'; this suggests it had already been built.
27 *Port Augusta Dispatch*, 23 November 1878, p. 3.
28 *SAC*, 24 March 1877, p. 17.
29 *SAC*, 6 May 1876, p. 22.
30 *SAC*, 24 March 1877, p. 17.
31 *SAC*, 26 October 1878, p. 21.
32 *Port Augusta Dispatch*, 28 March 1879, p. 2. According to John Mannion, a bell was never installed.
33 *Northern Argus*, 1 June 1880, p. 2.
34 *SAC*, 6 November 1880, p. 26.
35 *SC*, 3 July 1908, p. 11.
36 *SAR*, 19 August 1881, p. 2.
37 Margaret Press, *From Our Broken Toil: South Australian Catholics 1836–1906*, Archdiocese of Adelaide, 1986, p. 276.
38 *SC*, 28 February 1890, p. 8.
39 *SC*, 5 May 1893, p. 5.
40 See *Australian Town and Country Journal* of 27 December 1905, p. 57 for statement that in 1905 the diocese had 8 districts, 36 churches, 11 priests and 29 nuns.
41 *SC*, 25 October 1889, p. 4.
42 *SC*, 22 November 1895, p. 5.
43 *SC*, 24 January 1906, p. 8.
44 *SC*, 10 January 1919, p. 13.
45 *SC*, 17 April 1891, p. 5.
46 These related to the Port Augusta cathedral and the Kooringa church and amounted to £3500.
47 *SC*, 3 July 1908, p. 11.
48 See for example, *SC* of 31 July 1908, p. 11 (Yatina), *SC*, 14 August, p. 11 (Appila-Yarrowie).
49 *SC*, 6 July 1906, p. 5.
50 *SC*, 8 March 1907, p. 13.
51 *SC*, 25 May 1894, p. 8.
52 *SAR*, 26 March 1906, p. 7.
53 *SAR*, 20 November 1906, p. 3. For three months before the opening, Fr O'Flynn was in Ireland following ill health.
54 *Times and Northern Advertiser*, 13 February 1925, p. 3. In 1919 Booleroo was removed from the Pekina parish to become another parish. This might have reduced pressure on Pekina's church accommodation.
55 *SC*, 16 October 1925, p. 9.
56 *SC*, 16 December 1927, p. 13.
57 *SC*, 31 August 1928, p. 16.
58 SA *Advertiser*, 4 May 1881, p. 7.
59 *SC*, 25 May 1894, p. 8.
60 See *Evening Journal* of 11 November 1881, p. 3, *SAR*, 29 October 1883, p. 7 and *SC*, 9 November 1894, p. 9, 600 attended.
61 See *SC* of 4 August 1893, p. 8, 21 September 1894, p. 9, 2 September 1902, p. 9.
62 See *SC* of 2 October 1896, p. 10 (200 at Pekina Hotel), 14 October 1898, p. 12 (Booleroo Centre raised £13), *Petersburg Times*, 4 November 1898, p. 5 (first visit to Yatina, raised £9).
63 *Times and Northern Advertiser*, 19 April 1929, p. 2.

64 See Ann Herraman, '"A Certain Shade of Green": Aspects of Irish settlement in nineteenth-century colonial South Australia' in Jeff Brownrigg, Cheryl Mongan and Richard Reid (eds), *Echoes of Irish Australia: Rebellion to republic*, St Clement's Retreat and Conference Centre, Galong, 2007, pp. 141–142, for discussion of the order's educational and cultural impact in Macclesfield.
65 See *SC* of 25 July 1890, p. 9 for letter to the editor referring to Pekina branch being one of those started without input of central branch delegate.
66 SA *Advertiser*, 1 September 1881, p. 4. Given that Walshe had only reached Melbourne in June, this early Pekina recognition of his presence in Australia shows awareness despite issues of distance and communication.
67 *SAR*, 17 August 1882, p. 5.
68 *Evening Journal*, 12 November 1887, p. 5.
69 *SC*, 25 December 1889, p. 5.
70 *SC*, 13 September 1889, p. 8.
71 *SC*, 25 July 1890, p. 9.
72 *SC*, 4 October 1889, p. 9. The series was titled 'Travelling Notes: Flying trip through the north [by our special reporter].'
73 *SC*, 29 November 1889, p. 9.
74 Five guineas came from Fr Dunphy, chairman L. O'Loughlin and Michael Duffy and two guineas from Fr Maher.
75 *SC*, 22 May 1891, p. 7.
76 *SC*, 8 August 1890, p. 5.
77 Broken Hill *Barrier Miner*, 11 February 1892, p. 2.
78 *SC*, 30 June 1893, p. 8.
79 *Orroroo Enterprise and Great Northern Advertiser (OEGNA)*, 11 August 1916, p. 3.
80 *OEGNA*, 6 October, p. 4, 20 October, p. 4 and 27 October, p. 4 (meetings in support), 3 November 1916, p. 4 (anti-conscription). In 1911, the census revealed that only 239 of the County of Dalhousie's population of 6177 were Irish-born – only a small number would have been in Pekina.
81 *OEGNA*, 16 December 1917, p. 2.
82 *OEGNA*, 21 December 1917, p. 3.
83 *SC*, 7 October 1921, p. 9. The SDIL, promoted by de Valera, generated an impressive organisational approach resulting in large membership in city and country areas.
84 *SC*, 26 March 1897, p. 9.
85 *SAR*, 21 March 1905, p. 3.
86 *Quorn Mercury (QM)*, 18 March 1921, p. 2.
87 *QM*, 25 March 1921, p. 3.
88 *QM*, 24 March 1922, p. 3.
89 The Holy Hour devotion involved the whole congregation going to Communion in the morning and attending the Holy Hour in the evening; in Pekina this having happened for two years was judged as inspiring, not just to the clergy, but also to the community who could anticipate a special blessing for their display of faith.
90 *SC*, 13 December 1929, p. 19.
91 See endnote 80 for 1911 census details of County Dalhousie's population of Irish-born.
92 See Stephanie James, 'The Evolution of Adelaide's Irish National Association, 1918–1950: From security threat to cultural force?' in *Journal of the Historical Society of South Australia*, no. 45, 2017, pp. 31–49.
93 See *SC* of 2 May 1953, p. 5 for ongoing evidence in Nora Duffy's obituary. Between 1881 and 1888 (before her marriage) she was Fr Maher's housekeeper at Pekina and the item reports what she and others felt, that she reflected aspects of John O'Brien's poem 'The Little Irish Mother'.

94 Mannion, *No Place like Pekina*, p. 224.
95 *SC*, 29 November 1935, p. 15.
96 *SC*, 27 March 1936, p. 9.
97 *SC*, 2 August 1935, p. 15. See the *Times and Northern Advertiser* of 23 August 1935, p. 23 for lengthy verse about the picnic races based on 'It's a Long Way to Tipperary'.
98 *SC*, 2 August 1935, p. 15.
99 *SC*, 6 September 1935, p. 15.
100 *SC*, 8 May 1936, p. 17.
101 *SC*, 28 August 1936, p. 7.
102 *SC*, 28 August 1936, p. 7.
103 *SC*, 19 May 1939, p. 15.
104 *SC*, 29 January 1937, p. 8. Fr Prendergast stated that 'the local committee [had] promised the State Committee that they would hold a Centenary Celebration … during February 1937, and that promise will be fulfilled in the spirit and in the letter on the 20th of February'.
105 *SC*, 12 February 1937, p. 15. See John O'Brien, *Around the Boree Log and Other Verses*, Angus and Robertson Ltd, Sydney, 1921, pp. 69–74, 'The Old Mass Shandrydan', which recounts travelling 10 miles to mass.
106 *SC*, 12 February 1937, p. 15.
107 Port Pirie *Recorder*, 22 February 1937, p. 1. Only pilot surnames were provided: Anderson in a Fokker (winner of the £20), Kleinig in a Bristol and Warwick in a Fox Moth.
108 *SC*, 14 May 1937, p. 15.
109 *Times and Northern Advertiser* (*TNA*), 20 August 1937, p. 1.
110 *TNA*, 24 September 1937, p. 3.
111 *SC*, 6 July 1934, p. 5.
112 SA *Advertiser*, 21 June 1939, p. 11, *SC*, 19 July 1940, p. 15, *SC*, 11 July 1941, p. 4 and *SC*, 30, June 1943, p. 5.
113 *SC*, 12 June 1945, p. 9.
114 *TNA*, 20 August 1937, p. 1 and p. 29 SC, August 1941, p. 7.
115 *TNA*, 19 August 1938, p. 3.
116 *SC*, 23 August 1940, p. 11.
117 *SC*, 15 December 1933, p. 14.
118 *SC*, 29 November 1935, p. 15.
119 *SC*, 24 January 1941, p. 10.
120 See Mannion, *No Place like Pekina*, pp. 96–97 for discussion about the school closure.
121 *SC*, 29 June 1945, p. 11.
122 *TNA*, 28 February 1936, p. 1.
123 Ryan had bought the hotel in December 1925. His family was from Tipperary, and he had farmed in the Uroonda district near Cradock.
124 Mannion, *No Place like Pekina*, p. 96.
125 Pers. conversation, John Mannion and Suzanne Ryan, Archivist to Sisters of St Joseph, Adelaide.
126 *Government Gazette*, in *SAR* of 3 December 1880, p. 6.
127 Mannion, *No Place like Pekina*, pp. 241–243.
128 See John Mannion, 'History Through Monuments', 2009, copy in John Mannion's possession.
129 Pers. conversation, John Mannion and Bishop O'Kelly June 2018.

130 See Appendix Three (p. 116) for a poem about Pekina's Irish inhabitants. Its provenance is unknown; it was provided to John Mannion during the writing of *No Place like Pekina* in the 1990s.

Irish women in South Australia, 1836-1945

1   Hasia Diner, *Erin's Daughters in America: Irish immigrant women in the nineteenth century*, Johns Hopkins University Press, Baltimore, 1983; Janet Nolan, *Ourselves Alone: Women's emigration from Ireland 1885–1920*, University Press of Kentucky, Lexington, 1989.
2   Donald Harman Akenson, *The Irish Diaspora*, Institute of Irish Studies, The Queen's University of Belfast, Belfast, 1996; Breda Gray, 'Unmasking Irishness: Irish women, the Irish nation and the Irish diaspora', in Jim MacLaughlin (ed.), *Location and Dislocation in Contemporary Irish Society: Emigration and Irish identities*, Cork University Press, Cork, 1997, pp. 228–229; Patrick O'Sullivan (ed.), *Irish Women and Irish Migration*, Leicester University Press, London, 1995.
3   David Fitzpatrick, '"This Is the Place that Foolish Girls Are Knowing": Reading the letters of emigrant Irish women in colonial Australia', in Trevor McClaughlin (ed.), *Irish Women in Colonial Australia*, Allen & Unwin, Sydney, 1998, pp. 163–181; David Fitzpatrick, 'The Unimportance of Gender in Explaining Post-Famine Irish Emigration', in Eric Richards (ed.), *Visible Women: Female immigrants in colonial Australia*, Australian National University Press, Canberra, 1995, p. 146; Trevor McClaughlin, 'Barefoot and Pregnant?: Female orphans who emigrated from Irish workhouses to Australia, 1848–1850', *Familia* vol. 2 no. 3, 1987, pp. 1–5; Elizabeth Rushen, '"Not the Very Lowest and Poorest Classes": Irish female assisted immigration to Australia in the 1830s', *Australasian Journal of Irish Studies*, vol. 9, 2009, pp. 52–72; Elizabeth Rushen, *Colonial Duchesses: The migration of Irish women to New South Wales before the Great Famine*, Anchor Books Australia, Sydney, 2014.
4   Cherry Wedgwood Parkin, 'Irish Female Immigration to South Australia during the Great Famine', BA(Hons) thesis, University of Adelaide, 1964.
5   Stephanie Burley, 'Engagement with Empires: Irish Catholic female religious teachers in colonial South Australia 1868–1901', *Irish Educational Studies*, vol. 31 no. 2, 2012, pp. 175–190; Malcolm Campbell, 'Irish Women in Nineteenth Century Australia: A more hidden Ireland?', in Philip Bull, Chris McConville and Noel McLachlan (eds), *Irish-Australian Studies: Papers delivered at the Sixth Irish-Australian Conference July 1990*, La Trobe University, Melbourne, 1991, pp. 26–38; Jan Gothard, *Blue China: Single female migration to colonial Australia*, University of Melbourne Press, Melbourne, 2001; Dianne Hall, '"Now Him White Man": Images of Irish in colonial Australia', *History Australia*, vol. 11 no. 2, 2014, pp. 167–195; Dianne Hall and Elizabeth Malcolm, 'Diaspora, Gender and the Irish', *Australasian Journal of Irish Studies*, vol. 8, 2008/2009, pp. 3–29; Paula Hamilton, *No Irish Need Apply: Aspects of the employer–employee relationship Australian domestic service 1860–1900*, University of London, Australian Studies Centre, London, 1988; Chris McConville, *Croppies, Celts and Catholics: The Irish in Australia*, Edward Arnold, Melbourne, 1987, p. 87.
6   Trevor McClaughlin (ed.), *Irish Women in Colonial Australia*, Allen & Unwin, Sydney, 1998. See smaller studies such as Eric Richards and Ann Herraman, '"If She Was to Be Hard Up She Would Sooner Be Hard Up in a Strange Land than Where She Would Be Known": Irish women in colonial South Australia', in McClaughlin (ed.), *Irish Women*, pp. 85–86; Mark Staniforth, 'The *Inconstant* Girls: The migration experience of nearly 200 Irish orphan girls and young women sent to Adelaide in 1849 aboard the barque *Inconstant*', in Sue Williams, Dymphna Lonergan, Rick Hosking, Laura Deane and Nena Bierbaum (eds), *The Regenerative Spirit Volume 2*, Lythrum Press, Adelaide, 2004, pp. 27–42.

7   Margaret Barbarlet, *Far from a Low Gutter Girl: The forgotten world of state wards, South Australia, 1887–1940*, Oxford University Press, Melbourne, 1983; Brian Dickey, *Rations, Residences, Resources: A history of social welfare in South Australia since 1836*, Wakefield Press, Adelaide, 1986; Marie Steiner, *Servants Depots in Colonial South Australia*, Wakefield Press, Adelaide, 2009.

8   See, for example, Michael Cannon, *Australia in the Victorian Age: Who's master? Who's man?*, Viking O'Neil, Melbourne, 1988, pp. 137–140; Gothard, *Blue China*, pp. 41–44; Rushen, 'Not the Very Lowest and Poorest Classes', 2009, pp. 52–72; as well as newspaper commentaries such as A.T. Saunders, 'Irish Girl Migrants in 1855', *South Australian Register (SAR)*, 4 July 1924, p. 7; *SAR*, 28 June 1855, p. 2; *SAR* 3 April 1856, p. 3.

9   Official assisted passage passenger lists GRG35/48/1 number 8/1850 – *Tory*, State Records of South Australia (SRSA), (file for 'Arrivals *Tory*, August 27 1850 Female Emigration Fund list of 31 females embarked for Adelaide and Sydney on board the *Tory*, Captain Row' lists under 'for Adelaide' Bridget Donelly).

10 Alexander C. Wood and Frederic Rogers, 'Letter to the Right Honourable Earl Grey, Secretary of State, 11 August 1848', in *Irish University Press Series of British Parliamentary Papers: Correspondence and papers relating to emigration and other affairs in Australia, 1849–50*, vol. 11, Irish University Press, Shannon, 1968–1969, p. 351.

11 *Argus*, 24 January 1850, p. 3; *Goulburn Herald (GH)*, 2 March 1850, quoted in Emily Lieffers, 'Starving Ireland, Hungry Australia: The Irish female orphan emigration scheme, 1848–1850', *Constellations*, vol. 2 no. 1, 2010, pp. 1–31.

12 *Hobart Town Courier*, 4 July 1834, p. 4; *Launceston Advertiser* 27 December 1832, p. 4; 'Adelaide Hospital Admission Records', GRG 78/49 SRSA, (file for 18/2/1848 lists Richard Haimes, aged 25 yrs, surveyor).

13 *Kapunda Herald (KH)*, 4 August 1871, p. 2.

14 Mary Kent, née Murphy, pers. conversation 9 December 2014.

15 *KH*, 12 July 1871, p. 4.

16 *KH*, 28 July 1871, p. 3.

17 *South Australian Chronicle and Weekly Mail*, 29 August 1874, p. 7, 'Coroner's Inquest'.

18 *KH*, 14 December 1875, p. 3; *KH*, 20 June 1876, p. 2; *KH*, 23 June 1876, p. 2; *Kapunda Herald and Northern Intelligencer (KHNI)*, 27 April 1875, p. 3; *KHNI*, 14 August 1874, p. 2.

19 *Express and Telegraph*, 21 June 1876, p. 4; *KHNI*, 20 June 1876, p. 2.

20 *KHNI*, 16 January 1877, p. 3; *KH*, 9 January 1877, p. 3.

21 'John O'Connell was also teacher at Melrose. He later moved to Penola and was licensee of Royal Oak hotel from 1910', *Laura Standard*, 7 July 1910, p. 2.

22 Marie Therese Foale, *The Josephite Story*, St Joseph's Generalate, Sydney, 1989, p. 226; 'St. John's School, examined on 11th November, Sisters of St. Joseph, who also conduct the Kapunda school' *KHNI*, 12 November 1869, p. 3. Also noted in *Southern Cross (SC)*, 17 June 1949, p. 8.

23 See *Avoca Mail* of 30 May 1890, p. 2, 'The Wealthiest Man in South West Victoria' and *Evening Journal Adelaide*, 25 June 1890, p. 3.

24 Mary Ann Joyce, born 1841, married Austin O'Loughlin in 1858 at St John's. Austin O'Loughlin was born in 1837 in Ballyvaughan, County Clare (SA Genealogical Society records).

25 SA *Advertiser*, 30 March 1893, p. 6, 'Local Court – Adelaide'.

26 Madeline Sophie McGrath, *These Women? Women Religious in the History of Australia: The Sisters of Mercy Parramatta, 1888–1988*, New South Wales University Press, Sydney, 1989, p. 5.

27 Osmond Thorpe, *Mary MacKillop: The life of Mother Mary of the Cross*, Burns & Oates, London, 1957, p. 49.

28 Mary MacKillop 6 January 1885 to Archbishop Moran, in Sheila McCreanor, *Mary MacKillop in Challenging Times 1883–1899: A collection of letters*, Sisters of St Joseph of the Sacred Heart, Sydney, 2006, p. 77.
29 For more detail, see Cherrie De Leiuen, '"Corporal Punishment and the Grace of God": The archaeology of a 19th century girls' reformatory', *Archaeology in Oceania*, vol. 50 no. 3, 2015, pp. 145–152; Cherrie De Leiuen, 'Remembering the Significant: St John's Kapunda, South Australia', *Journal of Australian Catholic History*, vol. 36, 2016, pp. 43–60.
30 Margaret Barbarlet, *Far from a Low Gutter Girl*, p. xv.
31 Brian Dickey, *Rations, Residences, Resources*, p. 31.
32 *KH*, 27 October 1899, p. 3.
33 SC, 6 September 1907, p. 25; see for example, discussion of Irish women in Geoffrey H. Manning, *A Colonial Experience, 1838–1910: A woman's story of life in Adelaide, the district of Kensington and Norwood together with reminiscences of colonial life*, Gillingham Printers, Adelaide, 2001 and 'A Word for Irish Servant Girls', *Irish Harp (IH)*, 6 March 1874, p. 3a; 'No Irish Need Apply', *Adelaide Times (AT)*, 19 December 1855, p. 3.
34 Catherine Kovesi, *Pitch Your Tents on Distant Shores: A history of the Sisters of the Good Shepherd in Australia, Aotearoa/New Zealand and Tahiti*. Playright Publishing, Sydney, 2006, p. 287.
35 See 'Girls Absconding, St John's Reformatory for Girls, Sr Berchmans to State Children's Department', 24 June 1909, GRG 35/48/1 Unit 2, State Records of South Australia (SRSA) and various 'correspondence files' from 1908 to 1909, Berchmans to and from State Children's Department, GRG 27/1 SRSA.
36 'Mrs Mary Lee', SA *Advertiser*, 7 April 1902, p. 4; Helen Jones, *In Her Own Name: A history of women in South Australia from 1836*, Wakefield Press, Adelaide, 1986, p. 83; Elizabeth Mansutti, *Mary Lee, 1821–1909: Let her name be honoured*, E. Ho in association with Women's Suffrage Centenary History Sub-Committee, Adelaide, 1994; 'Lee, Mary (1821–1909)', *The Australian Women's Register, National Foundation for Australian Women*, http://www.womenaustralia.info/biogs/AWE0823b.htm accessed 12 March 2018.
37 *SAR*, 17 July 1893, p. 7.
38 Helen Jones, 'Lee, Mary (1821–1909)', in *Australian Dictionary of Biography*, National Centre of Biography, Australian National University (ANU), Canberra, 1986, http://adb.anu.edu.au/biography/lee-mary-7150 accessed 27 February 2018.
39 'The Women's Suffrage League, Women and Politics in South Australia', in *Parliament of South Australia, 2006*, https://www.parliament.sa.gov.au/ABOUTPARLIAMENT/HISTORY/WOMENINPOLITICSINSOUTHAUSTRALIA/Pages/TheWomensSuffrageLeague.aspx accessed 27 February 2018.
40 *SAR*, 15 January 1890 p. 6; Richard Froggatt, 'Mary Lee', *Dictionary of Ulster Biography*, http://www.newulsterbiography.co.uk/index.php/home/viewPerson/1934 accessed 12 March 2018.
41 Quoted in Eleanor Ramsay, 'Working Women and the Council, to Unite More Closely SA Unions History 1884–1984', 1984, http://www.saunions.org.au/Campaigns/Women/workingwomen.html accessed 1 March 2018.
42 *Adelaide Observer*, 22 March 1890, p. 8; for short summary see 'Working Women's Trade Union', State Library of South Australia (SLSA), 2007, http://www.samemory.sa.gov.au/site/page.cfm?u=675 accessed 2 March 2018.
43 'Mary Lee' in Women Shaping the Nation, *Victorian Honour Roll of Women, Volume 1*, Centenary of Federation, Victoria, 2001, p. 17, https://herplacemuseum.com/wp-content/uploads/2017/03/2001-Honour-Roll-Booklet.pdf accessed 27 February 2018.
44 Mansutti, *Mary Lee*.

45 Jones, 'Lee, Mary (1821–1909)'.
46 See, for example, *SAR*, 21 July 1888, p. 3; *SAR*, 27 July 1888, p. 7; *SAR*, 30 June 1896, p. 5; *SAR*, 20 September 1909, p. 4.
47 *Advertiser*, 7 April 1902, p. 3.
48 Patrick O'Farrell, *The Irish in Australia: 1788 to the present*, Third edition, University of New South Wales Press, Sydney, 2000, pp. 115–196.
49 Richards, *Visible Women*.
50 Mansutti and Jones both speculate. Also, after her death Mrs Nicholls of the Women's Christian Temperance Union stated, 'She was an eccentric, impulsive Irish woman. Her personality came much before the public, for she was a voluminous correspondent to the press. People used to talk and wonder about her. She was on a tram car one day when two women, discussing the suffragist, said, "She's just some crabby old maid." Miss Lee waited until she was getting off the car and then said, "You really are mistaken. I'm the crabby old maid; Mary Lee is my mother."' See *Crinoline Days – A Chat With Mrs E.W. Nicholls*, SLSA, http://www.slsa.sa.gov.au/manning/sa/women/suffrage.htm accessed 15 March 2018.
51 See, for more detail, De Leiuen, 'Corporal Punishment', p. 147.

The 'wrong kind of immigrant' : How existing prejudice on class, gender and ethnicity affected the reception of female Irish Famine orphans in South Australia under the Earl Grey Scheme

1 Eric Richards, 'Irish Life and Progress in Colonial South Australia', *Irish Historical Studies*, vol. 27 no. 107, 1995, p. 234.
2 Mark Staniforth, 'The *Inconstant* Girls: The migration experiences of 200 Irish orphan girls and young women sent to Adelaide in 1848 aboard the barque *Inconstant*', in Sue Williams, Dymphna Lonergan, Rick Hosking, Laura Deane and Nena Bierbaum (eds), *The Regenerative Spirit: (Un)settling, (dis)locations, (post-) colonial, (re)presentations – Australian post-colonial reflections*, Lythrum Press, Adelaide, 2004, pp. 27–41.
3 Cheryl Mongan, '"This Species of Immigration": The Irish famine orphans 1848–1850', in Jeff Brownrigg, Cheryl Mongan and Richard Reid (eds), *Echoes of Irish Australia: From rebellion to republic*, St Clement's Retreat and Conference Centre, Galong, 2007, p. 46.
4 Patrick O'Farrell, *The Irish in Australia: 1788 to the present*, University of New South Wales Press, Sydney, 1986, p. 65.
5 Joseph Robins, 'Irish Orphan Emigration to Australia 1848–1850', *Studies: An Irish quarterly review*, vol. 57 no. 228, 1968, pp. 372–387.
6 Eric Richards and Ann Herraman, '"If She Was to Be Hard Up She Would Sooner Be Hard Up in a Strange Land than Where She Would Be Known": Irish women in colonial South Australia', in Trevor McClaughlin (ed.), *Irish Women in Colonial Australia*, Allen & Unwin, Sydney, 1998, p. 86.
7 Trevor McClaughlin (ed.), *Barefoot and Pregnant?: Irish Famine orphans in Australia*, Genealogical Society of Victoria, Melbourne, 1991, p. R225.
8 Colonial Land and Emigration Commission (CLEC), *Tenth General Report of the Colonial Land and Emigration Commissioners*, William Clowes & Sons, London, 1850, p. 20, https://archive.org/stream/op1246959-1001#page/n0/mode/2up accessed 20 January 2018.
9 For a list of the ships that travelled to Australia under the Earl Grey Scheme, see the Sydney Irish Famine Memorial website at http://www.irishfaminememorial.org/en/orphans/ships/.
10 Robins, 'Irish Orphan Emigration', p. 378.
11 McClaughlin, *Barefoot and Pregnant?*, p. R225.

12 Kay Caball, *The Kerry Girls: Emigration and the Earl Grey Scheme*, The History Press Ireland, Dublin, 2014, pp. 115–116.
13 CLEC, *Ninth General Report of the Colonial Land and Emigration Commissioners*, William Clowes & Sons, London, June 1849, p. 13, https://archive.org/stream/op1246793-1001#page/n0/mode/2up accessed 20 January 2018. This statistic refers only to European immigrants in South Australia, and does not include Indigenous Australians who already lived on the land claimed by the colony.
14 Richards, 'Irish Life and Progress,' p. 216.
15 *Adelaide Observer (AO)*, 14 July 1849, p. 1.
16 *South Australian Gazette and Mining Journal (SAGMJ)*, 9 December 1848, p. 2.
17 *AO*, 14 July 1849, p. 1.
18 South Australian Migration Museum (SAMM), *From Many Places: The history and cultural traditions of South Australian people*, Wakefield Press, Adelaide, 1995, p. 238.
19 Eric Richards, 'The Importance of Being Irish in Colonial South Australia', in John O'Brien and Pauric Travers (eds), *The Irish Emigrant Experience in Australia*, Poolbeg Press, Dublin, 1991, p. 63.
20 Joseph Robins, 'The Emigration of Irish Workhouse Children to Australia in the 19th Century', in John O'Brien and Pauric Travers (eds), *The Irish Emigrant Experience in Australia*, Poolbeg Press, Dublin, 1991, p. 39.
21 Robins, 'Emigration of Irish Workhouse Children', p. 39.
22 *SAGMJ*, 28 October 1848, p. 3.
23 Robins, 'Emigration of Irish Workhouse Children', p. 43.
24 *South Australian Register (SAR)*, 25 October 1848, p. 2.
25 McClaughlin, *Barefoot and Pregnant?*, p. i.
26 McClaughlin, *Barefoot and Pregnant?*, p. ii.
27 McClaughlin, *Barefoot and Pregnant?*, p. i.
28 *SAR*, 25 October 1848, p. 2.
29 McClaughlin, *Barefoot and Pregnant?*, p. 1.
30 SAMM, *From Many Places*, p. 237.
31 *Goulburn Herald and County of Argyle Advertiser (GHCAA)*, 16 March 1850, p. 6.
32 *South Australian (SA)*, 24 November 1848, p. 2.
33 *SAR*, 2 September 1848, p. 2.
34 *SAGMJ*, 28 October 1848, p. 3.
35 *SAGMJ*, 28 October 1848, p. 3.
36 *GHCAA*, 16 March 1850, p. 6.
37 *SAR*, 21 January 1850, p. 3.
38 *SAR*, 21 January 1850, p. 3.
39 *SAR*, 24 January 1850, p. 3.
40 *SAR*, 24 January 1850, p. 3.
41 *SAR*, 25 January 1850, p. 2.
42 *SAR*, 6 February 1850, p. 2.
43 Robins, 'Emigration of Irish Workhouse Children', p. 42.
44 *SA*, 17 January 1851, p. 2.
45 *SAR*, 19 January 1850, p. 4.
46 *SA*, 17 October 1850, p. 4.
47 Richards and Herraman, 'Irish Women,' p. 86.
48 *SAR*, 27 October 1849, p. 4.
49 *SAR*, 27 October 1849, p. 4.
50 CLEC, *Ninth General Report*, p. 12.
51 CLEC, *Tenth General Report*, p. 19.

52 Richards and Herraman, 'Irish Women,' p. 86.
53 McClaughlin, *Barefoot and Pregnant?*, p. iii.

Irish lawyers and judges in South Australia, 1836-1914

1   R.M. Hague, *Portrait of a Judge*, Melbourne University Press, Melbourne, 1963 and, from J.M. Bennett's series, *Lives of the Australian Chief Justices*, Federation Press, Sydney: *Sir James Dowling: Second Chief Justice of New South Wales 1837-1844* (2001), *George Higginbotham: Third Chief Justice of Victoria 1886-1892* (2007), *Sir Frederick Darley: Sixth Chief Justice of New South Wales* ... (2016); Gerald O'Collins, *Patrick McMahon Glynn: A founder of Australian Federation*, Melbourne University Press, Melbourne, 1965; Ruth Campbell, 'Irish Lawyers in Victoria, 1838-60' in Philip Bull, Chris McConville and Noel McLachlan (eds), *Irish-Australian Studies: Papers delivered at the Sixth Irish-Australian Conference, July 1990*, La Trobe University, Melbourne, 1991, pp. 39-52.
2   Ann Daniel, 'Undermining British Australia: Irish lawyers and the transformation of English law in Australia', *Studies: An Irish quarterly review*, 84, 1995, pp. 61-70; Jarlath Ronayne, *First Fleet to Federation: Irish supremacy in colonial Australia*, Trinity College Press, Dublin, 2002.
3   Gerard Brennan, 'The Irish and Law in Australia', *The Irish Jurist*, 1986, p. 95; Alex C. Castles, 'Now and Then: Irish connections with Australian law', *Australian Law Journal*, vol. 66, 1992, p. 532.
4   Tony Earls, 'Irish Lawyers in Colonial Australia: "Significant yet indefinable"?', Global Irish Studies (UNSW) Symposium, 4 October 2012, https://hal.arts.unsw.edu.au/events/gist-irish-lawyers-in-colonial-australia-significant-yet-indefinable/ accessed 26 July 2017; Tony Earls, *Plunkett's Legacy: An Irishman's contribution to the 'Rule of Law' in New South Wales*, Australian Scholarly Publishing, Melbourne, 2009; Diane Campbell, 'Agents of Change and Civilisation: Anglo-Irish lawyers in Central Victoria, 1851-1886', ANZHS Conference, 2008.
5   Patrick O'Farrell, *The Irish in Australia*, University of New South Wales Press, Sydney, 1988 p. 142; Eric Richards, 'Migrants in the Mature Colony: South Australia c. 1840-c. 1877', *Journal of the Historical Society of South Australia*, vol. 45, 2017, p. 11.
6   Derived from Peter Moore's larger prosopography of all South Australian lawyers 1837-1945, and a comparative study of lawyers from New South Wales, South Australia and New Zealand, 1837-1861.
7   The Torrens system of land registration, indelibly associated with Kerryman, Robert Torrens, and in part inspired by Irish factors, was essentially English in legal principle and politically colonial in achievement, its German elements notwithstanding: Douglas Pike, 'Introduction of the Real Property Act in South Australia', *Adelaide Law Review*, 1960-1962, 1, pp. 169-89; Antonio Esposito, 'A Comparison of the Australian ('Torrens') System of Land Registration of 1858 and the Law of Hamburg in the 1850s', *Australian Legal History Journal*, vol. 7, 2003, p. 193; Greg Taylor, 'Is the Torrens System German?', *Journal of Legal History*, vol. 29, 2008, p. 253; Greg Taylor, 'Ulrich Hübbe's Doctoral Thesis – A Note on the Major Work of an Unusual Figure in Australian Legal History', *Legal History*, vol. 13, 2009, p. 121.
8   Compare Eric Richards, 'The Importance of Being Irish in Colonial South Australia', in John O'Brien and Pauric Travers (eds), *The Irish Emigrant Experience in Australia*, Poolbeg Press, Dublin, 1991 pp. 62-64, 94-95, and David Fitzpatrick, 'Irish immigration 1840-1914', in James Jupp (ed.), *The Australian People: An encyclopedia of the nation, its people and their origins*, Cambridge University Press, Sydney, 2001 pp. 451-456.
9   Legislation passed for England before the proclamation on 28 December 1836 applied if it suited the circumstances of the colony and, passed afterwards, only if it named the colony. The *Emancipation Act 1829* ('An Act for the Relief of His Majesty's

Roman Catholic Subjects', 10 Geo. 4 c. 7, assented 13 April 1829) applied in South Australia not because it affected Ireland, but because its terms applied it to England.

10   Ralph Hague, *Hague's History of the Law in South Australia, 1837–1867*, Barr Smith Library Press, Adelaide, 2005, vol. 2, p. 545.

11   Queen's Inn during the reign of Victoria, 1837–1901. On using the plural form, see Colum Kenny, *King's Inns and the Kingdom of Ireland: The Irish 'Inn of Court' 1541–1800*, Irish Academic Press, Dublin, 1992, and see https://www.kingsinns.ie/ accessed 22 August 2017.

12   The obligation to attend the Inns of Court in London for nine terms – a kind of 'Poynings Law' for the bar – dates from 1541 and was abolished in 1885, see Colum Kenny, *Tristram Kennedy and the Revival of Irish Legal Training, 1835–1885*, Irish Academic Press & Irish Legal History Society, Dublin, 1996. On the other hand, call to the English bar amounted to automatic admission to King's Inns: Act No. 32 Geo. III (1792).

13   Commonly called 'attorneys' until the 1870s in both Ireland and South Australia, most were admitted in Dublin as both attorneys and solicitors, as all had been in Adelaide since 1837.

14   Peter Moore, *The Roll of Practitioners Admitted to the Supreme Court of South Australia 1837 to 1945*, Australian Legal Heritage, Sydney, 2013, pp. 10–11.

15   '[L]egal enculturation transcended … national enculturation': Earls, 'Irish Lawyers in Colonial Australia – "significant yet indefinable"?'.

16   After them, no one of Irish extraction reached the Supreme Court bench until 1959 when Premier Thomas Playford appointed James Brazel QC in 1959 over the 'dead body' of Chief Justice Napier (Napier's words). Malcolm Playford, interview with Peter Moore, 15 May 2007.

17   His reverence reputedly trained four sons for the bar to help him contest his claim to a Scottish peerage: http://www.igp-web.com/Longford/crawf3.htm accessed 31 March 2018.

18   Earldom (Bellomont), viscountcy (Molesworth) and baronage (Mount-Florence), see William Courthope (ed.), *Debrett's Complete Peerage of the United Kingdom of Great Britain and Ireland*, 22nd edition, Rivington, London, 1838 and George Cokayne and Vicary Gibbs (eds), *The Complete Peerage: Or, a history of the House of Lords and all its members from the earliest times*, Second edition, St Catherine Press, London, 1910. Ponsonby Moore, barrister-cousin of the Earl of Drogheda, applied in 1850 and again in 1851 but died before he could be admitted, leaving his 'capital horse' and his gowns, bands and wig to be sold off, *South Australian Register (SAR)*, 8 October 1851, p. 4.

19   'Glynn, Patrick McMahon (Paddy) (1855–1931)', *Australian Dictionary of Biography*, vol. 9, Melbourne University Press, Melbourne, 1983.

20   Irish-born but not Irish qualified, Sidney Bernard is mentioned here because he started his training in Dublin but completed it in Adelaide: Supreme Court admission files, Bernard, S 1842, GRG 36/49/2, State Records of SA (SRSA); J.H. Bernard, *The Bernards of Kerry*, J.H. Bernard, Dublin, 1922.

21   Law teaching was not systemic until 1850, see W.N. Osborough, *The Law School of University College Dublin*, Four Courts Press, Dublin, Chapter 1, http://www.drb.ie/ new-books/the-law-school-of-university-college-dublin accessed 13 January 2018.

22   Supreme Court admission files, Molesworth, R 1852, GRG 36/49/2, SRSA.

23   Supreme Court admission files, Martyn, MJ 1853, GRG 36/49/2, SRSA.

24   O'Collins, *Patrick McMahon Glynn*, p. 19.

25   Supreme Court admission files, Bagot, JT 1851, GRG 36/49/, SRSA.

26   Bagot, Charles Hervey (1788–1880), *Australian Dictionary of Biography*, vol. 1, Melbourne University Press, Melbourne, 1966.

27 Robin Haines, *Life and Death in the Age of Sail: The passage to Australia*, University of New South Wales Press, Sydney, 2006; Robin Haines, *Doctors at Sea: Emigrant voyages to colonial Australia*, Palgrave Macmillan, Basingstoke, 2005, pp. 8–9; Katherine Foxhall, *Health, Medicine, and the Sea: Australian voyages, c. 1815–60*, Manchester University Press, Manchester, 2012 especially pp. 1–2, 16–20, 44–45, 79.
28 Supreme Court admission files, Lucas, T 1841, GRG36/49/2, SRSA.
29 A 'turn-about rule', asserted in Crawford's obituary – *SAR*, 28 September 1852, p. 3 – was endorsed by Ralph Hague, 'Mr Justice Crawford: Judge of the Supreme Court of South Australia 1850–1852', (unpublished), Ralph Hague, Adelaide, 1957 (typescript held at State Library of South Australia), and Crawford, George John (1812–1852), *Australian Dictionary of Biography*, vol. 3, Melbourne University Press, Melbourne, 1969.
30 Molesworth, Sir Robert (1806–1890), *Australian Dictionary of Biography*, vol. 5, Melbourne University Press, Melbourne, 1974.
31 *Adelaide Times*, 2 July 1853, p. 2; *SAR*, 2 July 1853, p. 2.
32 Edward later led a high-powered law firm in Melbourne's Chancery Lane, see *Argus*, 21 March 1890, p. 5 and 30 April 1890, p. 7. See also Fitzgerald, Nicholas (1829–1908), *Australian Dictionary of Biography*, vol. 4, Melbourne University Press, Melbourne, 1972.
33 *Adelaide Observer* 21 November 1896, p. 16; *Otago Daily Times*, 10 May 1898 p. 3, NZ *Evening Post*, 6 August 1921, p. 9.
34 *Local Courts Act* No. 5 of 1850, assented 12 March, 'District Courts [sic]', *SA Government Gazette*, 2 May 1850 in *South Australian*, 3 May 1850, p. 2.
35 See note 19 above.
36 *Argus*, 14 September 1907, p. 19.
37 Casey, James Joseph (1831–1913), *Australian Dictionary of Biography*, vol. 3, Melbourne University Press, Melbourne, 1969.
38 *SAR*, 17 June 1875, p. 1; *SAR*, 8 August 1881 p. 5. J.G. Daly, 'The South Australian Justices' Manual Compiled for the Information and Guidance of Magistrates, Their Clerks, and Others Assisting in the Administration of Justice', Government Printer, Adelaide, 1871; see *Evening Journal*, 9 May 1871, p. 2 for a review.
39 Both men re-signed the roll as Toler-Rowley in 1903, Moore, *The Roll of Practitioners* pp. 20, 45, 46, 48–49 (see note 12 above).
40 *SA Advertiser*, 31 July 1872, p. 2; *SAR*, 15 April 1889, p. 5; *Express*, 17 April, 1889 p. 5.
41 *SAR*, 13 Supplement, August 1870, p. 7.
42 *Southern Cross*, 22 March 1901, p. 4.
43 Publications about Kingston concentrate on his federal activism rather than the whole man: Margaret Glass, *Charles Cameron Kingston: Federation father*, Melbourne University Press, Melbourne, 1997; John Bannon, 'The Knight of the Realm and the Friend of Labor: The contrasting careers of Sir John Downer and Charles Kingston', *Journal of the Historical Society of South Australia*, vol. 36, 2008, pp. 8–23; Craig Campbell, 'Charles Cameron Kingston, Radical Liberal and Democrat: A contribution to the study of Australian liberalism with particular reference to Kingston's career in federal politics', BA(Hons) thesis, University of Adelaide, 1970.
44 Denny, William Joseph (Bill) (1872–1946), *Australian Dictionary of Biography*, vol. 8, Melbourne University Press, Melbourne, 1981.
45 Law Reform Bills October 1895 (HLA, Hansard, 6 to 11 November 1895) and August 1898 (HLA, Hansard, 31 August 1898 to 3 March 1899).
46 Trinity College and King's Inn exercised powerful influences on Australian public life, through its barristers and other professions. See Ronayne, *First Fleet to Federation*; Jarlath Ronayne, *The Irish in Australia: Rogues and reformers, First Fleet to Federation*, Second edition, Viking, Melbourne, 2003. See also Jarlath Ronayne and Robert Pascoe (eds), *The Irish Imprint in Australia*, Victoria University of Technology,

Melbourne, c. 1994. It is important to be wary of a tendency to over-emphasise, e.g. Chris McConville, 'Irish' in *eDictionary of Melbourne*, http://www.emelbourne.net.au/biogs/EM00763b.htm accessed 5 August 2018.
47 Hague, *Hague's History*, vol. 2, Law Club of Ireland, instituted 1791: *Pigot and Co's City of Dublin and Hibernian Provincial Directory*, J. Pigot, London, 1824.
48 His father George wore his 'Paddy' ambivalently, see *Express*, 26 January 1867, p. 2.
49 Peter Moore, *Thomas R. Bright: Reminiscences of 25 years of the law*, Australian Legal Heritage, Sydney, 2010, pp. 8–9.
50 *Frearson's Monthly Illustrated Adelaide News*, 1 March 1883, p. 2; *SAR*, 10 February 1883, p. 5; SA *Advertiser*, 1 July 1882, pp. 5–6; SA *Advertiser*, Supplement, 17 February 1883, p. 1.
51 Smith, Francis Villeneuve (1883–1956), *Australian Dictionary of Biography*, vol. 11, Melbourne University Press, Melbourne, 1988, and see J.M. Bennett and R.C. Solomon, *Sir Francis Smith* [forthcoming, Federation Press, Sydney, 2018].
52 *SAR*, 16 March 1839, p. 3.
53 See SA *Advertiser*, 28 December 1906, p. 4, 'Crown Solicitor in a Hole' published as Proclamation Day reading.
54 SA *Advertiser*, 18 August 1838, p. 2.
55 *SAR*, 27 March 1862, p. 2.
56 See for example, Peter Moore, *Charles Supple: A short life*, Australian Legal Heritage, Sydney, 2009.
57 Peter Moore, 'Scots Lawyers in Common Law Colonies', Australian & New Zealand Law & History Conference, University of Adelaide, 2015, and '"British" Law and Irish and Scottish Lawyers in Early South Australia', Australian & New Zealand Law and History Conference, University of Melbourne, 2010.
58 See *Australian*, 21 December 1832, p. 3 for editorial critique by Attwell Hayes from Cork on *Ex parte Dillon* (NSW Supreme Court, Banco, 14 December). 'Patlanders' was also used in South Australia, see *Chronicle*, 14 August 1875, p. 17.

South Australia's Irish colonial surgeons: The first 30 years, 1836-1866

1 'Torrens, Robert (1780–1864)', *Australian Dictionary of Biography*, adb.anu.edu.au/biography/torrens-robert-2740 accessed 12 January 2018; 'Glenelg, Baron (1776–1866)', *Australian Dictionary of Biography*, adb.anu.edu.au/biography/glenelg-baron-2101 accessed 12 January 2018. Irish-born Robert Torrens was chairman of the Colonisation Commission for South Australia. The *Mercury*, 13 August 1866, p. 3, 'Lord Glenelg'.
2 A.A. Lendon, 'Thomas Young Cotter, L.C.A., the First Colonial Surgeon for South Australia', unpublished manuscript, T.C. Borrow Collection, BORR/BOO5/01/02, Flinders University, South Australia, 1931; Ian L.D. Forbes, *From Colonial Surgeon to Health Commission: The government provision of health services in South Australia 1836–1995*, ILD Forbes, Adelaide, 1996, p. 1.
3 State Library of South Australia, 'Papers of Dr Alfred Austin Lendon 1854–1935', PRG 128.
4 Forbes, *From Colonial Surgeon*.
5 A.A. Lendon, 'Thomas Young Cotter'.
6 Marriage Entry, Thomas Young Cotter and Jane Nicholson, London Metropolitan Archives; London, England; *Church of England Parish Registers, 1754–1931*; Reference Number: p89/ctc/061 www.ancestry.com.au accessed 1 February 2018.
7 State Record Office of South Australia (SRSA) GRS 11897 Register of Medical Practitioners and Minutes of Medical Board to 1961.
8 Brian Dickey and Peter Howell (eds), *South Australia's Foundation: Select Documents*, Wakefield Press, Adelaide, 1986, pp. 51–52.

Notes

9   Dickey and Howell, *South Australia's Foundation*, pp. 51–52.
10   *Perth Gazette and West Australian Journal*, 17 January 1835, p. 425, 'Government Notice: Statement of the civil expenditure of the Colony of Western Australia for the quarter ending 31 December 1834'.
11   Brian Dickey, *Rations, Residence, Resources: A history of social welfare in South Australia since 1836*, Wakefield Press, Adelaide, 1986, p. 2.
12   SRSA GRG 24/4/B1837/13 Outwards Correspondence, Colonial Secretary's Office.
13   Forbes, *From Colonial Surgeon*, p. 1.
14   *Southern Australian (SA)*, 2 June 1838, p. 4, 'To the Working Classes of South Australia'. This was the first edition of the new newspaper.
15   House of Commons, 'Appendix to Second Annual Report of the Poor Law Commissioners for England and Wales together with Appendixes A B C D', *Parliamentary Papers*, vol. 29, part 1, 19 Aug 1836, pp. 45–47.
16   David Green and Lawrence Cromwell, *Mutual Aid or Welfare State: Australia's friendly societies*, George Allen & Unwin, Sydney, 1984, pp. 9–10. This was known as the Jones Wellwisher No. 1 Grand Lodge of South Australia.
17   *SA* 1 September 1838, p. 4; Geoffrey H. Manning, *A Colonial Experience 1838–1910*, Gillingham Printers, Adelaide, 2001, pp. 21, 608. According to Manning the first Infirmary was built at "Immigration Square".
18   J. Estcourt Hughes, *A History of the Royal Adelaide Hospital*, The Board of Management of the Royal Adelaide Hospital, Adelaide, 1967, p. 2.
19   *SA*, 1 September 1838, p. 4, 'Original Correspondence'. This contains copies of letters dated 20 January 1838, 9 April 1838 and 25 July 1838.
20   *SA* 1 September 1838, p. 4.
21   *South Australian Gazette and Colonial Register (SAGCR)*, 11 August 1838, p. 3, 'The Infirmary'.
22   *SAGCR*, 11 August 1838, p. 3.
23   *SAGCR*, 13 October 1838, p. 4, 'Mr Thomas Cotter and the Board of Enquiry into the State of the Infirmary'.
24   *SAGCR*, 13 October 1838, p. 4, 'Mr Thomas Cotter and the Board of Enquiry into the State of the Infirmary'.
25   *South Australian Register (SAR)*, 3 August 1839, p. 4, 'The Colonial Surgeon – Health of the Emigrants'.
26   *SA*, 6 October 1838, p. 3, 'To the Editor of the *South Australian Gazette and Colonial Register*', letter dated 1 October 1838.
27   *SA*, 16 January 1839, p. 3, 'The Colonial Surgeon'.
28   *SA*, 16 January 1839, p. 3, 'The Colonial Surgeon'.
29   *SAGCR*, 19 January 1839, p. 3, 'To Thomas Young Cotter, Esq., Colonial Surgeon'.
30   *South Australian Gazette (SAG)*, 18 July 1839, p. 5, 'Government Order'.
31   *SAR*, 3 August 1839, p. 4, 'The Colonial Surgeon – Health of the Emigrants'.
32   *SA*, 7 August 1839, p. 3, 'The Late Colonial Surgeon'.
33   Stevenson, George (1799–1856), *Australian Dictionary of Biography*, http://adb.anu.edu.au/biography/stevenson-george-2699 accessed 12 January 2018.
34   George H. Pitt, *The Press in South Australia 1836 to 1850*, Wakefield Press, Adelaide, 1946, pp. 2–3.
35   *South Australian Register*, 22 June 1839, p. 3, 'To Our Readers'.
36   Pitt, *The Press*, p. 11.
37   Pitt, *The Press*, p. 14.
38   Pitt, *The Press*, p. 11.
39   Pitt, *The Press*, p. 17.
40   *SAR*, 22 June 1839, p. 3, 'To Our Readers'.

41 Pitt, *The Press*, p. 19.
42 Genealogy SA Database, www.genealogysa.org.au/resources/online-databases.html accessed 1 February 2018.
43 'Advertisements', *Southern Australian*, 30 June 1838, p. 2, 'Advertisements'. Cotter, Thomas Young (1805–1882), *Australian Dictionary of Biography*, adb.anu.edu.au/biography/cotter-thomas-young-1923 accessed 1 February 2018.
44 *SA*, 8 May 1849, p. 2 'St Patrick's Society'.
45 'South Australia. Enclosure 1 in No. 10.' *Emigration: Papers relative to emigration to the Australian colonies*, London Her Majesty's Stationery Office, 1850, p. 199.
46 Dublin *Freeman's Journal*, 15 September 1849, p. 3, 'Foreign Intelligence: Colchicum a remedy for cholera'.
47 *Adelaide Times*, 7 January 1854, p. 4, 'New Councillor for Grey Ward'.
48 *SAA*, 20 March 1861, p. 1, 'Professional and Trade', *Adelaide Observer (AO)*, 29 March 1862, p. 8, 'Advertising', 'The Late Doctor Thomas Young Cotter', *Port Augusta Dispatch and Flinders' Advertiser (PADFA)*, 13 January 1882, p. 6, 'The Late Doctor Thomas Young Cotter'. Advertisements appeared in the press for a medical officer for the Great Northern Copper Company Mines in March 1861 to replace the incumbent who had returned to England. However, further advertisements were placed in March 1862.
49 *Port Augusta Dispatch and Flinders' Advertiser (PADFA)*, 13 January 1882, p. 6, 'The Late Doctor Thomas Young Cotter'.
50 *SAR*, 3 May 1850, p. 2, 'Saint Patrick's Society – Annual Dinner'.
51 *SAGCR*, 29 July 1837, p. 1, 'South Australian Church'.
52 *PADFA*, 13 January 1882, p. 6, 'The Late Doctor Thomas Young Cotter'.
53 Jennings, *An Annotated List,* p. 31, Dr. W. Gosse, M.D.', *SAR*, 1 August 1883, p. 2, 'Obituary'.
54 Forbes, *From Colonial Surgeon*, p. 23.
55 *SAR*, 8 December 1884, p. 6, 'The Late Dr Moore'.
56 Greta Jones, '"Strike out Boldly for the Prizes that are Available to You": Medical emigration from Ireland 1860–1905', *Medical History*, 2010, vol. 54, pp. 59, 68.
57 SRSA GRS 11897 Register of Medical Practitioners and Minutes of Medical Board to 1961.
58 A.A. Lendon, 'Robert Waters Moore. Colonial Surgeon', *Short Biographical Sketches*, PRG128/12/11, State Library of South Australia (SLSA), unpublished manuscript, 1933, *South Australian Gazette and Mining Journal*, 28 July 1849, p. 2, 'Advertising'.
59 A.A. Lendon, 'Robert Waters Moore'.
60 Genealogy SA Database, www.genealogysa.org.au/resources/online-databases.html accessed 1 February 2018. Luduvina's uncle, Francis Stacker Dutton was involved with the Kapunda mine with Irishman Captain Charles Harvey Bagot.
61 South Australian Parliamentary Papers (SAPP), 1867 Blue Book, 1868, p. 18, Lendon, 'Robert Waters Moore'.
62 *AO*, 13 March 1858, p. 5, 'The Government Gazette'.
63 *AO*, 13 November 1858, p. 7, 'Appointment of Colonial Surgeon'.
64 A.A. Lendon, 'Robert Waters Moore'.
65 Evelyn A. Shlomowitz, 'Nurses and Attendants in South Australian Lunatic Asylums, 1858–1884', *Australian Social Work*, December 1994, vol. 47, no. 4, p. 44.
66 Shlomowitz, 'Nurses and attendants', pp. 45–46.
67 Shlomowitz, 'Nurses and attendants', pp. 45–46.
68 SRSA GRG 24/6/A1852/367.
69 SRSA GRG 24/6/A1852/367.
70 SRSA GRG 24/6/A1852/367.
71 Lendon, 'Robert Waters Moore'.

72 *SAR*, 12 February 1861, p. 3, 'Law and Criminal Courts'.
73 *SAA*, 5 February 1862, p. 3,' Wilful Murder of Inspector Pettinger at Government House'.
74 *SAA*, 6 February 1862, p. 3, 'Adjourned Inquest on the Body of Inspector Pettinger'.
75 Adelaide *News*, 14 February 1942, p. 5, 'The Black Apron Murder at Government House'.
76 *SAR*, 26 September 1862, p. 2., 'Justices of the Peace'.
77 'Police Courts', *SAR*, 15 September 1864, p. 3, 'Police Courts'.
78 SAPP, Report on Adelaide Hospital by Commission appointed to Inquire into and Report on the Management, etc, of the Lunatic Asylum and Hospital, No. 31, Adelaide, 1864. See also Forbes, *From Colonial Surgeon*, pp. 98–193 which provides greater detail.
79 Forbes, *From Colonial Surgeon*, p. 100.
80 SAPP, 1864, no. 31, p. v.
81 *Express and Telegraph (ET)*, 18 February 1867, p. 2, 'The Hospital Enquiry', *ET*, 26 February 1867, p. 3, 'The Hospital Enquiry'.
82 *SAA*, 4 March 1867, p. 3, 'The Hospital Enquiry', *ET*, 5 March 1867, p. 3, 'The Adelaide Hospital', *South Australian Weekly Chronicle (SAWC)*, 9 March 1867, p. 6, 'To the Editor', *SAWC*, 11 May 1867, p. 4, 'The Hospital Enquiry'. Lawrence Healey may have been Irish. Benson refers to him thus: 'I don't think Healey can possibly be a genuine Paddy (as he would lead us to infer from speaking of our country) …' and later adds 'I should advise him the next time he emerges from his obscurity to be more careful in his observations, and sedulously avoid disclosing his nationality, as I am sure Ireland (in common with any other country) ought to be ashamed to own such a specimen'. This was in response to Healey's letter about Benson in March 1867 (see *South Australian Advertiser [SAA]*, 4 March 1867, p. 3, 'The Hospital Enquiry'), where Healey stated:.

'Let him stick to truth, and not give a helping base-hand in sinking, lower than it is our fallen country by such predisposition to falsehood, thereby justifying the necessity and propriety – however painful it may be – of that galling appendage which I am sorry to say we too often see attached to advertisements in the London, Liverpool, Edinburgh, and Glasgow newspaper – "Wanted, a confidential clerk, a superintendent, a housekeeper, a butler, a footman, e'en down to the servant of all work – 'No Irish need apply'.".'

83 *SAA*, 1 March 1867, p. 2, 'The Hospital Enquiry'. See Jennings, *An Annotated List*, p. 78 re Morgan Thomas.
84 Royal College of Surgeons Ireland (RCSI), RCSI Roll of Licentiates, www.rcsi.ie/roll_of_licentiates accessed 29 May 2016, 'Deaths', *Wexford Constitution*, 17 March 1869, p. 3, 'Deaths'. Death notice in this Irish newspaper states he was the son of the late Mr G. Tallis of Rossmore, County Kilkenny.
85 *Pettigrew & Oulton's Dublin Almanac & General Register of Ireland* 1846, www.findmypast.com.au accessed 20 November 2016.
86 *SAA*, 7 December 1860 p. 3, 'New Appointments'.
87 *Kapunda Herald and Northern Intelligencer*, 11 October 1867, p. 3, 'Public Meeting – Friends of Ireland'.
88 SRSA GRG 5/2/1868/539.
89 *Kapunda Herald and Northern Intelligencer*, 27 March 1868, p. 3, 'Indignation Meeting – Attack on the Duke of Edinburgh'.
90 *SAR*, 24 January 1863, p. 3, 'Local Courts'.
91 Genealogy SA database, www.genealogysa.org.au/resources/online-databases.html accessed 1 February 2018.
92 *Kapunda Herald and Northern Intelligencer*, 11 October 1867, p. 3, 'Public Meeting – Friends of Ireland'.

93 RCSI; Mary Clark, IE DCLA UDC/1, *Archives of the Rathmines and Rathgar Township (1847–1930)*, Descriptive List, Dublin City Archivist, 1982, pp. 7, 80.
94 'Death of Surgeon Benson', *Weekly Irish Times (WIT)*, 1 September 1877, p. 2, 'Death of Surgeon Benson', 'UK & Ireland, Medical Directories 1845–1942', www.ancestry.com.au accessed 28 January 2018; 'Ireland, Select Marriages, 1619–1898', www.ancestry.com.au accessed 28 January 2018.
95 *Star*, 17 March 1864, p. 3, 'Government Gazette'.
96 'Assistant Surgeon at the Hospital', *SAR*, 16 November 1864, p. 2, 'Assistant Surgeon at the Hospital', *Argus*, 16 November 1864, p. 5, 'South Australia', *AO*, 19 November 1864, p. 4, 'The Government Gazette'.
97 *WIT*, 1 September 1877, p. 2, 'Death of Surgeon Benson'.
98 South Australian Weekly Chronicle, 9 March 1867, p. 6, in 'To the Editor', Benson stated: 'To the indictment I am an Irishman I plead guilty (without any apology or extenuation); in fact I am rather proud of it.'

St Patrick's Day in South Australia from European settlement to World War II

1 *South Australian Register (SAR)*, 14 March 1840, p. 1.
2 *Southern Australian (SA)*, 17 March 1843, p. 3.
3 Bernard Whimpress, *The South Australian Football Story*, South Australian National Football League, Adelaide, 1983, p. 3.
4 *SAR*, 16 March 1844, p. 3.
5 *SAR*, 15 March 1845, p. 2.
6 *Adelaide Observer (AO)*, supplement, 14 July 1849, p. 1.
7 *SA*, 14 November 1850, p. 2.
8 Margaret M. Press, *From Our Broken Toil: South Australian Catholics 1836–1906*, Catholic Archdiocese of Adelaide, Adelaide, 1986, p. 133.
9 *SAR*, 11 March 1853, p. 2 ('Prince Patrick' refers to Prince Arthur William Patrick Albert). An article in the *Border Watch* of Tuesday 26 June 1923, p. 4, refers to the following: 'HOW THE DUKE OF CONNAUGHT WAS NAMED – While it is generally known that the Duke of Connaught, who has just celebrated his 73rd birthday, was christened Arthur, after his godfather, the Duke of Wellington, upon whose 81st birthday he was born, it is not so widely realised that he was christened Patrick as a sequel to an amusing incident in Dublin. Not so long before Prince Arthur's birth Queen Victoria was on a visit to the Irish capital, and as she drove through the streets she heard a man in the crowd yell out, "Call your son Patrick, Your Majesty, and all ould [sic] Ireland will die for ye!" The Queen recalled the request, and complied with it.'
10 *Adelaide Times (AT)*, 18 March 1853, p. 3.
11 *AT*, 18 March 1854, p. 3.
12 *AT*, 18 March 1856, p. 3. Governor MacDonnell was succeeded by another Irishman six years later, this time a Catholic, Governor Dominick Daly.
13 *South Australian Advertiser (SAA)*, 18 March 1856, p. 3.
14 *AT*, 19 March 1856, p. 3.
15 *SAA*, 10 March 1864, p. 3.
16 Cardinal Paul Cullen (1803–1878): Archbishop of Armagh (1850), Archbishop of Dublin (1852), Appointed Cardinal (1866). Brian Lalor (ed.), *The Encyclopaedia of Ireland*, Gill & Macmillan, Dublin, 2003, p. 262.
17 Dermot Keogh, *Ireland and the Vatican: The politics and diplomacy of Church-State relations, 1922–1960*, Cork University Press, Cork, 1995, p. 3.
18 Emmet Larkin, 'The Devotional Revolution in Ireland – 1850–75', *The American Historical Review*, vol. 77 no. 3, 1972, pp. 625–652.
19 *AO*, 29 March 1862, p. 7.

20 *SAA*, 20 March 1869, p. 3.
21 *SAA*, 16 March 1868, p. 2.
22 *Express and Telegraph (ET)*, 6 January 1879, p. 3.
23 *AO*, 21 March 1868, p. 3.
24 *Irish Harp*, 19 March 1870, p. 5.
25 *SAA*, 18 March 1878, p. 6.
26 *Evening Journal (EJ)*, 18 March 1879, p. 3.
27 *SAA*, 18 March 1880, p. 6.
28 *SAA*, 20 March 1882, p. 6.
29 *SAR*, supplement, 14 March 1881, p. 1.
30 *ET*, 16 March 1881, p. 2.
31 *SAR*, 19 March 1883, p. 7.
32 *ET*, 17 March 1884, p. 2.
33 *SAR*, 18 March 1890, p. 5.
34 *SAR*, 18 March 1890, p. 5.
35 *Adelaide Chronicle (AC)*, 21 March 1896, p. 17.
36 *ET*, 18 March 1897, p. 3.
37 The 'Men of '98' refers to the Irishmen involved in the Irish Uprising of 1798.
38 *Chronicle*, 19 March 1898, p. 17.
39 *Southern Cross (SC)*, 23 March 1900, p. 10.
40 *ET*, 18 March 1901, p. 3.
41 *SAR*, 18 March 1901, p. 6.
42 *AC*, 29 March 1902, p. 35.
43 The following is a list of known South Australian towns and areas that at some point in their history publicly celebrated St Patrick's Day:

Alawoona, Barmera, Berri, Booborowie, Calca, Caltowie, Ceduna, Chandada, Clare, Colton, Cradock, Cummins, Dawson, Edithburg, Echunga, Elliston, Farina, Farrell's Flat, Gawler, Georgetown, Goolwa, Hamley Bridge, Hammond, Iron Knob, Kadina, Kanmantoo, Kapunda, Karoonda, Kingscote, Kyancutta, Lameroo, Macclesfield, Maitland, Marrabel, Meningie, Millicent, Mintaro, Morphett Vale, Morgan, Mount Barker, Mount Gambier, Murray Bridge, Murrayville, Nairne, Naracoorte, Normanville, Ororoo, Panitya, Parilla, Penola, Pekina, Petersburg/Peterborough, Piednippie, Pinkerton Plains, Port Adelaide, Port Augusta, Port Broughton, Port Germein, Port Lincoln, Port MacDonnell, Port Pirie, Quorn, Renmark, Rhynie, Riverton, Saddleworth, Seven Hills, Snowtown, Spalding, Sutherlands, Tailem Bend, Tallala, Tarcoola, Thackaringa, Victor Harbor, Virginia, Wallaroo, Waikerie, Warooka, Waukaringa, Whyalla, Willochra, Willunga, Yankallila, Yarcowie, Yongala and Yorketown.

44 *Daily Herald*, 18 March 1912, p. 3.
45 *Advertiser*, 18 March 1914, p. 18.
46 *Advertiser*, 20 March 1916, p. 7.
47 A complete collection of Adelaide St Patrick's Day button badges (1917–1941), and an 1880 medal, is in the possession of Peter Moore of Katoomba, New South Wales. Peter, who was born and raised in South Australia (and who is a contributor to this book), inherited the collection pinned on black velvet cloth from his great-aunt, Miss Nora Mary Supple (1902–1982). According to Peter, Nora's parents kept hotels around Adelaide. She grew up at the Hampstead Hotel in Collingwood and then the Edinburgh Castle on the corner of Currie and Gray Streets. Nora attended St Mary's Convent, Franklin Street, and worshipped at both the old and new St Patrick's Church, Grote Street. With green paper shamrocks pinned to her first communion dress, she sang 'The Dear Little Shamrock' at a parish concert around 1911, and was known to hum, sing and even whistle 'Hail Glorious St Patrick' in her later years. The

family left the Edinburgh Castle in 1918, but continued to live in the city, until they moved to Prospect in 1930.

The author also has an almost complete collection (1917–1941, except 1930 and 1931) of Adelaide St Patrick's Day button badges, undated Irish Harps, symbolic Irish metal clasps, South Australian country town St Patrick's Day badges, a local Irish National Foresters badge, Home Rule for Ireland badge and Terence MacSwiney badges purchased individually in South Australia over many years.

South Australia was a prolific badge-making state. Local manufacturer A.W. Patrick and other firms produced thousands of badges for many different causes over many years.

48 *Daily Herald*, 28 January 1920, p. 1.
49 Margaret M. Press, *Colour and Shadow: South Australian Catholics 1906–1962*, Archdiocese of Adelaide, Adelaide, 1991, pp. 7–8.
50 *Mail*, 17 March 1917, p. 7.
51 *Chronicle*, 23 March 1918, p. 12.
52 *SC*, 20 March 1925, p. 14.
53 *Chronicle*, 22 March 1919, p. 10.
54 *Daily Herald (DH)*, 24 March 1920, p. 2; *EJ*, 9 March 1920, p. 1.
55 *Register*, 19 March 1920, p. 7.
56 *Advertiser*, 18 March 1920, p. 8.
57 *SC*, 11 February 1921, p. 4.
58 *SC*, 15 October 1920, p. 3.
59 *Register*, 16 February 1921, p. 9.
60 *Advertiser*, 23 February 1921, p. 7.
61 *DH*, 18 March 1922, p. 4.
62 Patrick O'Farrell, *The Irish in Australia*, New South Wales University Press, Sydney, 1986, p. 289.
63 *SC*, 22 July 1932, p. 9.
64 *Chronicle*, 30 June 1932, p. 46.
65 *SC*, 1 March 1935, p. 5.
66 *Advertiser*, 7 February 1938, p. 20.
67 *EJ*, 9 March 1920, p. 1.
68 *Advertiser*, 12 March 1921, p. 10.
69 *SC*, 1 March 1940, p. 15. See Josephine Laffin, *Matthew Beovich: A biography*, Wakefield Press, Adelaide, 2008, p. 14 for details about Archbishop Beovich's mother, Elizabeth Beovich (née Kenny), who was the daughter of Irish migrants from Ennis, County Clare, Ireland.
70 *SC*, 7 March 1941, p. 9.
71 *News*, 17 March 1942, p. 6.
72 The Australian Patrician Association, established 1949, became the Irish Australian Association in 1961, *Irish Australian Association, Adelaide*, https://www.irishclub.org.au/history-of-the-club accessed 5 August 2018.
73 Thank you to the following people for their kind assistance with editing and thoughtful suggestions: Dymphna Lonergan, Susan Arthure, Stephanie James, Fidelma Breen, Scott Durand and Peter Moore. Thank you to the following people for assistance in accessing the St Patrick's Day float image: Stephanie James, Lyn Dansie, St Mary's College, Adelaide (Principal, Mrs Clare Nocka and Principal's Executive Assistant/Registrar, Sandy Conroy). Thank you also to the following people for correspondence with queries: Loretta Ford, Terry Denneny, Felicity Savage and Sr Marie Foale RSJ. Last, but not least, thank you to Irena, Patrick and Bridget.

Varieties of Irish nationalism in South Australia, 1839 to 1950: Changing terms of engagement

1   The notion of Irish nationalism developing in late 19th-century Ireland and the diaspora incorporated a political philosophy and programme grounded in the understanding that national consciousness (that is the specific awareness and celebration of Ireland as reflected in the St Patrick's Society) could only be achieved within a separate nation state.

2   *South Australian Register* (*SAR*), 15 March 1851, p. 2. The document headed 'The St Patrick's Society' was signed by President G.S. Kingston and T.Y. Cotter, secretary.

3   Australia's Catholic Church was an Irish Church. Until the mid 20th century, most bishops were Irish-born (South Australia's first non-Irish archbishop – Matthew Beovich – was appointed in 1940).

4   Two other bodies, the Self Determination for Ireland League (SDIL), which existed from 1921 to 1922, and the Australian League for an Undivided Ireland (ALUI), founded after de Valera's 1948 visit and surviving until the early 1950s, will also receive brief mention.

5   The papers were the *Southern Cross and Catholic Herald* (1867), the *Irish Harp and Farmer's Herald* (1869–1872), the *Chaplet and Southern Cross* (1870–1872), the *Catholic Herald and Monthly Summary* (1870 but merging quickly with the *Irish Harp*), the *Irish Harp and Southern Cross* (1872–1875), the *Tablet* (1876–1877), the *Catholic Record* (1879–1881), the *Pilot* (1882) and the *Catholic Monthly and Messenger of the Sacred Heart* (1883–1889). No copies of either the *Record* or *Pilot* have survived. Although the *Catholic Monthly* existed during the visits from the Redmond brothers in 1883 and John Dillon in 1889, its focus, as the name suggests, was totally religious.

6   John Hirst, 'South Australia and Australia: Reflections on their histories' in Robert Foster and Paul Sendziuk (eds), *Turning Points: Chapters in South Australian history*, Wakefield Press, Adelaide, 2012, p. 118.

7   See *South Australian* of 12 March 1840, p. 2, advertising the dinner, and mentioning Kingston and John Brown; *SAR* of 21 March 1840, p. 6, for brief item regarding the dinner mentioning Captain O'Halloran and Kingston; *South Australian*, 9 March 1841, p. 2, advertising the dinner mentioning Kingston and Brown; *SAR*, 20 March 1841, p. 3, briefly reporting the dinner, referring to Kingston and Dr O'Hea (Mr Edwards sang); and *SAR*, 8 March 1845, p. 2, mentioning Kingston as 'Hon Secretary' advertising the dinner. There seemed no report of this event. Dr Henry Augustus O'Hea advertised his North Tce dispensary in *SAR* of 30 October 1839, p. 1.

8   *SAR* of 14 July 1849 supplement, p. 1, and 3 May 1850, p. 2, for names of committee members. Major O'Halloran, MLC (president), Captain W.L. O'Halloran, MLC, G.S. Kingston, C.B. Newenham (sherriff), R.R. Torrens (collector of customs) – vice-presidents. Committee members: A. Anderson, C. Bagot, Mr Blackham Snr, Mr Butler, C. Campbell, Mr Conway, Jas Clarke, E.B. Gleeson, Mr Hope, W. Mclean, P. Morris, James Nowland, J. Reid, H. Seymour, Drs Eades, Mahony, Moore, Macdonald, Rev G. Newenham were all known to be Protestant, while Mr Counsel, A. Fox, H. Johnson, E. McEllister, James O'Laughlin and Fr M. Ryan were Catholic.

9   Adelaide *Observer* Supplement, 14 July 1849, p. 1.

10   *South Australian*, 10 October 1850, p. 2.

11   Those advertised as stewards at the 1856 dinner were Torrens, Kingston, Major O'Halloran, J. Reid, R. Cotrell, H. Quin, Capt. Bagot, Gleeson, J.T. Bagot (Protestants), and Catholics, L. Cullen and E. McEllister.

12   See Patrick O'Farrell, *The Irish in Australia*, New South Wales University Press, Sydney, 1987, pp. 16–17.

13   See *Express and Telegraph* of 17 June 1875, p. 1, advertising a meeting on 22 June, and *Harp and Southern Cross* of 25 June 1875, p. 3, for report of meeting naming the subcommittee as T. Lonergan (chair), P. Healy, P. Martin, M. Walsh, W and T. Dixon

14   (the only Protestants) and M.H. Davis. See *Evening Journal* of 22 June 1875, p. 2 for names not listed in the *Harp*, L. Shinners and M.F. Shannon.
14   *SAR*, 6 July 1875, p. 6.
15   *Evening Journal*, 29 July 1875, p. 2.
16   *SAR*, 31 July 1875, p. 1.
17   *SAR*, 6 August 1875, p. 1. See *Evening Journal* of 5 August 1875, p. 2, for item stating that the 'front of the Town Hall' would be illuminated for the concert, and that a 'Mr Clint is preparing a large allegorical picture, and [that] a bust of the Liberator has been ordered from Melbourne to be used on the occasion'.
18   See *Border Watch* of 21 July 1875, p. 3, for advertisement for 6 August event, and 11 August 1875, p. 2, for report of Penola celebration, and 21 August 1875, p. 2, for very lengthy Mount Gambier report.
19   *Harp and Southern Cross*, 6 August 1875, p. 5. Gawler, Kapunda, Salisbury and Port Adelaide were listed. See Gawler *Bunyip* of 30 July 1875, p. 2, for surprise that no local celebrations were planned for Gawler.
20   *Kapunda Herald and Northern Intelligencer*, 10 August 1875, p. 3. The editor was not an Irishman.
21   See *Yorke's Peninsula Advertiser and Miners' and Farmers' Journal*, 13 July 1875, p. 3, *Express and Telegraph*, 30 July 1875, p. 3, and 2 August 1875, p. 3, *SAR*, 6 August 1875, pp. 4–5.
22   *Evening Journal*, 7 August 1875, p. 3.
23   Richard Vincent Comerford, 'Land League' and 'Land War' in S.J. Connolly (ed.) *Oxford Companion to Irish History* (2nd edition), Oxford University Press, Oxford, 2002, pp. 310–311 and 314–315.
24   Patrick Whelan to John Redmond, letter, 27 August 1900, MS 15,239/1, Redmond Papers, NLI. Whelan introduced himself saying, 'I presume you remember me as the founder of the first branch of the Land League in Australia at Adelaide SA and Honorary Secretary of same for 15 years …'.
25   F.B. Keogh, 'The Irish in South Australia. What They Have Done for Ireland. Interesting Reminiscences,' in *Southern Cross* (*SC*) of 21 December 1900, p. 16. Trove searches via the title and for the names of the three listed as founders in both South Australian and interstate papers have so far failed to reveal further details of the association.
26   See Stephanie James, 'Distress in Ireland 1879–1880: The unlikely activation of the South Australian community', in Philip Payton and Andrekos Varnava (eds), *Australia, Migration and Empire: Immigrants in a globalised world*, Palgrave (Britain and World Series), 2019 publication, for further details about this campaign.
27   SA *Advertiser*, 20 December 1879, p. 2.
28   Keogh, 'The Irish in South Australia'. The league was headed by J.A. Hewitt, M.M. Ryan was secretary, and early members included P. Healy, P. Whelan, H. Sheridan, J.S. McClory and J.B. Broderick.
29   To identify only a few examples that show O'Loghlin was monitoring what was said about Ireland in colonial newspapers, see the *Northern Argus*, 27 September 1881, p. 2 (Ireland and the Land League); *SAR*, 8 February 1883, p. 5 (Irish agitators); *SAR*, 14 March 1883, p. 1 (the Redmonds); *SAR*, 4 March 1884, p. 7 (the Irish Party); *SAR*, 23 December 1885, p. 6 (Irish independence); *Northern Argus*, 24 August 1886, p. 2 (Michael Davitt); and SA *Weekly Chronicle*, 14 May 1887, p. 6 (Mr Parnell and *The Times*).
30   Keogh, 'The Irish in South Australia,' p. 16.
31   See P.J. Naughtin, 'The Green Flag at the Antipodes: Irish nationalism in colonial Victoria during the Parnell Era 1880–1891', PhD thesis, University of Melbourne, 2011, p. 89.

32 This was something often commented on in the Irish-Catholic press, see Stephanie James, '"Deep Green Loathing"?: Shifting Irish-Australian loyalties in the Victorian and South Australian Irish-Catholic press 1868–1923', PhD thesis, Flinders University, 2013, pp. 17–18, 37 and 46 for further discussion of this issue.
33 Naughtin, *The Green Flag*, pp. 69–70.
34 Naughtin, *The Green Flag*, pp. 73–74, 79, 88–89.
35 Naughtin, *The Green Flag*, pp. 88. Pierce Healy was employed by the Victorian Land League Central Committee. A journalist, he was born in 1855 at Colac in Victoria, but spent most of his life in New South Wales. He was a prominent newspaper founder and proprietor at Musswellbrook where he died in 1932 according to the *Musswellbrook Chronicle* of 15 July 1938, p. 3.
36 From Tipperary, he had emigrated in 1840 with his father, Michael Hewitt.
37 *SC*, 3 April 1890, p. 8.
38 Melbourne *Advocate*, 8 July 1882, p. 8. The report was abridged from *SAR* of 1 July 1882, p. 6. Members included J.A. Hewitt as treasurer, Dr Gunson, T. Lonergan, W. Dixon, M.T. Montgomery, P. Whelan, J.B. Broderick, P. Egan, and J.S. McLory.
39 *SAR*, 1 July 1882, p. 6.
40 *SC*, 25 July 1890, p. 9. Treasurer Patrick Whelan acknowledged this had been the amount.
41 Booyoolee *Areas Express*, 5 August 1882, p. 2. Pekina also had 65 INL members. In addition to the locations named in the text, there were also branches at Carrieton, Millicent and Mount Gambier.
42 *SAR*, 15 July 1882, p. 2. Fidelma Breen, '"Yet We Are Told that Australians Do Not Sympathise with Ireland": A study of South Australian support for Irish Home Rule 1883–1912', MPhil, University of Adelaide, 2013, pp. 84–86, suggests that Clements was probably 'an embarrassment to Adelaide's Irish leaders'.
43 *Express and Telegraph*, 2 and 4 August 1882, pp. 1 and 2, *Evening Journal*, 22 August 1882, p. 2.
44 F.B. Keogh was named as secretary on 3 August; D. Creedon was shown as acting secretary in *Evening Journal* of 5 October 1882, p. 3. This item included the report of Pierce Healey's lecture about 'Robert Burns, the Scotch Poet.' See *Evening Journal* of 16 October 1882, p. 2, showing Thos Kildea as secretary.
45 Clements, a carpenter, was probably in South Australia from 1880, and involved in the Working Men's Political Association, before standing for parliament in 1886. Receiving only a fifth of votes in East Adelaide, he planned to move to Victoria.
46 See Gawler *Bunyip* of 23 November 1883 p. 4, and *Kapunda Herald* of 23 November 1883, p. 2, for reports of meetings at those centres.
47 See *SAR* of 10 February 1883, pp. 6–7, for report of town hall meeting chaired by Charles Cameron Kingston where Dr J.M. Gunson moved to dissolve the Land League and establish the INL, becoming its first president. Patrick Whelan was first secretary. Gunson was followed by John Hewitt and Wm Dixon.
48 See Breen, 'Yet We Are Told', p. 93, for comment that the 'antipodean Irish [were] handed the begging bowl and they repeatedly filled it,' a claim that does not fully accord with the repeatedly expressed regrets within various South Australian Irish organisations about the inadequacy of local support. See for example letters about this subject in *SC* of 1 August 1890, p. 8, and 31 October 1890, p. 7.
49 Adelaide *Observer*, 1 September 1883, p. 14.
50 See SA *Advertiser* of 2 February 1886, p. 2, for account of brief meeting between O'Doherty and league officials, and for wording of their address. Flexible plans were required because his ship was delayed by 24 hours. See J.G. O'Connor Scrapbook, National Library of Australia (NLA) MS9529 for copy of this address.

51 See SA *Advertiser* of 29 March 1887, p. 6, for account of the presentation of the address at the railway station, a hurried arrangement made because the INL had happened to find out about the visit.
52 Parnell, a Protestant landlord from Co Wicklow, became a Home Rule MP in 1875, and leader of the nationalist movement via the New Departure of mid 1879, president of the Land League in 1879 and chairman of the IPP in 1880. Charges made against him in 1887 letters to *The Times* led to a special commission, his vindication in 1890 managing to gather all nationalists in his support.
53 *Evening Journal*, 16 October 1888, p. 2. Patrick McMahon Glynn was to preside, and J.V. O'Loghlin, Rev W. Hopkins and B. Nash MP were listed as some of those who would address the meeting.
54 The figures came from the census of 1881 and 1891. In those years the colony's Catholic population – the only possible means of estimating second-generation Irish given most Catholics were Irish – was 42,628 and 47,179. Bishop Reynolds gave £20.
55 SA *Advertiser*, 12 April 1889, p. 7. The reports described huge crowds in Port Adelaide, and another 2000 to 3000 who gathered outside his city hotel.
56 See *SC* of 20 September 1889, p. 7, for names of South Australian delegates appointed by the INL: P. McMahon Glynn MP, B. Nash MP, Hon. J.V. O'Loghlin, C. Kelly, W. Dixon and P. Whelan. Owing to parliament being in session, the first three could not go, and ultimately only W. Dixon represented the colony. *SAR*, 27 September 1889, p. 4. This was largely a Victorian event with very few delegates from other colonies.
57 *SC*, 26 December 1890, p. 7.
58 *SC*, 2 and 9 January 1891, p. 7 and 8.
59 See *SC* of 12 December 1890, pp. 4–5, 26 December 1890, p. 7, 9 January 1891, p. 7–8, and 27 February 1891, p. 6. All three reported INL meetings, the second of which was a special meeting called to discuss the issues associated with Parnell. In 1916, after the rising, the same issue occurred: conflict over whether to cable local views to Ireland.
60 See *SC* of 10 July 1891, p. 5, for motion that Secretary P. Whelan communicate this 'to the Central Branch of the Irish National Federation in Dublin,' and see issue of 7 August 1891, p. 9 for his letter.
61 See *SC* of 26 June 1891, p. 2, for first advertisement proclaiming the South Australian Irish National Federation. Patrick McMahon Glynn was president for 10 years, J.V. O'Loghlin vice-president and Patrick Healy treasurer.
62 John Redmond's leadership of the minority that had followed Parnell was a challenging feature of the split for the local Irish community. He was an enormously popular local figure.
63 See *SC* of 22 May 1891, p. 7, for report of J.R. Cox MP's visit to Broken Hill where he spoke to 400 and collected £100, and Pekina, where a similar amount was subscribed. See issue of 29 June 1891, p. 6, for report of £600 draft sent to Evicted Tenant's Fund, Dublin. See issue of 20 November 1891, p. 7, for Cox's final remarks about having raised £3000 with South Australia 'undoubtedly ... giv[ing] the most generous response to his appeal'.
64 *SC*, 26 June 1891, p. 5.
65 See *Petersburg Times* of 21 August 1891, p. 4, for AGM of Petersburg INF to be held on 22 August 1891. See also Keogh 'What Australia Has Done'.
66 See *SC* of 7, 14, 21, and 28 June and 1 November 1895.
67 Michael Davitt, *Life and Progress in Australasia*, Methuen and Co, London, 1898, pp. 63, 65.
68 Brisbane *Courier Mail*, 20 July 1895, p. 6.
69 *SC*, 24 January 1896, p. 9.
70 *SC*, 31 January 1895, p. 7, 7 February 1896, p. 6, 14 February 1896, p. 9 and 21 February 1896, p. 4.

Notes

71 See James, '"Deep Green Loathing"?' pp. 125–177 for discussion of Irish-Australian responses to the South African War of 1899–1902.
72 An arrival of 1880, Glynn opened a Kapunda law firm in 1882, and edited the *Kapunda Herald* from 1883 to 1891. He was MHA for the electorate of Light from 1887 to 1890, then from 1895 until his 1901 election to the House of Representatives he represented North Adelaide. He was a South Australian delegate to the 1897/1898 Federal Convention.
73 *SC*, 30 March 1900, p. 5.
74 Gerald Glynn O'Collins, *Patrick McMahon Glynn: Letters to his family*, The Polding Press, Melbourne, 1974, p. 175. Some details in his account differ from that presented in the *SC* which suggest his vice-president, J.V. O'Loghlin, signed it, after Glynn refused, and in the issue of 6 April, p. 8, the editor revealed the governor 'could [not] receive it' owing to its political expression. The INF compromise was to send it to Dublin's lord mayor asking for it to be read to the Queen; in the issue of 14 September 1900, p. 7, a report noted enquiries about this but there was no further reference.
75 Some attitudes evident in Glynn's correspondence reveal his feeling superior to local colleagues and explain some of the later antipathy toward him.
76 See *SC* of 9 March 1900, p. 8, for jubilant editorial 'Re-united at Last' on the nationalists closing ranks.
77 See *SC* of 30 March 1900, p. 9, for the Sydney decision about forming the UIL, 29 June 1900, p. 6, for the Melbourne branch, *SAR*, 9 October 1900, p. 5, for the Western Australian branch, and the *SC* of 11 January 1901, p. 9, for the unanimous decision in Adelaide.
78 Patrick O'Farrell Papers, NLA MS6265/23/104. This letter was within a 'miscellaneous' file without any explanation about how it had come into O'Farrell's possession.
79 In 1906 Joseph Devlin MP and lawyer, J.T. Donovan, toured, and between October 1911 and August 1912, John Redmond's son, W.A.K. Redmond, Donovan and Richard Hazelton were the final IPP delegates.
80 Prime Minister Gladstone introduced the first and second Home Rule Bills in 1886 and 1893. They were defeated in the House of Lords. After the Liberals won government in 1910 with the support of the IPP, they were committed to Home Rule's introduction. This became possible after major reforms to the House of Lords, but the Bill had to pass in the House of Commons for three years in the life of one parliament before the measure could succeed.
81 The figures reflect Australian totals rather than South Australian amounts, and all figures are open to debate because sources differ.
82 *The Freeman's Journal* (Sydney), 10 June 1905, p. 33. The figure was cited at a farewell for J.W. Walshe.
83 See *SC* of 20 November 1891, p. 7 for INF President McMahon Glynn's estimate of £160,000 from Australia to Ireland in the previous 10 years, in which he included the famine fund of 1879–1880 of 'nearly £100,000'.
84 For further discussion of this event, see Stephanie James, 'Irish South Australians in 1914: Unconditional imperial loyalty?' in Melanie Oppenheimer, Margaret Anderson and Mandy Paul (eds), *South Australia on the Eve of War*, Wakefield Press, Adelaide, 2017, pp. 176–196.
85 *SC*, 8 May 1914, p. 14.
86 See James, '"Deep Green Loathing"?', pp. 178–230.
87 *SC*, 5 May 1916, pp. 5, 7, 10 and 12 May 1916, pp. 9, 10.
88 SA *Advertiser*, 28 April 1916, p. 7.
89 *SC*, 19 May 1916, pp. 10–11.
90 *SC*, 10 January 1919, p. 7.

91 *SC*, 16 January 1920, p. 7.
92 National Archives of Australia (hereafter NAA), (Adelaide) D1915 SA29, Pt.1, 'Irish National Association: Correspondence and reports,' circular 15, 17 November 1917. This had instructed security staff that 'it will be well to watch closely all persons known to be connected to the organisation [Sinn Fein]'.
93 NAA (Canberra): A8911/219, 'Sinn Fein, South Australia, General Reports on Organisation', 25 February 1918. Patrick O'Sullivan to P.E. O'Leary. O'Leary's request for a copy of Melbourne's Young Ireland Society (established 1916) constitution and a report of its activities led to O'Sullivan's reply which was intercepted.
94 *SC*, 29 October 1948, p. 11. Frank Doherty's name did not appear in subsequent newspaper accounts.
95 In June 1918, members of the Sydney, Melbourne and Brisbane INA were arrested following months of close surveillance. Imprisoned in Sydney, they faced a judicial enquiry. Although it was unable to establish the level of treachery wanted by the government, the enquiry endorsed the ongoing detention of these men.
96 See NAA: A8911/219, 'Sinn Fein, South Australia, General Reports on Organisation', 22 April 1918.
97 See NAA: A8911/219, 19 August 1918 and 25 September 1918.
98 See NAA: D1915 SA29 Pt.1, 15, 22 March, 24 May and 2 August 1920.
99 NAA: A8911/219, 27, 28 May, 4 June and 11 November 1918.
100 In addition to regular lectures, there was a dancing class, and an enormously successful three-day *feis* or festival of Irish music and dance in November 1921 – this included 165 separate events.
101 See James, '"Deep Green Loathing"?', Appendix N, 'Speakers and Topics at Adelaide ... Ireland-Related Meetings 1919–1923,' pp. 528–531.
102 In 1920 INA membership was 669, but only 109 in 1921, 44 in 1923 but 116 in 1924 before dropping to 36.
103 In 1927, the resignation of the president and secretary, the failure to hold the advertised AGM, and the need for the Irish Pipers (founded in 1912) to rescue the St Patrick's Day dinner all contributed to the crisis that precipitated the restructuring. An unnamed subcommittee's recommendations were followed – P.E. O'Leary became president and P.A. Greene treasurer and joint secretary.
104 In 1927 the Aeridheacht attracted 500, 1500 in 1928 and over 5000 in 1931 and 1932. Attendance figures were not always reported, but in 1941, 1949 and 1951, crowds exceeded 2000.
105 The 1928 AGM discussed the idea of asking 5CL to broadcast an Irish programme, the first three-hour 'Wireless Night' was on 12 June. By 1931 there had been seven and the ABC was asked about relaying the programme to Melbourne and Sydney.
106 The INA always had a clerical patron, and the major Aeridheacht address was from a priest. See *SC* of 26 May 1933, p. 4, for list of the 28 member INA committee names; eight were priests. While many positions were honorary, and the actual committee consisted of 10 (plus O'Leary and Greene), the clerical proportion was high.
107 In the *SC* of 25 September 1942, p. 5, it was said that the involvement of many INA and Irish Piper members 'in the fighting services and in other national works' was limiting INA activities.
108 The last reported AGM was in 1936. When P.A. Greene held the senior Hibernian role in 1937, it seemed to coincide with shorter *SC* reports, and a slow general decline.
109 See O'Farrell Papers, NLA, MS6265/19/41 'Correspondence South Australia [ALUI] 1948–1954', for an incomplete series of letters between Albert Dryer and P.E. O'Leary from March 1949 to June 1954. There were 23 letters from Dryer and 10 from O'Leary; his last was dated August 1951. In an important letter of 20 November 1949, O'Leary suggested reasons for the INA decline. For more detail about the

INA, see Stephanie James, 'The Evolution of Adelaide's Irish National Association 1918-c. 1951: From security threat to cultural force?' in *JHSSA*, vol. 45 1917, pp. 31–49.
110   Breen, 'Yet We Are Told', pp. 170–174.
111   See Keogh, 'The Irish'.
112   Healy (1846–1920) was born in County Clare and emigrated with his parents in about 1864; after goldmining in Victoria and Queensland, he established a very successful city boot-making business.
113   See note 72.
114   O'Loghlin's parents, both from County Clare, reached South Australia in 1840. Born in 1852, the youngest of six, J.V. was educated at Kapunda before farming with his father, working as a wheat agent, owning/editing a newspaper in Terowie, becoming a district councillor, and then a legislative councillor from 1888 to 1899 and member of the House of Assembly from 1910 to 1912. As first editor of the *Southern Cross* from 1889, he retained that role until 1896. Prominent in all Irish organisations, the Australian Natives Association and the militia, in 1915 he enlisted for service with the Australian Imperial Force. From 1913 to 1919 and 1922 to 1925 he was a Commonwealth senator.
115   O'Leary's father, Patrick, a noted musician, was born in County Cavan in 1851 and emigrated to South Australia in 1876 after four years in the US; he married Elizabeth O'Brien in 1882. He was the force behind the 1912 formation of the Irish Pipers Band. Patrick Eugene was born in May 1885, and was also a fiddler. Educated at CBC he was involved in the UIL before becoming a vice-president in 1914. He was Archbishop O'Reily's private secretary for some years, and as an accountant worked at the Mitcham Army Camp and State War Council during World War I. He was on the platform at the 1918 INA inauguration. At the age of 36 he married Mary Doherty who was 23. P.E. died on 7 August 1966 aged 81. Mary died on 2 December 1972.
116   Greene's parents were from County Clare and County Galway. P.A. was born in 1894 and died in 1983. Educated at CBC, but leaving at 15, he worked in the family's grocery shop, and then in other businesses. He had significant roles in a number of Catholic organisations as well as the Hibernians and Irish-focused groups. Irish dancing was of great importance for the Greene family. P.A. was INA treasurer and assistant secretary in 1919.
117   From this point, INA lectures were always presented by priests.

Ireland, Home Rule and the Orange Order in South Australia

1   In an effort to raise both awareness of the Home Rule cause and money, the IPP arranged a number of missions to Australasia and the United States. Irish parliamentarians and associated nationalist activists visited the colonies on several occasions – brothers John and William (Willie) Redmond (the Members for New Ross and Wexford respectively) came in 1883, followed by John Dillon (MP for Tipperary), John Deasy (MP for West Mayo) and Sir Thomas Esmonde (11th Baronet and MP for South Dublin) in 1889. By that time the first Home Rule Bill had been introduced and defeated in the House of Commons at Westminster. In 1895, two years after the rejection of the second Home Rule Bill by the House of Lords, the colonies received the renowned 'Father of the Land League', Michael Davitt, who toured to lecture and raise funds. Davitt's visit differed from the others on a number of levels. Firstly, Davitt himself was an amalgam of republican gunrunner, parliamentarian, journalist, social activist and renowned labour identity. Secondly, his tour did not commence in aid of the IPP. He initially intended to use the visit to raise personal capital after suffering bankruptcy, but the money raised went into the IPP campaign funds upon the announcement of a general election in Britain. In 1906 the MP for West Belfast, Joseph Devlin, accompanied by nationalist lawyer J.T. Donovan, visited a federated Australia. Five years later Donovan made a return visit, this time accompanying William Redmond Jnr (Member for Tyrone East) and

Richard Hazelton (Member for North Louth). Between these official delegations there were brief visits by other Irish nationalists, some of whom toured and collected funds, and others who came on recuperative or leisure trips.

2   Fidelma Breen, '"Yet We Are Told that Australians Do Not Sympathise with Ireland"; A study of South Australian support for Irish Home Rule, 1883 to 1912', MPhil thesis, University of Adelaide, 2013.

3   *Colonial Times*, 23 November 1847, p. 3, Orange Lodges.

4   *South Australian Register (SAR)*, 18 July, p. 1, 'Local Intelligence: Orange Lodge formed in Adelaide'.

5   *SAR*, 18 July 1849, p. 1.

6   *Moreton Bay Courier*, 8 September 1849, page 3, 'Summary of General News'.

7   Richard Davis, 'Orangeism in Tasmania, 1832–1967', Tasmanian Historical Research Association, *Papers & Proceedings*, vol. 55, no. 3.

8   *SAR*, 7 November 1871, p. 5, Orangeism in South Australia.

9   *SAR*, 7 November 1871, p. 5, A True Protestant. 'Orangeism', *Protestant Advocate*. 28 October 1871, p. 6.

10   *Maitland Mercury*, 11 June 1889, p. 6.

11   Lodges in existence in 1877: Derby Lodge No. 1, Adelaide; Vernu Lodge No. 2, Adelaide; Drumcalpin Lodge No. 3, Rice's Creek (now Auburn, 120 km north of Adelaide); Diamond Lake Lodge No. 4, Diamond Lake, near Honiton (240 km south-west of Adelaide); Enniskillen Lodge No. 5, Norwood; Royal Bismarck No. 6 Mount Gambier (435 km from Adelaide); and Duke of York No. 7, Alberton.

12   SA *Advertiser*, 16 July 1875, p. 14.

13   *Adelaide Observer*, 2 December 1876, p. 14.

14   SA *Advertiser*, 22 June 1883, p. 4.

15   *SAR*, 30 December 1922, p. 9.

16   *Northern Territory Times and Gazette*, 29 December 1883, p. 3, Our Adelaide Letter.

17   SA *Advertiser*, 18 October 1883, p. 5, T.K. Pater, 'Sawtell & Momphlait', To the Editor.

18   *Northern Territory Times and Gazette*, 29 December 1883, p. 3, Our Adelaide Letter.

19   SA *Advertiser*, 16 July 1875, p. 14.

20   A fragile connection may be formed between the very first *Biographical Index of South Australia (BISA)* entry for Adam Newell (listed as a draper from Norwood), and James Lugg. Both names appear on lists of supporters of candidates at various elections between 1870 and 1883. A report of the Duke of York Oddfellows lodges lists A. Newell as deputy grand master alongside the secretary J.S. Bagshaw. This reinforces the likelihood of Adam Newell as the 1875 Orangeman because no other A. Newells in *BISA* entries fit within these dates due to the recording of either their dates of birth or death.

21   David Fitzpatrick, 'Exporting Brotherhood: Orangeism in South Australia', *Immigrants & Minorities*, vol. 23, nos 2–3, 2005, p. 34.

22   SA *Advertiser*, 1 May 1903, p. 3.

23   *SAR*, 17 February 1883, p. 1.

24   *SAR*, 17 February 1883, p. 1.

25   Fitzpatrick, 'Exporting Brotherhood'.

26   *SAR*, 14 June 1890, p. 5.

27   The records mention brethren who, on occasion, could afford to lend their lodge substantial sums of money ranging from £10,000 to £15,000 to get them out of financial difficulty or even to purchase an organ. This indicates a reasonable amount of individual wealth among members.

28   State Library of South Australia, Adelaide, SRG/293, Box 3, Loyal Orange Institution of South Australia, Minutes of Loyal Orange Lodge No. 7, Port Adelaide, 6 July 1914.

29   SA *Advertiser*, 12 August 1903, p. 3 and SA *Advertiser*, 20 November 1903, p. 7.

30 It is marginally possible that in 1910 the notation 'Belfast in Ireland' was required to differentiate the northern Irish city from the town of Belfast in Victoria; it had been renamed Port Fairy in 1883.
31 *Chronicle*, 18 June 1887, p. 7.
32 SA *Advertiser*, 15 June 1900, p. 6.
33 *SAR*, 26 September 1900, p. 5.
34 *Barrier Miner*, 13 June 1900, p. 2.
35 The two detainees were John O'Donohoe, son of Patrick O'Donohoe from County Longford, who was both a gardener at the city's Botanic Gardens and a special constable, and Alfred John Adams, a schoolmaster.
36 *SAR*, 14 June 1900, p. 6.
37 *SAR*, 16 June 1900, p. 8, 'There are thousands in and about Adelaide who have been educated under the gentle rule and holy example of our nuns and brothers'.
38 The 1903 resolution was for an address to be presented to the king as was an earlier one of April 1882. Those of 7 May 1886 and 27 April 1887 were expressions of opinion to be forwarded to Salisbury, Gladstone and Parnell. See Jeff Kildea, '"That a Just Measure of Home Rule May Be Granted to the People of Ireland": The 1905 resolutions of the Australian parliament'. Paper presented at the 19th ISAANZ Conference, New Zealand, November 2012.
39 H.B. Higgins to J.E. Redmond, 10 December 1905 in Redmond, J.E. 'Correspondence, 1882–1919'. Kodak (Aust) Pty Ltd, 1976 held at National Library of Australia, Canberra.
40 SA *Advertiser*, 11 April 1906, p. 9.
41 *SAR*, 14 July 1906, p. 6.
42 Kildea, *A Just Measure*, p. 8.
43 O'Farrell, *Irish in Australia*, p. 233.
44 SA *Advertiser*, 13 July 1906, p. 6.
45 Patrick Ireland, *Only Distant Cousins: Irish Protestants and politics in the US, Canada, and Australia*. Draft paper for DIT: http://www.dit.ie/media/documents/psai/PatrickIrelandPSAIpaper82.pdf.

Cultural capital and Irish place names

1 John O'Donohue, *Eternal Echoes: Celtic reflections on our yearning to belong*, Bantam Press, London, 2000, p. 257.
2 Daryle Rigney, Steve Hemming and Shaun Berg, 'Letters Patent, Native Title and the Crown in South Australia', in Elliott Johnston, Martin Hinton and Daryle Rigney (eds), *Indigenous Australians and the Law*, Routledge-Cavendish, London, 2008, pp. 165–166.
3 *South Australian Register (SAR)*, 27 May 1843, p. 3.
4 David J. Towler, *A Fortunate Locality*, Peacock Publications, Adelaide, 1986, p. 26.
5 Robert P. Whitworth, *Bailliere's South Australian Gazetteer and Road Guide*, F.F. Bailliere, Adelaide, 1866.
6 Robert Torrens, *Emigration from Ireland to South Australia*, Dublin, 1839.
7 Greg Drew and Joyce Jones, *Discovering Historic Kapunda*, Department of Mines and Energy and the Kapunda Tourism Committee, Adelaide, 1988, p. 5.
8 Pierre Bourdieu, *Language and Symbolic Power*, Harvard University Press, Cambridge, Mass., 1995.
9 *SAR*, 10 October 1840, p. 1.
10 *Sunday Mail*, 17 March 1979.
11 The name Irishtown appears in *Balliere's* in 1866.

12 Keith D. Lilley, '"Non Urbe, Non Vico, Non Castris": Territorial control and the colonization and urbanization of Wales and Ireland under Anglo-Norman lordship', in *Journal of Historical Geography*, vol. 26 no. 4, 2000, pp. 517–531.
13 A. Norman Jeffares, 'Torrens: An Irishman in South Australia', in Colm Kiernan (ed.), *Australia and Ireland Bicentenary Essays*, Gill and MacMillan, Dublin, 1986, p. 175.
14 www.multicultural.sa.gov.au/__data/assets/pdf_file/0011/22034/Ireland-Dec-2014.pdf accessed 5 January 2018.
15 As late as 1886, the name was still being used in advertisements.

Author biographies

Susan Arthure is a doctoral candidate in archaeology at Flinders University. She is particularly interested in the nature of Irishness, the Irish diaspora with a focus on the Irish Australian experience, and how 19th-century Irish migrant communities lived and saw themselves once they moved from Ireland. Her research site is the 19th-century Irish community of Baker's Flat, located near Kapunda, South Australia. Her fieldwork there has identified the first *clachan*, a traditional Irish settlement pattern characterised by clusters of houses and cooperative farming, to be recognised in Australia. This research is supported by an Australian Government Research Training Program (RTP) scholarship. Susan was born and raised in Ireland, but has lived mostly in Australia since 1987.

Dr Fidelma Breen completed a Master of Philosophy in history studying Irish nationalism and loyalism in colonial South Australia at the University of Adelaide in 2013. Her chapter herein builds on the research she carried out on the development of the Loyal Orange Institution of South Australia for that thesis. Fidelma is a human geographer whose PhD (2018) investigated Irish migration to Australia between 2000 and 2015. She is currently a university postdoctoral fellow with the Hugo Centre for Population and Migration Research at the University of Adelaide. You can follow her on Twitter: @DivaDiaspora ORCiD: http://orcid.org/0000-0001-5469-2135 Researcher profile: http://researchers.adelaide.edu.au/profile/fidelma.breen#my-research

Dr Cherrie De Leiuen is an archaeologist and did her PhD at Flinders University. Her main interest areas are historical archaeology, women, and social justice. She has also worked in art museums and in the public service. She was first captivated by the stories of Irish in South Australia when working at St John's, Kapunda, and continues to work on the material culture of the Irish in Australia.

Bronte Gould is currently undertaking a PhD in history at Flinders University in Adelaide. Her thesis examines several women's organisations in South Australia and Western Australia between 1909 and 1939, including the Country Women's

Association, which was formed post-World War I. Her Honours thesis in 2013 highlighted a midwifery case at the Destitute Asylum in South Australia in the 1890s, and examined the changing roles of midwives and medical practitioners. Two medical officers who were featured were Irish born. This was followed in 2014 by an article based on that thesis, 'The Professional Midwife: Adelaide's Destitute Asylum and midwifery in South Australia 1880–1900' (*Journal of the Historical Society of South Australia*). Bronte's interest in medical and nursing history was borne out of her former nursing and midwifery career. The chapter in this publication is an extension of that interest, which has allowed her to research and present these doctors.

Jade Hastings has a Bachelor of Archaeology and Honours in History from Flinders University. She is a first year PhD student at Flinders University under the Australian Government Research Training Program scholarship, and this is her first official publication. Jade's contribution to this volume is based on her undergraduate research, which was centred on the experiences of female Irish Famine orphans who immigrated to colonial South Australia under the Earl Grey Scheme. Her current research examines the broader experiences of unmarried women in early colonial South Australia. It focuses on the strict moral opinions on the role of adult women outside of marriage, and how these opinions could affect the social and legal standing of single women in early colonial South Australia.

Dr Ann Herraman has developed detailed understandings of the long term demographic, economic and social characteristics of the Adelaide Hills communities through her experiences as a local resident, including engagement and leadership of the Mount Lofty Districts Historical Society Inc., through professional employment in regional economic development and through regionally focused postgraduate research at Flinders University. Her doctoral research projects have focused on development and implementation of global migration policy. The settlement patterns in South Australia in the colonial period, including arrivals of large numbers of Irish female immigrants, have been a major research focus. Ongoing research interests include analysis of vital registration documents aligned with collections of family and personal records to illustrate the impact of migration policy. Ann has received a range of awards from Flinders University, the government of South Australia and the Adelaide Hills Council for her contributions to academic excellence, community projects and innovative economic development.

Author biographies

Dr Rory Hope is a retired geneticist. After graduating with BSc (Hons) PhD from the University of Adelaide, he undertook postdoctoral research at the University of Oxford, United Kingdom. Appointed lecturer in genetics at the University of Adelaide in 1974, he went on to become an associate professor and head of the Laboratory of Molecular Evolution in the School of Molecular and Biomedical Science. He undertook collaborative research projects in London, Oxford, Detroit and Japan, and retired in 2002. Rory was a foundation member of the Human Genetics Society of Australia and is an honorary life member of the Genetics Society of Australia. He has a long-standing interest in the history of the Mid North of South Australia.

Dr Stephanie James has an abiding interest in the history of South Australia's Irish. Her strong Irish background, in association with her general passion for history, provides some explanation for this research direction. Her MA (2009) looked at the early history of the Irish in South Australia's Clare Valley while her PhD (2014) focused on issues of Irish-Australian loyalty during times of imperial crisis. Her publications have focused on Australasian Irish-Catholic newspapers, aspects of Irish colonist mobility, Irish-Australians during the Great War, exploring the extent to which they represented a security risk and how far, as 'outsiders', their experiences mirrored those of German-Australians. In addition to working toward a book with Rory Hope on his family's contribution to the Clare region, her current research also explores aspects of South Australian responses to the Irish famines of the 1840s and the late 1870s.

Dr Dymphna Lonergan was born in Dublin, and is a lecturer in academic and professional English at Flinders University. Her research focus is the Irish language in an English setting. Her Masters 'The Significance of Irish Gaelic in Anglo-Irish Literature 1800–1989' was followed by a PhD study that culminated in a book, *Sounds Irish: The Irish language in Australia* (Lythrum Press, 2004), a history of the language in Australia and an analysis of its effect on Australian English and literature. She has also written articles on the language as it appears in the Irish censuses, and on the global use of Irish words in English dialects. Her ongoing interest in Irish place names has resulted in a database at http://irishplaces.flinders.edu.au and is reflected in the final chapter of this book.

Described by ABC Radio's Peter Goers as 'a quiet achiever', Pekina farmer **John Mannion** has been recording South Australian regional history since 1974. In 1998, without any archiving or history training, John co-wrote a local history book, *No Place like Pekina: A story of survival*, commemorating the 125th anniversary of European settlement in the small town of Pekina 250 km north of Adelaide. This led to him being described as 'an improbable historian', and inspired him to enrol in the University of New England's Advanced Diploma in Local, Family and Applied History. He graduated in 2003 after five years of external studies. In 2001 John was instrumental in Pekina hosting the History Trust of South Australia's annual regional conference. In 2015 he received the History Council of SA Regional History Award, nominated by the South Australian branch of Oral History Australia, who described him as being 'a larger than life story teller who has a knack of finding stories that are quite humorous within a subject that is otherwise moving and serious'. The judges extolled him as 'the epitome of the local history activist who can keep the stories of a region alive and relevant today', promoting an awareness of the value of oral histories by conducting workshops, lecturing, and writing in the local press.

Janine McEgan returned to study in 2006, enrolling in a Bachelor of Arts at Flinders University after working in the science fields for many years. After graduating in 2010, majoring in archaeology and history, she continued her studies completing a Graduate Diploma in Cultural Heritage Management (CHM). She completed a Master of CHM in 2017. Janine took inspiration for her Master's research project from her family history, with three of her great-great-grandparents being Irish migrants to South Australia in the 1840s. She was keen to understand something about their lives and if any Irish cultural traditions were continued in their new country, focusing on Irish settlers in the Mid North of the state and the ways in which the deceased were memorialised. Her latest project is researching her family history from both sides of the Irish Sea.

Peter Moore is a fourth-generation Irish-Australian. An Adelaide lawyer with a strong interest in history, he spent two postgraduate years at University College Dublin, from 1978 to 1979, before returning to Australia to work as an archivist in Canberra and Sydney. Since 1992 he has worked as a Sydney publisher-editor specialising in multicultural Australian history, including numerous Irish-Australian titles, and authors in English as a second language. Peter has taught Irish history and Australian history at adult education centres in Sydney, Melbourne and Adelaide. Between-times, he has contributed papers at ISAANZ conferences since 1990 and since 1994 has led cultural tours of Ireland for small study groups. His principal research area is the legal professions in South Australia, New South Wales and New Zealand, with particular interest in the adoption and adaption of legal culture in the colonies.

Simon O'Reilley has a keen interest in the study and promotion of Irish South Australian history. Following years of independent research, he first spoke on the Irish settlement of Baker's Flat at the invitation of Dymphna Lonergan for the 2008 Oireachtas, Adelaide. This was followed by a presentation on the Irish in Kapunda at the Irish Australian conference Shamrocks in the Bush in New South Wales in 2009. Whilst an archivist at the Kapunda Museum he curated an Irish exhibition and facilitated items from the Kapunda area being loaned for the Irish in Australia exhibition at the National Museum in Canberra in 2011. Since 2012 he has enjoyed taking part in Susan Arthure's archaeological study of Baker's Flat. In 2016 he was a committee member of the 1916 Easter Rising commemorations in Adelaide, facilitating an evening of spoken presentations. He presented at the 22nd Australasian Irish Studies conference in Adelaide, speaking on 'St Patrick's Day in South Australia'. His chapter elaborates on this presentation.

Dr Neisha Wratten was born and educated in Ipswich, Queensland, and completed her medical studies at the University of Queensland in 1984. She moved to Adelaide in the early 90s to finish her training as a gynaecologist, a speciality in which she continues to actively practice. Her forays into history began as a form of 'mid-life crisis', initially focusing on her own family history and then progressing to the regional history of the south-east of South Australia, where she retreats to her beloved restored church, St Cedd's. Neisha is the proud descendant of Bridget Cannon, one of the 4114 Earl Grey orphans, whose life story she has researched for publication in Ireland in 2016. 'The Unexpected Irishmen', her first Australian piece, has been a brief hiatus from her current research, which aims to dispel the 'victimhood' myths which have been promulgated about the orphans and confirm their status as proud and valiant Australian pioneering women.

Acknowledgements

The genesis of this book was the 22nd Irish Studies Association of Australia and New Zealand (ISAANZ) conference in Adelaide, in 2016, the first time an ISAANZ conference had been hosted by South Australian members. The catalyst, however, was the meeting between Stephanie James and Dymphna Lonergan at the outset of their respective research. That meeting was facilitated by the late Pat Roberts of the South Australian Genealogy and Heraldry Society (SAGHS) who headed the Irish group there. In turn, they were introduced to Loretta Ford who has been a constant supporter of their work, and to Simon O'Reilley from Kapunda. Through Simon's interest and assistance, Susan Arthure's pioneering archaeological work in revealing the stalwart Irish presence on Baker's Flat was given a solid footing. Fidelma Breen's masters research on South Australian support for Irish Home Rule in the late 19th century progressed to a doctoral study of contemporary Irish migration using novel methodology. All of us benefitted greatly from earlier research by Eric Richards, Ann Herraman, and David Fitzpatrick. We also acknowledge our colleagues in ISAANZ who welcomed our work over the years for its value in creating a more balanced picture of Irish Australia. Our research demonstrates that while representationally small, South Australia's Irish story is unique.

We have individually acknowledged the help received from libraries and institutions in our respective studies, but here we wish to acknowledge especially Flinders University and the University of Adelaide whose postgraduate programs facilitated our coming together in the first place. They continue to serve this networking purpose as demonstrated in our chapters by new researchers in historical and archaeological fields. Our research group now has a name: the Irish Research Group of South Australia. This formalisation, we trust, will assist future researchers to get a foothold in what is still an under-researched area.

Acknowledgements

We thank Michael Bollen at Wakefield Press for his interest in the project and the History Trust of South Australia for providing financial support through the South Australian History Fund.

We give thanks for the gift of Irish ancestry, and the experience of migration that has formed who we are. We thank those who came before us, with us, after us, and to come.

Susan acknowledges, with thanks, her husband Hugh Kearns who travelled with her to Australia in 1987, and who has filled the intervening years with much love and laughter. Together they have raised Brendan and Darragh, splendid young Australian men with a strong sense of their Irish heritage. As a family, they have travelled frequently to Ireland, and treasure their Irish families and friends both 'back home' and in Australia.

Fidelma expresses her gratitude to her parents, Frances and Frankie, who first immigrated with her as a baby in 1973 and were later followed by various siblings, some of whom settled in Australia while others returned. Those who stayed formed an extended family that Fidelma is grateful for as it lessens the impact of being a migrant. Many years of back and forth migration cemented a firm footing in both Ireland and Australia for Fidelma and her sisters and frequent contact with 'home' in the days before contemporary communications technology allowed the family to preserve their sense of Irishness across the decades. Fidelma and her Irish husband, Don, have three wonderful 'Aussie' children who have variously expressed their pride in their Irish ethnicity.

Stephanie deeply values the legacies of her eight Irish-born great-grandparents – the courage of the families making the journey, their determination to make new lives in a distant place, their brave and constant commitment to education, and their contribution to the peopling of South Australia. The generations that followed in the wake of these passages from Ireland between the 1840s and the 1860s have increasingly cherished their Irish roots, and enjoyed the rich and diverse networks of relations they have inherited.

Dymphna wishes to thank that baby, John Lonergan, who made the long journey south to *deireadh an domhain* in 1972 with two naïve parents, and became a fine Australian, and Kate Lonergan who came afterwards and is living proof of the complexity of 'Irishness', and who has carried the fruits of that hybridity to her students and into the world.

Index

A

Adare 5, 234, 238, 247
Admella 53, 54
Advertiser, South Australian 128, 175, 206, 219
Allen's Creek 120
Anderson, Alexander 7, 16, 234, 236, 247
Anderson, Mary Eliza (née Milligan) 17–18
Anderson, Mary (née Greathurst) 16
Anderson, Matilda 19
Anderson/Milligan partnership 16, 18
Anderson, William 16–19
Around the Boree Log 90, 103, 104
Association, Protestant Defence 222
Australasian Catholic Benefit Society (ACBS) 176
Australian Labor Party 153, 154, 205
Australian-Patrician Association 188
Avoca 5
Ayers, Sir Henry 9

B

Bagot, Charles Harvey xv, 8, 9, 11, 58–63, 73, 148, 230
Bagot, Elizabeth and Christopher 58
Bagot, Harriet 59
Bagot, John 149, 152
Bagot, Mary 59
Bagshaw, John Stokes 217, 220
Baker's Flat xv, xx, 62–73, 88, 120, 235, 307, 311, 312
Balhannah 13
Bally Mckenny 10
Barlow, William 146, 148, 149, 157, 226
Battunga 17
Belvidere District Council 70
Benson, John 159, 169, 171–172
Beovich, Matthew (Archbishop) 187
Berchmans, Sister Mary 123–126, 129
Bernard, Robert 146, 147, 148, 157
Bernard, Sidney 146, 148, 150, 152
Bernard, Sister 70
Bernard, William 146, 148, 149
Birman xviii, 9, 59, 60, 63, 76, 235, 242
Blakiston 14, 15, 17, 246
Blood, Bindon 58, 59
Blood, Dr Matthew Henry Smyth 61, 65, 121
Blue Lake, Mt Gambier 52
Bolton, Ann 72
Booleroo Centre 96
Bool Lagoon 14
Bradley, John 198
Brady, Daniel and Rose 10
Brady, Peter 23, 24, 32, 34, 76, 77

Brennan, John 7
Brewer, Charles 50, 141
Briggs, Henry 168
Brightman 8, 254
Browne, William 46
Buffalo 5
Bugle Ranges 17
Bull, John Wraithall 14
Bungaree 14, 28, 29, 36, 152
Burra, Burra mine 3, 8, 26, 35, 76, 167
Butler, Patrick 7, 8, 23, 24, 25, 30, 31–33, 35, 38, 39, 40
Butler, Sarah 7, 25
Byrne, Fredrick (vicar-general) 177, 195

C

Cain, Edward and Mary 9
Calabar 218
Calaby family 16
Calcutta 6, 25, 237, 242
Callaghan, Mary 70
Caltowie xxii, xxiii, 92, 122, 124, 245
Carrieton xxiv, 92, 112
Cash, Kate 122
Catholic(s), Catholicism xiii, xiv, xv, 2, 6, 12–22, 31, 34, 39, 41, 43, 51, 56, 58, 60, 62, 70, 71, 72, 73, 74–89, 90–101, 103, 104, 106, 109, 111, 125, 129, 136, 147, 150, 171, 175, 183, 186, 187, 188, 193, 194, 212, 222, 224, 225, 232
Charles Forbes 7
Christ Church, O'Halloran Hill 6, 251
Church, Primitive Methodist 127
Clanfergil 9, 237
Clare 10, 23–40, 75
Clarke, Henry 7
Clarke, John 4, 5, 237
Clonlea 8, 238
Cloverdale 47
Coglin, Patrick Boyce 4, 175, 238

Collins, Bishop 107
Colonial Commissioners 59
Colonial Secretary 49, 50, 53, 160, 161, 163, 194
Colton 10, 235, 242
Conolan brothers 72
Considine, Martin 20
copper 9, 32, 35, 60, 61, 76, 121, 248
Costello, Martin 121
Cotter, Thomas Young 159, 160–167, 172
Courier 17
Cowan, Thomas 220, 221
Cox, J.R. xxv, 101
Cox, Mary. *See* Berchmans, Sister Mary
Craddock xxiv
Crawford, George John 145, 148, 155
Crocker, Jim 109
Cross Keys 10, 238
Crowe, Ellen 81
Crowe, Timothy 77
Cudmore, Daniel and Mary 5, 234, 237, 238, 247
Cullen, Luke 146–149
Cullen, Richard 148, 150, 156
Cygnet 1, 3, 5, 245, 251

D

Dalhousie County 91, 96
Davenport brothers 15–17, 19, 22
Davenport Special Survey 12
Delphi 7
Dempsey family 76, 151
Denny, William 151–156, 158
Dermody, Michael 83
Destitute Asylum 233, 308
Destitute Board 121, 167
Diadem 10, 254
Dillon, John xxv, 201, 205, 206, 222
Dismal Swamp 43–53, 239

Distressed Women's and Children's Committee 127
Dixon, William xxiv, 200, 201
Doherty, Frank 207
Downer, Sir John 226
Driscoll, Catherine 70
Driscoll, Daniel 70
Dry Creek xix, 10, 63
Dublin 6, 14, 29, 37, 60, 101, 123, 124, 144, 146–152, 157, 165, 170, 171, 182, 186, 203, 204, 206, 209, 212, 213, 231, 232, 239
Dublin Castle Hotel 12, 246
Duffy, Len 109
Duffy, Michael 92
Dundon, Patrick 65
Dutton, Francis Stacker 60, 167
Dutton, Frederick Hansborough 60
Dutton, Luduvina 167
Dyster, Tom 16, 19

E

Earl Grey Scheme 118, 131–142, 165
Easter Rising 102, 182, 206, 311
Echunga xxiv, 12
Elder, Captain William 17
Elgin 14, 133, 134, 141
Emerald Isle 6, 25, 76, 237, 242
Emu Hotel 7, 239
Encounter Bay xviii, 6, 237, 239, 241
Epaminondas 220

F

Farrell, Reverend James 9, 241
Faull, Jim 16
Fawcett, Robert 72
Female Emigration Fund 119
female immigrants (Irish) 15, 21, 49, 50, 133, 136, 137
Female Immigration Board 50

Fenians, Fenianism 170, 171, 176, 215, 216
Fisher, Charles 46
Fisher, James Hurtle 164
Fitzgerald, Edward 146, 149
Fitzgerald, James 149
Flaxley 17
Flynes, P. 65
Fordham's hotel 174
Foresters' Society 166
Fox, Bishop 107
Freemason's Tavern 174, 217
Friends of Ireland 170

G

Gawler 6, 7, 8, 10, 28, 35, 49, 156, 176, 238, 247, 252
Gawler, George 162, 164
Gazette and Register 162, 163, 164
Germain, Benjamin 53
Glandore 9, 242
Gleeson, Edward Burton 6, 7, 23–31, 35, 39, 76, 230, 234, 242, 243
Glen, George 56
Glynn, Patrick McMahon 70–73, 100, 146–158, 179, 203, 204, 210, 223, 242
gold rush 45, 61, 233
Goorty, Andrew 72
Gouger, Robert xi, xvii, 161, 163
Goulburn Herald and County of Argyle Advertiser 137
grave markers 74, 85, 87
Greathurst, Mary 16
Great Northern Mining Company 108, 165
Greene, P.A. 208, 210
Griffy, Andrew 72
Griffy, Thomas 64
Guiney, John 83

H

Hahndorf 12
Haimes, Bridget 120–123
Haimes, John 120, 122
Haimes, Margaret 120
Haimes, Richard 120
Haimes' store 120
Haimes, Susannah (Susan) 120, 122, 129
Hall, Ann 13
Hall, William 13
Hamilton, James Alexander Greer 170
Handley, Father 96
Hardy and Davis 70
Hart, Captain John 52, 55
Hartigan, Father John 90, 107
Hawker, Edward 151, 152
Hawker, George 14, 28, 36
Hayes, Mary 124
Healey, Pierce 100, 199, 200
Healy, Patrick 197, 198, 205, 206, 210
Helena, Sister (Mary O'Brien) 124
Hennis, Peter 4
Henty, Edward 42
Hewitt, J.A. 198, 199
Hibernian Australasian Catholic Benefit Society (HACBS) 176
Hibernian societies 156
Hibernian Society 20
Hickey, Michael 59, 60
Higgins, Bridget 43
Higgins, Ellen 10
Higgins, Henry Bourne 225
Higgins, Thomas 10, 247
Hindley Street 2, 4, 176
Hindmarsh County 12, 46
Hindmarsh, Governor 2, 161, 164
Hoare, Ann 70
Hoffmann, Chas 85

Holy Trinity Church, North Terrace 9, 17, 217
Home Rule 82, 102, 152, 178, 179, 182, 183, 184
Home Rule Association (HRA) 193, 197, 198
Hope, John 7, 8, 23, 23–25, 28–30, 33, 35–40, 252, 254
Hornsdale 108
Howard, Reverend Charles Beaumont 5, 6, 9
Howard, William 63
Hughes, Patrick and Christina 13

I

Inchiquin 7, 23, 25, 26, 27, 28, 230, 243
Inconstant 14, 15, 131, 133, 134, 141, 233
Independent Order of Rechabites (IOR) 219
Indian Civil Service 6
Irish Harp newspaper 120
Irish Harp hotel 7, 174, 243
Irish Land League 100, 193, 200
Irish National Association 104, 185, 188, 193, 206, 207
Irish National Federation 101, 178, 179, 193, 202
Irish National Land League 197
Irish National League 100, 101, 156, 178, 193, 200, 222
Irish National Society 185, 207
Irish Parliamentary Party xxiv, xxv, 101, 199, 212
Irish Pipe Band 182
Irish Relief Fund 177
Irishtown xxiii, 9, 232, 233, 243
Isabella 4

J

Jamestown xxii, xxiii, 107, 108, 122
Jeffcott Chambers 4
Jeffcott, John xv, 4, 145, 147, 248

Jeffcott Street 4
Jenkins, George Frederick 105
John and Sarah Saby 13
Johns, James 221, 223
Johnston, Charles 146, 149
Jose, Mary 70
Josephites, Josephite Convent xxiii, 20, 90, 94, 99, 104, 124

K
Kadina xxi, xxii, 176, 182, 239
Kain, Father 107
Kapunda 5, 6, 9, 58–73, 75, 91, 120, 121, 124, 150, 156, 158, 170, 171, 176, 196, 200, 230, 231, 235, 248, 252
Kapunda Herald 66, 70, 71, 121, 152, 242
Kapunda Philharmonic Society 6
Kauffmann, John 65, 66
Kavanagh, Mike 20
Kavanagh, Patrick 20
Keelan family 10
Kelly, John 121
Kennedy, James 146, 148, 149
Kenny, Michael 10, 214, 235, 242, 250
Keogh, F.B. 197, 198, 200, 209
Kermode Street 4
Kiernan, Mary 42
Killanoola 14, 156, 244, 245, 248
Killian, Archbishop 98, 187
Kingston, Charles Cameron 150, 152, 153, 154, 156, 179
Kingston, George Strickland xv, 1–3, 11, 27, 28, 35, 150, 151, 156, 174, 177, 194, 196, 198, 235, 244, 245, 248, 252
Kingston-on-Murray 3
Knowling, Alfred 122
Koolunga 8, 29
Koonunga 60, 241

L
Labatt, George 146, 148, 149
Labor League 176
Lacey, Mary 70
Lady Goderich 6
Lady Liverpool 4, 238
Landy, Father 20
lawyers and judges, Irish 143–158
League, Self Determination for Ireland 208
Leahan, Joseph 121
Leake, John 55
Leake, Robert Rowland 55
Lee, Mary 126–129
Lenane, John 64
A Letter from Sydney xi
Lewis, Margaret 15
Light, Colonel William xii, 1, 2, 232, 235
Light County xxii, 75, 76
Light, river 63
Little Dublin 12, 246
Little Para 10
Lizard Lodge 6, 246, 250
Lonergan, Timothy 195, 196
Loyal Orange Institution of South Australia (LOISA) 212–226
Lucas, Thomas 146, 148
Lugg, James 217, 218, 221
Lysander 9, 10, 252

M
Macclesfield 12–20, 22, 246, 250
MacDonnell, Governor Sir Richard 28, 52, 168, 175, 231, 239, 240, 246
Macgillivray, Leith 41, 44, 47
MacKillop, Mary 20, 70, 93, 123, 124
Magarey, A.T. 226
Magarey, Thomas 45, 246
Ma'guire, William 146, 149, 155
Maher, Bishop James 96, 97
Majors Road 6
Mallon, Corporal 121
Mann, Charles 163, 164

Marrabel 176
Martyn, Matthew 146–149
Mary Dugdale 8, 9, 10, 236, 250
Mary White 249
McAllister, M.J. 204
McCabe, Bishop 105, 108
McCormack, John 121
McEllister, Edward 174, 243, 250
McNamara family 18
McNamara, Joe 109
Mellish 43
Middlesex 42
Milligan/Anderson partnership 16, 18
Milligan family 19
Milligan, Mary Eliza 18
Milligan, Melville and Sarah 17
Mintaro xx, 24, 34–36, 75–79, 85, 124, 246
Mitchell, William 45
Molesworth, Robert 146–149
Montgomery, M.T. 198
Moore, Mrs 122
Moore, Robert Waters 159, 160, 166–169, 171, 172
Moran, Archbishop 124
Moreton Bay Courier 215
Morphett, John 7
Morrissey, Father 99, 103
Mosquito Creek (Naracoorte) 50
Motts 18
Mountain Hut 17
Mount Barker vii, xv, xix, xx, 12–22, 112, 148, 150, 158, 165, 239, 246, 250
Mount Benson 14, 248
Mount Gambier 41–46, 50–53, 57
Mount Jeffcott 4, 248
Mount O'Halloran 6
Mudge, Rev. Burnett Patch 217–219, 221
Muirhead, Henry 150, 151, 158
Muirhead, Mount 43

Murphy, Bishop Francis xviii–xx, 32, 38, 50, 175, 187, 191, 249
Myponga 4, 5, 248, 253

N
Nairne 12, 249
Nairne railway 19
Napoleon Hotel 4
Nash, James 163, 166, 168, 223
Nashwauk 25, 38, 240
Navan 75, 76, 85–87, 249
Ned Pront 17
Nesdale, Father 103
Neville, James 65
Nevin, Father Bernard 93, 96, 99
Nolan, Mortimer 7
Norton, Bishop John 96, 97
Nurney House 9, 230

O
O'Brien, Charles 146
O'Brien, Daniel 146, 147, 150, 156
O'Brien, Father Michael 16, 148
O'Brien headstone 85, 86
O'Brien, John. *See* Father John Hartigan
O'Brien, Mary. *See* Sister Helena
O'Brien, Michael, Jr 72
O'Brien, Richard 232
O'Brien, Thomas 72
O'Callahan, Annie 68
O'Callahan, Martin 72
O'Callahan, Mary 68
O'Connell, Daniel 82, 194, 195, 196
O'Connell, John 122
O'Connor, Pam and Brian 41, 48
Oddfellows' Society 166
O'Dea, John 9, 242
O'Doherty, Dr Kevin Izod 201
O'Driscoll, Daniel 72
O'Farrell, Henry 176, 215

O'Flynn, Father M.J. 98
O'Halloran, Thomas Shuldham 6, 151, 174
O'Halloran, William Littlejohn 8
O'Kelly, Bishop Greg 109
Oldham, William 60, 61
Oldham, William and Sarah 6
O'Leary, P.E. 207, 208, 210
O'Loghlin, James V. xxiv, xxv, 179, 197, 198, 200, 201, 207, 210
O'Loghlin, Sister Catherine 93
O'Loughlin, Laurence 179
O'Loughlin, Tom 20
O'Malley, John 20
O'Neir, Martin 122
Orange Lodge 126
Orangeman 17, 216, 218, 220
Orange Order 212–228
O'Reilly, Susan 124
O'Reily, Archbishop John xxv, 96, 178, 203, 210, 244
Orient 126
Orleana 7, 251
O'Rourke, Monsignor 107
Orroroo xxiii, 92, 94, 102, 109, 247
O'Sullivan, Florence 150, 152
O'Sullivan headstone 85
O'Sullivan, Honora and Ignatius 9

P

Paddy's Hill 12, 250
Paddy's Town 12, 19
Painter, William James 218
Paringa Hall 5
Parnell, C.S. 201, 202
Pekina 90–111, 200
Pekina Hotel 95, 100, 109
Pennefather, Frederick 146, 149, 157
Penola xxi, xxii, 50, 51, 53, 156, 170
Peterborough 75, 94, 113
Pettinger, Richard Palmer 168, 169

Phelan, Father 20
Phillips, Gladys 109
Pile, Anne 49
Pollitt, Rev. James 215, 217, 218
Poole, James 63
Poor Law (Irish) 8, 59, 132, 161
Port Adelaide 3, 9, 17, 36, 59, 60, 119, 124, 133, 134, 136, 200, 236, 245, 250, 254
Port Augusta xxiv, xxv, 96, 165, 166, 189, 244, 248
Port MacDonnell xxi, 176, 246
Power, David Herbert 41–57, 49
Power, Isabella 49
Power, Mary 49
Power, Robert H. 49
Power, Thomas Herbert 49
Prendergast, Father Michael Vincent 104, 105, 106, 107, 108, 111, 207
Prendergast, Rev. W. 20
Prince Regent 7, 25
Protestant Ascendancy 45, 58, 145
Protestant Defence Association 223
Protestant(s), Protestantism xvii, xx, 15, 21, 22, 30, 45, 58, 71, 73, 74, 79–85, 135, 145, 155, 174, 184, 187, 193, 194, 212–228
Purtle, Brigid 10
Purton, Brother D.G. 185, 207

Q

Quin, Hugh 3, 251

R

Rajasthan 6
Rapid Bay 4
Rechabite. *See* Independent Order of Rechabites
Recovery 7
Redden, Martin 107
Redmond, John 156, 183, 204, 206, 225

Redmond, John and William 156, 178, 183, 200, 205, 222, 225
Reeves, Elizabeth 16
Reid family 6–8
Reid, John 28, 234, 238, 247
religion, by county 77
Reynolds, Bishop Christopher xxiii, xxiv, 92, 93, 195, 196
Rhynie 176
Riley, E. 222
Riverland 5
River Torrens 2, 253
Robe xxi, 14, 50, 52, 165, 249
Rodgers, Catherine 121
Rodgers, Philip 121
Roman Emperor 14, 133, 136, 138, 141
Rostrevor College 8, 251
Russell, Mary Anne 64
Ryan, Father Michael 10, 51, 63, 174, 175, 198
Ryan, Thomas 109

S
Sacred Heart College 5
Saddleworth xx, xxii, 75, 76, 85
Salmon, Jack 20
Sawtell, Edith 219
Scott, Abraham and Henry 47
Scott, George Byng 53
Searle, Harriet 127
Self Determination for Ireland League 103
Sevenhill xix–xxi, xxiv, 33, 35, 38, 77
Seymour, Elizabeth 14
Seymour, Henry 14, 244, 248
Seymour, Henry, Jnr 14
Shannon, M.F. 196
Sherwin, Sarah Ann 121
Short, Bishop Augustus 52, 56
Siam 14, 244
Sinn Fein 104, 105, 206, 207

Sir John Franklin Hotel 120
Sisters of Saint Joseph 70
Slattery, Ann 70
Slattery lecture 224
Smith, Francis (Frank) Villeneuve 150, 156, 157
Smith, Henry 54
Smyth, Father John 171
Smyth, Rev. T. Jasper 65
Social Purity Society 127
Sons of Erin xviii, 3, 174, 194
South Australian 137
South Australian Colonisation Commission xi, 1, 2, 253
South Australian Protestant Federation 184
Stacey family 18
Stanley County 7, 25, 36, 75, 76, 152
St Catherine's Church 90, 93, 94, 98, 254
Stevenson, George 162–164
St Francis Xavier's Cathedral xx, 2, 175, 176
St James Anglican Church 14, 15
St John's cemetery 79, 120
St John's Reformatory 125
St Joseph's xxiii, 20, 109, 122
St Mary's Help of Christians Catholic Church 7, 9, 250
St Patrick's Day 3, 6, 26, 78, 90, 94, 98, 103, 108, 173–178, 194, 199, 203, 210
St Patrick's Hall 174
St Patrick's Society xix, xx, 3, 6, 7, 8, 9, 26, 134, 135, 165, 166, 172, 174, 192, 194
St Patrick's Temperance Association 176
Strangways Land Act 1869 33, 91
Strathalbyn xxiv, 12
St Rose's Catholic church 121
St Theresa's church 51
Sturt County 12

Sturt, Evelyn 42
Supple, Charles 151
Supple, Thomas 65
surgeons, Irish 159–171
Sutton, Anthony 41–57
Sutton, John and Honora 48
Sutton, Mary 48

T
Taggart, Catherine 4, 9
Tallis, George 159, 168–172
Tam O'Shanter 4, 237
Tara 5, 14, 253
Tarcowie 92, 99, 108
Tarpeena 51, 239, 240
Taylor, Henry 15
Tobin, Bart 20
Tomkinson, Samuel 213
Torrens, Colonel Robert 2, 8, 159, 246, 249, 253
Torrens, Robert Richard 11, 174, 175, 230, 232, 236, 254
Torrens Title 8, 236
Torrensville 2, 254
Tory 119
Trinity College Dublin 5, 9, 145, 244

U
Ulster Volunteer Force 222
Undalya xxiv, 75–77, 81, 83, 85
United Cabmen's Society 176
United Irish Association 193, 197, 200
United Irish League xxv, 179, 182, 193, 204
United Trades and Labour Council 128

V
Virginia 10, 176, 250, 254

W
Wakefield colonisation model 13, 21, 232
Wakefield, Edward Gibbon xi, xvii, 18, 19, 21
Walshe, John 100, 199, 200
Watson, Andrew 50
Wattle Flat 4, 5
Watt's Range school 122
Webb family 18
Wheal Coglin Mine 4
Whelan, Patrick xxiv, 101, 197, 200
White, James 69
William Nichol 8, 9, 17
Willunga xix, 17, 122
Women's Christian Temperance Union 127
Women's Suffrage League 127, 128
Woods, Father Julian Tenison xx, xxii, 20, 51, 122, 176
Working Women's Trades Union 127

Y
Yankalilla xx, 4, 253
Yarrowie xxiii, 92, 94, 96, 108
Yatala xxiii, 8, 237, 238, 244, 251, 253
Yatina xxiii, 92, 96, 108
Yongala xxiv, 5

MARY LEE
THE LIFE AND TIMES OF A 'TURBULENT ANARCHIST' AND HER BATTLE FOR WOMEN'S RIGHTS
Denise George

Irish-born suffragist and social justice advocate Mary Lee was determined to leave the world a better place than she found it. The feisty 59-year-old widow, of limited means, settled in Adelaide in 1879 and immediately set to work.

Undaunted by the opposition of antagonistic politicians and a conservative public, Mary thrust herself into high profile campaigns in support of female refuge, improving women's working conditions and gaining women's suffrage. In 1894, South Australia became the first place in the world to pass legislation giving women the right to vote and be elected members of parliament, thanks in no small part to Mary Lee's energy and committed determination.

The disappearance of Mary Lee's papers meant her contribution to history was not fully appreciated for 125 years. Undeterred, author Denise George travelled to Ireland and her painstaking examination of local records both there and in Adelaide revealed the compelling story of a woman who took on the Establishment, and won.

> '[Mary Lee] managed to leave this world, and most certainly South Australia, a better place than she had found it. And what a story it turned out to be!' – Nic Klaassen, *Flinders Ranges Research*

> 'A perfect companion to Clare Wright's recently published *You Daughters of Freedom* ... Denise George deserves all credit for unearthing the story from obscurity ... a very readable and totally inspiring biography.' – Lisa Hill, *ANZ LitLovers LitBlog*

For more information please visit www.wakefieldpress.com.au

GERMANS
TRAVELLERS, SETTLERS AND THEIR DESCENDANTS IN SOUTH AUSTRALIA
edited by Peter Monteath

From Beehive Corner and Bert Flugelman's polished balls in Rundle Mall to the vineyards, churches and cemeteries of the Barossa Valley, tangible signs of South Australia's Germans are everywhere. 'The Germans' are regarded as a single group in the state's history: the truth is more complex and intriguing.

Those who first came to the colony mostly spoke a common language, but were divided by differences of culture and class. They were farmers from Silesia and Brandenburg, missionaries from Dresden, liberals from Berlin, merchants from Hamburg, miners from the Harz mountains or erudite graduates from the best universities. They brought a wide variety of knowledge and talents, and made a difference in many fields.

Germans have been praised as model citizens, even as over-achievers. But at times they have also been accused of divided loyalties or barefaced treachery. Part celebration and part sober assessment, this book helps make sense of South Australia today.

'This publication [provides] those of us who have lost touch with our heritage a more complete picture in which to see ourselves and the experiences of South Australians of German origin.' – Heidi Ing, *Transnational Literature*

'The book constitutes a meticulously researched source for everyone interested in the intricate relationship between Germany and (South) Australia. The clear style and absence of jargon as well as the breadth of themes render [this] a worthwhile compendium for scholars and general readers alike.' – Oliver Haag, *Reviews in Australian Studies*

For more information please visit www.wakefieldpress.com.au

Foundational Fictions in South Australian History

edited by Carolyn Collins and Paul Sendziuk

In this lively, provocative collection, some of Australia's leading historians challenge established myths, narratives and 'beautiful lies' about South Australia's past. Some are unmasked as false stories that mask brutal realities, like colonial violence, while others are revealed as simplistic versions of more complex truths.

'Each generation writes history that speaks to its own interests and concerns,' write historians Paul Ashton and Anna Clark. In *Foundational Fictions in South Australian History*, which grew out of a series of public lectures at the University of Adelaide, an impressive range of contributors suggest different ways in which familiar narratives of South Australia can be interpreted. These essays tap into wider debates, too, about the nature and purpose of history – and the 'history wars' first flamed by John Howard.

'*Foundational Fictions* brings together some key (mis)conceptions about South Australia and allows the reader to reinvestigate the past record and query just who makes history, and how history is passed down to successive generations. This book would be a really useful resource for developing students' understanding of the historical concepts proposed by the Australian history curriculum: "evidence, continuity and change, cause and effect, significance, perspectives, empathy and contestability".' – Helen Eddy, *ReadPlus*

For more information please visit www.wakefieldpress.com.au

Wakefield Press is an independent publishing and
distribution company based in Adelaide, South Australia.
We love good stories and publish beautiful books.
To see our full range of books, please visit our website at
www.wakefieldpress.com.au
where all titles are available for purchase.
To keep up with our latest releases, news and events,
subscribe to our monthly newsletter.

Find us!

Facebook: www.facebook.com/wakefield.press
Twitter: www.twitter.com/wakefieldpress
Instagram: www.instagram.com/wakefieldpress

www.ingramcontent.com/pod-product-compliance
Lightning Source LLC
Chambersburg PA
CBHW021341300426
44114CB00012B/1031